VERB CONSTRUCTIONS IN GERMAN AND DUTCH

Volume 242

Pieter A.M. Seuren and Gerard Kempen (eds.)

Verb Constructions in German and Dutch

VERB CONSTRUCTIONS IN GERMAN AND DUTCH

Edited by

PIETER A.M. SEUREN
Max-Planck-Institut für Psycholinguistik, Nijmegen

GERARD KEMPEN
Universiteit Leiden
&
Max-Planck-Institut für Psycholinguistik, Nijmegen

JOHN BENJAMINS PUBLISHING COMPANY
AMSTERDAM/PHILADELPHIA

™ The paper used in this publication meets the minimum requirements of American National Standard for Information Sciences — Permanence of Paper for Printed Library Materials, ANSI Z39.48-1984.

Library of Congress Cataloging-in-Publication Data

Verb constructions in German and Dutch / edited by Pieter A. M. Seuren and Gerard Kempen
    p.   cm. -- (Amsterdam studies in the theory and history of linguistic science. Series IV, Current issues in linguistic theory, ISSN 0304-0763 ; v. 242)
Includes some of the papers presented at the Colloquium on Verb Constructions in German and Dutch held Feb. 2-3, 2001, at the Max Planck Institute for Evolutionary Anthropology in Leipzig.
    Includes bibliographical references and index.
    1. German language--Verb. 2. Dutch language--Verb. 3. German language--Verb phrase. 4. Dutch language--Verb phrase. I. Seuren, Pieter A. M. II. Kempen, Gerard, 1943- III. Series.
PF3318.V47 2003
439.31'5--dc21   2003050288
ISBN 90 272 4754 4 (Eur.) / 1 58811 401 5 (US) (Hb; alk. paper)

John Benjamins Publishing Co. • P.O.Box 36224 • 1020 ME Amsterdam • The Netherlands
John Benjamins North America • P.O.Box 27519 • Philadelphia PA 19118-0519 • USA

Table of contents

Introduction

The present book originated in the *Colloquium on Verb Constructions in German and Dutch*, held at the Max Planck Institute for Evolutionary Anthropology in Leipzig, 3–4 February 2001, and organized by the editors. The purpose of that Colloquium was to bring together representatives of various schools of linguistic thought and see what they would have to say on questions of German and Dutch verb constructions. Yet the group of contributors to this volume does not entirely coincide with the group of those who presented papers at the Leipzig Colloquium. Of the contributors to this volume, Gosse Bouma, Arnold Evers, Hubert Haider, Gerard Kempen, Karin Harbusch and Pieter Seuren actually took part in the Colloquium and presented papers. Ronald Kaplan, Annie Zaenen, Andreas Kathol and Owen Rambow were not present in Leipzig but were later invited to contribute to the volume.

The result is a collection where a number of different schools is represented. Bouma (Chapter 1) and Kathol (Chapter 5) analyse the German and Dutch verb constructions from the perspective of Head-driven Phrase Structure Grammar (HPSG). Evers and Haider present versions of current Generative Grammar in the Chapters 2 and 3, respectively. A Lexical Functional Grammar (LFG) view on the phenomena in question is developed by Kaplan and Zaenen in Chapter 4. Kempen and Harbusch (Chapter 6) show the results of their analysis in terms of a psycholinguistically motivated formalism called Performance Grammar. Rambow analyses the facts from the point of view of a modified version of Tree Adjoining Grammar (TAG) in Chapter 7. Seuren, finally, applies the Semantic Syntax model, his version of erstwhile Generative Semantics, to the phenomena in question in Chapter 8.

Organizational problems made it impossible to extend the range of theories to be represented. Categorial Grammar, for example, would have figured well in the present collection, but mundane factors of workload made that impossible. Other theories might have been represented as well. The fact that they are not will hopefully stimulate their practitioners to publish their accounts of the syntactic phenomena highlighted in this volume elsewhere.

The topic is interesting enough, for a number of reasons. First, the German and Dutch verb constructions show up a rich array of syntactic phenomena that have so far been distinctly underexposed in the literature, despite the fact that they have proved to be a source of substantial problems in theoretical grammar. Since the phenomena in question are to a significant extent replicated in a great many other languages, it seems that they can do with some publicity, so that the attention will be diverted a little from English, which is an all too exclusive subject of syntactic discussions but lacks phenomena typical of German, Dutch and many other languages as well. We, the editors, hope that the publication of the present volume will contribute to a more even distribution of the interest shown by theoretical syntacticians in the different language types of this world.

The publication of the papers at hand may, furthermore, help to disabuse both traditional and more theoretically oriented grammarians of German and Dutch of the still widespread but nevertheless false notion that the complementation system in these two languages is basically identical to what is found in English, or, for that matter, in Latin. English and Latin belong to the group of languages where the overtly expressed semantic *subject* of a non-finite complement clause has the grammatical status of direct object of the superordinate verb (the so-called accusative-cum-infinitive construction). German and Dutch, on the other hand, belong to a different group of languages where the semantically subordinate *verb* is united with the higher verb (most theories speak of a 'cluster'), while the argument terms of the subordinate verbs are amalgamated with those of the higher verb. It is time that this fact should finally be given full recognition in the many grammars and grammatical treatises, both traditional and theoretical, that appear on the market.

A further, equally important, reason lies in the fact that there is relatively little interaction among the various schools of linguistic thought. For the past decades, general or theoretical linguistics has been characterized by the parallel existence of a fairly large number of distinct communities, each united by a specific approach or theory, which show a lively pattern of citation and communication within the groups concerned but largely fail to interact across group boundaries. We consider this to be an undesirable state of affairs, though perhaps inevitable as a transitional phase in the discipline's development to full maturity. It is the express purpose of the present volume to cut through those group barriers.

We realize, however, that this is easier said than done. Habits as well as prejudices are hard to eradicate and feelings of loyalty easily grow into firm doctrinal convictions. Realizing that any possible improvement in this respect will inevitably have to be a long-term process, we decided that it would be premature, and probably futile, to try to get an actual discussion going in the present volume. All we have done, therefore, is simply bring together the various analyses into one volume, hoping and expecting that their mere juxtaposition will provide material for future comparative evaluations.

The relevant facts of German and Dutch verb constructions have not been known very long. Until the middle of the 20th century it was commonly thought, in European linguistic circles, that syntax, in the sense of combining words into larger wholes, be they sentences or texts, was mostly a matter of individual, stylistic creativity, belonging to the study of 'parole' rather than of 'langue'. As a result, there were hardly any serious attempts at investigating the structural properties of sentences beyond the crudest level. During the 1930s isolated pockets of linguistic structuralism were found in Europe, in particular in the Dutch- and German-speaking world, and it is here that the first inklings are found of there being a system behind the apparent chaos of German and Dutch verb constructions. One thinks, for example, of Overdiep's *Stilistische grammatica van het moderne Nederlandsch* (1936), which, despite its title, was in fact an incipient syntactic description.

Then, after the second World War, European linguists began to develop a greater sensitivity as regards the formal properties of syntactic structures. In Dutch linguistics one finds Paardekooper (1955) as an early harbinger of the new, postwar European structuralism, which even allowed for a modest degree of formalization. In German linguistics it was Gunnar Bech who, in his monumental (1955), presented the first arguments to show that there is a basic distinction, in German, between what he called 'incoherent' and 'coherent' constructions, the latter corresponding to what we now call verb clusters. Since, however, he did not have at his disposal a clear notion of syntactic rule, and even less of tree structure, as instruments of linguistic analysis and description, he was unable to cast his ideas into the format of a formally precise description.

It was not until the 1970s, when the ideas and techniques of Transformational Generative Grammar began to be widely known this side of the Atlantic, that modern, theoretically oriented grammarians started to observe the data more precisely and more systematically. This quickly led to the first formal analyses and descriptions of the German and Dutch verb constructions, based on then current versions of Transformational Generative Grammar. For a while, Dutch linguists (Evers 1975; Seuren 1972) took the lead, presenting transformational descriptions of verb constructions, especially verb clusters, not only in Dutch and German, but also in French, Japanese and other languages (see Kuroda 1965 for what probably constitutes the very first discussion of verb clustering in the transformational literature). As regards German, a new generation of German linguists quickly followed (see in particular Heidolph et al. 1981). This led to a constant stream of publications in the same tradition, including Haider (1986, 1990, 1993, 1994), Den Besten and Rutten (1989), and many others.

For some strange reason, however, these transformational descriptions, though remarkably successful on current criteria, met with a lukewarm reception in the dominant centers of Generative Grammar in America. In Germany, Austria and the Low Countries (including Flanders), however, the facts were studied ever more systematically in ever wider circles, until they found their way into what may be considered the national standard grammars of German and Dutch (though, for obvious reasons, without any formal theoretical framework). The German Duden Grammar has, in its 1995 edition, a marvellously complete and systematic survey (due to Horst Sitta) of the verb cluster data in standard modern German. (Zifonun et al. 1997, though voluminous, is curiously lacking in this respect.) The latest (1997) edition of the 'national grammar' of Dutch, the *Algemene Nederlandse Spraakkunst* or ANS, again has prolific data surveys.

At the same time, the striking facts of the Dutch and German verb constructions began to attract the attention of other, newly founded, schools of syntactic theory. Thus one finds Steedman (1983, 1984) and Moortgat (1988), where the Dutch (right-branching) verb clusters with their troublesome nesting dependencies are subjected to an analysis in terms of Categorial Grammar. Joshi (1985:245–249) considers the same Dutch nesting dependencies, in a global way, in terms of Tree Adjoining Grammar. Then, during the 1990s, Hinrichs and Nakazawa, in a number of publications, presented analyses of the German verb constructions in terms of Head-driven Phrase Structure Grammar. Kaplan and Zaenen followed suit, now in the terms of Lexical Functional Grammar. Kempen and Harbusch, with Performance Grammar, and Rambow, presenting his D-Tree Substitution Grammar (DSG) as a variant of Tree Adjoining Grammar, have recently joined the list.

This is, in rough outline, the context in which the present volume came into being. It explains the selection of authors and schools, and our regret at having been unable to cover a wider range. It is hoped that this book will contribute not only to a better knowledge and a better understanding of the facts concerned but also to a better mutual understanding of the various schools of linguistic thought.

Pieter A. M. Seuren
Gerard Kempen

CHAPTER 1

Verb clusters and the scope of adjuncts in Dutch

Gosse Bouma
Rijksuniversiteit Groningen

1. Introduction

The Dutch cross-serial dependency construction is characterized by the fact that complex clauses may be formed in which arguments precede verbal predicates in a non-nesting fashion. In the subordinate clause in (1), for instance, the NP *Anne* is the subject of the modal *mag*, and the NP *deze film* is the direct object of the verb *zien*.

(1) dat Anne *deze film*   mag *zien*
     that Anne this   movie may   see
     that Anne is allowed to see this movie

The classic transformational analysis of this construction was given in Seuren (1972) and Evers (1975). An underlying structure was proposed in which *deze film zien* would be a VP left-adjacent to the modal *mag* and a 'Verb-raising' transformation moved the main verb to the right of the modal. A further transformation, called *pruning*, removed spurious phrase structure nodes, and created a situation where *mag* governs *deze film*. Lexicalist analyses of this construction have either employed a syntactic operation called '*function composition*' which allows the syntactic valency of verbs to be combined, or a closely-related operation known as '*division*' or the '*Geach-rule*' in Categorial Grammar and as '*argument composition*' in Head-driven Phrase Structure Grammar. This mechanism allows the valency of a *Verb-raising* verb to depend on the valency of its (lexical) verbal argument.

The transformational as well as the lexicalist traditions face certain problems when trying to account for the distribution of adjuncts in the context of verb clusters. Adverbial phrases may either precede or follow complements:

(2) a.   dat   Kim   **regelmatig**   haar   moeder   bezoekt
        that   Kim   regularly   her   mother   visits
        that Kim visits her mother regularly
   b.   dat Kim haar moeder **regelmatig** bezoekt

The same freedom can be found in clauses containing a verb cluster.

(3) a.   dat   Kim   Anne   **aandachtig**   het   scherm   zag   bestuderen
        that   Kim   Anne   attentively   the   screen   saw   study
        that Kim saw Anne study the screen attentively
   b.   dat Kim Anne het scherm **aandachtig** zag bestuderen

The adverb *aandachtig* in (3) clearly modifies the main verb *bestuderen*, and thus it is to be expected that it may either precede or follow the direct object of *bestuderen*. In other cases, the adverbial phrase is most naturally interpreted as taking scope over the verb cluster as a whole:

(4) a.   dat   Kim   Anne   **niet**   het   huis   hoorde   verlaten
        that   Kim   Anne   not   the   house   heard   leave
        that Kim did not hear Anne leave the house
   b.   dat Kim Anne het huis **niet** hoorde verlaten

What is striking about the word order in (4b) is that the complement of the main verb precedes an adjunct which takes scope over the verb cluster as a whole. Cases where the scope of the adjunct is actually ambiguous, can easily be constructed as well:

(5) a.   dat   Kim   **regelmatig**   haar   moeder   wil   bezoeken
        that   Kim   regularly   her   mother   wants   visit
        that Kim regularly wants to visit her mother
        that Kim wants to regularly visit her mother
   b.   dat Kim haar moeder **regelmatig** wil bezoeken

In (5a) and (5b), the same ambiguity is present. The adverb *regelmatig* can be interpreted as taking scope over the verb *wil*, but also as taking scope over the main verb *bezoeken* only.

In transformational frameworks, examples such as (2a) and (4b) have been used as argument for a *scrambling* transformation, which moves an object, originally generated adjacent to the verb, to the left, and Chomsky-adjoins it to a vp-node (Webelhuth 1992; de Hoop 1992). The derivation of (6a), given in (6b) illustrates that scrambling must be able to move an object past adjuncts of a higher clause as well.

(6)   a.   dat Anne deze film   waarschijnlijk mag zien
             that Anne this movie probably   may see
             that Anne is probably allowed to see this movie

     b.

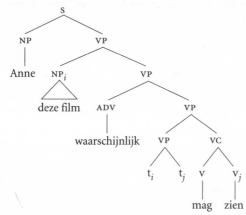

Note that both elements of the vp *deze film zien* have been moved. The head has been adjoined to the right of the modal verb by *V-raising* and the object has been *scrambled* out of the complement vp to a position left of the adverb which modifies a projection of the modal verb *mag*. The ambiguity in examples like (5a) and (5b) can now be accounted for by assuming that the adverb was either adjoined to the embedded vp headed by (a trace of) *bezoeken*, or to the vp headed by *wil*. In both cases, the object-adverb order is obtained by scrambling.

    In Head-driven Phrase Structure Grammar (HPSG; Pollard & Sag 1994), *argument composition* has been widely used to account for the syntactic valency of verb clusters like *mag zien* in (6). It is assumed that the complements of the modal *mag* (defined by the COMPS-feature) consist of a (lexical) verbal complement *plus* all the elements on the COMPS list of that verbal complement. As *zien* is a simple transitive verb, the COMPS list of *mag* in (6) consists of a verbal complement and an accusative NP:

(7) $\begin{bmatrix} \text{PHON} & \langle mag \rangle \\ \text{HEAD} & V \\ \text{COMPS} & \left\langle \boxed{1}\text{NP}, \begin{bmatrix} \text{HEAD} & V \\ \text{COMPS} & \langle \boxed{1}\text{NP} \rangle \end{bmatrix} \right\rangle \end{bmatrix}$

Specific grammar rules for combining a head with one or more complements are defined in HPSG as instantiations of a *head-complement-structure*: a structure consisting of mother, a head daughter and one or more complement daughters. The actual selection of complements follows from the *valence principle*: the value of the valence feature COMPS on the mother is equal to COMPS on the head daughter, minus all selected complements. A complement is selected if it occurs as a non-head daughter in a head-complement-structure, and its feature structure can be unified with an element on COMPS of the head daughter.

While there is a broad consensus about the lexical aspects of *verb clustering*, different analyses have been proposed for the syntactic structure of the construction. One approach is to assume that there is a rule, instantiating a head-complement-structure, which allows a lexical verbal head to combine with a lexical verbal complement to form a verb cluster, and another rule which accounts for the selection of non-verbal complements (the head of the rule is underlined):

(8)   *head-complement-structure*: V[+LEX] → $\underline{V}$[+LEX] V[+LEX]

(9)   *head-complement-structure*: V[−LEX] → XP $\underline{V}$

A standard approach to adjunct word order in the VP simply allows adjuncts to be adjoined to arbitrary verbal projections (by means of a rule instantiating a *head-adjunct-structure*, which requires that the MOD value of the adjunct be unifiable with the feature structure of the head)), where the adjunct semantically takes scope over the constituent it is adjoined to:

(10)   *head-adjunct-structure*: V → AdvP $\underline{V}$

Thus, the derivation of the VP in (6) is as follows:[1]

(11)

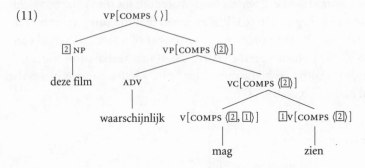

The adverb-object word order is derived similarly, by assuming that the adverb modifies a saturated VP (i.e. v[COMPS ⟨ ⟩]).

In van Noord and Bouma (1994) it is observed that cases where an adverb modifies the governed verb, as in (12) and (3a) and (3b) above, are problematic for accounts based on argument inheritance. The manner adverb *hard* in (12) clearly modifies the event denoted by the embedded verb. However, in a non-transformational, surface oriented, framework, the adverb can only be analysed as a sister of a verbal projection headed by *laat*, and thus, as modifying the semantics of *laat* rather than *straffen*.

(12)   dat de   minister de   misdadigers **hard** laat straffen
       that the minister the criminals   hard lets punish
       that the minister makes the criminals be punished hard

A solution for this apparent mismatch between syntax and semantics can be found if adjuncts may be added lexically to the syntactic valency of a verb. By introducing adjuncts lexically on COMPS, they can be selected in syntax by the head-complement rule responsible for selection of non-verbal complements. In (12), the verb *straffen* is therefore now assigned an 'extended' COMPS-list including an adjunct. Furthermore, as adjuncts are present on COMPS, they participate in *argument composition*. The *argument composition* verb *laat* in (12) gets assigned the following COMPS-list:

(13) $$\begin{bmatrix} \text{PHON} & \langle laat \rangle \\ \text{HEAD} & v \\ \text{COMPS} & \left\langle \boxed{1}\text{NP}, \boxed{2}\text{ADV}, \begin{bmatrix} \text{HEAD} & v \\ \text{COMPS} & \langle \boxed{1}\,\text{NP}, \boxed{2}\,\text{ADV} \rangle \end{bmatrix} \right\rangle \end{bmatrix}$$

As adjuncts are no longer distinct from complements at the level of syntax, it can be assumed that they are all selected in the Mittelfeld by means of a single head-complement rule:

(14)   *head-complement-structure*: V[COMPS ⟨ ⟩] → XP⁺ V

The example in (12) can now be analysed as follows:

(15)

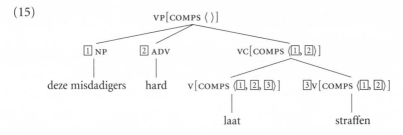

In the *adjuncts-as-complements* analysis it is assumed that an adjunct modifies the semantics of the head which lexically introduces it. Thus, even though the adverb *hard* is selected in syntax by *laat*, semantically it modifies the main verb *straffen*. Similar examples where an adverb takes wide scope (such as (6)) are accounted for by assuming that in those cases the lexical argument structure of the modal verb has been extended with an adjunct.

In de Hoop (1992), de Hoop and van der Does (1998), and elsewhere, it has been argued that *object scrambling* interacts with semantics. In particular, they assume that scrambling of an indefinite NP forces a '*quantificational*' reading of that NP, and that the possibility of scrambling depends on focus and presuppositional structure. Another clear semantic difference between scrambled and non-scrambled word order is described in Ruys (2001): whereas (16a) is ambiguous between a *de re* and *de dicto* reading of the object, the scrambled (16b) only has a *de re* reading.

(16) a. dat Jan   vaak een meisje zoekt
          that John often a   girl   seeks
          that John often seeks a girl
          that there is a girl which John often seeks
      b. dat Jan een meisje vaak zoekt
          that there is a girl which John often seeks

The literature on scrambling does not provide a clear answer to the question how to account for this difference exactly, but at the very least examples like these suggest that the relative order of adjuncts and complements must be closely linked to a semantic account of scope. It should also be clear that the adjuncts-as-complements analysis as it stands does not provide such an account, as it allows adjuncts to be interspersed with complements freely on COMPS, and only stipulates that the inserted adjuncts must take scope over the lexical semantics of the verb on whose COMPS-list they originate.

In this paper, I extend the adjuncts-as-complements analysis with an explicit account of semantics which supports a detailed account of the interaction of word order and scope for adjuncts, complements, and *argument raising* verbs. In HPSG, quantifier scope can be accounted for by means of explicit storage and retrieval of NP-meanings, or by means of underspecification. The latter approach constructs underspecified meaning representations which can be resolved in one or more ways, depending on the constraints imposed on such structures. One of the attractive features of underspecification semantics is that it suggests a framework in which word order may impose constraints on semantic representations. Below, I will develop an underspecified semantics for a fragment of HPSG with adjuncts-as-complements, and propose a scopal constraint which accounts for the word order phenomena observed above. In the next section the HPSG analysis of Dutch verb clusters is reviewed in more detail. In Section 3 I outline the essentials of Lexical Resource Semantics (Richter & Sailer 2001b), the underspecified semantics formalism I will be using. In Section 4, the treatment of adjuncts as complements along the lines of Bouma, Malouf, and Sag (2001) is shown to be compatible with the data above. Furthermore, an underspecification semantics for both scopal and non-scopal, intersective, modifiers is presented, and integrated with the adjuncts-as-complements analysis.

In the final three sections, several implications of the proposal are considered. One prediction is that adjuncts in general may take wide or narrow scope with respect to the matrix verb. It is argued that this is correct for a range of adjunct types. Furthermore, the analysis predicts that adjuncts modifying a matrix verb may appear between dependents of the lower verb. Evidence for this prediction is presented. Finally, I address the semantics of clauses containing an *argument inheritance* verb and more than one adjunct (potentially modifying two different predicates) or a combination of an adjunct and a quantified NP complement. In such cases, the scope of the adjuncts relative to the other dependents is completely determined by word order. To account for this restriction, a constraint on the dependency structure of verbal lexical entries is proposed.

2.   Dutch cross-serial dependencies in HPSG

The syntax of the so-called verbal complex in Dutch and German with its notorious crossing dependencies has received ample attention in theoretical linguistics, at least since Seuren (1972) and Evers (1975). Within the framework of Head-driven Phrase Structure Grammar (Pollard & Sag 1994), Hinrichs and Nakazawa (1994) have proposed a lexicalist analysis of this construction in terms of *argument inheritance*, thereby following earlier work in Categorial Grammar in terms of function composition (Steedman 1984). Various aspects of their analysis have been elaborated in a number of publications (Kathol 1998; Kiss 1994; Nerbonne 1994; Müller 1996; Müller 1999; Meurers 1999; Bouma & van Noord 1998; van Noord & Bouma 1997).

The core observation of Hinrichs and Nakazawa (1994) is that argument inheritance allows complements of one verbal head to be inherited (lexically) by a governing verbal head, thus allowing the governing verbal head to select

the complements of that head. This in turn opens up the possibility of complement word orders where *inherited* complements occur between *true* arguments
and the verbal head itself.

Below, I present a grammar fragment for Dutch modal and *accusativus cum
infinitivo* verbs. Crossing dependency word orders are accounted for by means
of argument inheritance.

Following Bouma, Malouf, and Sag (2001), I assume that the valency of
lexical items is determined by a mapping from *argument structure* to *dependency structure* and from *dependency structure* to (grammatical) valency. The
list of dependents consists of the list of arguments, possibly extended with adjuncts. The valence features SUBJ and COMPS correspond to the head and the
tail of the list of dependents, respectively.[2]

The lexical entry for the transitive verb *bestuderen* given in (17) has an
argument structure consisting of a nominative and an accusative NP. The semantics of the verb is represented by the head-feature MAIN, whose function
is explained in more detail in the next section. Its value is a three-place relation *study*, including a Davidsonian event variable. The other arguments of the
relation are unified with the semantic index of the nominative and accusative
NP, respectively.

$$
(17) \quad
\begin{bmatrix}
\text{PHON} & \langle \textit{bestuderen} \rangle \\[2pt]
\text{HEAD} & \begin{bmatrix} \textit{verb} \\ \text{MAIN study}(e,i,j) \end{bmatrix} \\[12pt]
\text{ARG-ST} & \left\langle \begin{bmatrix} \text{HEAD} \begin{bmatrix} \textit{noun} \\ \text{CASE} \quad \textit{nom} \\ \text{INDEX } i \end{bmatrix} \end{bmatrix} , \begin{bmatrix} \text{HEAD} \begin{bmatrix} \textit{noun} \\ \text{CASE} \quad \text{ACC} \\ \text{INDEX } j \end{bmatrix} \end{bmatrix} \right\rangle
\end{bmatrix}
$$

The values of DEPS and the valence features SUBJ and COMPS are determined
by general *mapping* constraints. A mapping constraint is expressed as an implication on (typed) feature structures. For now, I assume the constraint in
(18), which requires that feature structures of type *word* must have identical
values for DEPS and ARG-ST. The constraint in (19) states that, for verbal lexical
entries, the single element of SUBJ corresponds to the first element on DEPS,
whereas the tail of DEPS corresponds to COMPS:[3]

$$
(18) \quad \textit{word} \rightarrow
\begin{bmatrix}
\text{DEPS} & \boxed{1} \\
\text{ARG-ST} & \boxed{1}
\end{bmatrix}
$$

$$(19) \quad \begin{bmatrix} word \\ \text{HEAD } v \end{bmatrix} \rightarrow \begin{bmatrix} \text{SUBJ} & \langle \boxed{1} \rangle \\ \text{COMPS} & \boxed{2} \\ \text{DEPS} & \langle \boxed{1} \rangle \oplus \boxed{2} \end{bmatrix}$$

The constraints above imply that the lexical entry for *bestuderen* can therefore be as follows:

$$(20) \quad \begin{bmatrix} word \\ \text{PHON} & \langle bestuderen \rangle \\ \text{HEAD} & verb \\ \text{SUBJ} & \langle \boxed{1}\,\text{NP}[nom] \rangle \\ \text{COMPS} & \langle \boxed{2}\,\text{NP}[acc] \rangle \\ \text{DEPS} & \langle \boxed{1}, \boxed{2} \rangle \\ \text{ARG-ST} & \langle \boxed{1}, \boxed{2} \rangle \end{bmatrix}$$

Heads may project *head-complement* and *head-subject* structures. A head-complement rule for building VPs was given in (14). Head-subject structures are similar to head-complement structures, except that in this case the non-head daughter is a subject, and therefore has to unify with an element on SUBJ. The fact that subjects are normally selected after all complements, can be implemented by requiring that the COMPS value of the head must be the empty list:

(21) *head-subject-structure:* V → NP $\underline{V}$[COMPS ⟨ ⟩]

As both head-complement and head-subject structures are *headed* structures, the value of the attribute HEAD is unified on the mother and head daughter. An example is given in (22).

(22)

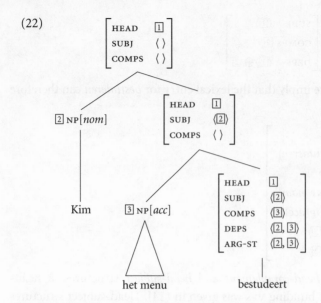

Argument inheritance verbs differ from ordinary verbs in that their argument structure depends on the valence of the verbal complement they combine with. Formally, this can be represented by defining the argument structure of inheritance verbs as the *append* ($\oplus$) of three lists: a list containing a subject argument, possibly a direct object argument (for object control verbs), a list of inherited complements whose value is identical to the COMPS-list of the verbal complement, and a list containing the verbal complement itself:[4,5]

(23)
$$
\begin{bmatrix}
\text{PHON} & \langle moeten \rangle \\
\text{HEAD} & \begin{bmatrix} verb \\ \text{MAIN} \ \text{must}(e, i, \alpha) \end{bmatrix} \\
\text{ARG-ST} & \left\langle \begin{bmatrix} \text{HD} \begin{bmatrix} noun \\ \text{CASE} \ nom \\ \text{INDEX} \ i \end{bmatrix} \end{bmatrix} \right\rangle \oplus \boxed{1} \oplus \left\langle \begin{bmatrix} word \\ \text{HD} \begin{bmatrix} verb \\ \text{VFORM} \ inf \\ \text{TOP} \ \alpha \end{bmatrix} \\ \text{SUBJ} \ \langle \text{INDEX} \ i \rangle \\ \text{COMPS} \ \boxed{1} \end{bmatrix} \right\rangle
\end{bmatrix}
$$

(24)
$$
\begin{bmatrix}
\text{PHON} & \langle zien \rangle \\[2pt]
\text{HEAD} & \begin{bmatrix} verb \\ \text{MAIN} \ \text{see}(e, i, \alpha) \end{bmatrix} \\[4pt]
\text{ARG-ST} & \left\langle \begin{bmatrix} \text{HD} \begin{bmatrix} noun \\ \text{CASE} \ nom \\ \text{INDEX} \ i \end{bmatrix} \end{bmatrix}, \begin{bmatrix} \text{HD} \begin{bmatrix} noun \\ \text{CASE} \ acc \\ \text{INDEX} \ j \end{bmatrix} \end{bmatrix} \right\rangle \\[8pt]
& \oplus \boxed{1} \oplus \left\langle \begin{bmatrix} word \\ \text{HD} \begin{bmatrix} verb \\ \text{VFORM} \ inf \\ \text{TOP} \ \alpha \end{bmatrix} \\ \text{SUBJ} \ \left\langle \begin{bmatrix} \text{INDEX} \ j \end{bmatrix} \right\rangle \\ \text{COMPS} \ \boxed{1} \end{bmatrix} \right\rangle
\end{bmatrix}
$$

The argument structure of argument inheritance verbs is flexible, and depends in part on the syntactic valence of the verbal complement they combine with. Consequently, the value of DEPS and COMPS is also flexible. The examples below therefore represent only two possibilities for instantiating the flexible lexical entries in (23) and (24). In (25), it is assumed that the verbal complement of *moeten* is a transitive verb, having a single element on COMPS. In (26), *zien* takes an intransitive verb (whose COMPS list is empty) as verbal complement.

(25)
$$
\begin{bmatrix}
\text{PHON} & \langle moeten \rangle \\
\text{SUBJ} & \langle \boxed{1} \rangle \\
\text{COMPS} & \langle \boxed{3}, \boxed{2} \rangle \\
\text{DEPS} & \langle \boxed{1}, \boxed{3}, \boxed{2} \rangle \\
\text{ARG-ST} & \langle \boxed{1} \text{NP}[nom], \boxed{3}, \boxed{2} \, v[\text{COMPS} \ \langle \boxed{3} \rangle] \rangle
\end{bmatrix}
$$

(26)
$$
\begin{bmatrix}
\text{PHON} & \langle zien \rangle \\
\text{SUBJ} & \langle \boxed{1} \rangle \\
\text{COMPS} & \langle \boxed{2}, \boxed{3} \rangle \\
\text{DEPS} & \langle \boxed{1}, \boxed{2}, \boxed{3} \rangle \\
\text{ARG-ST} & \langle \boxed{1} \text{NP}[nom], \boxed{2} \text{NP}[acc], \boxed{3} \, v[\text{COMPS} \ \langle \ \rangle] \rangle
\end{bmatrix}
$$

These lexical entries can be used to derive the following examples:

(27)

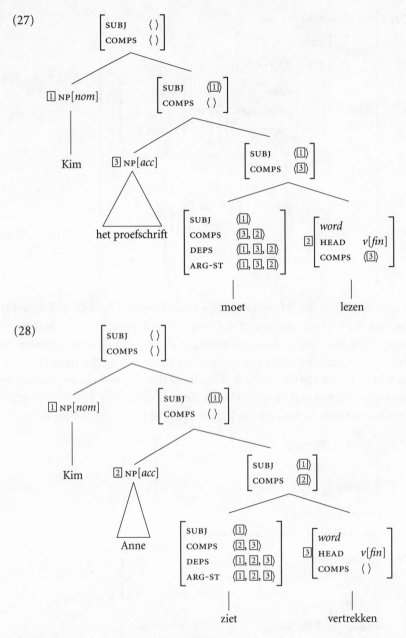

Word order is accounted for by means of *linear precedence* constraints, which may impose ordering constraints on sister nodes. For the purposes of this paper, it suffices to assume that non-verbal complements are realized in the same order as they appear on COMPS of the head, and that they must precede the head. Verbal complements inside the verb cluster must normally follow the head. In Bouma and van Noord (1998), an analysis of word order in Dutch and German verbal complexes is presented, which accounts for the order of verb clusters consisting of more than two verbs, and for such phenomena as 'AUX-flip' and *'Oberfeldumstellung'* in German, and the distribution of separable verb-particles in Dutch.

3. LRS Semantics

Underspecification semantics accounts for the ambiguity of natural language expressions by assigning such expressions underspecified or quasi logical forms which correspond to one or more fully specified formulas. Ambiguity is expressed by a single (underspecified) formula and thus can be the result of a single grammatical derivation. Ambiguity resolution amounts to instantiating the underspecified representation into a fully resolved formula. Underspecification semantics is particularly popular in computational semantics (Alshawi & Crouch 1992; Frank & Reyle 1995; Bos 1995; Copestake et al. 1999) as it supports architectures in which grammatical analysis only produces different analyses if there are genuine syntactic ambiguities. Reduction of syntactic ambiguity in general has a positive effect on parsing efficiency. Ambiguity resolution amounts to selecting the syntactically correct parse and instantiating its meaning. In many cases, only a partial resolution of the underspecified result is necessary. In an automatic translation system, for instance, it may be necessary to select the correct syntactic structure and to resolve underspecified lexical predicates, but resolving quantifier is not always required.

In this section, I introduce the basic concepts of Lexical Resource Semantics (LRS) (Richter & Sailer 2001a, 2001b), a recent member of the family of underspecified semantics formalisms. LRS allows (standard, fully specified) logical formulas to be described by means of underspecification. The constraints make use of the machinery of constraint-based grammar formalisms as much as possible. In particular, the theory is integrated in the grammar framework of HPSG. I will be mostly concerned with underspecified representations of the scope of quantifiers and scopal adverbs.

The semantics of words and phrases in LRS is encoded by means of the features TOP, PARTS, MAIN, and INDEX. The value of TOP and MAIN is a logical form. The value of PARTS is a list of terms. The value of INDEX is a logical variable. The TOP of a clause is its logical form. It has to consist of all and only the terms in its PARTS list. If PARTS can be assembled into a logical form in various ways, an ambiguity arises. MAIN is the element of PARTS which corresponds to the meaning of the lexical head of the phrase. In *headed structures*, the value of TOP, MAIN and INDEX is identical on mother and head daughter. For this reason, I assume that these features are present under HEAD.

Words typically introduce a single semantic term. The lexical entry for *lezen* (*read*) in (29) has a PARTS attribute containing a term consisting of the relation name *read*, and arguments e, i, and j.[6] The argument e stands for a Davidsonian event variable. The other two arguments are co-indexed with the the INDEX values of the two NP-arguments.

$$(29) \quad \begin{bmatrix} \text{PHON} & \langle lezen \rangle \\ \text{HEAD} & \begin{bmatrix} \text{TOP} & lf \\ \text{INDEX} & e \\ \text{MAIN} & \boxed{1} \end{bmatrix} \\ \text{ARG-ST} & \left\langle \begin{bmatrix} np \\ \text{INDEX } i \end{bmatrix}, \begin{bmatrix} np \\ \text{INDEX } j \end{bmatrix} \right\rangle \\ \text{PARTS} & \langle \boxed{1}\, read(e,i,j) \rangle \end{bmatrix}$$

I will assume, following the MAIN principle of (Richter & Sailer 2001b), that in every lexical entry and every phrase, MAIN is required to be a component of TOP.

Scope-taking elements, such as quantifiers, and certain verbs and adverbs, are associated in the lexicon with underspecified terms, containing one or more arguments whose value is required to be a semantic term again. Such arguments are indicated with letters $\alpha, \beta, \ldots$

$$(30) \quad \begin{bmatrix} \text{PHON} & \langle een, boek \rangle \\ \text{HEAD} & \begin{bmatrix} noun \\ \text{TOP} & lf \\ \text{MAIN} & \boxed{1} \\ \text{INDEX } x \end{bmatrix} \\ \text{PARTS} & \langle \exists x(\alpha \wedge \beta), \boxed{1}\, book(x) \rangle \\ & \& \boxed{1} \lhd \alpha \end{bmatrix}$$

In quantified noun phrases, the semantic head of the noun is required to be a component of the restriction of the quantifier. The constraint $T \lhd U$ is used to express that a term T must be a component of a larger term U. Complex constraints of this type, which cannot be expressed as feature values or reentrancies, are added to a feature structure with the prefix &.

The PARTS value of a phrase is simply the concatenation of the PARTS attributes of the daughters. Therefore, a standard derivation of (31) will give rise to the PARTS in (32a).

(31)   alle studenten lezen een boek
       all students read a book

(32)   a.
$$\begin{bmatrix} \text{HEAD} \begin{bmatrix} \text{TOP} & \boxed{1} \\ \text{INDEX} & e \\ \text{MAIN} & \boxed{4} \end{bmatrix} \\ \text{PARTS} \left\langle \forall x(\alpha \to \beta), \boxed{2}\,\text{student}(x), \exists y(\gamma \wedge \delta), \boxed{3}\,\text{book}(y), \boxed{4}\,\text{read}(e,x,y) \right\rangle \\ \& \boxed{2} \lhd \alpha \,\& \boxed{3} \lhd \gamma \end{bmatrix}$$

       b. $\boxed{1}\,\forall x(\text{student}(x) \to \exists y(\text{book}(y) \wedge \text{read}(e,x,y)))$
       c. $\boxed{1}\,\exists y(\text{book}(y) \wedge \forall x(\text{student}(x) \to \text{read}(e,x,y)))$

The semantics of an utterance is the value of its TOP. This value is constrained to consist of all and only the terms in PARTS. Furthermore, all scopal constraints must be satisfied. The logical forms in (32b) and (32c) are the result of two ways to instantiate the value of TOP in (32a), compatible with the principles and constraints.[7]

As the scope of quantifiers is not subject to restrictions, the analysis also accounts for the fact that quantified NPS may in general take wide or narrow scope with respect to a modal verb. Modal verbs, such as *wil* in (33), are assumed to be control verbs, i.e. they express a relation between an entity and a VP meaning, where the subject argument of lexical head of the VP is required to be identical to the index of the subject of the modal verb.

(33)
$$
\begin{bmatrix}
\text{PHON} & \langle wil \rangle \\[4pt]
\text{HEAD} & \begin{bmatrix} verb \\ \text{TOP} \quad \boxed{1} \\ \text{INDEX } e \\ \text{MAIN} \quad \boxed{2} \end{bmatrix} \\[4pt]
\text{ARG-ST} & \left\langle \begin{bmatrix} \text{HD} \begin{bmatrix} noun \\ \text{INDEX } i \end{bmatrix} \end{bmatrix} \right\rangle \oplus \boxed{3} \oplus \left\langle \begin{bmatrix} \text{HD} & \begin{bmatrix} verb \\ \text{TOP } \alpha \end{bmatrix} \\ \text{SUBJ} & \langle \text{INDEX } i \rangle \\ \text{COMPS} & \boxed{3} \end{bmatrix} \right\rangle \\[4pt]
\text{PARTS} & \langle \boxed{2}\,\text{want}(e, i, \alpha) \rangle
\end{bmatrix}
$$

In examples like (34) the direct object argument of the embedded verb *vervangen* may take either wide or narrow scope with respect to the modal verb *wil*. Given the lexical entry for *wil* in (33), a derivation of (34) gives rise to the semantic representation in (35a). The value of TOP in this representation can be either (35b) or (35c).

(34)   dat   Kim   een   computer   wil   vervangen
       that Kim   a   computer   wants   replace
       that Kim wants to replace a computer
       that there is a computer that Kim wants to replace

(35)   a.
$$
\begin{bmatrix}
\text{HEAD} & \begin{bmatrix} \text{TOP} \quad \boxed{1} \\ \text{INDEX } e \\ \text{MAIN} \quad \boxed{2} \end{bmatrix} \\[4pt]
\text{PARTS} & \langle\, \boxed{2}\,\text{want}(e, k, \alpha),\ \boxed{3}\,\text{replace}(e', k, x),\ \boxed{4}\,\text{computer}(x),\ \exists x(\beta \wedge \gamma)\,\rangle \\
& \&\ \boxed{4} \lhd \beta
\end{bmatrix}
$$

   b. $\boxed{1}$ want$(e, k, \exists x(\text{computer}(x) \wedge \text{replace}(e', k, x)))$

   c. $\boxed{1}$ $\exists x(\text{computer}(x) \wedge \text{want}(e, k, \text{replace}(e', k, x)))$

Note also that semantic construction does not need to take into account the fact that the embedded VP *een computer vervangen* is discontinuous and that the direct object is inherited on the argument structure of *wil*. The meaning of a phrase is determined by the PARTS list, which is simply the concatenation of the PARTS of the daughter phrases, and the lexical semantics of the words involved. This schema is general enough to support the syntactic analysis of argument inheritance verbs without extra stipulations.

4. Adjuncts as complements

In this section, Argument Structure Extension as defined in Bouma, Malouf, and Sag (2001) is introduced. I demonstrate that this operation, which allows adjuncts to be selected as complements, enables an account of the fact that adjuncts may appear left of a verb cluster and still take scope over only a part of that cluster. Furthermore, I show that the underspecified semantics introduced in the previous section allows the adjuncts as complements analysis to be combined with an explicit semantics.

4.1 Syntax

The adjuncts-as-complements hypothesis makes the selection of adjuncts a lexical property of the verbs involved, and allows adjuncts to be selected by the same rule mechanism responsible for selection of complements. Arguments for selecting adjuncts as complements in HPSG have been presented for French (Miller 1992; Abeillé & Godard 1994), Japanese (Manning, Sag, & Iida 1999), Polish, Finnish (Przepiórkowski 1999a, b) and English (Bouma, Malouf, & Sag 2001). In van Noord and Bouma (1994) it is argued, on the basis of examples like those presented in the introduction, that the distribution and scope of adjuncts in the context of Dutch verb clusters also provide evidence for lexical selection of adjuncts as complements. By treating adjuncts as complements, selected lexically by the heads which they modify, adjuncts become visible for argument inheritance. This basically allows adjuncts in the Mittelfeld to act as adjuncts of an embedded verb.

In van Noord and Bouma (1994) the valency of verbs is extended by means of a (recursive) lexical rule which adds adjuncts to COMPS. In Bouma, Malouf, and Sag (2001) an alternative is proposed, in which adjuncts are introduced in the mapping from argument structure to dependency structure (DEPS). The *Argument Structure Extension* principle defines this mapping:

(36)   **Argument Structure Extension:**

$$word \rightarrow \begin{bmatrix} \text{HEAD} & \boxed{2} \\ \text{DEPS} & \boxed{1} \bigcirc list(\begin{bmatrix} \text{MOD} \begin{bmatrix} \text{HEAD} \boxed{2} \end{bmatrix} \end{bmatrix}) \\ \text{ARG-ST} & \boxed{1} \end{bmatrix}$$

Note that Argument Structure Extension is defined as an implicational constraint: each feature structure of type *word* must satisfy the feature structure in the implication. The value of DEPS is defined as the *sequence union* (or *shuffle*) of two lists: ARG-ST and an arbitrary list of adjuncts. This essentially allows any number of adjuncts to be interspersed with arguments on DEPS, while leaving the relative order of ARG-ST unchanged.[8] The mapping of dependents to SUBJ and COMPS remains as before. A transitive verb like *bestuderen* can now be instantiated with a two element DEPS-list as before, but also with a three element list, as shown in the examples below.

(37)

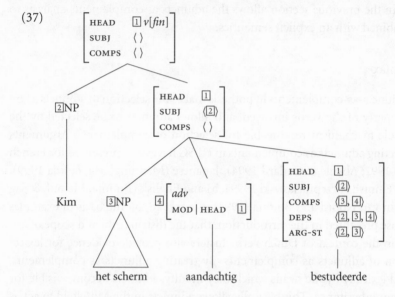

Note that argument structure extension requires the MOD|HEAD value of the adjunct to unify with the head features of the head which is being modified. The fact that adverbs typically modify verbs, but not nouns or prepositions, is accounted for by restricting MOD|HEAD of adverbs to the type *verb*.

The formulation of Argument Structure Extension in (36) does not impose any restrictions on the ordering of adjuncts with respect to arguments, and thus in general allows adjuncts to precede subjects (the initial element of ARG-ST) as well. In Dutch, adjuncts may precede subjects (in subordinate clauses) only if certain conditions are met. It seems possible to formulate the relevant constraints on adjunct-subject word order in terms of the framework presented here, but this falls outside the scope of the present paper.

As selection of adjuncts is subsumed by the same mechanism responsible for the selection of complements, inheritance of COMPS-lists consisting of both arguments and adjuncts is predicted. This is illustrated in the example below.

(38)

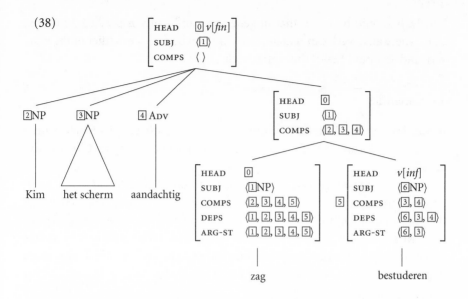

In those cases where the adverb clearly modifies the matrix verb, it is assumed to be introduced on the DEPS list of the matrix verb, and it is not inherited from the COMPS list of the governed verb.

(39)

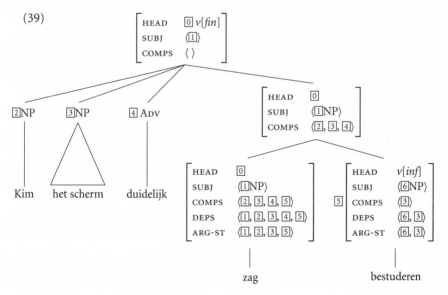

Finally, it should be noted that in general an ambiguity is predicted in those cases where an adverb can semantically function both as a modifier of the main verb and as a modifier of the matrix verb.

4.2 Semantics

In this section the adjunct-as-complements analysis is supplemented with a semantics in terms of LRS. I will analyze both scope-taking and intersective adjuncts.

Scope-taking adverbials, such as negation, modal adverbs (*mogelijk, possibly*), and frequency adverbs (*vaak (often), nooit (never)*), must take scope over the predicate introduced by the verb they modify. Furthermore, unlike quantified NP's, which in general can take arbitrary wide scope, adjuncts must take scope within the clausal or verbal projection of the verb of which they are a dependent:

(40) Kim gelooft dat de trein naar Amsterdam **vaak** te laat is
      Kim believes that the train to   Amsterdam often   late   is
      Kim believes that the train to Amsterdam often is late
      Kim often believes that the train to Amsterdam is late

These two constraints on adjunct scope can be implemented in LRS by assuming that adverbials must take scope over the MAIN of the head they modify, and must take scope within the TOP of the head they modify. This is exemplified in (41), which gives the semantics of the lexical entry for *regelmatig (regularly)*, which is assumed to introduce a unary operator.

$$
(41) \quad
\begin{bmatrix}
\text{PHON } \langle regelmatig \rangle \\[2mm]
\text{HEAD} \begin{bmatrix} \text{TOP} & \boxed{1} \\ \text{MAIN} & \boxed{3} \end{bmatrix} \\[4mm]
\text{MOD} \begin{bmatrix} \text{HEAD} \begin{bmatrix} verb \\ \text{TOP} & \boxed{1} \\ \text{MAIN} & \boxed{2} \end{bmatrix} \end{bmatrix} \\[6mm]
\text{PARTS } \langle \boxed{3}\text{regularly}(\alpha) \rangle \\[1mm]
\& \boxed{2} \vartriangleleft \alpha
\end{bmatrix}
$$

The fact that the scope of an adverb is limited to the TOP of the verb it modifies is a consequence of the fact that the TOP values of both are unified. Thus, the MAIN term introduced by the adverb must be within the semantic domain of the verb. Note also that if *geloven* (*believe*) selects for a clausal argument whose TOP is unified with one of the arguments of the *believe* relation (i.e. *believe* functions like a modal operator much like *must* in (34)), the adverb *vaak* (*often*) in (40) can take scope over *te laat zijn* (*be late*) but not over *gelooft*.

Example (42) contains a scopal adverb preceding a quantified NP. In such cases, the NP may take either wide or narrow scope with respect to the adverb.

(42)   dat   Kim   regelmatig   een   arts   bezoekt
        that Kim   regularly   a   doctor   visits
        that Kim regularly visits a doctor
        that there is a doctor which Kim regularly visits

In the adjuncts-as-complements analysis, the DEPS-list of the verbal head, *bezoekt*, needs to be instantiated to a list containing one modifier, as shown in (43). This gives rise to the derivation shown in (44). The TOP-value can be resolved to a well-formed logical formula in two ways (45a, b). Note that in both cases the scopal constraints on various parts of the structure are respected. In particular, as long as *regularly* scopes over the main verbal predicate *visit*, the quantifier may take either wide or narrow scope with respect to the adverbial operator.

(43)

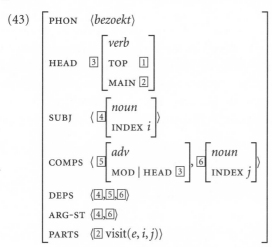

(44)

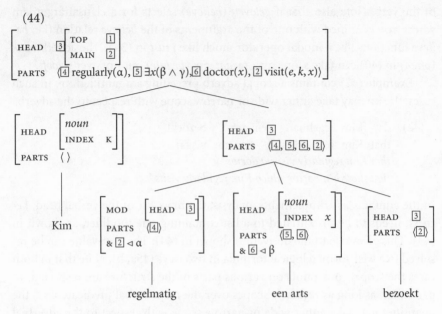

(45) a. $\boxed{1}$ regularly$(\,\exists x(\mathrm{doctor}(x)\wedge\mathrm{visit}(e,k,x)))$

b. $\boxed{1}$ $\exists x(\mathrm{doctor}(x)\wedge\mathrm{regularly}(\mathrm{visit}(e,k,x)))$

Intersective modifiers are characterized by the fact that they introduce a predicate which takes the event introduced by the verbal predicate as argument. Intersective modifiers do not seem to give rise to ambiguities with respect to quantified NP arguments (46a). Furthermore, if an intersective adverb co-occurs with a quantifier, it seems the event predicated over by the adverb cannot be bound by an existential quantifier scoping over the quantified NP (46b).

(46) a. dat Kim vandaag een arts   bezoekt
          that Kim today   a   doctor visits
          that Kim visits a doctor today
      b. dat Kim vandaag geen arts   bezoekt
          that Kim today   no   doctor visits
          that Kim does not visit a doctor today
          that there is a moment today where Kim does not visit a doctor

These observations motivate the analysis of intersective adverbials exemplified in (47) below. The relation symbol $\unlhd$ is defined as follows: $f \unlhd g$ holds if $f = g$ or if $g = g' \wedge g''$ and $f \unlhd g'$ or $f \unlhd g''$. In other words, the adverbial predicate must be conjoined with the MAIN predicate introduced by the verb, possibly in conjunction with other predicates.

(47)

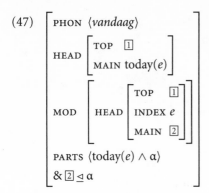

$$
\begin{bmatrix}
\text{PHON} & \langle \textit{vandaag} \rangle \\
\text{HEAD} & \begin{bmatrix} \text{TOP} & \boxed{1} \\ \text{MAIN} & \text{today}(e) \end{bmatrix} \\
\text{MOD} & \begin{bmatrix} \text{HEAD} & \begin{bmatrix} \text{TOP} & \boxed{1} \\ \text{INDEX} & e \\ \text{MAIN} & \boxed{2} \end{bmatrix} \end{bmatrix} \\
\text{PARTS} & \langle \text{today}(e) \wedge \alpha \rangle \\
& \& \boxed{2} \trianglelefteq \alpha
\end{bmatrix}
$$

The effect of this constraint is to effectively force narrow scope for the adverb in those cases where an ambiguity would otherwise be conceivable. The example in (46b) gives rise to the semantic structure in (48a), whose TOP can only be resolved as shown in (48b).

(48)   a.
$$
\begin{bmatrix}
\text{HEAD} & \begin{bmatrix} \text{TOP} & \boxed{1} \\ \text{MAIN} & \boxed{2} \end{bmatrix} \\
\text{PARTS} & \langle \neg \exists x (\alpha \wedge \beta), \boxed{3}\, doctor(x), today(e) \wedge \gamma, \boxed{2}\, visit(e,k,x) \rangle \\
& \& \boxed{3} \triangleleft \alpha \, \& \boxed{2} \trianglelefteq \gamma
\end{bmatrix}
$$

   b. $\boxed{1}\ \neg\exists x(doctor(x) \wedge today(e) \wedge visit(e,k,x))$

The ambiguity of adverbial phrases in the context of argument inheritance verbs can now be described precisely. If a scopal adjunct is introduced on the lower verb, it must take scope over the predicate introduced by that verb and within the semantic domain defined by that predicate (i.e. TOP). The derivation with the narrow scope reading for *regelmatig* in (49) is given in (50).

(49)   dat   ik   Kim   regelmatig   zag   studeren
         that   I   Kim   regularly   saw   study
         that I saw Kim study regularly

(50)

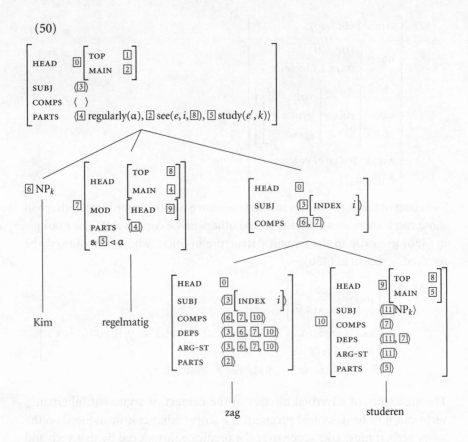

An adjunct is introduced by Argument Structure Extension on the DEPS list of the verb *bestuderen*. Argument Structure Extension unifies the MOD|HEAD value of the adjunct with the HEAD of the verb. The adjunct is inherited by the verb *zag*. When this verb combines with its complements, the feature structure of the adverb *regelmatig* is unified with the adjunct on COMPS of *zag*, which is the same as the adjunct introduced originally on the DEPS list of *studeren*. As the MOD|HEAD value of the adverb *regelmatig* is unified with the HEAD value of *studeren*, constraints on the relative scope of *regelmatig* are interpreted relative to *studeren*. As the TOP value of *studeren* is an argument of the matrix predicate *see*, the adverb must have narrow scope with respect to *see*. Thus, the only way to resolve the TOP value of the VP is as shown in (51).

(51) $\boxed{1}$ see$(e, i, \text{regularly}(\text{study}(e', k)))$

The wide scope reading differs from the structure given in (50) only in that Argument Structure Extension introduces an adjunct on DEPS of *zag* in that case.

The semantic constraints on the scope of *regelmatig* would apply relative to *see*, and therefore only the wide scope reading would be available (as *regelmatig* has to outscope the MAIN predicate of *zag* in that case).

In this section, it has been demonstrated that Argument Structure Extension allows adjuncts to be added to the syntactic valence of verbal heads. LRS provides the tools to provide a semantics for adjuncts selected as complements as well. The relative order of adjuncts and arguments, as well as the interaction between scope and word order, has been left almost completely unconstrained, however. In the remainder of this paper, I will be concerned with the question to what extent additional constraints on the word order and scope of adjuncts need to be imposed.

5. The scope of adjuncts with respect to the matrix verb

The theory outlined in the previous sections makes a number of predictions about word order and scope of adjuncts in the Mittelfeld preceding a verb cluster consisting of an argument inheritance verb and a main verb. Adjuncts are introduced lexically, and are freely added to DEPS of either the matrix or the governed verb. Argument inheritance accounts for the inheritance of arguments as well as adjuncts. The analysis therefore predicts that adjuncts in the Mittelfeld may take either wide or narrow scope with respect to the matrix verb. In this section, I argue that this prediction is correct for various types of adjuncts.

Adverbials to the left of a verb cluster may in general take wide or narrow scope with respect to the matrix verb. This is not to say that all examples involving adverbials and verb clusters are ambiguous. In some cases the relative scope of an adverbial is hard to determine, and does not seem to have an impact on semantics. In other cases, there is a clear preference for interpreting an adverbial as taking either wide or narrow scope. However, genuinely ambiguous cases exist as well.

In cases involving a simple temporal or locative adjunct, it may be hard to determine whether an adjunct restricts the event introduced by the matrix verb, or only the event introduced by the embedded verb:

(52)   dat Sanne Kim **gisteren**   een artikel zag schrijven
        that Sanne Kim yesterday a   paper saw write
        that Sanne saw Kim write a paper yesterday

It is almost impossible to think of situations where the temporal adverb applies strictly to either the matrix verb or the embedded verb. In other cases, the adverb is most naturally interpreted as restricting the event introduced by the embedded verb:

(53) dat Kim het artikel **morgen**   af   wil   hebben
      that Kim the paper   tomorrow PRT wants finish
      that Kim wants the paper finished tomorrow

Ambiguous examples can be found as well:

(54) dat Kim Sanne **in de tuin**   hoorde zingen
      that Kim Sanne in the garden heard   sing
      Kim heard Sanne sing in the garden
      In the garden, Kim heard Sanne sing

Here, the adjunct may restrict either the location of the event introduced by the perception verb *horen* or the event introduced by the main verb *zingen*.

Operator adverbs, like negation, modal adverbs, and adverbs quantifying over events, tend to take scope over the matrix verb, although narrow scope readings are not excluded.

(55) Ik heb Johan **nooit** horen klagen   over   geld
      I have Johan never   heard complain about money
      I have never heard Johan complain about money

(56) dat Kim Sanne de opdracht   **niet** zag inleveren.
      that Kim Sanne the assignment not   saw hand in
      that Kim didn't see Sanne hand in the assignment

(57) dat Sanne deze film   **waarschijnlijk** mag zien
      that Sanne this movie probably   may see
      that Sanne probably is allowed to see this movie

(58) Zuid-Afrika is een staat die   zich **niet** laat intimideren door
      South Africa is a   state which self not   lets intimidated by
      dreigementen
      threats
      South Africa, is a state which doesn't let itself be intimidated by threats

The examples above illustrate that operator adverbs tend to take scope over perception, modal, and causative verbs. However, in some cases an operator adverb can take either wide or narrow scope:

(59)   dat Kim de boeken **nooit** wil   controleren
       that Kim the books   never wants check
       that Kim never wants to check the books
       that Kim wants to never check the books

(60)   dat Kim het verslag **wekelijks** wil   ontvangen
       that Kim the report   weekly   wants to receive
       that Kim weekly wants to receive the report
       that Kim wants to receive the report weekly

Manner adverbs tend to impose strong restrictions on the kind of verbs they can modify. The adverb *wild*, for instance, can modify *zwaaien*, but not the *accusativus-cum-infinitivo*-usage of *zien*. Therefore, (61) only has a reading where the manner adverb takes narrow scope with respect to the matrix verb.

(61)   dat Cathy hen   **wild** zag zwaaien.
       that Cathy them wild saw wave
       that Cathy saw them waving wildly

More examples are presented below:[9]

(62)   Ik heb de minister **schouderophalend** horen zeggen dat er
       I   have the minister shruggingly   hear   say   that there
       een grens is.
       a   border is
       I heard the minister say shruggingly that there is a limit

(63)   de beestjes   die   ze   **dartel**   naderbij zien fladderen
       the small creatures which they playfully closer   see   fly
       the small creatures which they see fly towards them playfully

(64)   Het is vreemd dat Stegemann Schubert **uitvoerig** laat   praten
       It   is strange that Stegemann Schubert extensively allow talk
       It is strange that Stegemann allows Schubert to talk extensively

While verbs of saying combine frequently with the adverb *schouderophalend* (*shruggingly*), this adverb cannot normally co-occur with *horen* (*hear*). Similarly, the adverbs *dartel* (*playfully*) and *uitvoerig* (*extensively*) can be used in conjunction with *fladderen* and *praten*, but not with *zien* and *laten*. Thus, only the narrow scope readings are possible.

The dependency between the embedded verb and some manner adverbs can also be demonstrated by examples like (65) and (66) below. The adverb *hard* can mean both *fast* and *strongly, fiercefully, severely*. Only the first reading is available in (65), whereas only the second reading is available in (66). As the matrix verb is identical in both cases, this difference in interpretation must be due to differences in meaning of the embedded verb, thus providing evidence for the fact that the manner adverb modifies the embedded verb.

(65) Kim heeft Anne **hard** zien weglopen
       Kim has   Anne fast   see run-away
       Kim has seen Anne run away fast

(66) Kim heeft de politie de demonstranten **hard** zien aanpakken
       Kim has   the police the demonstrators severly see deal-with
       Kim has seen the police deal with the demonstrators severly

The conclusion to be drawn from the examples above is that adjuncts in the Mittelfeld in general may take wide or narrow scope over a matrix verb. If either a wide scope or narrow scope reading is excluded, this is due to the lexical semantics of either the verb or adjunct involved. It is not the case that scopal ambiguity is restricted to particular classes of adjuncts.

6. Scrambling of adjuncts and arguments

The analysis outlined above introduces adjuncts lexically, by adding adjuncts freely to DEPS. Thus, it is predicted that adjuncts and arguments in principle can occur in both orders. As arguments are inherited on ARG-ST by argument-inheritance verbs, it is predicted that matrix adjuncts may follow arguments of the embedded verb. The examples below provide evidence that this is correct.

Adjuncts of the matrix verb may clearly appear in a position immediately preceding the verb cluster, and possibly following inherited arguments:

(67) dat Kim de kinderen het boek **niet** zag lezen
       that Kim the children the book not saw read
       that Kim didn't see the children read the book

Here, an operator adverb follows the direct object of the embedded verb *lezen*.

As adjuncts are mixed freely with non-adjunct dependents of a verb (i.e. both arguments and inherited arguments), the analysis also predicts that matrix adjuncts may occur between arguments of the lower verb. The following example shows that this is indeed possible:

(68) dat Kim de spelers de bal **niet eerder** zo hard zag raken
       that Kim the players the ball not before so hard saw hit
       that Kim never before saw the players hit the ball so hard

Adjuncts which take narrow scope, on the other hand, cannot precede arguments of the matrix verb. This is illustrated in the example below:

(69) *dat Anne **hard** Piet zag weglopen
       that   Anne fast   Piet saw run away
       that Anne saw Piet run away fast

In (69), the adverb *hard* precedes *Piet*, the direct object of *zag*. The argument structure of a perception verb like *zien* consists of a subject, an object, inherited arguments, and a verbal complement, in that order. Inherited adjunct complements can therefore never the object. The adverb *hard* in (69) can therefore only be interpreted as modifying the matrix verb *zien*, a reading which is semantically anomalous.

Finally, note that this analysis of adjunct word order differs from scrambling in that it does not involve movement of arguments in the Mittelfeld. This appears to be a welcome result in light of the discussion in Neeleman (1994), who criticizes scrambling analyses of adjunct placement. In particular, he notes several data that argue against the fact that scrambling involves movement of argument NP's. For instance, the order of arguments in Dutch, compared to a language like German, is relatively fixed. In general it is not possible to reorder arguments with respect to each other. However, the examples in (68) and below show that an adjunct may follow one or more arguments:

(70) a. dat Kim **niet eerder** de spelers de bal zo hard zag raken
       b. dat Kim de spelers **niet eerder** de bal zo hard zag raken

If all orders are derived by means of scrambling of one or more argument NPs, one would expect the following examples to be grammatical as well:

(71) a. *dat Kim de bal **niet eerder** de spelers zo hard zag raken
       b. *dat Kim de bal de spelers **niet eerder** zo hard zag raken

The ungrammaticality of the examples in (71) (under the reading given in (68), i.e. with *de bal* as object of *raken*) shows that scrambling overgenerates in this respect.

The adjuncts-as-complements analysis, does not have this problem, as it does not presuppose that arguments can be reordered freely. Instead, it assumes a lexical mechanism that allows adjuncts to be added to DEPS. Neeleman (1994) proposes a transformational analysis where adjuncts may be added to verbal projections at D-structure, and where selection of arguments, by means of θ-role assignment, is formulated so as to allow adjuncts to intervene between predicates and arguments at D-structure. This seems to be a transformational analogue of the analysis proposed here.

7. A constraint on word order and scope

A number of authors have observed that, while the position of adjuncts in the Mittelfield appears to be relatively free, there is a strong relation between the position of an adjunct and its potential to take scope over other adjuncts and arguments. In this section, I review the data and point out that constraints on scope can be observed both in simple clauses and in clauses containing a verb cluster, where adjuncts and arguments may be licenced by different verbal predicates.

A constraint on the scope of elements on DEPS is proposed, which has the effect that adjuncts may only take scope over other dependents to their right. The constraint generalizes over clauses with a single predicate and verb clusters. It rules out the apparent cases of overgeneration of the account so far.

7.1 Multiple adjuncts

If a clause contains two adjuncts in the Mittelfeld, reordering of the adjuncts has an effect on scope:

(72) a.   dat Jan   **met tegenzin vaak** pizza eet
           that John unwillingly   often pizza eats
           that John unwillingly often eats pizza
      b.   dat Jan **vaak met tegenzin** pizza eet
           that John often unwillingly eats pizza

Ackema and Neeleman (to appear) present the following example:

(73) dat we **in die   dagen volgens   Marleens plan** op vakantie
      that we in those days according to Marleen's plan on holiday
      gingen
      went
      that we used to go on holiday in accordance with Marleen's plan in those days

(74) dat we **volgens Marleens plan in die dagen** op vakantie gingen
      that, in accordance with Marleen's plan, we went on holiday in that period

They conclude that, in the Mittelfeld, the relative scope of adjuncts is strictly determined by word order, with the leftmost adjunct always taking scope over any following adjuncts. Ackema and Neeleman (to appear) also present the following example:

(75)   dat   ik   Jan   het   project   **regelmatig gedurende een   tijdje** zag
        that   I   Jan   the   project   regularly   for   some time   saw
        hinderen
        hamper

They observe that in this example, the adverb *regelmatig* has to take scope over the phrase *gedurende een tijdje* (76a). Note, however, that the example actually contains a verb cluster. The adjuncts can therefore in principle take scope over either the matrix verb *zien* or the embedded verb *hinderen*. The narrow scope reading for both adjuncts seems possible (76b), as well as the reading where *regelmatig* takes wide scope over the matrix verb and *gedurende een tijdje* takes narrow scope (76c). The reading where both take wide scope seems semantically odd, but not impossible in principle (76d). Readings where the adjunct *gedurence een tijdje* takes wider scope than *regelmatig* are completely excluded, however (76e–g).

(76)   a.   *that I regularly saw Jan hamper the project for some time*
        b.   *that I saw Jan regularly for some time hamper the project*
        c.   *that I regularly saw Jan for some time hamper the project*
        d.   ?*that I regularly for some time saw Jan hamper the project*
        e.   *that, for some time, I regularly saw Jan hamper the project*
        f.   *that I saw Jan for some time regularly hamper the project*
        g.   *that I for some time saw Jan regularly hamper the project*

The example shows that the observation that adjunct scope follows word order applies both to adjuncts modifying the same predicate and to adjuncts in the Mittelfeld modifying different predicates.

The following examples also demonstrate the similarity of simple clauses and clauses containing a verb cluster in this respect.

(77)   a.   dat   de   speler   de   bal   **waarschijnlijk snel**   afspeelt
             that   the   player   the   ball   probably   quickly   passes
             that the player probably passes the ball quickly
        b.   dat de speler **waarschijnlijk snel** de bal afspeelt
        c.   dat de speler **waarschijnlijk** de bal **snel** afspeelt
        d.   *dat de speler de bal **snel waarschijnlijk** afspeelt
        e.   *dat de speler **snel waarschijnlijk** de bal afspeelt
        f.   *dat de speler **snel** de bal **waarschijnlijk** afspeelt

Examples (77a–c) illustrate that adverb combinations may precede or follow the direct object. Examples (77d–f) show that manner adverbs cannot precede an operator adverb. This is probably due to the lexical semantics of manner adverbs. Manner adverbs tend to co-occur only with specific verbal predicates. If a modal adverb intervenes, and if adjunct scope follows word order, the manner adverb would modify the semantics of the adverb rather than the verbal predicate. This leads to semantic anomaly.

Example (78) shows that exactly the same orders are possible in clauses with a verb cluster.

(78) a. dat de speler de bal **waarschijnlijk snel**   leert   afspelen
         that the player the ball probably   quickly learns pass
         that the player probably learns to quickly pass the ball
         that the player probably quickly learns to pass the ball

    b. dat de speler **waarschijnlijk snel** de bal leert afspelen

    c. dat de speler **waarschijnlijk** de bal **snel** leert afspelen

    d. *dat de speler de bal **snel waarschijnlijk** leert afspelen

    e. *dat de speler **snel waarschijnlijk** de bal leert afspelen

    f. *dat de speler **snel** de bal **waarschijnlijk** leert afspelen

In this case, the manner adverb may either modify the matrix verb or the embedded verb.[10] Under a reading where the modal adverb modifies the matrix verb *leert*, and the manner adverb *snel* modifies *afspelen*, one can only explain the ungrammaticality of (78d–f) if constraints on the scope of adjuncts apply to adjuncts licenced by different verbal predicates as well.

The conclusion of this section is that, although adjuncts of a matrix predicate may freely mix with arguments of a lower clause in Dutch verb raising constructions, they may not follow adjuncts of the lower clause. A potential explanation for this fact requires that the constraint which accounts for the fact that adjunct scope follows word order, applies to adjuncts of a single predicate as well as to adjuncts which are licenced by different members of a verb cluster.

7.2 Scope of adjuncts and arguments

Although adjuncts can mix with arguments rather freely in Dutch, the various word order possibilities do have an effect on semantics. Much of the literature on object scrambling is concerned with the question how to characterize the semantic effects of scrambling exactly. Here, I will focus on scope effects only.

The following example illustrates that the scope of an adjunct in the Mittelfeld depends on its position with respect to other arguments:

(79) a. dat Kim **regelmatig** twee computers verplaatst
         that Kim regularly   two   computers moves
         that Kim regularly moves two computers
         that there are two computers which Kim moves regularly
      b. dat Kim twee computers **regelmatig** verplaatst
         that there are two computers which Kim moves regularly

The adverb may only take scope over the indefinite argument NP if it precedes the argument. Ruys (2001) notes that a similar effect can be observed in the context of intensional predicates:

(80) a. dat Jan **met een verrekijker** een eenhoorn zoekt
         that Jan with binoculars   a   unicorn   seeks
         that, with binoculars, Jan searches for a unicorn
      b. dat Jan een eenhoorn **met een verrekijker** zoekt
         that there is a unicorn which John seeks with binoculars

The first example is ambiguous between a *de dicto* and *de re* reading for the existential, whereas the second only has a *de re* reading.

In those cases where a subject can be non-initial, the interaction of word order and scope can also be demonstrated for subjects.

(81) dat er   **regelmatig** een dokter bij Kim op bezoek komt
      that there regularly   a   doctor at   Kim on visit   comes
      that regularly, a doctor visits Kim
      that there is a doctor which regularly visits Kim

(82) dat een dokter **regelmatig** bij Kim op bezoek komt
      that a   doctor regularly   at   Kim on visit   comes
      that there is a doctor which regularly visits Kim

The first example, involving an existential *there* construction, is ambiguous, whereas in the second example only the wide scope reading for the subject is possible.

The observations concerning adjunct and argument scope apply to verb clusters as well.

(83) a. dat Kim **regelmatig** minstens twee computers moet repareren
         that Kim regularly   at least two   computers must repair
         that Kim regularly has to repair at least two computers
         that there are at least two computers which Kim has to repair regularly

      b.   dat Kim minstens twee computers **regelmatig** moet repareren
           that there are at least two computers which Kim has to repair regularly

(84) a.   dat Jan **waarschijnlijk** een pizza wil   bestellen
           that Jan probably   a   pizza wants order
           that Jan probably wants to order a pizza
           that there is a pizza which Jan probably wants to order
      b.   dat Jan een pizza **waarschijnlijk** wil bestellen
           that there is a pizza which Jan probably wants to order

(85) a.   dat ik Kim **regelmatig** minstens twee computers zie
           that I   Kim regularly   at least   three computers see
           verplaatsen
           move
           that I regularly see Kim move at least two computers
           that I see Kim move regularly at least two computers
           that there are at least two computers, which I regularly see Kim move
           that there are at least two computers, which I see Kim regularly move
      b.   dat ik Kim minstens twee computers **regelmatig** zie verplaatsen
           that there are at least two computers, which I regularly see Kim move
           that there are at least two computers, which I see Kim regularly move

The examples illustrate that the interaction between adjunct and argument scope applies equally to cases where an adjunct and an inherited argument co-occur in the Middlefield. Example (85b) is ambiguous where the scope of the adverb with respect to the matrix predicate is concerned. Under both readings, however, the adverb may not take scope over a preceding argument.

7.3   A semantic constraint on dependency structure

The observations in the two preceding paragraphs suggest that adjunct scope needs to be constrained in such a way that adjuncts may not take scope over preceding adjuncts and arguments. Furthermore, the constraint should generalize over both simple clauses and clauses with verb clusters.

    The adjuncts-as-complements analysis treats adjuncts and arguments as lexically selected dependents of a verbal predicate. Furthermore, I have assumed that the order of elements on DEPS directly reflects word order in the Mittelfeld. Scope ambiguities are accounted for in underspecified semantics by assuming that the constraints on the logical form of a phrase leave room for different hierarchical orderings of the semantic elements which give rise to the ambiguity. Constraining the scope of adjuncts so that they may not take scope over preceding dependents (arguments or adjuncts) can therefore be achieved by imposing additional constraints on the scope of adjuncts, relative to their position on DEPS.

The following constraint on verbal lexical entries implements this:

(86)
$$
\begin{bmatrix} word \\[4pt] \text{DEPS} \quad \Big[\ldots, \boxed{1}\big[\text{HEAD} \mid \text{MAIN}\boxed{2}\big], \ldots, \boxed{3}\big[\text{HEAD} \mid \text{MAIN}\boxed{4}\big], \ldots\Big] \\[8pt] \text{ARG-ST} \; \boxed{5} \\[4pt] \&\ \boxed{2} \lhd \boxed{4} \end{bmatrix} \rightarrow \boxed{3} \in \boxed{5}
$$

The idea is that for each pair A, B, of elements on DEPS: if B follows A and outscopes A, B must be an argument (i.e. a member of ARG-ST). This basically ensures that adjuncts can only scope over depedents which follow them on DEPS, while it does not impose such a constraint on arguments. Note that the constraint prevents adjuncts from taking scope over preceding adjuncts as well as over preceding arguments. Arguments, on the other hand, can still take arbitrary scope.

Consider the lexical entry for the verb *eet* in (87), for example. It will contain a DEPS list containing two adjuncts (eventually instantiated with the MAIN values given) and a direct object (88). The constraint in (86) prevents the adjunct *met tegenzin* to take scope over *vaak*.

(87)   dat Jan **vaak met tegenzin** pizza eet
        that John often unwillingly eats pizza

(88)
$$
\begin{bmatrix} \text{DEPS} \quad \langle \boxed{1}, \big[\text{HD}\,[\text{MAIN often}(e)]\big], \big[\text{HD}\,[\text{MAIN unwillingly}(e)]\big], \boxed{2} \rangle \\[6pt] \text{ARG-ST} \; \langle \boxed{1}\text{NP}, \boxed{2}\text{NP} \rangle \end{bmatrix}
$$

An example involving a verb cluster is given in (88). If both adjuncts are introduced on either the matrix verb or the embedded verb, the scope constraint clearly prevents a reading where *waarschijnlijk* takes scope over *snel*. The situation where *waarschijnlijk* is introduced on the matrix verb, and *snel* is inherited is sketched in (90).

(89)   *dat de speler de bal **snel**   **waarschijnlijk** leert   afspelen
        that the player the ball quickly probably   learns pass

$$(90) \quad \begin{bmatrix} \text{DEPS} & \langle \boxed{1}, \boxed{2}, \boxed{3}, \begin{bmatrix} \text{HD} \begin{bmatrix} \text{MAIN probably}(e) \end{bmatrix} \end{bmatrix}, \boxed{4} \rangle \\ \\ \text{ARG-ST} & \langle \boxed{1}\text{NP}, \boxed{2}\text{NP}, \boxed{3} \begin{bmatrix} \text{HD} \begin{bmatrix} \text{MAIN quickly}(e) \end{bmatrix} \end{bmatrix}, \boxed{4} \begin{bmatrix} \text{COMPS} \langle \boxed{2}, \boxed{3} \rangle \end{bmatrix} \rangle \end{bmatrix}$$

Here, *waarschijnlijk* cannot take scope over *snel*, as *waarschijnlijk* is not an argument.

The fact that argument inheritance is implemented using ARG-ST instead of DEPS may suggest that inherited adjuncts are mistakenly treated as arguments in (86). While this is true in principle, no overgeneration results, as the scope of inherited adjuncts is always restricted to the TOP of the verb which introduces them. Thus, an inherited adjunct can never scope over a matrix verb (or any of its arguments) to begin with.[11]

The constraint proposed above only restricts the scope of adjuncts. It is compatible, however, with a proposal for German in Kiss (2001). Kiss argues that in clauses with a canonical word order, i.e. SUBJ < I-OBJ < D-OBJ, scope follows linear order. The scope of an adverb, which can intervene between any of the arguments, is also strictly determined by linear order. Ambiguity arises only in cases where there is a mismatch between obliqueness and linear order. If a subject follows the direct object, scope may either follow linear order or respect obliqueness. Steedman (2002) speculates that a similar situation might hold for certain Dutch constructions as well.

8. Conclusions

In this paper, a lexicalist, surface-oriented, account of adjunct word order and scope in the Mittelfeld has been proposed. It differs from most of the transformational literature by not assuming a *scrambling* transformation, or alternative mechanism, for reordering arguments. Instead, it has been assumed that adjuncts may be freely inserted in the lexical dependency structure of verbal predicates. While most of the literature on scrambling has focussed on simplex clauses, I have argued that constraints on the relative scope of adjuncts and arguments generalize to clauses involving verb clusters as well. Adjunct scope in the Mittelfeld strictly follows word order. In the analysis proposed here, which combines a lexical treatment of adjunct selection with underspecification semantics, this constraint can be expressed as a general constraint on the dependency structure of lexical entries.

Acknowledgements

I would like to thank the participants of the Leipzig Colloquium on the Grammar of German and Dutch Verbal Constructions (February, 2001), the members of the Groningen Semantics Lab, and Pieter Seuren for their helpful comments on previous versions of this paper.

Notes

1. The labels vc and vp are used for expository reasons only, where vc (*verbal complex*) is used for phrases consisting of a lexical verbal head and a lexical verbal complement, and vp is used for all other verbal phrases.

2. In Bouma, Malouf, and Sag (2001), a unified account of subject, complement, and adjunct extraction is given by assuming that dependents may be realized on slash (the feature used to register non-local dependencies) instead of on one of the (local) valence features. This possibility is ignored in the presentation below.

3. In (19) $A \oplus B$ denotes the concatenation or 'append' of the two lists A and B.

4. The representation of *argument inheritance* verbs in the architecture proposed by Bouma, Malouf, and Sag (2001) is also addressed in De Kuthy and Meurers (1999, 2001). In their proposal, *argument structure* does not include inherited arguments. Instead, arguments which must be inherited from a verbal complement are incorporated in deps by means of the constraint which defines the mapping between arg-st and deps. I believe their formulation is essentially correct, especially if binding phenomena (which must most likely be accounted for in terms of arg-st) and extraction are taken into account as well. As the formulation of a mapping constraint which extends deps both with adjuncts and inherited arguments is complex, I will assume, for ease of exposition, that the effect of argument inheritance is encoded lexically in arg-st.

5. The head feature top contains the semantics of a phrase, as explained in the next section.

6. The parts lists in (Richter & Sailer 2001b) contain elements corresponding to relation names and individual arguments as well. Here, I refrain from including that level of decomposition.

7. Note that the event variable of the verbal predicate remains unbound. I will assume that its proper interpretation can be arrived at by replacing it by a Skolem constant dependent on the (non-existential) quantifiers which take scope over it.

8. The sequence union or shuffle of two lists A and B consists of a list containing all and only the elements of A and B. Furthermore, if A_1 precedes A_2 on A, it must also precede A_2 in the result. Similarly for list B. The operation resembles shuffling two decks of cards.

9. The examples were extracted from a Dutch newspaper corpus (*de Volkskrant op cd-rom 1997*) using the Gsearch corpus tool (Corley et al. 2001).

10. A narrow scope reading of the modal adverb is again excluded for lexical semantic reasons, i.e. the object of learning can be an verbal predicate, but is unlikely to be a modal predicate.

11. A more elegant account can perhaps be obtained by following the suggestions in De Kuthy and Meurers (2001) (see also Note 4). Another option is to introduce a binary feature to distinguish between arguments and adjuncts.

CHAPTER 2

Verbal clusters and cluster creepers

Arnold Evers

UiL OTS

1. The issue and the gambits

1.1 Core examples

The term 'verbal cluster' will be used here as an informal observational indication for complex predicates in Dutch, c.q. West-Germanic. Complex predicates consist of a linear array of predicative heads <+V>. The <+V> heads are in a strict linear order that reflects a selectional hierarchy. The last selected and rightmost <+V> element in Dutch may select a particle or some other <–V> predicative head. This <–V> element is indicated here as the cluster creeper. It may take position in front of any <+V> element in the cluster without any semantic effect whatsoever. See the examples in (1).

(1) Het labyrinth waar ik hem niet

     stranded P   *creeper*

  a. [$\bullet^5$ over $\bullet^4$ zal $\bullet^3$ hoeven $\bullet^2$ laten $\bullet^1$ na<+P>   denken]

  b. [$\bullet^5$ in $\bullet^4$ mag $\bullet^3$ gaan $\bullet^2$ horen $\bullet^1$ fluit<+N>   spelen]

  c. [$\bullet^5$ mee $\bullet^4$ moet $\bullet^3$ willen $\bullet^2$ blijven $\bullet^1$ bezig<+A> houden]

  d. [$\bullet^5$ uit $\bullet^4$ had $\bullet^3$ kunnen $\bullet^2$ zien $\bullet^1$ weg<+Adv> vliegen]

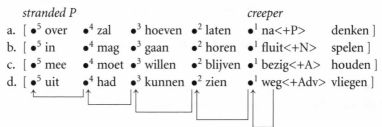

  The labyrinth where I him not

  a.   about   will   need   let   re-   flect

  b.   in   may   begin   hear   flute   play

  c.   with   must   want   stay   busy   keep

  d.   not   out   had   can   see   away fly

The term 'verbal cluster' does not imply a constituent structure for the predicative heads, such as a V^0 stack or a VP stack. See (2a) or (2b).

(2)   a. V^0 stack   b.   VP stack

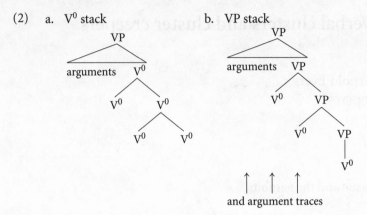

and argument traces

The distribution of the $<-V>$ element also holds for the past participle, a matter that will be discussed later. There is an additional position of the cluster creeper besides the four in front of a $<+V>$. The preposition at the beginning of each pattern in (1) has been stranded by wh-movement. This preposition is always unstressed, whereas the cluster creeper is invariably stressed. The unstressed, stranded preposition cliticizes on the verbal cluster. It may, but need not, cross the cluster creeper, cf. (3b/c), where (3a) repeats (1d).

(3)   Het labyrinth waar ik hem niet (the labyrinth where I him not)

    a.   uit had kunnen zien *weg* vliegen
       out had can   see away fly

    b.   uit *weg* had kunnen zien vliegen
       out away had can   see fly

    c.   ??*weg* uit had kunnen zien vliegen
       away out had can   see fly

The other variants of (1d), the forms (4a) and (4b) have the cluster creeper half-way. They are claimed to be grammatical as well.

(4)   Het labyrinth waar ik hem niet (the labyrinth where I him not)

    a.   uit had kunnen *weg* zien vliegen
       out had can   away see fly

    b.   uit had *weg* kunnen zien vliegen
       out had away can   see fly

The grammaticality of types like (4a) and (4b) is controversial. Van Riemsdijk (1978) and Koster (1978) rejected them as substandard. Bennis (1992) and Evers and Huybregts (1972, published as 1977) consider them as fully acceptable and derive them by an ad hoc rule. Koopman in Koopman and Szabolcsi (2000:229) objects to position superscript 2 in (1) and observes that the quality difference is subtle, but persistent. As such, this is not remarkable. Plausibly, somewhat top-heavy verbal clusters must have a preference for adjacencies as they appear in simpler contexts. Another point may be relevant. The more complex verbal clusters cannot have been an acquisition context. Nevertheless, they exhibit a linear structure that is quite rigid, excepting the creeper distributions. Any change in the position of the finite verb results in straightforward ungrammaticality, cf. (5a). Any switch between the infinitives yields a different meaning or makes no sense at all, cf. (5b). Any change such that the last infinitive comes to the left of the cluster creeper is crushingly ungrammatical, cf. (5c).

(5) Het labyrinth waar ik hem niet (the labyrinth where I him not)
   a. *uit kunnen had zien weg   vliegen
       out can   had see   away   fly
   b. *uit had zien kunnen weg   vliegen
       out had see   can   away   fly
   c. *uit had kunnen zien vliegen weg
       out had can   see   fly   away

The various distributions of the cluster creeper in (3) and (4) are by comparison nearer to, or simply within, the domain of stylistic preferences. The linear structure of a three- or four-membered verbal cluster is rigid with the exception of the cluster creeper. An analysis should preferably clarify both points, the linear rigidity as well as the exception of the cluster creeper. Below I will consider all cluster-creeper positions in (1) as fully grammatical. They will be derived in a uniform way. The possible preference in example (1) for the positions superscripted 5, 4, 3 and 1, over the position superscripted 2 is left unexplained, though the preferences do exist. It is suggested here that they are of a non-grammatical nature.

1.2 Crossing relations

The Dutch/German verbal cluster was well-known in structuralist grammar (Bech 1955; Paardekooper 1955). Several heads within the verbal cluster select their own arguments and all arguments are lined up in front of the verbal cluster. The left-right order of arguments reflects the same hierarchy as the left-right order of the heads. Members originating from higher VP structures precede the members originating from more embedded lower VP structures that are selected later. See diagram (6) with A_n for argument and V_n for argument selecting predicative head. Both originating from the structure VP_n .

(6)   A1 ... A2 ... A3 ... . V1 ... V2 ... V3

This arrangement guarantees the maximal amount of crossing between head-argument relations. Arguments and heads are ordered in two successive arrays. Each array imposes an internal left-right order that derives from the original selectional VP hierarchy. The repetition of an identical order is a weird effect for any theory of language. See the example in (7).

(7)   toen   [ik] [jou] [Icarus] [de afsprong] [meer steil] zag leren maken
              1-   2-   2-   3-   3-   -1   -2   -3
       when   I   you   Icarus   the take-off   more steep   saw teach make
       (when I saw you teaching Icarus to make the take off steeper)

In general, it is not so that each argument needs to be licensed by the head it has been selected by. Consider the English example *Ike had not yet been seen to fly such a steep take-off.* The subject *Ike* is basically selected by *fly*, and ultimately licensed by *has*, a few predicative heads higher. Dutch examples like those in (1) and (7) are more extreme due to the combined effect of two factors. The Dutch set of such verbs not only contains auxiliary and semi-auxiliary verbs. It also contains content verbs, such as *laten* (let), *zien* (see), *leren* (teach), *leren* (learn), *proberen* (try), that bring in their own argument frames. Furthermore, and more importantly, none of the arguments within the complements of Dutch raising verbs are ultimately licensed within the complement. There seems to be a total argument exodus. This holds for structural arguments, inherent arguments, and small clause phrases as well as for external arguments. The sentence splits up in an array of arguments and a corresponding array of predicative heads. This is the basic issue, stated in (8).

(8)   How can more established ways of argument licensing be extended in such
       a way that Dutch, c.q. West-Germanic, comes out as a 'natural' variant?

There are basically three gambits for the problem in (8). All of them have been tried out in the literature.

(9) Gambit *i*   Direct compounding of <+V> heads
                    (Di Sciullo & Williams 1988)
    Gambit *ii*   Argument raising for bare VP complements
                    (Zwart 1996; Koopman & Szabolcsi 2000)
    Gambit *iii*   Head-to-head raising for bare VP complements
                    (Seuren 1972; Evers 1976/1975; Baker 1988)

Verbal clusters are relevant for all principles that interact with the set-up of argument structure: {... (restrictions on the domain of lexical selection, restrictions on long and short reflexivization, restrictions on passive and clitic movement, extended scope of negation, nominalization and gapping of the verbal cluster, extended scope of Extraposition) ...}. I will first formulate the major perspective for each approach, as well as its major disadvantages. It stands to reason that the proponents of each approach have found or will find ways to overcome associated disadvantages. Moreover, solutions within each approach have a natural tendency to become rather theory-internal. Hence it is interesting to confront the existing approaches with new requirements. Two will be presented below. Both will be related to the cluster creeper. It will be argued that a successful analysis should anticipate the stress constancy of the cluster creeper (Section 2) as well as its distributional freedom (Section 3). The outcome will be that both requirements fit in with the first generative solution (Seuren 1972; Evers 1976). This gambit (cf. (9-iii), a cyclically repeated head-to-head raising, will subsequently be extended (Section 4) in order to include the distribution of past participles, reconsidered as a kind of cluster creepers (Section 4.1), and the VP raising of southern Dutch, reconsidered as VP segment raising (Section 4.2).

1.3 Gambit (9i): Direct compounding

A morphological approach is taken by Di Sciullo and Williams (1988) in their analysis of the verbal cluster of Romance causatives. The general perspective of this approach is that the licensing within head-argument structures is sufficiently local so as to require no transformational rearrangements. Di Sciullo and Williams did not attempt to apply this idea to Dutch. One might nevertheless imagine the following. Suppose it were possible to join verbal heads together into a compound. Suppose further, and more crucially, that the argument carrying potential of the verbal heads in (7) could be added up within the compound as diagrammed below in (10).

(10)

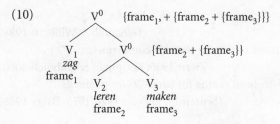

One might now imagine how the argument frame of V_2 contains a position 'theme' for the frame of V_3 to fit in. This is to be repeated for each segment of a compound structure like (10). The full structure of an example like in (7) may now emerge from a compound as in (10). Small wonder all arguments appear to the left of V^0 and in due order. There has been no argument-selecting substructure VP_1, VP_2 or VP_3. Hence it is not necessary or even possible to organize the full argument exodus proclaimed by gambit (9-ii) or the full head exodus proclaimed by gambit (9-iii). It is a minor point that non-verbal compounds in Dutch are left-branching whereas (10) is right branching. More serious must be that compound formation in the Germanic languages is quite free, but not if the highest head is <+V> and projecting for a VP. Compound formation is in principle blocked for such cases. For example, one might design a glider to escape from a labyrinth, and sell the thing as an *escape glider*. Yet, Germanic grammars do not allow a construct like *to escape glide*. This remarkable restriction was explained by Lieber (1983). She argued that the verb *glide* would insist on the full argument structure within its syntactic VP domain. That would make the morphological companion '*escape*' within the compound uninterpretable. Although this was not exactly her point, Lieber easily and correctly invites the observation that deeper-down heads in compounds are unlikely to have a theta grip on phrasal structure outside the compound. For example, a glider may allow one to escape from a labyrinth, but *an escape glider from the labyrinth* adds the direction one must look in to see the thing. It does not indicate its purpose. This differs from *an escapee from the labyrinth*. It suggests that the deeper-down 'relativized' heads in (10) will not have a theta effect outside of (10) unless by some quite construction-specific ad hoc stipulation. The most serious difficulty for the morphological approach in gambit (9i) is the monoclausal argument structure in (10). Sometimes reflexives and quantifiers appear to hang around in some clause as a substructure. See, for example, the sentence in (11), where the co-reference between two surface co-arguments hem_i ('him') and *de vader$_i$* ('the father') does not trigger a reflexivization failure.

(11)   omdat de vader$_i$ zijn zoon niet naar hem$_j$ [hoorde schreeuwen]
        because the father$_i$ his son   not to him$_j$ [heard scream]
        (because the father did not hear his son scream to him)

Di Sciullo and Williams (1988:88) recognize this type of problem for verbal clusters in Japanese, Hopi, Quechua, French, and Italian. They admit that the quasi- morphological analysis of the verbal cluster by a V^0 stack needs support by an alternative syntactic analysis. One that distributes the arguments over a VP stack such that some arguments are real co-arguments, whereas others are not or less so. The two simultaneous analyses are clearly a type of transformational variants. This is exactly the point of the transformational approaches by gambit (9-ii) and gambit (9-iii).

1.4 Gambit (9ii): Full argument exodus

It is quite common to assume that one argument in every predicative structure – the external argument – is to be licensed outside of the <+V> projection by which it is selected. There are more subtle cases but most of the time a lexical <+V> projection is grammatically wrapped into an I^0<tense/agr> projection. This IP configuration will get the external argument licensed outside of the selecting VP. Arguments in the subject function require external licensing. It has been considered whether any syntactic argument were to ask for such an external licensing configuration. This conception has been worked out for Dutch under the banner of 'minimalism' in Zwart (1996) and Koopman and Szabolcsi (2000). It would lead to configurations like in (12).

(12)

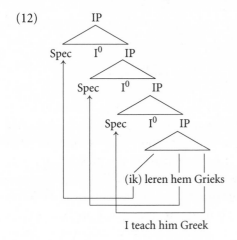

I teach him Greek

Suppose further that all clause-like complements, the set of CP's, IP's or VP's, originate or end up to the right of their selecting <+V> matrix verb. The bare VP complements will by assumption lack a <+C> and <+I> shell. Hence they will not be able to license their arguments. If the arguments raise until they meet a licensing IP configuration, they will raise into shells that belong to the matrix <+V>. Suppose this has happened in structures like (1) and (7). The verbal cluster in the predicate-final position although bereft of its arguments remains a VP stack. It might be seen as a former storehouse of the selected arguments. These arguments themselves have been raised into the newly stipulated set of IP shells. These now overarch the lexical matrix verb, see example (7) now analyzed as (13).

(13)

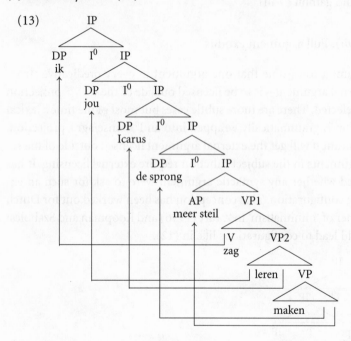

The postulation of multiple IP projections is quite a change. It used to be assumed that the syntactic identity of a lexical item was constituted and learned by its subcategorization frame. The subcategorization frame seemed to select as well as to license its arguments. This is changed in the present approach. The two functions for argument handling, selection and licensing, are separated. In a sense, the following transformational extravaganza will be introduced. Lexical items select subcategorizing arguments but will not license them ever, whereas functional items license such arguments but do not select them. This implies a massive argument reordering for any predicative structure. Assume this to be the case, i.e. not only for the so-called external argument but for any <+V> subcategorizing phrase XP. The proposal for verbal clusters already diagrammed in (12) and (13) now follows in a more principled fashion. The projection of any <+V> item has to be covered by as many IP umbrellas as it selects subcategorizing constituents. The order of arguments no longer follows from a subcategorization frame. The order of arguments follows from the hierarchy of its argument-licensing IP shells. The hierarchy is the familiar one of surface subject, indirect object, surface object, prepositional object or small clause predicate. Structures like (12) and (13) remind one of function/slot templates in structuralist grammar. The lexical verbs that select a bare VP complement, i.e. a complement without functional shells of its own, show full argument exodus. Yet, this is not so surprising. Within the present view, all lexical V^0 projections will do the same. Subcategorizing arguments of a bare VP complement only have the additional peculiarity of raising into the functional facilities of the matrix structure. Otherwise, the arguments could not be licensed. A bare VP has by assumption no functional shells of its own. Nevertheless the arguments of the bare VP raise into the nearest-by functional structures. These happen to be provided by the matrix structure. The nice point of this view is that the argument exodus in (1) or (7) is not a peculiarity of Dutch at all. It is, rather, a property of any predicate in any language. It only shows up in languages like Dutch that seem to have an almost unhealthy fondness for bare VP stacks.

Let this whole minimalist set up and its additional measures be granted. Consider then the following difficulty. The arguments are licensed upstairs in an order that reflects the downstairs hierarchy of the lexical <+V> heads. See the numbers under example (7). The maximal crossing of argument-head relations is factually a major consequence of full argument exodus. Yet, *de jure*, crossing does not follow from anything assumed so far. There is no reason why some downstairs 'theme' should become an upstairs Spec.IP$_1$, Spec.IP$_2$, Spec.IP$_3$, etc. None of the umbrella IP's in the matrix structure has a predetermined relation with a downstairs VP. Arguments have a thematic <+V> related status somewhere downstairs within a bare VP stack. Upstairs they have syntactic status as specifiers somewhere within an IP stack. What they have not, is a predetermined syntactic relation between these two positions, as the formerly unique 'external' argument had. There is only the following paradoxical instruction: Assign a non-licensing linear argument order within each VP and realize full argument exodus by a maximal crossing of head argument relations. That restates the problem in (8). The usual argument licensing chain had its source position defined in a configurational subcategorization frame and A-chains did not cross each other in principle. The maximal and systematic crossing of head argument relations exemplified in (7) is still beyond explanation.

1.5   Gambit (iii): Full exodus of heads

Finally, it is not uncommon for a head <+V> to raise outside of its bare VP into the first governing position <+I>. Verbs will adjoin the <+I> element that governs their VP if they themselves are to become, c.q. to be checked as <+fin>. Suppose, this is generalized to all <+V> heads of bare, i.e. <–I>, VP's. Each grammatically unmarked <+V> will raise and adjoin to its selecting governor, just like in the common case of <+fin> formation, cf. Evers (1981). See the VP stack in (14).

(14)

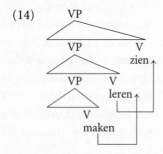

Diagram (14) assumes that Dutch is OV. This is at present a provisional assumption only. It is not crucial to the main argument below, but will greatly simplify its exposition. New and more principled support for the OV order will be summarized at the end of Section 3. The OV subcategorization frame will be maintained for nominal (PP, DP, NP) and clausal objects (CP, IP, VP) alike. The <+I> marked CP and IP objects will shift to the right later on due to a rule of Extraposition. Assuming the OV order, Extraposition will cross a <+I> marked V^0 head stack. See (15).

(15)

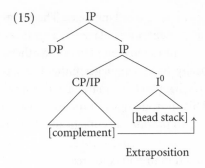

Extraposition

Extraposition will not take place until some later cycle has turned the V^0 stack into a $<+I>$. According to the present view, argument selection and argument licensing is the same thing. Licensing of arguments must take place within the same VP that selects the arguments. Minimal though this may be, minimalism it is not. Nevertheless the present view entails that Extraposition cannot be understood in terms of argument licensing. The clause-like complements are to be licensed within the VP that has selected them, whereas Extraposition is not in evidence before there is an IP. I have two remarks about Extraposition: it can be independently motivated and, as a movement to the right, it has the excuse of being a minor movement rule in de sense of Emonds (1976). It switches the positions between an I^0 and its CP/IP governee and neighbor for reasons of scope structure.

The bare VPs in (14) do not trigger Extraposition. There is no $I^0–I^0$ dependence in (14). Structure (14) is supposed to trigger V^0-to-V^0 raising instead. This is gambit (9-iii). Its strong point is the line-up of arguments. One gets that for free. The first question is why bare VP structures should react with such an outrageous rearrangement at all. I propose the following provisional answer in terms of argument licensing. A $<+V>$ projection is a subcategorization frame that selects and licenses its deictically marked arguments DP/PP and IP/CP on the spot to its left. By contrast, the bare VP, although selected, lacks deictic $<+I>$ marking and hence cannot be licensed on the spot. The $<+V>$ projection line of the bare VP is insufficiently visible. It lacks the fiber of grammatical $<tense/agr>$ features. This looks again like the separation of a selection structure from a licensing structure. Yet, the problem is more manageable than the one that came up with full argument exodus. A strict locality of licensing can be maintained.

Any bare VP phrase gets all of its material licensed within the matrix projection it is selected by, due to the restructuring. The trigger for predicate raising as proposed here is different from McCawley's (1968b) proposal and also different from Baker's (1988) proposal for polysynthetic languages. Their triggers are placed in morphology, whereas the present one is placed in a syntactic licensing theory. Baker proposed that head-to-head movement in polysynthetic languages might be triggered morphologically. In his languages, either the matrix head or the complement's head, or both, happen to be marked with a morphological subcategorization property. This morphological property ensures that head-to-head raising must follow so as to produce a syntactically derived lexical item. Fortunately, the raised head in Baker's analysis leaves a trace. The head-to-head relation as such could not function in syntax for reasons of morphology (the stray affix filter). Yet this head-to-head relation can be preserved by traces supported by a binding theory with somewhat more muscle.

(16)

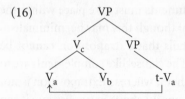

The upstairs matrix head Vc in (16) identifies the downstairs trace just like a local head governor should do. At the same time, the same matrix head functions as the antecedent of the downstairs trace. Due to the head-to-head adjunction, the governing matrix head has incorporated the material Va appropriate for a good antecedent (the non distinctness property). It has never become quite clear, in Baker's analysis, why his downstairs heads are systematically lexical and not <+C> or <+I> marked elements. The verbal clusters in the West-European languages contain the same modal, aspectual and causative material and show the same lack of <+I> or <+C> elements in the complement. Yet, the European verbal clusters would be highly atypical if taken as morphological constructs. For that reason it is better to consider all V^0-head stacks in terms of bare VP complement licensing. Later on, some language types may package their V^0 stacks in a morphological construct, but that then is a side issue. The diagram of head-to-head raising in (14) has been expanded in (17) and makes use of traces. One may now assume with Baker (1988) that the head cluster functions as antecedent and local governor of the downstairs trace. As one may easily see the repeated V^0-to-V^0 raising is bound to build up intermediary traces with an internal structure of subordinated traces.

(17)

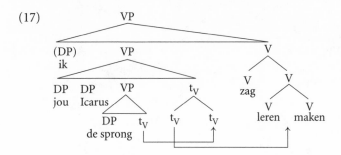

Such constructs are necessary if one wants to keep track of the well-formed build-up of the V^0 stack by means of delayed LF rules. Minimalism allows layered traces, but minimal in the naïve sense they are not. It was argued in Evers (1993) that the emergence of such constructs was an unacceptable consequence of Baker's cyclic head raising by means of traces. Suppose now that the raised infinitives leave no trace for the very reason they could not be licensed either. Leaving a trace is for structurally licensed items only and being licensed requires deixis. Deixis by assumption was lacking in the bare VP projection line. One might see this whole argument as a simplification and strengthening of the Empty Category Principle. It now follows that raising the infinitive will lead to the disappearance of the head of the VP projection line and hence to the disappearance of that projection line itself. A blessing, since the thing was unlicensable anyway. The maneuver boils down to a reintroduction of Kuroda's (1972) Guillotine Principle: removal of the (unlicensed) head will lead to removal of its projection line. The dependents of the removed projection line will have to be reattached. Proposals to that end have been made by Seuren (1996:51) as 'reattachment rules'. In line with the present approach I will reinterpret them as 'relicensing rules'. The V^0-to-V^0 raising creates the head stack as the new head. The arguments orphanaged by the pruning can be relicensed by the new head. The relicensing is structure-preserving. No rearrangement is necessary and the same categories enter the same configurations with a head on the right. The tree in (17) now reappears as (18).

(18)

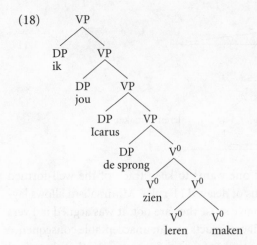

McCawley's Predicate Raising, Kuroda's Guillotine Principle and Seuren's Reattachment Rules have been interpreted in terms of argument licensing. Although Pruning may seem a wild gesture it is not that far from other analyses in present-day syntax. A key analysis by Pollock (1989:372) argues that the infinitive in French cannot leave a trace such that the VP structure remains recoverable. This explains why it is possible to raise the auxiliaries *être* and *avoir* over the negation element, as in (19), whereas it is impossible to do so for the lexical infinitive, as in (20).

(19) a. ne   pas être heureux
         n'être pas t   heureux
         (not be happy)

     b. ne   pas avoir eu d'enfance heureux
         n'avoir pas t   eu d'enfance heureux
         (not have had a happy childhood)

(20) ne   pas pleurer en lisant 'Les Misérables'
      *ne pleurer pas *t   en lisant 'Les Misérables'
      (not cry when reading 'Les Misérables')

Raising the lexical infinitive would destroy the licensing frame for its infinitival arguments. This might be generalized and rephrased as follows. A bare infinitive will not leave a trace. It lacks the grammatical body for such an impact, whereas a finite verb will leave a trace. If the infinitive does not leave a trace, its stranded argument structure is no longer licensed. Perhaps better: the projection line of the bare VP complement is no longer supported by a head or its trace and disappears. The NEG-element fails to preserve its VP complement when the infinitive moves out and it blocks relicensing. Pollock's analysis of deficient traces was at the basis of present day reasoning about the verbal cluster in English.

1.6 Conclusion

Three approaches to the verbal cluster in Dutch have been considered shortly, see (9). The first approach, gambit (9-i), is nontransformational and assumes a base-generated compound structure. There are difficulties for this approach relating to what is known about compounds in general, and also with regard to *ad hoc* reference to an alternative syntactic analysis. The two other approaches are transformational. Both start with a VP stack and organize a full argument exodus, as in (9-ii), or a full head exodus as in (9-iii), respectively, both for presumed reasons of argument licensing. The full argument exodus will probably have severe problems with the linear line-up of arguments in the derived structure. The full head exodus must develop an argument for the pied-piping of heads in V^0-to-V^0 raising and their stranding in V-second (I^0-to-C^0 raising). Besides that problem, there are problems it shares with the monoclausal analysis by Di Sciullo and Williams (1988). An account is needed for the binding and scope phenomena that rely on the VP complements that have been pruned. These problems for the approach in gambit (9-iii) will be dealt with in Section 3.

At the same time, two new arguments will be seen to support the gambit (iii) derivation of the verbal cluster as a V^0 stack. The first new argument will follow from a rule for stress assignment (Section 2). The second will follow from pied-piping in head-to-head raising (Section 3). Both arguments get their cutting edge from the appearance of 'cluster creepers', as shown in the *creeper* column of (1). Four empirical properties of the Dutch cluster creeper are listed in (21).

(21) a. The categorical status of the cluster creeper is a X^0 <–V>.
      b. The cluster creeper is licensed directly in front of any V^0 of the cluster it belongs to and the distributional variation has no semantic effect whatsoever.
      c. The cluster creeper attracts the cluster stress in any of its positions.
      d. The cluster creeper is selected idiomatically by the most embedded verb only.

It stands to reason that these four properties of the cluster creeper are to be derived in a principled way. The two last properties (stress and selectional hierarchy) are looked at in Section 2, where the stress assignment of the verbal cluster is derived. The first two properties (category status and licensing) play a part in Sections 3 and 4, where the distributional properties within the verbal cluster are derived and the underlying principles are applied to other cases.

2. Stress assignment

2.1 Grammatical distinctions for metrical trees

There appears to be a difference between a stress assignment in compounds and stress assignment in phrases. The stress in compounds falls to the left of the construct (*an oil-lamp*), at least in the Germanic compounds. The stress assignment for phrases points to the right hand side (*a lamp with* **oil**).

As argued by Cinque (1993), the left/right guidance in these descriptions is less than fortunate. Stress assignment is better controlled by structure, than by left/right linearity. This is suggested by the fact that, roughly speaking, SOV and SVO languages tend to stress the object, in spite of the difference in the object's linear position. The question is which aspect of the syntactic structure will suffice for a general principle of stress assignment. Cinque (1993:244) proposes that 'depth of embedding' is the best candidate, although there is a problem with 'depth of embedding'. It is not a property immediately available from the syntactic analysis. One rather needs a fairly elaborate procedure to find out about the hierarchy of embedding. Cinque (1993) proposes such a procedure. The grid theory of stress assignment will sift out the most embedded constituent. It is clear how this will work in configurations of type (22a). The complement YP will take precedence over a head X^0. It is less clear how things will work for the adjunct structure (22b), the specifier structure (22c), or the compound structure (22d).

(22) a. [X^0 complement]$_{XP}$
      b. [X'   adjunct   ]$_{XP}$
      c. [Spec.X   X'   ]$_{XP}$
      d. [Y^0 X^0]$_{XP}$

We may assume that the complement within (22a) is a maximal projection YP. It will boast more labels than its X^0 counterpart, and attract the stress assignment accordingly. This solves configuration type (22a). The *de facto* outcome of (22b) and (22c) is that stress assignment falls respectively in the direction of the non-adjunct, and the direction of the non-specifier. Cinque (1993:246,

268), who is oriented at depth of embedding, is somewhat uneasy about the
following examples.

(23) a.   [[the man from Philadelphia]_{DP} ['s **hat**]_{D'}]_{DP}
      b.   [[the author of several articles about reincarnation]_{DP} [**died**]_{I'}]_{IP}

In these examples a highly complex specifier phrase or a highly complex adjunct will not attract the major stress, even when their X' counterparts are
single words. The problem reappears when compounds display a structure
as in (22d), but in such a way that the head structure X^0 contains considerable internal compound structure, whereas the qualifying element Y^0 is a
single ele-ment. Yet, complement Y^0 bears the compound stress in spite of its
simplicity.

Cinque (1993) makes several provisions to overcome this problem. As far
as compound structure is concerned, he boldly proposes to reject the head-
to-head adjunction in (22d) as an admissible structure anyway. Cinque observes that in several cases the Y^0 part of the compound must have been an YP,
e.g. the PP in the compound *an* [[*over-the-fence*]_{PP} [*gossip*]_N]_N. If, by assumption, the qualifier Y^0 could always count as a maximal projection (because it
is so sometimes), it would invariably have more labels, that is more embedding, than a simplex X^0 head and attract the stress assignment as needed. At
least some of the (22d) cases have now been reduced to the ideal case (22a).
Nevertheless, the X^0 head within (22d) may have internal structure. Consider,
for example, the complex compound *an* [[*over-the-fence*]_{PP} [[*nasty neighbor*]_{NP}
[*gossip*]_N]_N]_N. Stress within the complex X^0 will be on the qualifying XP's. The
next step brings in a new competition for the title 'most embedding structure'.
The competition is now between the PP *over the fence* and the N *nasty neighbor
gossip*. These cases of (22d) remind of (22b) and (22c). Two constituents, each
allowing an arbitrary amount of possible structure, are combined. The one that
includes the simplex head wins out. Why should that be?

Cinque (1993:269) proposes that the projections in specifier and adjunct
positions (22b/c) are not embedded "in the relevant sense". What really counts,
he argues, is depth of embedding on the recursive side, "assuming recursion to
be fixed to the right". Hence, "having more depth of embedding" as such is not
relevant. What seems to matter is the distinction between complements versus
adjuncts and specifiers. As long as stress assignment searches for the complement within the complement, things run smoothly. The notion *complement*
belongs to the standard syntactic distinctions, whereas the notion *depth of embedding on the recursive side, whether there is recursion or not* must count as a
more doubtful vehicle (but see Seuren 1996:72–79 for the similar notion of

"spine"). In principle, complements are head-governed, whereas specifier and adjunct phrases are not. Let us formulate the Phrasal Stress Principle as in (24). It is based on head government and assumes that complex heads and complex phrases are labeled binary trees.

(24)   *The Phrasal and Compound Stress Principle*
    a. Each pair of branches that shares a label differs internally as s versus w.
    b. The branch to a new projection line is s iff head-governed and w otherwise.

The principle in (24) applies a strong/weak distinction directly to syntactic head-oriented X-bar representations. This procedure turns syntactic trees into metrical trees of the kind proposed in Giegerich (1985). Giegerich controls the strong/weak assignments by rules like the 'compound stress rule' and the 'nuclear stress rule'. It is possible, though, to control these assignments by means of grammatical distinctions common to compounds and phrases. This was the core of Cinque's proposal. Cinque (1993: 256) prefers metrical grids to metrical trees, since the grids keep track of the amount of embedding. Yet, it may rather count as a virtue of metrical trees that they reflect the syntactic tree directly. Suppose that the principle of phrasal stress in (24) is sufficiently informed about syntax to know that the X^0 in (22a–d) is a head, and hence to know that the Y^0 in (22d) and the [complement] in (22a) are head-governed elements, that merit to be stressed. By the same expertise, the principle knows that adjuncts and specifier elements will not be head-governed, and hence will not get assigned major stress. Principle (24) can now be applied to the structures in (22). The result is shown in diagram (25).

(25)
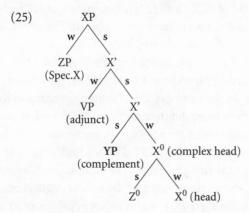

The specifier-DPs in (23) are not head-governed. The labels I' and D' contain inner deictic agreement elements (I⁰ agr and D⁰ agr) and these direct the neutral stress towards their lexical sister, respectively *hat* and *died*.

Nominal compounds in Dutch and German stress leftwards, because they have their heads on the right side. Although stress falls on the qualifying part of the compound, it is not crucial to (24) that this part surpasses the head by a certain amount of internal structure. This is illustrated by the difference between the structures in (26) and (27).

(26)   trek-vogel-vlucht-studie (migratory-bird-flight-study)

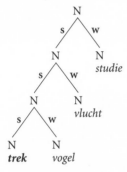

(27)   veiligheids-vleugel-arm-band (safety-wing-arm-band)

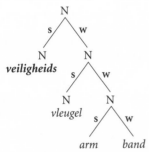

The deepest embedded qualifier in (26) is [*trek*]ᵥ ('migrate'), whereas the deepest embedded qualifier in (27) is [*arm*]ₙ ('arm'). Both are three branches down from the top of the compound. Nevertheless, [*arm*]ₙ in (27) does not get the compound main stress, whereas [*trek*]ᵥ in (26) does. The relevant point of difference must be that [*trek*]ᵥ is the qualifier within a qualifier, within a qualifier and as such dependent on strong branches only. The qualifier [*arm*]ₙ, by contrast, is qualifier within a complex head, see (27). Hence, it is dependent on mainly weak branches.

Cinque (1993) discusses more subtle cases of compounding. If the first element of the compound indicates a place or a possessor, it tends to evade compound stress. An example is [*world* [*saving-day*]] probably a worldwide day devoted to difficulties with saving versus [[*world-saving*] *day*], rather a day devoted to the saving of the world. If the compound structure could be qualified such that *world* is recognized either as a thematic argument or as a place adjunct, it should or should not attract stress according to that structure. I do not see how the X^0 labeling system that is applied here could make such a distinction.

(28)   a.   b.

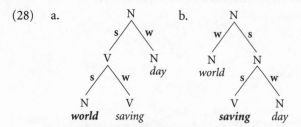

Fortunately, that problem can be left aside here. All X^0 elements in the V^0 head stack are of the thematic complement type. Consider diagram (29).

(29)

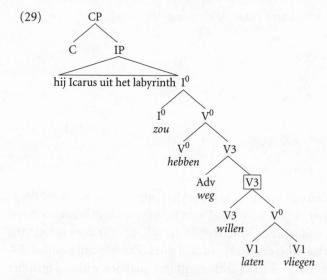

If, and only if, the V-clusters in (30) and (31) below are analyzed as V^0 stacks, the Giegerich type approach in (24) predicts that the <–V> cluster creepers will get the main stress of the V-cluster. Consider the V^0 stack (32) as a representation for the verbal cluster in (30). The cluster creeper *weg* ('away') has been placed in position marked in (30) by superscript 3. The choice between the five cluster-creeper positions in (30) is free.

(30)   als hij Icarus uit het labyrinth

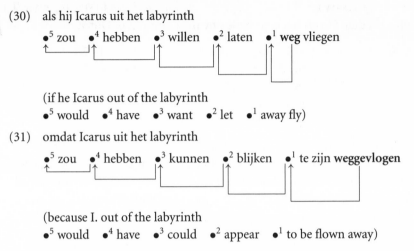

(if he Icarus out of the labyrinth
•⁵ would   •⁴ have   •³ want   •² let   •¹ away fly)

(31)   omdat Icarus uit het labyrinth

(because I. out of the labyrinth
•⁵ would   •⁴ have   •³ could   •² appear   •¹ to be flown away)

Any of the numbered positions above in (30) and (31) adjoins the cluster creeper to a V^0 constituent on the right. I claim that all variants in (30) and (31) are clear cases of grammaticality in standard Dutch. Assume now this constituent is a V^0, see (32).

(32)

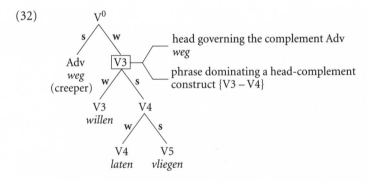

The revised Cinque principle in (24) predicts that the immediate complement of the boxed V^0 head will get (compound) stress. Hence, the cluster creeper Adv will get the stress. Within a VP stack, the revised Cinque rule makes a different prediction. Now the rule will continue its search for the most embedded V^0. It will predict, contrary to fact, that the stress in (30) and (31) is invariably on the rightmost V^0. It is not. This I do not hold against the revised Cinque rule, but against the analysis of the verbal cluster as a VP stack.

The example in (31) contains a further distributional nicety, observed by Den Besten and Rutten (1989). The past participle itself selects a cluster creeper. It is not necessary for the two creepers, *weg-* and *gevlogen* to stay together. The flight schedule (33) is freely provided by the grammar of Dutch.

(33)   If *gevlogen* is on 1:   *weg*   is allowed on   1 - 2 - 3 - 4 - 5
                   on 2:   *weg*   on   - 2 - 3 - 4 - 5
                   on 3:   *weg*   on   - 3 - 4 - 5
                   on 4:   *weg*   on   - 4 - 5
                   on 5:   *weg*   on   - 5

All in all, the verbal cluster in (31) allows 15 synonymous distributions (out of a total of 7! = 5040 imaginable ways to line up the 7 predicative heads (*gevlogen, weg, zijn, blijken, kunnen, hebben* and *zou*)). The stress of the cluster in all 15 variations is on the leftmost cluster creeper *weg*. This structure develops into a final variant of the stress argument against the VP stack analysis. See (34).

(34)   a.

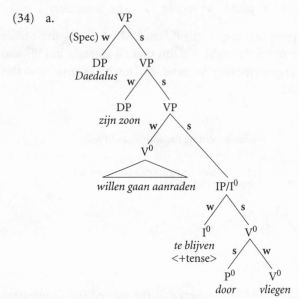

   b.   Zou Daedalus zijn zoon

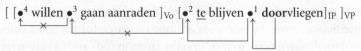

(Would Daedalus his son [[want go advise] [to continue through fly?]])

There is in (34) a final group with again 7 predicative heads. It is known independently that a particle verb like $[[aan]_P[raden]_{V_0}]_{V_0}$ ('advise') may have an IP complement, but cannot be in the initial or intermediate position within any cluster (Evers 1975:41). This motivates the two verbal clusters in (34). A crashing ungrammaticality would result if one were to move the cluster creeper *door* ('through') into the first group, labeled here V^0. The main stress of the entire construction is on *door*, regardless of whether *door* is in front of *vliegen* ('fly') or in front of *te blijven* ('to continue'). This again follows from the revised Cinque stress rule. Stress is correctly predicted to fall into the IP complement of the (complex) V^0. Structure (34) is a group with 7 predicative heads like (31) is. Yet, this time cluster stress must be on the second creeper *door*, rather than on the first creeper *aan*. It is clear that one needs a major boundary between *aanraden* ('advise') and *te blijven* (to continue') in order to direct movement and stress assignment for cluster creepers in the appropriate way. Fortunately, this boundary between the two V-to-V domains was already known to be present in the verbal cluster of (34), just as it was already known to be absent in the verbal cluster of (31) (Evers 1975). The distributional variability of the cluster creeper within each domain will be derived in Section 4 below as an automatic effect of V^0-to-V^0 raising.

2.2 X^0 heads and XP phrases

The arrangement with stress rule (24) above turns on X-bar conventions. Its application to the structures above seems to play fast and loose with the notions head and phrase. For example, the boxed label V3 above in diagram (29), repeated here as (35), is a head and as such it correctly assigns stress to its complement, which happens to be the cluster creeper *weg* ('away').

(35)

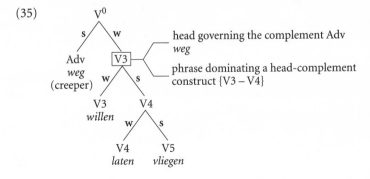

At the same time, boxed V3 dominates a substructure of the head stack. This substructure is characterized by a head-complement set-up of its own. This will guide a renewed application of the same stress rule. The subordinated stress is on its way to V5. Now, one may wonder how boxed V3 may qualify as a X^0 if it dominates at the same time a head-complement phrase structure. What kind of additional property is needed to give XP phrasal status and why is dominating a head-complement structure, as boxed V3 does, not sufficient? If it weren't for such an additional requirement for XP status, boxed V3 would turn into an XP and the effective application of stress rule (24) would be lost.

The labeling problem is not restricted to stress assignment. Roberts (1991) pointed out that the finite verb in root clauses is clearly extracted from the verbal cluster by the V-second rule. The V-second rule strands the rest of the cluster. If the verbal cluster had been a V^0 stack, Roberts argues, it must be a morphological unit as well. Obviously, a syntactic rule should not extract morphological units out of a X^0 with word status (the excorporation problem). In order to account for the verbal cluster as a syntactic unit, Roberts proposes that the adjacent V^0 elements are connected by a construction-specific indexing. This indexing stops short of sucking the whole thing into the Charybdis of morphology. For good measure, Roberts explicitly legislates against the possibility of X^0 adjunction in syntax (Roberts 1991: 426, condition 6b). A syntactic X^0 must have word status and be a syntactic atom. Hence it would not allow extractions like the V-second rule.

The insistence that a V^0 head stack must be a morphological construct is probably due to Baker's (1988) analysis of polysynthetic verbs. Baker (1988) builds up a V^0 stack in syntax. Yet, the landing site is marked by a morphological slot. Baker's analysis meets the opposite problem (the incorporation problem). The head incorporated in a V^0 stack must sustain a syntactic head-movement chain. Baker stipulates that the incorporated relativized head may bind the trace in its former position. This can be done if its virtues as an antecedent are projected to the top of the V^0 stack (cf. Baker 1988: 64, 'non-distinctness condition').

In order to preserve the various advantages of a X^0 head stack, including the beneficial effects of the stress rule (24), I propose (36), (37) and (38). These deny, among other things, that a X^0 head stack needs word status.

(36) a.   Syntactic principles may refer to a difference X^0 / XP.
      b.   They will never refer to a difference X^0 <terminal element> versus X^0 <head stack>.

(37) Let at least syntactic constituents that lack internal syntactic structure –
i.e. syntactic terminal elements – have X^0 status.

A projection of a X^0 must dominate Y, an additional part of the syntactic structure. This additional part Y may or may not contain a deictic marker $\{D^0, I^0,$
$Degr^0\}$, see the diagrams in (38).

(38) a. If the complement Y contains no deictic marker, the projection of X^0
has again X^0 status.

    b. If the complement Y does contain a deictic marker, the projection of
X^0 has XP status.

    c. The top segment of a deictic projection gets XP status.

a.

V^0

    Adv V^0
    weg   *vliegen*

(away fly)

b.

IP

    PP I^0

    met zijn vader Adv I^0
                 weg

             I^0 V^0
             zou

             V^0 V^0
             willen *vliegen*

(with his father away would want (to) fly)

c.

IP

    DP/D^0 IP
    he

        IP/I^0 $DgrP/Dgr^0$
        flies   *more*

Particles and Adverbs often allow for idiomatic intensifiers *far away, flat down,*
straight up, etc. If one considers these as deictic degree assigners, they will turn
the cluster creeper into an XP. An XP cannot enter the V-cluster. It would turn
the V^0 stack into a (bare) VP structure according to (38b), which does not fit
the licensing XP conditions. This is correct in so far as the XP phrase cannot

enter the cluster, whereas the single head can. See (39). The present arrangement about heads and phrases still fails to predict Roberts' 'excorporation'. The V-second rule will not move the head-cluster Xo. Any attempt to do so results in a crashing ungrammaticality. This demonstrates an unexplained difference between the <+wh> movement to C and the <+fin> movement to C. Both are deictic features, but the first pied-pipes, the second does not. The <+wh> feature moves the extended projection DP/PP within a CP projection. The <+fin> feature rearranges a head within its own extended projection. An arrangement about heads should have anticipated the pied-piping difference, but it does not.

(39)   als Icarus

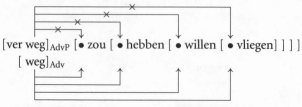

[ver weg]$_{AdvP}$ [● zou [● hebben [● willen [● vliegen]]]]
[weg]$_{Adv}$

(if Icarus (far) away ● would ● have ● want ● fly)

The labeling principles make crucial reference to the distinction <+/–deictic>. The distinction <+/–deictic> will reappear in the next section as the key distinction in argument and predicate licensing. This may be close to Williams (1994: Ch. 6), who argues that the theta relation of external and internal arguments implies referentiality.

3.   The mechanics of head raising

3.1   An option between V⁰ heads

Consider the example in (40). It contains the cluster creeper adverb *weg* ('away'). The cluster creeper is selected by the movement verb *vliegen* ('fly').

(40)   a.   Hij kon Icarus uit Kreta   **weg**   zien   vliegen
            He could Icarus out of Crete   away   see   fly
       b.   Hij kon Icarus uit Kreta   zien   **weg**   vliegen
            He could Icarus out of Crete   see   away   fly

Besides the 'telic' result-indicating particle *weg*, the selection by *vliegen* must also have included a source PP *uit Kreta* ('out of Crete') and an agent *Icarus*. The structure (40a) shows that these selected labels are licensed left of the verbal cluster, where they are also separated from the selecting item *vliegen* ('fly'). There is a variant though, (40b), where the particle remains positioned next to its selector. The diagram in (41) presents a potential selection structure from which (40a) and (40b) are to be derived.

(41)

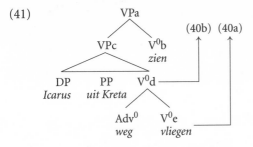

a.   Icarus uit Kreta [**weg** zien vliegen] (I. from Crete away see fly)
b.   Icarus uit Kreta [zien **weg**vliegen] (I. from Crete see away fly)

The higher matrix structure in (40) is *hij kon VPa* ('he could VPa'). It will select VPa (41), but is otherwise irrelevant for the derivation of the cluster-creeper variants (40a) and (40b). The sub-constituent V^0d *weg-vliegen* ('away fly') contains the cluster creeper *weg* ('away'). It does not contain a deictic category. Hence, it must be a V^0 and not a VP, if one were to accept the X^0/XP deictic phrase effect in (38a). The full selection structure of *vliegen* ('fly') is VPc in (41). This is a VP, since it contains the deictically marked DP *Icarus* and the deictically marked PP *uit Kreta*. Nevertheless, the projection line of this VPc itself is without deixis, i.e. without I^0. The VPc is selected by V^0b *zien* (see (41)) but cannot be licensed by it. A deixis-less VP projection-line might be selected by some verbs. I add the crucial stipulation in (42).

(42)   a.   A projection line XP cannot be licensed unless it is marked by deixis.
b.   A non deictic head can be theta licensed by adjunction to its governor.

The relation in (42) between deixis and licensing may remind of, and is inspired by, Williams's contention (1994: Ch. 6) that the theta relation of external and internal arguments implies referentiality.[1] The intention with structure (42) is that its bare VPc can be transformed into a licensable variant. The transformation is local, within the domain of the selector V^0b *zien*. To that end, the V^0 head of VPc in (41) must be head-to-head moved to the selector V^0b and get licensed within a compound head-head configuration. The projection line VPc will be pruned by the Guillotine Principle and the VPc subcategorization string, already licensed within VPc, is re-licensed within VPa. See diagram (43).

(43)

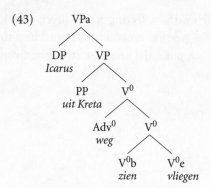

(Icarus out-of Crete [**away** see fly])

The projection-line VPc from (41) has disappeared. According to (43) the constituents $[Icarus]_{DP}$, $[uit Kreta]_{PP}$ and $[weg]_{Adv}$ are relicensed *in situ* by the new V^0 head stack. I come now to the relevant point of the present section. According to the labeling convention above in (38), there are two candidates for head-to-head raising in (41). Besides V^0e *vliegen* (fly), there is in (41) V^0d *weg-vliegen* (away fly). Raising the one V^0, or raising the other V^0 makes no difference for the licensing conditions. Both will lead to the pruning of the obnoxious VPc projection line. Hence, besides (43) one may also derive (44).

(44)

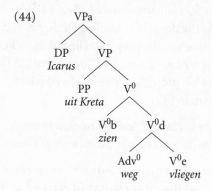

(Icarus out-of Crete [see **away** fly])

Raising the higher V^0d [*weg vliegen*] in (41) will also raise the cluster creeper *weg* (away). The subsequent adjunction of V^0d to its governor V^0b *zien*, will lock up the cluster creeper within the head stack, see diagram (44). By contrast, raising the lower V^0e *vliegen*, as in (43), will strand the cluster creeper on the left hand side of the head stack. A renewed raising of this head-stack V^0 will reopen the option between locking up the cluster creeper on the right hand side or letting it creep further to the left. The procedure predicts correctly that a cluster creeper may eventually take position to the left of any V^0 in a head stack. The distributions of the cluster creeper have been derived as an unintended side effect of the whole licensing arrangement. If *weg* ('away') and *vliegen* ('fly') had not been united within a V^0 and if the licensing rearrangements had not been a head exodus based on head-to-head movement, the cluster-creeper effect would have required a separate *ad hoc* statement, as in Evers and Huybregts (1972/1977: 23), Bennis (1992). I add two closing remarks about raising or stranding of predicate final material.

First, raising a V^0 may cause the stranding of a cluster creeper on the left. Raising a head stack V^0 does not allow for stranding a V^0 member of the head stack. The head stack has to move as a unit. If it were to strand one of its V^0 members, the pruning of the bare VP projection line could not follow and the structure would continue to contain an unlicensable constituent. Secondly, it is sometimes possible to adorn the cluster creeper with a deictic element or a complement of its own, e.g. *ver weg van het labyrint* ('far away from the labyrinth'). In such cases the former cluster creeper has been turned into a subcategorizing XP. That offers no possibility for a labeling convention to get a V^0 that incorporates the cluster creeper. Hence there is in such cases no cluster-creeper effect whatsoever.

3.2 Predicate licensing and the Extended Projection Principle

The licensing arrangement above dealt with verbs that restructure their clause-like complement. It has been implied that these verbs, the V^0-to-V^0 raising verbs, are subcategorized for a bare VP complement. Many of the V^0-to-V^0 raising verbs allow their clause-like complement to vary between bare VP, IP or CP, with no or hardly any semantic difference. The same theta relations must be at work to make sense out of the constructs. Sentence-qualifying verbs like *schijnen* ('seem') vary between a CP complement (the a-variant) and a bare VP complement (the b- and c-variants).

(45) a. toen het scheen dat Icarus weg vloog
          when it   seemed that Icarus away flew

      b. toen Icarus weg scheen te vliegen
          when Icarus away seemed to fly

      c. toen Icarus had weg   schijnen te vliegen
          when Icarus had away seem   to fly

Some exceptional Case marking verbs like *zien* ('see') vary as well between a CP (the a-variant) and a bare VP complement (the b- and c-variants).

(46) a. toen   ik   zag   dat   Icarus   weg   vloog
          when   I   saw   that Icarus   away flew
      b. toen   ik   Icarus   weg   zag   vliegen
          when   I   Icarus   away saw   fly
      c. toen   ik   Icarus   had   weg   zien   vliegen
          when   I   Icarus   had   away see   fly

A small set of at most ten Control verbs, for example *proberen* ('try') optionally functions as a restructuring verb (Rutten 1991:79).

(47) a. toen   Icarus   probeerde   weg   te vliegen
          when   Icarus   tried   away to fly
      b. toen   Icarus   weg   probeerde   te vliegen
          when   Icarus   away tried   to fly
      c. toen   Icarus   had   weg   proberen   te vliegen
          when   Icarus   had   away try   to fly

The usual Control verb in Dutch prefers the extraposition of its IP complement. It does not allow V^0-to-V^0 raising, but it does allow a VP-segment raising. The VP-segment raising is indicated by Rutten (1991:61) as "third construction". I do not know how to analyze the third construction in terms of plausible principles and categories.[2]

Control verbs like the one in (47) harbor a conceptual difficulty that is quite instructive. The description of Control by means of the element PRO is not convincing. If a complement is to be restructured, it is unlikely to offer PRO a shelter or a unique position against outside governors. For that reason, I once proposed (Evers 1986:173) that Control should be seen as a case of (bound) 'anaphoric I^0'. Anaphoric I^0 would have underspecified features of <agr> and <tense>. Anaphoric I^0 is incompatible with a Spec.I position, like any bound anaphor is incompatible with an apposition. By contrast, free anaphoric I^0 (pro-drop) is specified for <agr> and <tense> and does allow an apposition in Spec.I. The locality of Control would coincide with the locality of anaphoric binding, since the anaphoric IP projection line is a constituent within the controlling matrix structure. An intervening CP label is rare and a-typical for controlled complements, see (48).

(48)

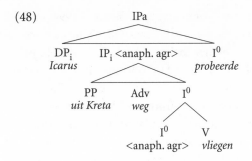

If present, it could be irrelevant and on a par with the PP label of reflex-ivized propositional objects. The absence of Control in small clauses (no I^0 available) and finite clauses (I^0 available but not anaphoric) follows as wanted. The proposal extends naturally to the cases of logophoric Control in Williams (1994: 85). The element PRO may have been a bad answer to a good question. So, I prefer to stick to the interpretation of Control as anaphoric I^0 agreement. Yet, the incompatibility of I^0 anaphoric Control and restructuring reappears in the present context. Control is interpreted as obligatory binding of the (bound) anaphoric <+I> projection line. Restructuring is seen as pruning the comple-ments <–I> projection line. Hence, it is either the one solution <+I, *te*> or the other solution <–I, *te*>, but not both. I now propose the following. The infini-tival prefix '*te*' may function as <+anaphoric I^0>, but it appears between brack-ets (<+anaphoric I^0>). The brackets mean that the element '*te*' may, but need not, be read as anaphoric I. Below, I will use the same device of optional func-tional features for past participle properties. If the positive option is chosen the complement projection line becomes <+I>. The complement turns into a de-ictically identified IP that will not be restructured. The external theta role of the controlled complement will be assigned to the anaphoric <agr> index within '*te*'. The anaphoric <agr> index will be bound (controlled) within the matrix structure. If by contrast, the option <anaphoric I^0> is not read, the comple-ment turns into a bare VP with a merely idiomatic head prefix '*te*'. There is no anaphoric index to assign the external argument to, and there will be no Control. The complement will be restructured. Yet, as soon as the predicate head is licensed, it will assign its external argument requirement to the licenser. The licenser of the raised infinitive is not the functional category <+I> but the restructuring matrix verb.

This offers a new perspective. Licensing the predicate either by a <+I> or by a restructuring verb implies as well defining a structural subject position for that predicate. The subject is in the first structurally identifiable position the predicate licenser can define. By definition, a subject could never be present within the VP from where its theta role originates. See Williams (1994: 141) for the tenability of this position. There are some problems with a single structural position for subjects regardless of whether their predicate is I^0 marked or restructured. The restructuring verbs in (45b) and (47b) transmit the subject for the downstairs predicate to their own external argument position. This may fit the proposal. They have no other argument positions. The 'exceptional Case marking verbs' in (46b) do not react that way. Their argument frame suddenly offers the subject *Icarus* a matrix object position. Probably the object position relates to the DP or CP object of *zien* ('see') in (46a).

Another difficulty is that the ambiguous *te* predicts that all Control verbs are in principle restructuring verbs. This wild prediction, already present in Evers (1975), is difficult to maintain empirically, as was pointed out by Rutten (1991: 78). These uncertainties do not seem to me to diminish the positive point. All theta-marked referential subjects get the theta role from their predicate and due to the licenser of that predicate. No licenser fails to offer the same structural position. The subject has to be the first new argument configuration defined by the licenser of the theta-assigning predicate. This licenser may be a restructuring verb in the matrix construction or the regular I^0 licenser in an extended V-projection.

Predicate licensing and the definition of a structural subject position are now identified. The V^0-to-V^0 raising serves to realize the subject function. The difference between Control complements and restructuring complements can now be defined in a more principled way. The controlled infinitival complements have IP status. They function as clause-like arguments in the matrix construction. The subject theta role of these infinitival IP complements is assigned internally to their I^0 head, a <+anaphoric agreement> that projects to the IP top. By contrast, infinitival complements that are bare VP cannot absorb the complement-subject role internally. These infinitival complements are restructured. That way they avail themselves of the matrix verb as an operator that must define their subject. This move is not needed or even possible for the IP complements. One can now easily imagine the following corollary of the Extended Projection Principle. A predicate is always and only licensed by a subject defining operator (I^0 or V^0). This view on the matter may clarify the licensing account of restructuring in the following way. The IP complements are licensed as arguments, but the bare VP complements are licensed as predicates. The bare VP lacks deictic marking and cannot be licensed as an argument. Yet, in principle, it is or can be licensed as a predicate. To that end, it must be seen to enter a construct based on a subject-defining operator.

It is here that Dutch V^0-to-V^0 raising comes in. The Dutch V^0-to-V^0 raising realizes a solution recommendable for SOV languages. It maintains the O – V frame for argument licensing but succeeds to combine that with an optimal predicate licenser. One that is adjacent to, and left of, the predicates <+V> head. The viability of this solution is proved in early child language. The O – V frame almost exclusively dominates the first year of child language acquisition. This is the period when the primary verbal lexicon and its subcategorization frames are established, roughly from the 18th to the 30th month. The last four to five months of that period show the amazing rise of predicate licensing from far below 10% to well above 90% of the predicative constructs. See Evers and Van Kampen (2000) for a full exposition. The predicate-final position of V^0 and I^0 in Dutch and German has now been established by a learnability argument.

4. Extensions

The maximal crossing of argument-head relations indicated by (1) and (2) has been clarified as a local cross-over in cyclic V^0-to-V^0 raising. The whole head-argument rearrangement has been interpreted as a licensing mechanism for bare VP complements. Crucial devices for the licensing mechanism were a structure building V^0-to-V^0 raising (McCawley's Predicate Raising), a structure-destroying Pruning convention (Kuroda's Guillotine Principle) and again a structure-building reattachment of stranded material (Seuren's Reattachments Conventions). The pruning of the bare VP label happens to have an additional effect as well. The cluster creeper can get optionally stranded at each cycle. Subsequently, the labeling convention for head-head dependencies will inevitably reattach the cluster creeper to the new V^0 head stack. The curious and useless cluster-creeping phenomenon now follows as a non-intended side effect of the licensing mechanism. Solutions that do not apply pruning may need a somewhat weird and language-specific statement to get the cluster creeper moving.

Koopman and Szabolcsi (2000: 26) observe that head movement by V^0-to-V^0 raising cannot strand any of the adjoined infinitives, whereas head movement by I^0-to-C^0 (the V-second rule) is different. It has to strand them all. At first, the V^0 head stack proves itself to be a new and tight structure. It raises as a unit from predicate-final position into predicate-final position. Then, it cracks into two parts. The cause is the V-second rule (I^0-to-C^0). It raises the finite head out of its V^0 head stack and lands it into the initial <+C> operator position. The infinitival part of the V^0 head stack must now be stranded. It cannot be pied-piped ever. The difference between I^0-to-C^0 raising and V^0-to-V^0 raising is the difference between a head extraction and a head pied-piping. A successful analysis should of course derive this effect, not stipulate it.

(49) a.   b.

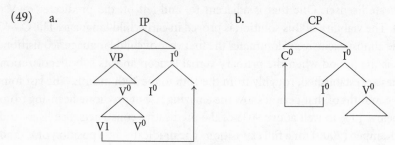

tree a. V^0-to-V^0 raising pied-pipes the whole V^0 stack.
         It cannot strand a V^0 element.
tree b. V-second must strand the V^0 head stack.
         It cannot pied-pipe a single X^0 element.

As we see now, pied-piping of the V^0 stack versus stranding of the V^0 stack follows naturally from the pruning requirement. If the bare VP-projection line were still supported by a remnant V^0 with head status, no pruning could follow. The structure would continue to contain the non-licensable VP complement. For the same reason, the V^0 stack should not leave a trace when it is raised. This comes close to Pollock's misgivings about traces left by infinitives. By contrast, if the finite verb (I^0) is moved in French or Dutch – but not in English – there is a deictic grammatical marking <+fin> of sufficient strength. This yields enough marking for leaving a trace. Hence, the Dutch V-second rule moves I^0 <+fin> out of its IP and leaves its trace. Consequently, it need not and will not pied-pipe the full V^0 stack, nor will the move I^0-to-C^0 cause a pruning of the IP projection line. The trace for the I^0 will preserve the I^0 projection. All of this follows from fairly general assumptions, i.e. prospective UG principles.

There was another objection to the pruning of the bare VP complements. Pruning removes structure that is relevant for rules of binding and scope assignment (Haegeman 1992: 127). The objection is correct but not necessarily relevant. If the grammatical derivation has to result in an integrated semantic representation, it surely would be better not to prune the complement structure. In such a case, one had better keep track of the underlying complement structure, e.g. by means of A-traces. If so, the insertion of binding and scope indices by a later LF component could subsequently lead to a single integrated semantic representation. If, by contrast, separation of rule components is an artificial restriction, matters are different. Then it is better to take a derivational view of the matter. The relevant binding and scope properties have to be stated the moment the relevant structure is represented. Not later. They are no longer a concern when the structure has been converted into something else, some other phonological or syntactic representation. In fact, abolishment of rule components might be the best way to understand Chomsky's (1995) minimalism. The X-bar principles, lexical insertion principles, movement principles and morphological checking principles are not ordered by statements about rule components. Each principle applies as soon as there is a structure to which it is applicable. It seems there is but one exception. The phonological rules for phrasal stress and assimilation have to be delayed until the final linear arrangement is there. This is brought about by a strange and atypical concession. Phonological spell-out of lexical options can be, and often must be, delayed. Nevertheless, let me take the minimalist perspective that the function of a rule or principle offers no reason for its extrinsic ordering. Then it is not necessary, or even possible, to preserve the complement structure for a later interpretation by an LF component. Such LF interpretations do not have to be later. The Theta Criterion and its A-traces can be given up. Pruning shows the simplifying effect of infinitival movement.

The pruning analysis of the Dutch verbal clusters can be extended. It is possible to derive the distribution of the Past participle as an <+A> cluster creeper (Section 4.1). Finally, the VP-raising in southern Dutch and its strange argument distribution (Haegeman 1992: 185) follows fairly well (Section 4.2).

4.1 The past participle as a cluster creeper

The properties of the cluster creeper listed in (21) and repeated here as (50), also hold for the past participle.

(50) a. The categorical status of the cluster creeper is a X^0 <–V>.
 b. The cluster creeper is licensed in front of any V^0 of the cluster it belongs to and the distributional variation has no semantic effect whatsoever.
 c. The cluster creeper attracts the cluster stress in any of its positions.
 d. The cluster creeper is selected idiomatically by the most deeply embedded verb only.

There is a historical as well as a synchronic parallel between the past-participle prefix and the particle (Hoeksema 1988). The two elements add a terminative function <+Adv/state> to the predicate. The past-participle prefix adjoins to a <+V> in morphology, the particle adjoins to a <+V> in syntax.

The properties of the cluster creeper (21)/(50a) to (21)/(50d) hold for both, particle and past participle. Both elements, the morphological one and the syntactic one, characterize an argument as <+resulting state>. That type of theta role may require that the complement be DP or IP. This at least is a fact. The <+V> that has selected a particle prefix or a particle adverb is disqualified as a governor in the verbal cluster. Both constructs insist on an IP complement, even if the <+V> element itself might have allowed for a bare VP. Hence, the past participle gets cluster-creepers property (21)/(50d). It has to be last selected element of its V^0 stack. At the same time, the past participle demonstrates the stress constancy (21)/(50c) and the creeper distribution (21)/(50b). See for the latter (51).

(51) omdat   Icarus uit het labyrinth   **weg**
      because Icarus out of the labyrinth away

a.	zou	kunnen	zijn	**gevlogen**
	would	may	be (have)	flown
b.	zou	kunnen	**gevlogen**	zijn
	would	may	flown	be (have)
c.	zou	**gevlogen**	kunnen	zijn
	would	flown	may	be (have)
d.	**gevlogen**	zou	kunnen	zijn
	flown	would	can	be (have)

Arguably, the past participle is a <+A>. If so, it is a <–V> and satisfies the creeper property (21)/(50a). The past participle differs from the lexical/idiomatic cluster creepers on two points. Its strands its arguments and it may as well adjoin to the right of its <+V> governor. Both properties are exemplified in (51). The subcategorizing constituents [*uit het labyrinth*]PP ('out of the labyrinth') and [*weg*]Adverb ('away') have been selected by the past participle [*gevlogen*] ('fly') but they have been stranded by their selector. The structure (51a) demonstrates that the past participle can be placed to the right of its perfective auxiliary *zijn* (be). These two properties, adjunction to the right and stranding of arguments, have so far been related to the raising of <+V> heads only. What is at issue here, is the somewhat ambiguous categorical status of the past participle. I will argue the <+A> status of the past participle first and consider the objections against it thereafter.

Traditional grammar suffers as much from less inspired moments as any other type of grammar. It tends to make a distinction between the past participle Passive, the past participle Perfect and the past participle 'used as an adjective'. The striking fact is that nearly all periphrastic verbal systems in Indo-

European seem to insist on such a triple categorical ambiguity, from Hittite fifteen centuries BC (Sturtevant 1933:267; Benvéniste 1962:40–65) to Afrikaans (Conradie 1979; Robbers 1997) more than thirty centuries later. Several of these periphrastic systems must have emerged independently from each other, when the verbal inflection of Proto-Indo-European failed to survive. Moreover, within each system, the morphological forms of the past participle are a swamp of irregularity, but the triple categorical ambiguity is almost without exception. Historical doublets have not been used to disambiguate categories. It seems reasonable to derive the differences between the perfect, passive and attributive construction from the surrounding functional categories (*have, be,* A-agreement) only. The past participle itself should be an identical common core. I will not attempt within the present context to discuss the possible mechanics, interesting though they are. Clearly, the past-participle morphology blocks <+I> verbal agreement, whereas it does not block the adjectival A-agreement morphology as in standard written German and even, in a rudimentary fashion, in highly deflected Dutch. Why does the past-participle morphology not block the A-agreement morphology whereas it does block the V-agreement morphology? The straightforward answer would be that the past-participle morphology is a <+V> adjectivizer. Its outcome is a category <+A>. Small wonder it blocks V-agreement and welcomes A-agreement. The <+A> status is also confirmed by the use of the copula for predicates with a past-participle head. This property is without exception. Finally of course, there are the two facts that concern us here immediately. The <+A> status of the past participle predicts its striking appearance as a cluster creeper in the right-branching V^0 stacks of Dutch. It also predicts that the past participle cannot function as a <+V> governor whether in the right-branching V^0 stacks of Dutch or the left-branching V^0 stacks of German. Hence, it has to be the last selected element in the verbal cluster. So far, the <–V> / <+A> status of the past participle has been supported by access to the copula constructs, attributive agreement and cluster-creeperhood, as well as by its access to the verbal cluster as last selected element only. The state assigned by the past participle is event-related and allows a '*by+* agent' phrase. This may be irrelevant. Lexical theta structure is in principle not sensitive to category status as is proved by category conversions, a quite general property in any grammar.

The <+A> status of the past participle has its problems. It got bad marks from Beedham (1982) for the following reason. The past participle refuses to enter syntactic and morphological constructs of Dgr^0, although these are prototypical adjectival constructs. Yet, this specific objection to the <+A> status of past participles may not be decisive. The realization of the past-participle morphology may follow from consulting a lexicon. The same may hold for the realization of Dgr^0. If so, they have no access to each other's products. By contrast, both Degree and past-participle morphology do have access to the A-agreement morphology. Let the A-agreement be a categorical consequence of <+A> status rather than a lexical provision for underived <+A> elements. If so, absence of Dgr^0 morphology need not be much of an argument against the <+A> status of past participles. More awkward problems are the two apparently <+V> properties of the Dutch past participle in (52).

(52) a. As last selected element, the past participle need not but may very well adjoin to the right of its <+V> governor.
      b. If the past participle is raised into the verbal cluster and adjoined to its governor, either to the left or to the right, it strands its arguments.

The options in (52) are available for any participle, see (53b) and (54b). At the same time they are not at all available for <+A> elements, see (53a) and (54a).

(53) a. omdat Icarus   t kan zijn [** roekeloos]A
          because Icarus can be   reckless
      b. omdat Icarus   t kan zijn [weggevlogen] Past Part
          because Icarus can be   away flown

(54) omdat de vader (as the father)

      a. [t op het oordeel van zijn zoon] kan ** trots   zijn
          of the judgement of his son   can   proud be
      b. [op het oordeel van zijn zoon t] kan afgegaan zijn
          on the judgement of his son   can relied   be (have)

There is a more or less plausible way to get around the last objection. The impossibility of stranding the arguments of a <+A> predicative head can be related to the directionality of argument licensing. The lexical <−V> heads would license their arguments to the right, whereas the <+V> heads would license their arguments to the left. If so, the raising of a <−V> head into a <+V> cluster on the right would block the relicensing of its stranded arguments. These do not fit a (cluster) head on the right. They expect, as of old, a head on the left. If the past-participle phrase, although <+A>, licenses its arguments on the left, as its underlying VP complement did, it follows that these arguments can be stranded and relicensed in a head-to-head raising movement, see (55).

(55) [arg$_1$ arg$_2$ past participle]$_{\text{Past P phrase}}$ [....]V stack

licenser to the right   rasing to the right

This changes the objection. The question is why the adjectivation of a
<+V>/bare VP projection did not change the direction of the argument licens-
ing. It may be that all functional categories that operate on <+V> predicates
in Dutch are in the same predicate-final position as <+I>. They govern their
complement to the left. Only <+A> signs with lexical content license their argument to the right. Assuming this, it follows that the past participle, although
a <+A> may preserve the licensing direction of the <+V>, may raise into the
verbal cluster and will strand its arguments. Let me disregard for a moment the
objection (53a/b) that the past participle may raise to the right of its governor,
whereas a regular <+A> may not, see example (53a). It seems then that the
past participle is a state-assigning participle <+A>. Due to this initial status, it
probably enjoys a high learnability in early child language, and a corresponding
long historical standing in Indo-European grammar. Its striking appearance as
a cluster creeper in the context of Dutch V^0-head stacks is highly language specific but now predicted from general principles. This was the main point of
the present section. Nevertheless, it might be useful to say something about the
anomaly in (53b).

The exceptional position of the past participle in (53b) may indicate that
its <+A> status can be overruled in certain contexts. Imagine a rule like (56).

(56) Past participle <+A> → <zero> / [V ___]$_V$

A past participle <+A> drops its categorial feature <+A> if governed from
the left by a V. The past participle itself has been derived from a head <+V>
and this category now takes over by default. Unpleasant ad hoc tinkering as
this may be, part of the situation is not uncommon. The categorial marking of <+V> elements in a verbal chain is often somewhat ambiguous. Under
contextual pressure Modals tend to become mere <+I> from <+V>, Gerunds
<+V> from <+N>, past participles <+V> from <+A>, and infinitival mark-
ers *te* <zero> from <+P>. The morphological ending may in all these cases
remain and preserve its grammatical function of predicate marking. Yet, it
may drop its categorial feature and the <+V> head takes over. In order to
express this, I once proposed the following descriptive possibility. Functional
morphemes may contain a categorial feature that is optional and written
as (<+A>), (<+N>), (<+P>), (<+V>), cf. Evers (1993). The claim is that
categorial status can be conditional on a context. See Van Kampen (2000),

who argues for an acquisitional point of view. The categories of lexical items <+/–N>, <+/–V> are inevitably idiomatic and have to be learned from a narrow, highly repetitive, grammatical context. Historically, periphrastic forms may lose category features and develop a categorial <+V> uniformity for the verbal paradigm. If the categorial feature <+A> due to (56) is not read, the past participle becomes <+V>. Yet, as a member of the verbal cluster, the past participle maintains its grammatical functions. It continues to mark its complements as <+state>, continues to be the last selected element in the verbal cluster, and continues to need selection by a tense auxiliary (*have, be*). There is worse to come.

The <+A, +state> past participle cannot function as governor in a verbal cluster. This implies that the <+V> governors in a verbal cluster must have defective paradigms. They cannot be marked as passives or perfectives. As far as passives are concerned this is according to fact in Dutch and German (but not in Italian). The perfective has given rise to an alternative that has baffled grammarians since it was first observed by Grimm (1837: 168–169). It is known as Infinitivus Pro Participio. See the following examples.

(57) a. als hij zijn zoon [heeft *ge -zien neerstorten]
          if   he   his   son   has   seen   crash
      b. als hij zijn zoon [heeft - -zien neerstorten]
          if   he   his   son   has   see   crash
      c. toen hij [is *ge-bleven doorvliegen]
          when he   is   continued   through fly
      d. toen hij [is - blijven   doorvliegen]
          when he   is   continue through fly

In terms of the present approach, one might attempt the following ad hoc statement. The past participle morphology is not spelled out at all and turns into a <zero>, given the context: bare VP complement that has to be restructured. Suppose the arrangement in (58).

(58) *Infinitivus Pro Participio*
      Assume that
      a. the past participle has the form [(<+Past P>) <+V>].
      b. its presently relevant context is [VP [___ <+V>]PastP]PastP. phrase
      c. the morpheme reduction rule is
          <+Past Part> → <zero> / [VP [___ <+V>]Past P]Past P. phrase

Grimm characterizes the Infinitivus Pro Participio as "*widersinnig*" ('crazy'). It cannot be an infinitive, he insists. One would like to agree. Especially the later selection by *have* depends on the information <+past part>. Nevertheless, the form becomes <+V> and infinitival. One might also expect that an arrangement like in (58) is not particularly learnable. The opposite appears to be true. The very well informed Grimm shows how the phenomenon appears from medieval texts up to the present in the whole continental West-Germanic dialect area. Obviously, we have missed out on something.

4.2 The VP raising

Southern Dutch allows the same restructuring of bare VP complements as northern Dutch. In addition, it allows restructuring by raising one of the bare VP-segments, or even the whole VP, see (59) and (60).

(59)

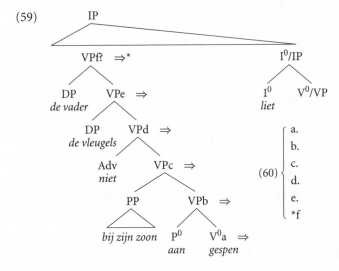

(60) omdat ik
  a. de vader die vleugels   niet bij zijn zoon   aan   **liet** gespen
  b. de vader die vleugels   niet bij zijn zoon   **liet**   aangespen
  c. de vader die vleugels niet   **liet**   bij zijn zoon   aangespen
  d. de vader die vleugels **liet**   niet   bij zijn zoon   aangespen
  e. de vader **liet** die vleugels   niet   bij zijn zoon   aangespen
  f. *__liet__ de vader die vleugels   niet   bij zijn zoon   aangespen
    (because I did not let the father clasp on those wings to his son)

The external argument of the bare VP (*de vader* 'the father') in (59f)/(60f) appears only as an argument of the matrix construction. This could be a consequence of the definition for subject, as proposed above. Its position as subject can only be defined by the licenser *liet* ('let').

The option of restructuring by VP-to-V^0 raising in Southern Dutch holds for all V^0-to-V^0 raising verbs, i.e. all verbs subcategorized for a bare VP complement. The VP-to-V^0 raising will give rise to Pruning of the bare VP label and Reattachment of the stranded argument material as above in cases of licensing by V^0-to-V^0 raising. See the variants in (59), (60) above. Raising a VP-segment has the advantage that no longer all head argument relations cross. Arguments quite close to a V^0 may remain adjacent to it. This new VP-licensing configuration corresponds a bit with English The licensing operator is on the left hand side and allows a VP with some internal argument structure. There is a difference as well. Southern Dutch preserves the O – V frame for the VP. Hence the VP licenser is no longer adjacent to the <+V> head of the bare predicate VP that was to be licensed. There is a curious fact supporting the view that VP-to-V^0 raising is on a par with V^0-to-V^0 raising. The Infinitivus Pro Participio applies in cases of predicate raising, i.e. in cases with a bare VP complement. As mentioned in Rutten (1991) the Infinitivus Pro Participio appears in cases of V^0-to-V^0 raising as well as in cases of VP-to-V^0 raising. See (61), taken from Rutten (1991:69).

(61) a. $^?$dat Jan zijn broer heeft *proberen* [naar het zwembad te krijgen]$_{VP}$
          (Southern standard Dutch)
          that John his brother has try [to the swimming pool to get]$_{VP}$
      b. da Marie hem ee proberen [nen brief (?te) schrijven]
          (West Flemish dialect)
          that Marie him has try [a letter to write]

It is interesting to see how the dialect is more firm in its option for the Infinitivus Pro Participio and prefers to drop the <–I> prefix *te* as spurious. The *ad hoc* statement for the Infinitivus Pro Participio in (58) remains effective as stated. It remains unclear why standard northern Dutch does not restructure by VP-segment raising like southern Dutch. The following speculation may apply. The VP-segment is a phrase. Suppose that the southern/Belgian infinitive <+V> is marked by the optional feature (<tense>), whereas the northern infinitive <+V> is not. The tense option is between brackets and becomes visible if he projection line is governed from the right, i.e. after raising. If no such <tense> marker becomes visible, then, as in northern Dutch, head–head interaction continues until the level I^0 has been reached. The I^0 is <+tense> and <+agreement> by definition.

Haegeman (1992) handles the VP raisings of her native dialect in a different way. She assumes that DP and PP arguments can be scrambled out of any VP, by optional movement. The scrambled arguments may land to the left of the negation and sentence adverbials. Suppose scrambling is a result of some leftward movement. Then the following sequence for southern Dutch VP raising becomes imaginable. The DP and PP arguments may or may not scramble out into a VP matrix constituent. Subsequently, the VP complement is raised out, somewhat tattered maybe by a previous argument scrambling. The raised VP lands to the right of the matrix verb and seems licensed. See the diagram in (62) for the examples.

(62)

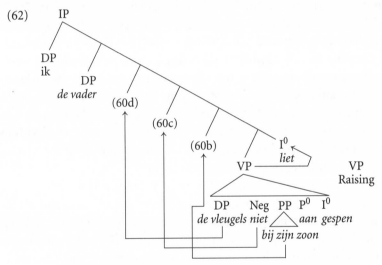

Cumulative but optional scrambling out

The nice point is now that all variations of VP raising are derived without reference to VP-segments. Haegeman considers for a moment to derive all raising variants from scrambling variants, including V^0-to-V^0 raising. She rejects this approach *inter alia* because the cluster creeper will not scramble, but insists on its V^0 adjacency. The idea of a "generalized scrambling out" returns in Koopman and Szabolcsi (2000). One should realize though, that the scrambling out of DP and PP arguments brings in problems of its own. Scrambling cannot easily be presented as some belated movement into a licensing position beyond the VP. Scrambling out arguments in an optional and cyclic fashion belies an account by argument licensing. Nor can scrambling be convincingly presented as an A-bar movement towards some topic position. Rearrangements for an A-bar topicalization should permit argument crossing with a certain disregard for A-binding relations. This is not born out by the facts. Scrambling would represent a third type of movement, as Haegeman (1992:161) points out, referring to Den Besten and Rutten (1989). Neeleman (1994: Ch. 3) enters into an extensive discussion of this problem. He eventually rejects scrambling as a movement. The present context of VP-raising seems to enhance Neeleman's (1994) position. Consider diagram (62) again. A DP and a PP argument have just been scrambled into the matrix frame VPb. This frame is in turn being inserted in VPa. The DP and PP argument that have just been scrambled out of VPc need not be scrambled out again. Yet, they may be. See (64f/e) for this option. The resulting optional leftward drift of the arguments in (64) was already noticed in Haegeman and Van Riemsdijk (1986). Haegeman (1992:185) is careful to point out that her VP raising/Extraposition analysis captures all the distributions, by repeated and optional scrambling. Haegeman, it must be added, certainly does not invoke the licensing account of scrambling. Nevertheless, her optional scrambling out of arguments, under whatever triggers, is a kind of argument exodus. Hence, it comes into the problems of gambit two, the argument exodus. It must explain why and how the original line-up of arguments is preserved. Leftward scrambling, whatever its adventures with adverbial material, does preserve the argument line-up of the original subcategorization statement (Neeleman 1994, 1998).

The scrambling facts as such hold as well for standard Dutch. They are in fact characteristic for the whole continental West-Germanic area and are obvious candidates for some type of typological explanation. Suppose we accept the account of scrambling by Neeleman (1994). It is Neeleman's contention that the subcategorization frame in certain language types is characterized by linearity but not by a strict adjacency. Adverbial and negation elements can be added during the build-up of a VP subcategorization frame. The advantages pointed out by Neeleman (1994) merit some consideration. One gets a typological perspective and one needs no triggers, domains, traces and landing sites for scrambling movements. Finally, and more immediately relevant here, one gets the immutable line-up of DP and PP arguments for free. This approach, if supplemented by VP-segment raising, will cover the same distributional material.

5.   Conclusion

The maximal crossing of argument-head relations was exemplified in (1) and (7) and stated as a grammatical problem in (6) and (8). Three potential generative approaches were listed in (9). The analysis in the sections above has tried to construe this as a Goldilocks situation. The porridge on a Di Sciullo and Williams (1988) plate (9-i) is too cold. One might eat it, but it may not taste good, neither for a morphologist nor for a syntactician. The one that comes out of the Minimalist kitchen (9-ii), whether cooked by Zwart (1996) or by Koopman and Szabolcsi (2000), is too hot. It simply cannot be eaten. But, the product prepared by means of systematic head exodus (9-iii) turns out to be just right. The systematic argument exodus used in the minimalist product (9-ii) can as yet not guarantee the line-up of arguments and heads. It stipulates that order, since it fails to explain it. Hence, it is in its present state no competitor yet. By contrast, the two other approaches derive the argument-head line-up in a principled way. Both make use of a V^0 head stack. Both derive the monoclausal character of the eventual construction. Both share the advantage of handling the stress constancy of the cluster creeper in a straightforward way. The further adventures of the two V^0 head stack gambits are different. The Di Sciullo and Williams (1988) recipe has the bad luck of introducing the V^0 stack as a kind of verbal compound. This leads to questionable morphology. The cluster-creeper distributions are atypical for a morphological construct. More serious, the theta assignment by subordinate 'relativized' heads contradicts what is known about compounds in general (Lieber 1983). Finally, the strict monoclausality of the derivation by Di Sciullo and Williams (1988) runs into difficulties with restrictions on binding and scope elements. These rather suggest underlying clausal structures. The solution by head exodus as defended here, is more fortunate. It builds up the V^0 stack in syntax. This brings in a threefold advantage over the morphological approach by Di Sculllio and Williams (1988). (i) There are underlying clausal structures to refer to for scope and binding restrictions, (ii) the curious distribution of the cluster creepers can be made to follow from the V^0-to-V^0 raising alone, and (iii) there is no need to worry about the contrasting properties of theta assignment by morphological compounds. The head exodus (9-iii) outperforms its competitors of head compounding (9-i) and argument exodus (9-ii.) This may give one pause to think. How did the earlier solution, one from thirty years ago (Seuren 1972; Evers 1976, 1975), regain its force? The answer must be this.

The in-between period has been dominated by empty place arrangements. All distributional variation in syntax was to be constrained by binding principles. These did not apply on the spot. They belonged to a separate rule component LF, which – due to its task – had to come in late. The LF component was to compose an integrated semantic representation as derived from all syntactic information. The delayed LF binding requirement imposed a strict representational view on syntax (cf. Koster 1987). All the in-between positions touched by a syntactic derivation had to be preserved by traces. The full preservation of structure by traces was guaranteed by an overarching convention, the Theta Criterion. It required that each movement should leave a structure preserving trace. Only for such representations, LF rules could retrace the actual distributions to their original theta assignment configurations. As soon as the idea of a separate LF rule components is given up, things change. Grammar could return from a basically representational view on grammar to a far more derivational one. The Theta Criterion, its associated A-traces and binding as a general constraint on distributional variation became questionable. They have in fact been given up in the analysis above. The cyclic locality restrictions on head-to-head movement are understood as the outcome of mere crossing constraints. The elegance of a McCawley type of Predicate Raising (McCawley 1968) could be reconsidered. Structure building and structure pruning, as well as the immediate interference of lexical insertion, and syntactic derivation remind one of the same romantic period. The in-between period (Government and Binding) developed the awareness that each step in a rearrangement must serve a separate licensing condition. The earliest derivation of the Dutch infinitival distributions by predicate raising and pruning has now been rephrased according to these more contemporaneous concerns. The analysis has been extended with parallel derivations of stress assignment (Section 2), cluster creeping (Section 3), past participle distribution (Section 4.1), and VP raising (Section 4.2).

Notes

1. I am aware of the fact that the structure in (41) assumes the selection of a bare VP. It introduces an underlying syntactic representation which, as such, is not directly licensable. This is not at all in the spirit of Williams's (1994) proposals and in fact exactly the type of animal he wants to get rid of. It is not obvious though, how the approach taken by Di Sciullo and Williams (1988) should proceed here, cf. above gambit (9-i). The argument structure around the Dutch verbal cluster strongly suggests rearrangements on an underlying structure.

2. Rutten describes "the third construction" as "remnant Extraposition". Structural arguments would scramble out of the IP complement into the matrix structure. Subsequently, the IP would be extraposed. A V^0-to-V^0 raising that would have stranded cluster-creepers and comparable material, cannot apply if one assumes with Rutten that V^0-to-V^0 raising is triggered only by a rule feature $<+aux>$ on the matrix verb. I suggest, but cannot prove, the following alternative. V^0-to-V^0 raising is in principle possible for all infinitival complements. Most Control verbs, but not those that allow V^0-to-V^0 raising, have an alternative subcategorization for an oblique object or predicative adjunct, e.g. *verlangen naar een*

omhelzing ('long for an embrace') versus *verlangen om te omhelzen* ('long to embrace'). Such Control verbs seem to be unable to relicense the oblique object/adjunct of a restructured complement VP. The fact that they allow a VP-segment raising that is blocked for regular V^0-to-V^0 raising verbs, may point to a blocking of the former option by the latter. I have no theory to back this up.

CHAPTER 3

V-clustering and clause union
Causes and effects

Hubert Haider

1. Overview: Descriptive generalizations and their theoretical implications

The background assumptions and claims defended in this paper are as follows:

- In Dutch and German, clustering involves *any* dependent *verbal* category (i.e. V_{Inf}, V_{PII}, $zu_{Germ.}/te_{Du.}$ + V_{Inf}): Clustering is *obligatory* with non-sentential complements, that is, with bare V_{Inf} and V_{PII} heads.[1]

- In German, in contrast to Dutch, infinitival complements with zu + V_{Inf} are *optionally* clustering if the superordinate verb selects a sentential infinitival complement.[2] As in Dutch, clustering is *obligatory* for subsentential ('raising' predicates) complement types.

- Derivational accounts in terms of phrasal movements (of remnant clauses or remnant V-projections) prove empirically inadequate.[3]

- Clause-union effects are predicted, if clustering starts from a base-generation option of head-to-head selection and merger. Serialization patterns follow from local head movement (adjunction, cliticization, VP-shell formation).

- German and Dutch represent minimally different grammatical implementation options of clustering: Both employ verbal cliticization to the right. As to rearrangements targeting the left side, Dutch implements head-movement by adjunction to the left whereas German uses (directionally non-canonical) VP-shell projections.

- Clustering is a property of recursive head-final projections: V-clustering has the effect of minimizing center embedding for V-projections and their lexical or functional extensions. It follows from a UG-principle that guarantees parser-friendliness.

Grammar theory offers in principle three different ways of modeling the V-clustering phenomenon and its relation to the non-clustering variant. One possibility is that clusters are clusters from the beginning, that is, cluster formation is a base-generation option (*head-to-head merging*), and that the non-clustering construction is a separate construction from the beginning. Second, clusters can be derived from the non-clustering construction by movement operations, either in terms of *phrasal movement* (for instance by *CP- or VP-evacuation and movement of the remnant CP or VP*, respectively) or by *head-movement* (for instance by *V-to-V adjunction* or *head chains in a VP-shell projection*) with or without restructuring (cf. Wurmbrand 2001).[4] Third, cluster formation may involve a combination of cluster base generation and head movement. Here, it will be argued that minimally different implementations of the third approach are necessary and adequate for an empirically adequate coverage of both the German and the Dutch variants of clustering, respectively.

2.   A descriptive survey of V-clustering and clause union in German

2.1 The structure of the clusters

The data reviewed in this section are core data for the construction and they provide evidence for the crucial question: What is the phrasal architecture of the cluster? Does it involve more complex, phrasal projections or is it simply a cluster of X^0-type elements?

The evidence to be discussed here is drawn from three independent sources. First, there is comparative OV-VO evidence: In German and Dutch, clustering is reflected by a strict adjacency requirement for the verbs in the cluster. This is not expected if the cluster consists of stacked projections (including remnant CPs or VPs). Second, left dislocation and topicalization provide evidence for V-clusters as head clusters, rather than V-projections, and third, clustering affects the argument structure of dependent verbs (clause union effects), which is unexpected if the cluster consists of projections. Additional, independent evidence for a monoclausal structure is reviewed briefly at the end of the subsection.

Let us start with the robust and characteristic adjacency property of the elements in the cluster. A comparison of English and German reveals a clear difference in the organization of V-projections that involve auxiliaries. In English, they behave as is expected for stacked VPs, in German (and Dutch), however, they do not. The verbs seem to cluster.

(1) a. The new theory certainly may *possibly* have *indeed* been *badly* formulated   (Quirk et al. 1986: §8.20, p. 495)

    b. daß die Theorie wohl   tatsächlich schlecht formuliert (*)
        that the theory possibly indeed   badly   formulated
        worden (*) sein (*) mag
        been   be   may

The fact that it is possible to separate auxiliaries by intervening adverbials tells
that the structure for (1a) is one with stacked phrasal projections. Each auxiliary projects a VP (and functional layers on top of it, if you like) and selects
a VP (or a functional extension thereof) as its complement. In German, the
series of verbs is the mirror image of the English pattern, but intervening material is strictly excluded. This is indicated by the bracketed asterisks in (1b).
Adverbials must precede the chain of verbs. This is not at all a peculiarity of
adverbs, but it holds for any potentially postverbal material as potential intervener. A comparison with topicalized (remnant) VPs is instructive. These data
show that (remnant) VPs may contain extraposed material, hence potential
postverbal interveners in clusters.

(2) a. [*Gerechnet damit*]$_i$ hat sie nicht mehr e$_i$
        reckoned   *it-with* has she not   anymore

    b. *daß sie nicht mehr   *gerechnet damit* hat
        that she not   anymore *reckoned it-with* has

    c. daß sie nicht mehr *gerechnet* hat *damit*

    d. [*Gesagt, wie es funktioniert*] hat er dem Kollegen
        told   *how it works*   has he to the colleague
        leider   nicht
        unfortunately not

    e. *daß er dem Kollegen leider   nicht *gesagt wie es*
        that he the   colleagues unfortunately not   *told*   *how it*
        funktioniert hat
        works   has

    f. daß er dem Kollegen leider   nicht *gesagt* hat *wie es*
        that he the   colleagues unfortunately not   *told*   has *how it*
        funktioniert
        works

Note furthermore, that clustering is not a by-product of raising heads out of
the VP to a higher functional head position on the right.[5] This can be demonstrated with the following set of data.

Note first, that the VP is a potential extraposition site for (relative) clauses, as in (3a). But extraposed material cannot be sandwiched between verbs in the cluster. Overt reconstruction of (3a) into its extraction site is ungrammatical (3b). The extraposed (relative) clause is clause-final (3c). If clustering were a side effect of something like V-to-I clustering, an extraposed relative clause should be able to occur right before the raised sequence of verbs, as in (3d). This is the counterpart of (3a), with a VP-internal extraposed relative clause, but with the verbs raised to a clause final functional head. Note that moving the verb out of the VP would not prohibit extraposition, as illustrated by (3e), where the verb moved to the top functional-head position.

(3) a. [$_{VP}$ *Jenen* etwas gegeben *die ihn darum gebeten haben*] hat er noch nie
         those [who him it-for asked have] something given has he yet never
         'that he has never yet given something to those who asked him for it'

     b. *daß er [$_{VP}$ *jenen* etwas gegeben [*die ihn darum gebeten haben*] hat
         that he those something given [who him it-for asked have] has

     c. daß er *jenen* etwas gegeben hat, *die ihn darum gebeten haben*
         that he those something given has [who him it-for asked have]

     d. *daß er [$_{VP}$ *jenen* etwas e$_i$ [*die ihn darum gebeten haben*]] gegeben$_i$ hat
         that he those something [who him it-for asked have] given has

     e. Er gab$_i$ [*jenen* etwas e$_i$, [*die ihn darum gebeten haben*]]
         He gave those something [who him it-for asked have]

What these data show is, first, that the cluster structure of auxiliaries and the main verb does not leave any room for intervening material. There would be enough room, however, if the clusters consisted of stacked (remnant) projections, because, on the one hand a (remnant) VP allows extraposed material (see VP-Topicalization with extraposition in (2a, d)), and on the other, English shows that V-projections (plus their functional extensions) allow intervening material. So, the 'no intervener' property is not reducible to a constraint that would hold for Vs selecting V-projections or their functional extensions.

Second, the effect cannot be reduced to head-movement since the 'no-intervener' property already holds for the base positions (see (3d)). Head-movement would not destroy the base constellation of the V-projections and therefore would not account for these side effects.

Let me emphasize that the 'no-intervener' property is clear counterevidence to any analysis of cluster construction that operates with V-projections (or higher ones) as minimal building units of clusters. This applies to Koopman and Szabolcsi (2000) as well as to Wurmbrand (2001). Unfortunately, both publications pay no attention to this crucial property of clusters.

Let us now compare topicalization and left dislocation (LD). As discussed in Haider (1990), there is a mismatch between VP-topicalization and VP-in-situ. In situ, the auxiliaries are obligatorily clustered (see also Haider 1993: Chapter 9) but VP-topicalization seems to display a stacked-VP structure. However, left-dislocation is a good source of evidence for deciding between a clustering analysis and one that assumes remnant VPs. The examples in (4) show that a verb cluster can be topicalized or left dislocated. In the first option, the verb cluster is moved to the Spec position of the functional head that hosts the finite verb. In the latter option, the Spec position contains a pronominal bound by the left-dislocated phrase.

(4) a. [Wiedererkennen können]^i (das^i) müßte er sie schon
         identify   be-able   (this)   must he her well

     b. [Vorsingen lassen müssen]^i (das^i) wird man ihn schon
         audit   let   must   (this)   shall one him well
         'One will have to let him audit'

     c. [Übersehen haben]^i (das^i) wird man sie sicher nicht
         overlooked have   (this)   will one her surely not

     d. [Übersehen worden]^i (das^i) ist sie noch nie
         overlooked been   (this) has she never ever

     e. [Zu reparieren versucht]^i (das^i) hat man ihn nicht
         to repair   tried   (this)   has one it not

In these examples, the argument structure of the main verbs is of the unmarked transitive format, that is, the argument structure contains only arguments without lexical specifications. Interestingly, only the left dislocation option becomes ungrammatical once the argument structure of the verb contains lexical specifications, for instance, *lexical case features* or selection requirements for *wh-features* (in case of selected *wh*-complements). In this case, only topicalization is allowed, but not left-dislocation.

(5) a. *[Zeigen müssen] (*das) hätte er es ihr sofort
         show   must   (this) had   he it her immediately
         'he had have to show it to her immediately'

     b. [Sagen müssen], (*das) hätte er aber   schon, ob   er
         tell   must   (this) had   he however well, whether he
         will
         wants

c. [Sagen müssen, ob   er will]   (das) hätte er aber
    tell   must   whether he wants (this) had   he however
    schon
    well

d. [Interessieren müssen] (*das) hätte ihn doch, ob   das
    interest   must   (this) had   him well   whether the
    Ergebnis stimmt
    result   correct-is

e. [Zu zeigen versucht] (*das) hat er ihr nicht, wie es funktioniert
    to show tried (this) has he her how it works

Obviously, left dislocation is more restricted than topicalization. The predicate
pro-form *das* (= *this/it*) does not transmit argument structure specifications to
the chain headed by the pronominal predicate. This is the crucial fact. Another
way of looking at it is this: whenever the LD-construction is acceptable, the LD-
constituent is optional. In other words, dropping the LD-constituent leaves the
sentence grammatical. So we expect that the restriction that holds in (5) is the
same as the restriction in anaphoric sequences as in (6):

(6) a. Hat er Maria wiedererkannt?   – Das hat er sie sicher nicht.
         has he Mary identified   this has he her surely not
     b. Hat er Maria das Bild gezeigt? –*Das hat er es ihr sicher nicht.
         has he Mary the picture shown   this had he it her surely not
     c. Hat ihn etwas interessiert?   –*Ob das Ergebnis stimmt, das
         has him something interested   whether the result holds, this
                                           hat ihn nicht
                                           has him not

The fact that left-dislocation involves a predicate pro-form and that this pro-
form does not transmit the full argument structure of the left dislocated cluster
indicates that the left-dislocated constituent is a verbal cluster and not a remnant VP. The left dislocated constituent cannot be a remnant VP because it does
not fully reconstruct. Hence the traces of arguments in the remant VP could
not be bound. The crucial difference between topicalization and LD is easy
to identify. The topicalized element is the head of a chain, the left-dislocated
constituent does not head a chain. It is anaphorically construed by means
of a pronominal. Additional and independent evidence comes from split-NP
constructions (see Haider 1990):

(7) [Aufsätze publiziert] (*das) hat er nur zwei kurze
     papers   published   (this) has he only two short$_{AGR}$

The predicate pro-form obviously does not establish the relation between the N in the left dislocated V-projection and the rest of the NP. This is additional evidence that the pronominal that links the LD constituent to the clause blocks reconstruction and that the LD-constituent is an independently generated constituent.

Note that this result cuts both ways. If the LD constituent is a verbal cluster rather than a remnant VP, then the topicalized constituent may be a cluster, too. The differences between the two constructions reduce to an independent fact: The topicalized cluster is related to its base position by a chain dependency. The LD constituent is related by means of a bound pro-nominal, which itself is a predicate proform selected by the auxiliary. The chain dependency allows reconstruction, the pronominal dependency does not. This is the independent source of the differences with respect to the argument-structure selectivity illustrated by the examples above. So we may conclude that V-clusters in the LD-constituent as well as in the topicalized V-projection are not remnant VPs but smaller units.

Occasionally, clustering affects the projection of the argument structure. This is the so-called clause-union property. This property becomes particularly perspicuous if one compares a clause with a sentential infinitival complement and the V-clustering counterpart.

Höhle (1978) discovered a phenomenon that is now known as 'long distance passive' (see the discussion of (8) below): passivizing the matrix verb triggers subject case for the object of the infinitival complement. In Haider (1986), this peculiarity is derived as a by-product of the V-cluster variant of the infinitival complementation constructions. By virtue of being members of a head-to-head clustering structure, the argument structures of the verbs in the cluster are pooled into a single argument structure format for the cluster as an effect of selecting a head rather than a phrasal complement. The concomitant clause-union effect is best illustrated with optionally clustering infinitival constructions (see Haider 1993: Ch. 9; 1994). In this construction, the direct object of the dependent, infinitival verb ends up in the nominative when the matrix verb lacks a nominative argument. This happens when the matrix verb is transitive and passivized, or, when the matrix verb is unaccusative. In each of the two constellations, the object of the infinitive is the only active structural-case-checking argument in the pool and therefore ends up in the external case, that is, nominative, when the clause is finite.

(8) a. daß *den*$_{ACC}$/*der*$_{NOM}$ Wagen zu reparieren versucht wurde
         that the   car   to repair   tried   was

b. daß versucht wurde, den_{ACC}/*der_{NOM} Wagen zu reparieren
   that tried   was   the   car   to repair

c. [Zu reparieren versucht] wurde *den_{ACC}/der_{NOM} Wagen nicht
   to repair   tried   was   the   car   not

d. daß uns der_{NOM}/den_{ACC} Erfolg auszukosten   erlaubt
   that us the   success to-test-to-the-full permitted
   wurde
   was

e. daß uns erlaubt   wurde, den_{ACC}/*derNOM Erfolg
   that us permitted was   the   success
   auszukosten
   to-test-to-the-full

f. [Auszukosten   erlaubt] wurde uns *den_{ACC}/der_{NOM} Erfolg
   to-test-to-the-full permitted was us   the   success
   nicht
   not

g. daß uns den_{ACC}/*der_{NOM} Erfolg auszukosten   *nicht/selten*
   that us the   success to-test-to-the-full not/rarely
   erlaubt   wurde
   permitted was

The case alternation in (8a, d) is a consequence of the ambiguous structure. The infinitival verb can be the lexical head of a sentential infinitival complement. In this case, the direct object surfaces as accusative and the subject of the sentential infinitival complement is PRO, that is, the covert infinitival subject. The other possibility is the clustering construction. In this case, the infinitival verb is part of the verbal cluster. It does not project a separate VP and hence no separate infinitival clause is projected. The arguments of the infinitival verb and the matrix verb are pooled, and the subject argument of the infinitival is directly identified with the controlling argument. It thereby becomes syntactically inactive and is not projected. In the argument pool, a single candidate for structural case is left. By virtue of the priority of external case checking over internal checking ('Burzio's Generalization', see Haider 1999) it must surface with nominative case. This 'case conversion' is a straightforward consequence of the lack of sentential embedding of the infinitive. So the clustering construction behaves like a simple clause, not like a clause with an embedded infinitival clause.

In (8b, e) the infinitival clause is extraposed, so it is sentential and consequently case conversion is not possible. This shows that the case switch presupposes cluster formation. This is confirmed by (8c, f): Topicalization of the cluster is correlated with the case switch. This is a straightforward result: if the cluster is topicalized, there must be a cluster, and hence nominative is the only option. (8e), finally, shows that without clustering there is no case switch. If the verbs are not adjacent there can be no cluster (see the 'no intervener' property, above). If they cannot cluster, there is no way of assigning nominative to the object of the infinitival verb because it is the object of an infinitival sentential complement clause.

The same patterns are predicted for *impersonal unaccusative* matrix verbs like *gelingen* (succeed) and *mißlingen* (fail) since they start out with an A-structure format that a passivized transitive verb ends up with:

(9) a. daß ihm   nicht gelungen ist [den_{ACC}/*der_{NOM} Text zu
         that him_{DAT} not   succeeded is   the   text to
         entziffern]
         decipher
         'he did not manage to decipher the text'
     b. Zu entziffern gelungen ist ihm der_{NOM} Text nicht
         to decipher succeeded is him   the   text not

In both verb classes, the clausal infinitival is the direct object of the matrix verb. The difference between the unaccusative verb and the transitive verb is simply that the former lacks the designated argument, that is, the would-be subject. Passivization turns a transitive argument format into an unaccusative one, whence the parallel behavior in clustering and clause union.

It is easy to provide further independent evidence for the clause union effect of clustering, and its consequence, the pooling of the argument structures once the verbs belong to a cluster. Verbs in the cluster by definition do not project their argument structure separately; otherwise a cluster could not remain a cluster. Two independent pieces of evidence will be called upon. First, reflexives need antecedents. If a reflexive is bound by the PRO subject in the clausal construction, it will lose its antecedent in the clustering construction and become ungrammatical. Second, a clause is a domain of sentential negation. Sentential infinitives are separate domains of negation, clustering infinitives are not.

(10) a. daß $ihnen^i$ nicht erlaubt   wurde [PRO^i $sich^i$/es zu entfernen]
          that them   not   permitted was   [themselves/it to remove]

    b. daß [PRO^i sich^i/es zu entfernen] ihnen^i (nicht) erlaubt
       that [themselves/it to remove]   them (not) permitted
       wurde
       was

    c. [Zu entfernen erlaubt]   wurde *es/*sich*   ihnen nicht
       to   remove permitted was   it/themselves them not

    d. daß ihr^i [PRO^i sich^i/ihn zu befreien] gelang
       that her [herself/him to free]   succeeded

    e. [Zu befreien gelungen] ist *er/*sich*   ihr nicht
       [to liberate succeeded is he/herself her not

In the clustering construction (10c, e), the infinitive is part of the VC of the matrix clause. There is no PRO-subject projected. Control is handled by identification of the respective arguments in the pooled argument structure of the VC. As a consequence, reflexives become ungrammatical.[6] In (10c, e), the reflexive would have to be directly bound by the dative objects, but reflexives cannot be bound by datives in German, for independent reasons. In (10a, b, d), the reflexive is bound by PRO, which is controlled by the dative object of the matrix verb. In the clustering construction, the dative argument and the reflexive are co-arguments. The reflexive is the single structural argument that would surface as nominative. This is the second source of ungrammaticality. When the reflexive is replaced by a personal pronoun in (10c, e), the sentence is grammatical. The pronoun, however, switches into the nominative, which cannot be seen in the case of *es* (it) in (10d), because the form remains the same in nominative and accusative, but in (10e), the switch from accusative to nominative (*ihn* vs. *er*) is obvious.

    The scope of sentential negation is a clear indicator of clause union triggered by clustering. As in English, the combination of a negative indefinite DP with the negation particle (Ger. *nicht*) in a simple clause amounts to negation canceling by double negation (i.e. $\neg\neg p \equiv p$), since standard German does not allow negative concord. In the clause union construction, there is only a single negation domain since there is only a single sentence, whence the canceling effect.

(11) a. daß keiner [ihn nicht zu stören] versuchte
         that nobody [him not   to disturb] tried

    b. Keiner hat versucht [ihn nicht zu stören]
       nobody has tried   [him not   to disturb]

    c. ??[Zu stören versucht] hat ihn keiner   nicht (negation cancelled)
       to   disturb tried   has him nobody not

    d. daß keinem   [ihn nicht zu stören] gelang
       that nobody$_{DAT}$ [him not to disturb] succeeded

    e. ??[Zu stören gelungen] ist er keinem nicht (negation cancelled)
       to   disturb succeeded is he nobody not

In Haider (1993, 1994) additional evidence for the clause-union effect induced by clustering, originally noted by Bech (1955), is discussed. The matrix verb is in the scope of the negation of an object of the infinitival (12).

(12) a. daß ihr niemand zu beleidigen gelang   (narrow/wide scope)
       that her nobody to insult succeeded (she did not succeed in insulting anybody/she succeeded in insulting nobody)

     b. daß ihr niemand zu beleidigen oft gelang   (narrow scope only)
       that her nobody to insult often succeeded

     c. Zu beleidigen gelungen ist ihr niemand   (wide scope only)
       to insult succeeded is her nobody (she did not succeed in insulting anybody)

The scope ambiguity of (12a) is due to the structural ambiguity. The negated indefinite in the sentential infinitival complement in (12c) has, as expected, narrow scope only. Crucially, the cluster construction in (12c), does not allow the narrow scope reading.

    Pronominal serialization is another source of evidence. In the simple clause, they are serialized in the order NOM-ACC-DAT. When a series of pronominals is not ordered this way and the clause is grammatical (see (13b)), the pronouns cannot be clause mates. The fact that (13a) is grammatical shows that the two pronouns are clause mates, and hence that the verbs are clustering. Long distance extraction is not a possible source, as (13c) demonstrates. The verbs are not adjacent, so they are not clustering and pronoun fronting turns out to be blocked.

(13) a. Zu entziffern gelang   *es ihr / *ihr es*
       to decipher succeeded it her / her it
       'she managed to decipher it'

     b. daß *ihr* [*es* zu entziffern] gelang
       that her [it to decipher] succeeded

     c. *daß es$_i$ den Experten [e$_i$ zu entziffern] *nicht/oft* gelang
       that it the experts$_{DAT}$ [to decipher] not/often succeeded

Yet another independent source of evidence for clustering is locality constraints. If the locality domain is the domain of the simple clause, it is different for the clustering and the non-clustering construction. This can be shown with the extraposition constructions (14a, b). Extraposition of argument clauses is clause-bound. The cluster construction is a simple clause, hence the extraposition of an argument of the infinitival verb remains clause-bound. (14b) is a clear case of sentential embedding, and it respects the locality constraint on extraposition. The sentence is ungrammatical because of the violation of this constraint. Only local extraposition, that is, within the embedded clause is possible, as in (14c).

(14) a. daß uns   nie [[zu erklären] versucht wurde], *warum man uns*
          that us$_{DAT}$ never [to explain tried was]   why   they us
          festhielt
          detained

      b. *daß [uns zu erklären] nie   versucht wurde, *warum man uns*
          that [us to explain]   never tried   was   why   they us
          festhielt
          detained

      c. daß [uns zu erklären *warum man uns festhielt*] nie   versucht
          that [us to explain why they us detained]   never tried
          wurde
          was

Let us finally turn to a clear contrast between the cluster construction and a construction with sentential complement. The infinitival verb may appear topicalized if it is part of the cluster but not if it is the head of a sentential infinitival (15).

(15) a. *Zu erklären$_i$ hat man gar nicht versucht [uns das Problem e$_i$]
          to explain   has one not at all tried [us the problem]

      b. Zu erklären$_i$ hat man uns das Problem gar   nicht
          to explain   has one us the problem at all not
          [e$_i$ versucht]
          [tried]

      c. *Zu erklären$_i$ hat [uns das Problem e$_i$] man gar   nicht
          to explain   has [us the problem]   one at all not
          versucht
          tried

      d. daß [uns das Problem zu erklären] man gar   nicht versucht hat
          that [us the problem to explain] one at all not   tried   has

The main verb or a projection of it cannot be extracted out of an infinitival clause (15a, c). (15c) is a derivational variant of (15d). The apparent exception

(15b) is not an exception if the infinitival verb is not part of an infinitival clause but rather a part of the cluster. In this case, it is a variant of topicalizing a part of the verbal cluster as in (16).

(16) a. [Erklären]$_i$ müßte   man das [e$_i$ können]
       explain   must$_{SUBJUNCTIVE}$ one that   be-able
       'One ought to be able to explain it'
    b. [Erklären können]$_i$ müßte man das e$_i$
       [explain   be-able]   must   one   that

The comparison of Dutch and German in the following section will help to identify the crucial differences that reflect different derivational histories of derivations starting with a base generated V-cluster. A good starting point for a comparison of the Dutch and German V-clustering properties is the IPP-phenomenon since the clear and robust contrasts between German and Dutch provide insights into the minor but far-reaching differences in the grammatical set-up for the given grammars.[7]

2.2 Comparison of German and Dutch VCs, especially with respect to IPP

2.2.0 *Introduction*

In the grammar of German, the term *Infinitivus pro Participio* (IPP, Dutch grammar tradition) or *Ersatzinfinitiv* (German grammar tradition) refers to the switch from the participial form to the bare infinitival form on the dependent verb when the (auxiliary) verb that governs the participial form precedes rather than follows the dependent verb:[8]

(17) a. daß er sie nicht hätte fragen *können*   (??fragen gekonnt hätte)
       that he her not had ask   can$_{INF}$
    b. daß er sie nicht hätte zu fragen brauchen
       that he her not had to ask   need
                                 (??zu fragen gebraucht hätte)
    c. daß er sie nicht hätte fragen lassen   (??fragen gelassen hätte)
       that he her not had ask   let$_{INF}$
       'that he would not have let her ask'

In German, the class of verbs subject to the IPP construction is restricted in the following way: The *dependent verbs*, with the exception of the 'raising' predicate *brauchen* (17b),[9] govern a bare infinitive, that is, modals, verbs of perception (*sehen*-see, *hören*-hear), and the causative/permissive *lassen* (let). The *fronted verb* is the perfective auxiliary *haben* (see (17)), – not the perfect auxiliary *sein* (be) or the passive auxiliary (details below) – or the future auxiliary *werden*. Since the latter auxiliary governs bare infinitive anyway, fronting does not change the verbal morphology on the dependent verb.

(18) a. daß er sie nicht wird fragen können   (or: fragen können wird)
          that he her not   willl ask can_{INF}
      b. daß er sie nicht wird zu fragen brauchen
          that he her not   will to ask   need
                                              (or: zu fragen brauchen wird)
      c. daß er sie nicht wird fragen lassen   (or: fragen lassen wird)
          that he her not   will ask   let

However, fronting plus IPP is ungrammatical with the passive auxiliary *werden*,[10] and, more interestingly, the perfect auxiliary *sein*. German, in comparison to Dutch (see §2.2.5 below), is exceptional with respect to the exclusion of the perfect auxiliary *sein* (see (19d)).

(19) a. daß in diesem Jahr viele Vorhaben fallen gelassen wurden
          that in this   year many   projects fall let_{PII} were
          'that in this year many projects were cancelled'
      b. *daß in diesem Jahr viele Vorhaben *wurden* fallen *lassen*
          that in this   year many   projects were   fall let_{INF}
      c. daß er nicht arbeiten gegangen ist
          that he not $work_{INF}$ gone   is
          'that he has not gone to work'
      d. *daß er nicht *ist* arbeiten *gehen*
          that he not   is $work_{INF}$ go_{INF}

Finally, when the triggering verb is embedded in the verb cluster, reordering starts with the top verb in the cluster and proceeds until the triggering verb is fronted. In (20a), the trigger is the perfective auxiliary, governed by the future auxiliary. In the result (20b), both auxiliaries end up in the inverted, mirror image order. More complex clusters tend to become clumsy in the result, but the pattern is nevertheless uncontroversial (20d):

(20) a. daß er sie nicht fragen gedurft   haben wird
          that he her not   ask   be-allowed have   will
      b. daß er sie nicht *wird haben* [fragen *dürfen*]
          that he her not   will have   ask   be allowed
          both: 'that he will not have been allowed to ask her'
      c. daß er ihn nicht weglaufen gesehen haben müssen würde
          that he him not   run-away   seen   have $must_{INF}$ would

d. daß er ihn nicht *würde müssen haben* [weglaufen *sehen*]
that he him not would must$_{INF}$ have run-away see
both: 'that he would not have had to see him run away'

Let us recapitulate. In descriptive terms, a German verbal cluster starts out in the order (21), with right-to-left dependencies between the verbs. This order may be replaced (when the conditions described above are met) by an inverted order in which the original order is mirrored. In (22), this is illustrated for a sequence of 5 verbs. The minimal sequence left in the original order consists of at least two verbs (22d). This is a simple consequence of the fact that IPP-triggers are verbs that select verbs in a cluster (modals, etc.). In German, IPP is inapplicable to main verbs.

(21) $V_1 \leftarrow V_2 \leftarrow V_3 \leftarrow V_4 \leftarrow V_5 \ldots$

(22) a. $[V_1 \leftarrow V_2 \leftarrow V_3 \leftarrow V_4 \leftarrow V_5]$ [untersucht worden sein müssen wird]
examined been be must$_{INF}$ will$_{INF}$
'will have to have been examined'
  b. $V_5 \ldots [V_1 \leftarrow V_2 \leftarrow V_3 \leftarrow V_4]$ wird [untersucht worden sein müssen]
  c. $V_5V_4 \ldots [V_1 \leftarrow V_2 \leftarrow V_3]$ wird haben [untersuchen lassen müssen]
  d. $V_5V_4V_3 \ldots [V_1 \leftarrow V_2]$ wird müssen haben [weglaufen sehen]
will must have run-away seen
'will have to have seen run away'

The pattern in (22) is a pattern of 'full inversion', that is, the fronted verbs are fronted across the entire cluster. Another possibility is splitting the cluster by inversion, as illustrated in (23). In this case, the inverted auxiliaries follow the main verb. I use the term *splitting*, because the adjacency requirement is not lifted. The main verb that precedes the inverted auxiliary in (23a–c) therefore cannot be analyzed as the left edge of a VP, whose verb does not participate in clustering. (23d) illustrates that the minimal requirement is that the auxiliary that would trigger the participial form is fronted across its dependent verb.

(23) a. … für jemanden, der öffentlich in Stücke geschnitten *hätte*
… for someone, who publicly in pieces cut$_{PII}$ had$_{SUBJ}$
werden sollen[11]
be$_{INF}$ shall$_{INF}$
'… for someone who should have been cut in pieces in public'
  b. … sondern was gemacht *hätte* werden sollen[12]
… but what done had$_{SUBJ}$ be$_{INF}$ shall$_{INF}$
'… but what should have been done'

    c. ... ob   die Todesgefahr   erkannt *hätte*   werden müssen[13]
       ... whether the mortal-danger realized had$_{SUBJ}$ be$_{INF}$ must$_{INF}$
       '... whether the mortal danger should have been realized'
    d. ... ob   die Todesgefahr   erkannt werden *hätte*   müssen
       ... whether the mortal danger realized be$_{INF}$ had$_{SUBJ}$ must$_{INF}$
       '... whether the mortal danger should have been realized'

As with full inversion (cf. (20)), the roll-up variation is also found with split-inversion (see §2.2.1 for details). This is illustrated in (24). In the main-clause order, that is, with the finite verb in the verb-second position, the split pattern may appear as if the auxiliary had been wrongly sandwiched, but a comparison with the corresponding base order reveals the regular pattern: compare (24b) with (24c).

(24) a. daß er es (nicht) *würde haben* in die Tasche stecken
        that he it (not)   would have into the pocket put$_{INF}$
        müssen
        must$_{INF}$
    b. daß er es (nicht) in die Tasche stecken *würde haben* müssen
      both: 'that he would (not) have had to put it into his pocket'
    c. Er *würde*ᵢ es (nicht) in die Tasche stecken eᵢ *haben* müssen
        he would it (not) in the pocket put$_{INF}$ have must$_{INF}$
        'He would not have had to put it into his pocket'

2.2.1 *IPP with non-verbal interveners (non-adjacency) in German, but not in Dutch*

The sequence of verbs in the IPP-construction does not form a cluster in German. This is reflected by the fact that non-verbal material may intervene between the fronted auxiliaries and the left edge of the original cluster. In Dutch, this is ungrammatical.

(24) a. daß er für ihn nicht *hatte* die Firma   am Leben halten
        that he for him not had the company alive   keep
        wollen
        want$_{INF}$
        'that he had not wanted to keep the company alive for him'
                             (Th. Mann)

b. Gerda, die   sie nicht *hatte* in der Familie grau werden
Gerda, whom she not   had in the family grey turn
sehen
see
'Gerda, whom she had not seen turn grey in the family' (Th. Mann)
c. daß der Tod   ihr *werde* in unabsolviertem Zustand auflauern
that the death her would in unabsolved   state   wait-for
dürfen
may_INF
'that death should be allowed to lie in wait for her while she was
unabsolved'   (F.Werfel)
d. *dat hij graag   wilde   de kraanvogels fotograferen
that he with-pleasure wanted the cranes   photograph
'that he would like to photograph the cranes'   (ANS:949)
e. *... wil   *naar huis* gaan   (Koopman & Szabolcsi 2000:151)
   ... want to   home go
f. ... wird *nach Hause* gehen wollen
   ... will to   home go   want

The pattern illustrated in (24a–c) is not restricted to single fronted auxiliaries.
Additional slots are opened if more than one auxiliary is fronted.[14] The clear
contrast between German and Dutch in terms of admissible, non-verbal interveners is evidence for a structural difference that calls for a principled solution
(see Section 3).

2.2.2 *No clustering with particle verbs as governing verbs in Dutch*
If the selecting verb is a particle verb, clustering is ungrammatical in Dutch, but
not in German. This can be tested only with the optionally clustering infinitival
constructions, since there are no auxiliaries of this type:

(25) a. *dat Anita de kinderen ophield te verwennen
        that Anita the children stopped to pamper
        'that Anita stopped pampering the children'   (Hoeksema 1988:157)
     b. [Zu verwöhnen aufgehört] hat sie die Kinder nie
        [to pamper   stopped]   has she the children never
        'Stopped pampering is what she never did to the children'

The relevant difference between clustering in Dutch and German is the word
order change in Dutch. In German, the cluster variant and the non-cluster variant do not differ in word order. A governing particle verb would produce a
cluster with a stranded particle within the cluster since the word-order opera-

tions in the cluster strand particles, as can be observed with *dependent* particle verbs (see below). The offending property is that the fronted verb would cross the particle. Licit stranding does not cross. Stranding by fronting is possible for particle verbs that precede the particle (as in English), or by moving to the right for particle verbs that follow (as in Dutch, see below). In each case, the particle is not crossed.

2.2.3   *No topicalization (out) of the inverted VC in Dutch (and German)*

This is a contrast that can be reduced to the property identified in §2.2.1. Topicalization of the cluster is possible only for the non-inverted part. Since in Dutch, the cluster tends to be inverted completely. as in (26a), topicalization is impossible, as shown in (26b). German provides the testing ground because it provides uninverted and inverted clusters, as in (26c) and (26d), respectively.

(26) a. dat hij het boek zeker zou   willen lezen
          that he the book surely would want   read$_{INF}$
          'that he would surely want to read the book'

      b. *[Willen lezen] zou hij het boek zeker

      c. [Lesen wollen] würde er das Buch sicher
          read   want   would he the book surely

      d. *[Haben lesen   wollen] wird er das Buch sicher
          have read$_{INF}$ want   will he the book surely

The ungrammaticality of (26b) and (26d) is due to the ungoverned trace of the topicalized constituent. The trace follows the base position of the finite verb. In Dutch and German, the canonical government for verbs is from right to left. Clustering inverts the canonical order in Dutch. Immediate evidence is the contrast in (27a) and (27b). Topicalization is possible, if it starts from the canonical serialization:

(27) a. Stelen heeft ze   nooit e$_i$ gewild/*willen e$_i$
          steal has she never   wanted/want$_{INF}$

      b. Werken$_i$ heeft Pieter nooit e$_i$ gehoeven/*hoeven e$_i$
          work   has   Pieter never   needed/need$_{INF}$

                                                (Hoeksema 1988:159)

2.2.4   *No IPP with zu + Aux in German*

A particularly clear-cut contrast between Dutch and German is the ban against infinitival IPP constructions in German. IPP in German is confined to finite clauses and is ungrammatical in sentential infinitival constructions, as shown in (28c, d).

(28) a. zonder hem *te* hebben laten wachten
         without him to   have   let   wait
         'without having let him wait'
      b. om   de ontwikkelingen *te* hebben kunnen   volgen
         so-as-to the developments   to   have can_{INF} follow
         'so as to have been able to follow the developments'
      c. *ohne   ihn *zu haben* warten lassen
         without him to have   wait   let
      d. *um   die Entwicklungen zu haben verfolgen können
         so-as-to the developments to have   follow can_{INF}
      e. ohne   daß man ihn *hat* warten lassen
         without that one him has   wait   let
      f. ohne   daß man die Entwicklungen *hat* verfolgen können
         without that one the developments has follow can_{INF}

As noted already by Bech (1955), there is a compromise construction that switches the infinitive marker *zu* from the inverted auxiliary to the right-most verb in the verbal cluster. In my judgment, the construction is nevertheless deviant:

(29) a. ??ohne/anstatt   ihn *haben* warten *zu* lassen   (cp. (28c))
         without/instead him have   wait   to let
      b. ??um   die Entwicklungen *haben* verfolgen *zu* können (cp. (28d))
         so-as-to   the developments have   follow   to can_{INF}

This contrast highlights the different status of the IPP construction in Dutch and German. The infinitival verb cannot be removed out of the verbal cluster. In Dutch, it remains within the cluster, as the no-intervener property betrays. In German, it would be removed in the IPP construction (since IPP allows non-verbal interveners). Removal, a case of head-movement, would strand the infinitival particle. This is the source of the compromise construction. The stranded particle is precliticized to the verb to its left.

One might feel tempted to entertain the alternative hypothesis that IPP is the result of moving the finite auxiliary to a tense-head position, that is T^0, and that this differentiates correctly between a tensed auxiliary and an untensed infinitival form that must stay in situ. But this hypothesis fails in view of the following contrast: if the perfect tense auxiliary is *sein* (be), IPP is ungrammatical. Movement to T^0 would not differentiate between the two perfect auxiliaries.

2.2.5   IPP with all auxiliary types in Dutch, but not in German
As noted already in Section 2.2.0, the inverted order in the V-cluster (with IPP)
is not found with the auxiliary *sein* (be) in German, but only with *haben* (have)
and the future auxiliary *werden*.

(30)   a.   dat   hij   het   boek   was   komen   halen
            that   he   the   book   was   come$_{INF}$ fetch
            'that he had come to fetch the book'
       b.   *daß   er   das   Buch   war   holen   (ge-)kommen
            that   he   the   book   was   fetch   come
       c.   dat   hij   is   blijven   liggen
            that   he   is   remain$_{INF}$ lie-down
            'that he has continued to lie down'
       d.   *daß   er   ist   liegen   bleiben/geblieben
            that   he   is   lie-down   remain/remained
       e.   dat   hij   is   weggestuurd   (geworden)
            that   he   is   away-sent   (been)
            'that he has been sent away'
       f.   *daß   er   ist   weggeschickt   worden/werden
            that   he   is   away-sent   been/be

An automatic IPP rule that fronts the finite auxiliary in the sequence V_{INF} +
V_{PART} + Aux_{TENSE} would produce correct results with perfective *haben* (have),
but not with perfective *sein* (be).

2.2.6   No infinitival clauses in the midfield in Dutch
In Dutch, sentential infinitival complements cannot be projected in the position nominal complements would be projected in. They are either replaced by
a clustering construction or extraposed.

(31)   a.   *dat   Jan   [het   boek   terug   te   geven]   (niet)   vergat
            that   Jan   [the   book   back   to   give]   (not)   forgot
       b.   daß   Jan   [das   Buch   zurückzugeben]   (nicht)   vergaß
            that   Jan   [the   book   back-to-give]   (not)   forgot
       c.   eine   Kür,   die$_i$ sicher   [PRO e$_i$ spektakulär zu nennen]
            a   free-exercise,   that   surely   [spectacular to call]
            nicht   übertrieben   wäre[15]
            not   exaggerated   would-be

For verbs that optionally allow a clustering construction in German, these sentences are systematically ambiguous between a construction with clausal embedding and a simple clause structure with V-clustering.

(32) a. daß uns [zwischen zwei Strukturen zu wählen] erlaubt   wird
that us [between two structures to choose] permitted is
'that we are allowed to choose between two structures'

   b. daß uns zwischen zwei Strukturen [zu wählen erlaubt   wird]
that us between two structures [to choose permitted is]

This ambiguity is the source for the case alternation in the construction with a matrix passive or a matrix unaccusative verb:

(33) a. daß der$_{NOM}$/den$_{ACC}$ Brief einzuwerfen vergessen wurde
that the   letter to-post   forgotten was
'that one forgot to post the letter'

   b. daß uns (?)der$_{NOM}$/den$_{ACC}$ Text zu entziffern gelungen ist
that us$_{DAT}$ the   text to decipher succeeded is
'that we succeeded in deciphering the text'

If the clausal construction is forced by splitting the potential verbal cluster, the nominative option is canceled, as expected, since the nominative is licensed only in the clustering construction.

(34) a. daß [*der$_{NOM}$/den$_{ACC}$ Brief einzuwerfen] *leider*   vergessen
that [the   letter to post] unfortunately forgotten
wurde
was

   b. daß uns [*der$_{NOM}$/den$_{ACC}$ Text zu entziffern] *endlich* gelungen
that us$_{DAT}$ [the   text to decipher] finally   succeeded
ist
is

It is not evident what could be the (micro-)parametric source of this grammatical contrast between the German and the Dutch system of sentential complementation.

2.2.7 *No particle stranding in German V-clusters*

V-movement strands particles both in Dutch and German when the verb moves to the clause-initial position in finite clauses (35). So, particle stranding is an indicator of movement because the particles themselves do not move.[16]

In Dutch, but not in German, particles may be stranded in the V-cluster. This is a good indicator of re-arrangement processes within the V-cluster in Dutch.

(35) a. Hij *legde*$_i$ iets   *weg*-e$_i$
     b. Er *legte*$_i$ etwas   *weg*-e$_i$
        he put$_{PAST}$ something   away

(36) a. dat hij het boek *weg* had moeten hebben *gelegd*
        that he the book away had must$_{INF}$ have   put$_{PII}$
     b. daß er das Buch hat weggelegt   haben müssen
        that he the book had away-put$_{PII}$ have   must$_{INF}$
     c. *daß er das Buch *weg* hat *gelegt* haben müssen

The fact that the particle may surface in between the verbs of the cluster in Dutch indicates that there must be a possible position for the verbal companion of the particle as well, which is indeed the case (Seuren, this volume). (37) lists but a subset of possible patterns, since the verb does not necessarily have to end up as the final element in a cluster. It may be placed in prefinal positions as well but it must follow the particle in each case.

(37) a. dat hij het boek *weg*   had moeten hebben *gelegd*
        that he the book away had must$_{INF}$ have   put$_{PII}$
        'that he should have put away the book'
     b. dat hij het boek *weggelegd* had moeten hebben
     c. dat hij het boek had *weg* moeten hebben *gelegd*
     d. dat hij het boek had *weggelegd* moeten hebben
     d.$^{(?)}$dat hij het boek had moeten *weg* hebben *gelegd*
     e. dat hij het boek had moeten *weggelegd* hebben
     f. dat hij het boek had moeten hebben *weggelegd*

The descriptive generalization is simple: The particle position is a possible position for the particle verb, and moving the verb strands the particle. Note, first, that the verb must not precede the particle. Hence there must be movement to the right within the cluster.[17] Second, nothing else than a verbal particle may occur within the cluster. Hence it is safe to conclude that we are dealing with a cluster internal process.

3. Towards an empirically adequate modeling of the clustering phenomena

The discussion above highlighted empirical generalizations that must be captured if the theoretical reconstruction of the phenomenon is to meet the indispensable standards of empirical adequacy.

- *No non-verbal interveners in the cluster*, except particles in Dutch. [Implication: a cluster cannot consist of stacked phrasal projections, that is, (remnant) VPs or higher projections, since these would provide positions for interveners, such as adverbials or extraposable material.]
- *A main verb in the cluster is mobile* in Dutch (for cliticization), but *not* in German. [Implication: no particle stranding can occur in German clusters, but it can in Dutch clusters.]
- *Position of fronted auxiliaries in IPP*: the fronted auxiliaries in the IPP construction in Dutch are left-adjoined to the cluster, and are thus cluster-internal. In German, the auxiliaries are projected in a VP-shell structure, whence the possibility of intervening non-verbal constituents in German. [Implication: no IPP-fronting with infinitivals in German, because of stranding of the infinitival particle in a V-chain.]

With particle stranding as prime evidence for movement within the cluster, the conclusion will be unavoidable that Dutch and German clusters involve *two* types of *head* movement, namely *left adjunction* to the root node of the cluster and local *right-adjunction* (verbal cliticization) to the right adjacent verbal head. The various possible combinations of these two independent processes are responsible for the puzzling variety of patterns in the cluster constructions.

Let us start with the basic patterns in German and Dutch. These are identical structures, namely clusters that result from merging verbal heads, with the dependent element preceding the selecting head. In Dutch, the basic order is ill-formed as a surface order (see (38b)) when the cluster contains bare infinitives. A possible surface order is (38c):

(38) a. daß er das Buch [$_{V^0}$ *weggelegt* [$_{V^0}$ *haben* [$_{V^0}$ müssen wird]]]
          that he the book away-put$_{PII}$ have   must$_{INF}$ will
          'that he will have to have put away the book'
      b. *dat hij het boek [$_{V^0}$ *weggelegd* [$_{V^0}$ hebben [$_{V^0}$ moeten zal]]]
          that he the book away-put$_{PII}$ have   must   will
          'that he will have to have put away the book'

c. dat hij het boek zal   moeten hebben *weggelegd*
    that he the book will must   have   away-put$_{PII}$

In German, the base order is a possible surface order (except for IPP triggers). In Dutch, a licit surface order is illustrated by (38c): the base order is mirrored by switching the sister constituents in the cluster (which consists of binary mergers of V^0s) from top to bottom. Technically, this requires left-adjunction (V^0 to V^0) to the top node of the basic cluster. For (38c), this is indicated, step-by-step in (39).[18]

(39) a. dat hij het boek [$_{V^0}$zal$_i$[$_{V^0}$*weggelegd*[$_{V^0}$moeten[$_{V^0}$hebben e$_i$]]]]
          that he the book will   away-put$_{PII}$ have   must

      b. dat hij het boek [zal$_i$ [moeten$_j$ [*weggelegd* [hebben [e$_j$ e$_i$]]]]]

      c. dat hij het boek [zal$_i$ [moeten$_j$ [hebben$_k$ [weggelegd [e$_k$[e$_j$ e$_i$]]]]]]

3.1 Deriving the Dutch cluster – left-adjunction and/or cliticization to the right

That (38b) must be the base order becomes evident not so much on the basis of comparing German and Dutch, but on the basis of genuine Dutch evidence, namely the particle distribution. The fact that a particle may appear in a cluster-initial position shows that this is a possible position for the particle verb (see (37a)). If the cluster were structured as a right-branching, left-to-right selecting head-to-head merged structure, the lexical main verb would always be at the cluster-final bottom position. In this case, the word order of (39c) would be the only available serialization.[19]

Particle stranding is obviously a process of stranding the particle by moving the verb to the *right*, since the verb never crosses and thereby precedes the particle, and since particles do not move. The adequate theoretical tool for modeling this process seems to be verbal *post-cliticization*, that is, strictly local head-to-head adjunction to the right of the adjacent verbal head. The particle is stranded, once the verb cliticizes to the right. This is the second crucial process responsible for the sequencing of verbs in the cluster (the first one being left adjunction). Since this process of verbal cliticization may apply iteratively, that is, a clitic complex may be cliticized again. The overall result may be a mirror image sequence of the verbal cluster, as in the left adjunction option, but with the particle stranded in the initial position:

(40) a. *dat hij het boek [*weggelegd* [hebben [moeten [zal]]]]   (= 38b)
          that he the book away-put   have   must   will

b. *dat hij het boek [*weg* [hebben+*gelegd* [moeten zal]]]
c. *dat hij het boek [*weg* [moeten+hebben+*gelegd* zal]]
d. dat hij het boek [*weg* [zal+moeten+hebben+*gelegd*]]

Note that verbal cliticization is a process that in principle may affect the whole cluster, as in (40). The part of the cluster that is not mirrored by top-down inversion is inverted by bottom-up cliticization. But cliticization is not a fully obligatory process.[20] It may, therefore, come to a halt before the whole cluster is affected. This, plus the combination with left adjunction is the grammatical source of the great variety of possible surface linearizations in the verbal clusters.

Let me illustrate the combination of the two processes illustrated with the examples (37d, e), repeated for convenience in (41a, b):

(41) a. [(?)]dat hij het boek had moeten weg   hebben gelegd
            that he the book had must$_{INF}$ away have   put$_{PII}$
      b. dat hij het boek had moeten weggelegd hebben

In both sentences, the two top auxiliaries are inverted by top-down left adjunction. In (41a), the particle verb is cliticized and hence the particle is stranded. In (41b) cliticization is not applied; hence the bottom of the cluster remains in the base order. Note that the order in (42) is the result of only top down inversion, without cliticization, since the particle is not stranded:

(42) dat hij het boek had moeten hebben weggelegd
      that he the book had must   have   away-put$_{PII}$

The somewhat marginal status of the construction (41a), which is judged acceptable by Pieter Seuren (this volume), but claimed to be close to deviant by Hans den Besten, indicates that there seems to be a preference for inversion by adjunction rather than by cliticization. (43) presents a systematic survey of the derivations starting with the same base configuration as in (38b), with another example:

(43) a. *dat ze   deze liedjes meegezongen hebben kunnen
            that they these songs   together-sung have   can$_{INF}$
            zouden   base order
            would
      b. dat ze deze liedjes *zouden kunnen hebben* meegezongen
                                                        3x inv. by adj.
      c. dat ze deze liedjes *zouden kunnen* meegezongen hebben
                                                        2x inv. by adj.

    d.   dat ze deze liedjes meegezongen *zouden*+[*kunnen*+*hebben*]

                                                    2x clit. (not main verb)

    e.   dat ze deze liedjes mee *zouden*+[*kunnen*+[*hebben gezongen*]]

                                                     3x clit.

    f.   dat ze deze liedjes *zouden kunnen* mee *hebben*+*gezongen*

                                                    2x inv., 1x clit.

    g.   dat ze deze liedjes *zouden* mee *kunnen*+[*hebben*+*gezongen*]

                                                    1x inv., 2x clit.

    h.   dat ze deze liedjes *zouden* meegezongen kunnen+*hebben*

                                             1x inv., 1x clit. (not m.v.)

Seuren (this volume) and Kempen and Harbusch (this volume) list three additional patterns, namely (44a–c), but some appear to be controversial and likely to be rejected by some speakers.[21] In the system proposed above, (44a) and (44b) could be derived, but only with an additional assumption, namely, that the first step of cliticization may be *pre*-cliticization to the right rather than *post*-cliticization, that is, the participle is pre-cliticized to the following verb, as in German. The following cliticizations are regular post-cliticizations. (44c), however, is underivable and is, therefore, paragrammatical in the system proposed here.[22]

(44) a.   dat ze deze liedjes mee *zouden*+[*kunnen*+[*gezongen*+*hebben*]]
            that they these songs together should be-able-to sung have
      b.   dat ze deze liedjes *zouden* mee *kunnen*+[*gezongen*+*hebben*]
      c.   dat ze deze liedjes mee *zouden* gezongen *kunnen hebben*

On the basis of the system proposed above, these examples are predicted to be rated from marginal to unacceptable, a prediction that could be checked with a dialectally representative sample of native Dutch evaluators.

3.2 The German cluster structure and IPP inversion

The three crucial micro-parametric differences that separate German from Dutch are the following. First, inversion in German is obligatory only for a subset, namely the combinations of participles of infinitive-selecting verbs (modals, causative, verbs of perception), as illustrated in (45a, b). Second, a main verb is *immobile* in the German verbal cluster. Unlike Dutch, it cannot be cliticized (see the discussion above).

(45) a.   daß man nicht schlafen können wird
            that one   not   sleep   can$_{INF}$ will

    b. *dat   men   niet   slapen   kunnen   zal
       that   one   not   sleep   can$_{INF}$ will

Third, the structure of the inverted cluster is different. In Dutch, fronting is left-adjunction to the cluster. In German, the position of the fronted auxiliaries is cluster-external. This is evidenced by the contrasting data for nonverbal interveners in the cluster. In German, but not in Dutch, IPP movement creates a VP-shell structure. Thus, German and Dutch represent two different grammatical implementation possibilities for fronted heads: In Dutch it is local adjunction of a head to a complex projections of head-elements (i.e. a head-head cluster). In German, it is the recruiting of a structural option that is the standard structure for complex head-initial projections namely the projection of a lexical V-projection shell. To be more precise, it is on a par with a VO language VP-shell structure with a stranded element in the base position as a non-verbal intervener.

(46) a. [$_{VP}$ send$_i$ [$_{VP}$ the clients [$_{V'}$ e$_i$ *out* a letter]
      b. [$_{VP}$ hätte$_i$ [$_{VP}$ *aus*   *der Tasche* [$_{V^0}$ [$_{V^0}$ [$_{V^0}$ ziehen] müssen] e$_i$]
         had   out-of the pocket   pull   must$_{INF}$

The particle distribution in English and in Scandinavian languages provides immediate evidence for the empty verb positions in the VP-shell structure, if the language allows stranding particles (like English and Norwegian). The particles can be stranded in either position and their distribution reflects the distribution of verb positions (details in Haider 1997). (46a) represents a VP-shell with the fronted V^0 belonging to a minimal cluster, that is a combination of verb plus particle. The particle is stranded in (46a), and so is the cluster in (46b).

Even if the German construction employs an admissible option in terms of the universal syntactic repertoire, this option does not fully fit. IPP fronting deprives the auxiliary verb of its directional licensing domain by moving it across its selected head. This is on the one hand the source of the switch from the participle form to the neutral form (i.e. bare infinitive). On the other hand, the structure remains a patch-up option (as a kind of last resort effort) because the shell-structure is not triggered, as in English, by the fronted element (i.e. by its directionality requirement), but by an avoidance requirement, that is, by grammatical altruism. The result is a grammatical compromise: the recruited structure is admissible, but it is not canonical, that is, it is peripheral. A directionality exception is admitted in order to avoid an ineffability situation, in order to be able to form a pluperfect with modals.

The fact that IPP is a non-canonical option is instrumental for the understanding of the existence of the cliticization option. Both in Dutch and German, inversion in the cluster destroys the directionality relation for the inverted
elements, and so does cliticization. If cliticization is the solution for the serialization in (47a, b) in German, it starts from the base version (47c), and by
reordering avoids the selection of the participial form for the modal. (47d)
illustrates the other option, namely the VP-shell option.

(47) a.   erkannt   *hätte*+[werden+müssen]
           recognized had   be   must$_{INF}$
           'would have had to be recognized'
      b.   erkannt werden *hätte*+müssen
      c.   *erkannt [[[werden] gemußt] *hätte*]
      d.   *hätte*$_i$ [erkannt werden müssen e$_i$]
      e.   ??/*erkannt *hätte*+[müssen+werden]

The fact that (47e) is deviant shows, however, that cliticization cannot work as
it does in Dutch. (47e) results when post-cliticization is applied iteratively, as
in Dutch. (47e) is generated if only post-cliticization is applied: first the passive
auxiliary is post-cliticized to the modal, followed by post-cliticization of the
clitic complex to the finite auxiliary, just as in Dutch.

The situation in German is as follows. Cliticization is pre-cliticization, except for the immediate IPP-context, that is, in avoidance of participle selection.
This yields (47a) and avoids (47e).[23] Thus, cliticization, being string-vacuous,
becomes identifiable only when there is a clitic complex (as in (47a)) that ends
up as a post-cliticized element.

Note once more that the crucial difference between the shell-structure and
the clitic structure is the fact that in German, the former allows non-verbal
interveners between the fronted auxiliary and the rest, the latter, of course, does
not. Consequently, the latter cannot be a derivational variant of the former.

The fronted heads in the auxiliary shell are heads without a specified A-
structure, and hence the shell-structure and the V-cluster structure are equivalent in terms of the A-structure properties projected. The German IPP structure is equivalent to an English complex VP consisting of a main verb projection selected by a non-finite auxiliary:

(48) a.   that the theory could well
           [$_{VP\text{-}be}$ be [$_{VP\text{-}formulate}$ much more carefully [formulated]]]

b. daß die Theorie nicht [$_{VP-hat}$ hätte   [$_{VP-cluster}$ besser
    that the theory   not   had$_{SUBJ}$ better
    [formuliert werden können]
    formulated be   can$_{INF}$
    'that the theory could not have been formulated better'

The question of whether the Dutch and the German implementation are two independent alternative choices from the pool of available structuring options, I prefer to leave open. At the moment, I am not in a position to produce reasons for a deterministic account, i.e. an account that would demonstrate that for Dutch only the adjunction option, and for German, only the shell option is admissible, given the determinants of the two grammatical systems. In other words, one would have to produce reasons as to why the converse situation, German with the Dutch and Dutch with the German implementation, is ruled out.

3.3 The grammatical causality of clustering

The clustering constructions raise several non-trivial questions for an adequate grammar-theoretic coverage and modeling. First, what is the grammar-theoretic motivation for the existence of cluster constructions instead of stacked V-projections? Second, why is clustering correlated with head-final projections?[24] Third, why is clustering obligatory in some contexts (bare infinitival and participle selection) and optional in others (clausal infinitival construction in German)?

Let us start with the first two questions and a comparison of the structures found with auxiliary plus main verb combinations. In English, as mentioned at the beginning, there is good evidence for stacked VPs, as in (49a), whereas in German, the evidence points to the conclusion that the verbs are clustering, as in (49c) rather than projecting separate VPs, as in (49b).

(49) a. [$_{VP}$ V$_1$ [$_{VP}$ V$_2$ [$_{VP}$ V$_3$ ...]]]
      b. [$_{VP}$ [$_{VP}$ [$_{VP}$ ... V$_1$] V$_2$] V$_3$]
      c. [$_{VP}$ ... [$_{V^0}$[$_{V^0}$ V$_1$ V$_2$] V$_3$]]

A look at the bracketed representations in (49) provides a first cue. In (49a), but crucially not in (49b), the left-to-right order corresponds to the top-to-bottom organization of the phrase. (49a) is a syntactic structure that is friendly to a parser (more below).[25] In a right branching structure, the parser can unambiguously identify the top-most node of the projection after encountering the first element of the projection, i.e. V_1. (49b), however, is not parser-friendly. The parser would have to guess how many brackets there might be, because their number – or in other words, the depth of embedding of the left-most element – depends on the number of verbs to come. General top-down information on the possible structure of a VP will not help guessing, because the number of auxiliaries is not context-dependent. Structure (49b) is a case of centre-embedding by stacking instances of the same category, namely VP. This is known to be an extremely parser-unfriendly data structure.

The clustering construction narrows down the domain of structural uncertainty from an unbounded phrasal domain (e.g. stacked VPs) to a local domain, namely the verbal cluster. When the parser meets V_1 and it cannot decide whether this is the main verb or not, the decision can be made in the next step.

These considerations suggest an answer to the first question: clustering constructions enhance parser-friendliness for head-final projections. It does not yet answer the second question, however. Parser-friendliness is not sufficient for establishing a grammar-driven condition. If there is a context of obligatory clustering there must be a *grammatical* principle that enforces clustering. Parser-friendliness by itself is a performance property and would not be strong enough to yield obligatoriness. Only in the perspective of the cognitive evolution of grammars, parser-friendliness could have been a driving force in the selection of UG-principles. A UG principle to this extent, the BBC, was proposed in Haider (1992) and in later papers:

> BBC (*Basic Branching Constraint*):
> Projection-internal branching nodes of the (functionally or lexically extended) projection line follow their sister node.

This principle of phrase structuring forbids right-branching basic projections and its functional or lexical extensions. Therefore, the BBC rules out a structure like (49b) if the VP-nodes belong to an *extended projection* of a VP.

An extended projection is either a *functionally extended projection* or a *lexically extended projection*. The functional extension is the cascade of functional projections on top of the lexical projections targeted by overt head movement of the head of the lexical projection. The lexical extension is a cascade of selected lexical projections whose pooled lexical features are equivalent to the feature format of a single verb. This amounts to the following situation:

The verbs in the stacked VP do not introduce arguments, or else the arguments are pooled. The verbs are related by morphosyntactic government relations and argument merger. There is only one verb that introduces an event variable.

These conditions single out auxiliary and modal verbs (no argument structure, no event variable), and verbs of perception, if the event variable is not
instantiated.[26] These are obligatorily clustering verbs in German. The types of
obligatorily clustering verbs are listed in (50) and illustrated in (51):

(50) a. V^0 governs bare infinitival V^0: *werden* (future tense aux.), modals,
          causative verbs.[27]
      b. V^0 governs past participle V^0: *werden* (passive aux.); *haben, sein*
          (perfect tense aux.).
      c. V^0 governs bare infinitival zu+V^0: *scheinen* (seem); *haben, sein*
          (deontic).

(51) a. daß sie ihn *fragen* wird/kann/ließ
          that she him ask   will/can/let
      b. daß er *gestoppt* hat/wurde
          that he stopped has/was
      c. daß er *zu stoppen* scheint   'that he seems to be stopping'
          that he to stop   seems
      d. daß er *zu stoppen* hat   'that he has to stop'
          that he to stop   has
      e. daß er *zu stoppen* ist   'that he [is to be/can be] stopped'
          that he to stop   is

Having briefly introduced the necessary background, we can return to the
question under discussiony: why is clustering in the relevant contexts obligatory in German and Dutch (and other OV-languages)? The answer is this:
clustering is obligatory in an extended V-projection because BBC rules out
VP-stacking for head-final projections:

(52) a. *$[_{VP} [_{VP} [_{VP} \ldots V_1] V_2] V_3]$
      b. $[_{VP} V_1 [_{VP} V_2 [_{VP} V_3 \ldots]]]$
      c. $[_{VP} \ldots [_{V^0} [_{V^0} V_1 V_2] V_3]]$

(52a) is ruled out because BBC forbids right-daughter nodes of nodes on the
main projection line of a projection. (52b), a head-initial (extended) projection
is well-formed with respect to BBC: there are no left brackets adjacent to each
other. This is just another way of expressing the fact that there are no right
daughters of nodes on the main projection line. The right daughter is always a
node on the projection line.

(52c), as the grammatical alternative for (52a), does not violate BBC. The
projection line of the VP starts with the highest V^0 node. It is the projection line

of a simple VP. This is the answer to the third question raised at the beginning of this subsection.

Let us summarize and recapitulate the main points by means of the tree diagrams in (53): (53a) is a subtree of a stack of V-projections in a head-initial projection. It respects BBC and it is parser-friendly. Once the parser reaches V_1 in the input, it can project the top VP-node, proceed to the next item and instantiate the next VP, and so forth. Compare this with (53b), the structure of stacked VPs in a head-final projection. One difference is immediately obvious, namely the difference in depth of embedding: Before the parser can reach the head node of the top VP it must have parsed the dependents of the top VP plus all embedded VPs. This is just the burden of centre-embedded structures.

What is more crucial, however, is the following difference. In (53a), the parser can postulate the top node once it reaches the first element of the top projection. In (53b), however, it would have to guess how many verbs there will come in order to be able to decide how many V projections need to be projected once 'XP' is reached.

The V-projection with the cluster (53c) reduces the potential VP-stacks considerably. The structural complexity is shifted from the phrasal projections to the V-cluster. But this is a local domain, which makes backtracking easy.[28]

(53)   a.   VO   b.   * OV

    c.   OV + clustering

These considerations indicate that clustering contributes to parser-friendliness. This notwithstanding, the grammatical causality of clustering is BBC, not the enhancement of parsing. Parsing functionality comes into play only in an evolutionary perspective as the selecting force of the cognitive environment on UG as the grammatical source for data structures.

(53c) still is a sub-optimal solution. The optimal structure is a completely right-branching cluster as in (54). This is the Dutch solution of the problem. In Dutch, the verbs not only cluster (as in (53c)) but also raise within the cluster (by adjunction or cliticization). The resulting structure of a fully inverted cluster (traces omitted) is (54):

(54)   Dutch raising (by adjunction and/or cliticization)

$$
\begin{array}{l}
\boxed{VP_3} \\[4pt]
\quad\big| \\
XP \dots\dots V^0 \,\text{---}\, V^0 \,\text{---}\, V^0_3 \\[4pt]
\quad\big| \qquad \big| \qquad\quad \big| \\
\triangle \quad \boxed{V^0_1} \quad V^0_2
\end{array}
$$

What remains to be accounted for is the third question. Why is clustering optional for sentential infinitival constructions in German? The trivial answer is: in Dutch, but not in German, sentential arguments are ungrammatical in clause internal positions, that is, not extraposed nor topicalized. The non-trivial answer, namely the answer that uncovers the grammatical causality of this contrast between German and Dutch, I am unable to provide for the time being.

Finally, it is a positive outcome that V-clustering in head-initial V-projections is unexpected. Why is it unexpected? Because the resulting cluster would be left-branching, given the directionality of licensing. Therefore, the clustering option would violate the constraint against left-branching structures, whereas the stacked-VP option is perfect.

4.   Grammar-theoretical afterthoughts

The devices proposed in this paper (X^0-to-X^0 adjunction, X^0-to-X^0 cliticization) are means that belong to the standard tool kit of grammar theory. What may be considered non-standard is the assumption of head-to-head merger as a base-generation option that produces the initial verb-cluster constituent.

Head-to-head merger seems to presuppose licensing conditions that single out verbs as the only candidates for clustering:

– The selected heads have selectable morphosyntactic features.[29]
– Head selection is an equivalence relation with argument selection.

The latter property guarantees that the monoclausal, clustering construction is semantically equivalent (as far as the A-structure projections are concerned) with a biclausal construction. Technically, the argument management in the cluster is implementable as functional composition,[30] properly constrained by the morphosyntactic selection properties (see Haider 1994, 2001).

Notes

1. PII is an abbreviation for the *second participle*, that is, the perfect & passive participle.

2. However, clustering is possible only for an unmarked argument, that is, the argument without specific lexical requirements in terms of case marking or subcategorization. This is – in surface grammar terms – the direct object argument or the unaccusative subject argument.

3. Fanselow (1989) suggested an analysis of verbal clustering in terms of remnant clausal constituents (IPs). Koopman and Szabolcsi (2001) develop a similar analysis in terms of remnant V-projections. Both accounts fail to capture the relevant generalizations (details below). The need for ad hoc 'complexity filters' for adjusting structures to the data is a sign of a poor coverage of the empirical generalization by a phrasal movement analysis.

4. This solution was first proposed by Seuren (1972) and Evers (1975).

5. This applies both to analyses in terms of V-movement to a clause-final functional head position, as well as to an analysis that derives the German/Dutch patterns from English-like patterns by movement to the left (see Zwart 1993).

6. Analogously, principle B effects arise: a *coreferent* bound pronoun is well-formed in the bisentential construction, but not in the clustering, that is, monosentential, variant (reason: principle B violation in the monosentential structure):

(a)   Max^i hat (uns^j) [PRO^j ihn^i zu zitieren] nicht erlaubt
      Max has (us) [him to quote] not permitted

(b)   Zu zitieren erlaubt hat ihn^{*i} (uns) Max^i nicht
      to quote permitted has him (us) Max not

7. For a comprehensive description of the phenomena in German, Bech (1956) still is the classic source to consult.

8. In spoken Austrian vernacular, especially in the Viennese variety, IPP is found even without inverted verb order: daß er sie nicht fragen *können* / *müssen* / *lassen* hätte (that he could / should not have asked her / that he would not have let her ask).

9. In dialects, *brauchen* is used with bare infinitive:

(i)   Das brauchst Du nicht tun (this need you not do).

10. 'Passive' is the effect of combining a participle (as the unaccusative verbal variant) and an auxiliary with an unaccusative format. IPP would destroy the effect of the participle, namely the blocking of the external argument. Therefore, passive must be spared by IPP in German and in Dutch.

11. From a newspaper report (*Stuttgarter Zeitung* 10/89, p. 4).

12. *Die Zeit* Nr. 52, 10 Dec. '85, p. 34, 2nd col.

13. *Evening News*, 3 July 2001, Austrian Radio.

14. This holds likewise for clusters with more than one fronted verb, such as the cluster in (i), where the "+" sign marks alternative positions for inserting e.g. *damit* (with-it):

(i)   daß er ihn + nicht + *würde* + *müssen* + *haben* + [weglaufen *sehen*]

The intervening prepositional object can follow the first, second or third of the fronted auxiliaries. The resulting patterns are restricted variants of the so-called 'V-projection raising' construction (Van Riemsdijk & Haegeman 1986). The difference between standard German and varieties with 'V-projection raising' seems to be just the range of the fronting construction in terms of the participating verbs and the scope of fronting.

15. Commentary (Eurosport channel, 22 Febr. 2002) on gold-medal-winning Sarah Hughes' performance.

16. This is true also for particle stranding in English and other VO-languages. As argued in Haider (1997), the stranded particle marks a possible V-position in the VP-shell structure of complex, head-initial V-projections.

17. Note that this phenomenon is direct counterevidence for approaches that take fronting to be the only source of the verb cluster patterns in Dutch (or German), as in various antisymmetry-based accounts (Zwart 1993; Koopman & Szabolcsi 2000).

18. Note that the technical implementation is either an iteration of merger plus left-adjunction, or the generation of a verbal cluster in which every left-branch head (except the lowest) is related to a gap in the right-hand complement selecting position (= base-generated filler-gap structure).

19. It is presupposed that particles do not move by themselves. If particles moved, they ought to be found within the middle field as well as in the sentence-initial spec-position. A detailed analysis of particle distribution in English as well as in Scandinavian languages in terms of stranding rather than particle shift is presented in Haider (1997).

20. It is obligatory only if the selected verb is infinitival.

21. I want to thank Henk van Riemsdijk for helpful information on 'cluster creeper' data.

22. In order to derive it, the clitic cluster [gezongen+hebben] would have to be first pre-cliticized to *kunnen* followed by excorporation plus post-clitization of *hebben*. This is definitely beyond a resonable and plausible account, in my opinion.

23. An apparent Dutch order could be seen in constructions like (i), derived from the basic order (ii). This impression is deceptive, however, because (ii) requires double inversion, since the IPP-triggering auxiliary is selected by the matrix verb, so both need to be inverted (as in the V-shell construction (iii)).

(i) daß er sie nicht fragen wird haben dürfen
     that he her not ask will have may$_{INF}$
(ii) daß er sie nicht fragen dürfen haben wird
(iii) daß er sie nicht *wird haben* [fragen *dürfen*]

24. Contrary to Koopman and Szabolcsi's claim (2000), Hungarian should be analyzed as an OV-language, with DP-fronting into pre-VP topic and focus positions. As for the verbal complex formation, the obligatory order of verb and particle (namely V+particle, e.g. be (*in*) menni (*go*$_{INF}$) vs. *menni be; see Koopman & Szabolcsi 2000:16f.) is evidence for an OV base order. In VO, particles follow the position of the verb. The possible reorderings are the result of two processes: (a) fronting of the finite verb, and (b) optional reordering in the verbal complex of the Dutch type, that is left adjunction. Koopman and Szabolcsi's account in terms of remnant VPs overgenerates massively. For this reason they suggest a number of filters.

25. The data-to-parser fit is optimal if the parser – a left corner parser – can simultaneously operate bottom-up and top-down, i.e. continuous data processing (bottom-up) plus grammar guidance (top-down information on possible structures). This presupposes right-branching structures.

26. Note that this is an explanation for the well-known peculiarity of infinitival perception verb constructions, namely, the direct perception quality:

(i) I heard that he worked in his office (direct or indirect perception)
(ii) I heard him work in his office (direct perception only)

27. Perception verbs and *lassen* (let) cluster, but they do not obligatorily yield a passive effect. This means, the subject of the infinitival is not obligatorily inactivated, which implies that the cluster is either not base-generated or that the ecm-construction they instantiate is the result of an exceptional argument pooling.

28. Note that the indices of the verbs only refer to the relative order in the input, not to the dependency relations. V$_1$ is the first verb in the input. In VO, this is the highest, in OV it is the lowest one.

29. In Bech's original terminology this is the category of verbal status (bare infinitive, supine, *zu*+infinitive). He explicitly refers to 'status government' as the verbal equivalent to case government.

30. The familiar head-complement relation corresponds to functional application.

CHAPTER 4

West-Germanic verb clusters in LFG

Ronald M. Kaplan and Annie Zaenen
Palo Alto Research Center

1. Introduction

In a previous paper (Zaenen & Kaplan 1995; henceforth ZK) we developed a general LFG account of West Germanic sentence structure, concentrating on the order of nominal arguments in the forefield and the middlefield. The account was based on the interactions between functional uncertainty equations, functional precedence constraints, and phrase structure rules. It proposed general rules for non-extraposed, extraposed and third-construction infinitival complements. In this paper we start from that account and refine the proposed rule set to account for the order and form variation found in Dutch and German verb clusters.

2. West Germanic Infinitival Complements as described in ZK: Dutch

Ignoring adjunct material, embedded extraposed and non-extraposed clauses in Dutch can be represented by the annotated phrase structure rules in (1) and lexical entries of the type illustrated in (2). Rules (1a) and (1b) correspond to ZK (27) and ZK (13) respectively, and the lexical entries correspond to ZK (3).

(1) a. $\text{VP} \rightarrow$ NP^* V'   (VP)

           $(\uparrow \{\text{XCOMP}|\text{COMP}\}^* \text{NGF}) = \downarrow$ $(\uparrow \text{XCOMP}^* \text{COMP}) = \downarrow$

     b. $\text{V'} \rightarrow$ V   (V')

              $(\uparrow \text{XCOMP}) = \downarrow$

              $(\uparrow \text{XCOMP}^+ \text{NGF}) \neg <_f (\uparrow \text{NGF})$

(2)   a.   willen   ($\uparrow$ PRED) = 'want<($\uparrow$ SUBJ) ($\uparrow$ XCOMP)>'
                      ($\uparrow$ SUBJ) = ($\uparrow$ XCOMP SUBJ)
      b.   laten   ($\uparrow$ PRED) = 'let<($\uparrow$ SUBJ) ($\uparrow$ XCOMP)>($\uparrow$ OBJ)'
                      ($\uparrow$ OBJ) = ($\uparrow$ XCOMP SUBJ)
      c.   studeren ($\uparrow$ PRED) = 'study<($\uparrow$ SUBJ) ($\uparrow$ OBJ)>'

As motivated by ZK, rule (1a) provides a flat constituent structure for zero or
more NP's in the middlefield and relies on the functional uncertainty equa-
tion ($\uparrow$ {XCOMP|COMP}* NGF) = $\downarrow$ to assign each NP to some nominal gram-
matical function (drawn from the set SUBJ, OBJ, ... denoted by NGF) in an f-
structure that can be reached on a path consisting of an indeterminate number
of XCOMPs and/or COMPs. This specification by itself does not correlate the linear position of a particular NP with the depth of embedding of the verb that it
can relate to. The (somewhat loose) correlation between NP position and level
of embedding is provided by the verb-cluster rule (1b). This rule provides a
right-branching structure for the verbs in a V' cluster, and the next lower verb
becomes the head of the XCOMP assigned at each level (by virtue of the equation
($\uparrow$ XCOMP) = $\downarrow$). The f-precedence requirement ($\uparrow$ XCOMP$^+$ NGF) $\neg$ $<_f$ ($\uparrow$ NGF)
imposes a simple constraint on the relation between the NP's and the verbs.
Of all the ways that rule (1a) allows particular NP's to be linked to particular
verbs, those possibilities in which an NP linked to a lower verb via XCOMP$^+$ NGF
comes before an NP linked to a higher predicate are unacceptable. The negative
statement of the precedence condition, as ZK explain, gives the desired result
in the vacuous cases when particular nominal functions are not present in a
given sentence.

The lexical entries in (2) classify both *willen* and *laten* as verbs that take
functionally-controlled open complements. The functional control equation
($\uparrow$ OBJ) = ($\uparrow$ XCOMP SUBJ) marks the fact that *laten*'s object serves as the understood subject of its complement, while the SUBJ of *willen* plays that complement role. *Laten* is also a raising verb, since the ($\uparrow$ OBJ) appears outside the angle brackets that enclose the thematic arguments in its semantic-form. *Willen*
is marked as an equi verb since its subject is included within the thematic
argument list.

These rules and lexical entries will analyze sentences like the following:

(3)   ...dat Jan   Marie geneeskunde wil   laten   studeren.
      ...that John Marie medicine   wants let-INF study.
      ...that John wants to let Marie study medicine.

The sentence in (3) will be associated with the c-structure and corresponding f-structure in (4).[1] This diagram shows in addition the structural correspondence mapping between the nodes of the phrase structure and the units of the f-structure; this correspondence plays a crucial role in the formal definition of f-precedence that we give below.

(4)

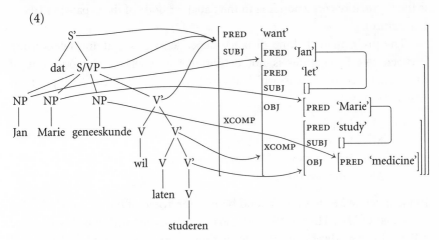

ZK note that the optional VP at the end of rule (1a) also provides for extraposed complements, as in (5a), and the COMP alternative in the NP functional uncertainty equation offers a simple account of the Third Construction (5b). We briefly discuss these sentence patterns later on in this paper, after we have examined the range of verb-cluster variations.

(5) a. ...dat Jan heeft getracht   Marie te helpen.
         ...that Jan has   tried-PART Marie to help.

     b. ...dat Jan Marie heeft getracht   te helpen.
         ...that John Marie has   tried-PART to help.

         ...that John has tried to help Marie.

We begin by reviewing the formal properties of functional uncertainty and f-precedence, the key elements of our verb-cluster analysis. Functional uncertainty is the standard formal device in LFG for characterizing dependencies that relate functional units expressed by constituents that do not stand in a locally specifiable phrase-structure configuration. Kaplan and Zaenen (1989) introduced this device originally to give a natural, functional account of the long-distance dependencies that appear in topicalization, questions, and relative clauses, but it has found many other uses (see e.g. Dalrymple 1993; Nordlinger

1998). Functional uncertainty is a straightforward extension to the basic mechanism for describing simple functional relationships in LFG. A basic equation such as ($\uparrow$ XCOMP) = $\downarrow$ appearing in a phrase-structure rule is satisfied just in case the f-structure corresponding to the mother node of the c-structure expansion (the f-structure denoted by $\uparrow$) has an XCOMP attribute whose value is the f-structure corresponding to the daughter node of the expansion (the $\downarrow$ f-structure).

The problem with long distance dependencies is that the relationship between two f-structures is not determined uniquely by the positions of the phrasal constituents to which they correspond. Consider the topicalized sentences in (6):

(6)   Mary John likes.
   Mary John says that Bill likes.
   Mary John says that Bill believes that Henry likes.
   Mary John says that . . .

In the first one *Mary* is understood both as the TOPIC of the sentence and also as the OBJ of *likes*. The equation ($\uparrow$ OBJ) = $\downarrow$ associated with the fronted *Mary* NP would properly characterize this within-clause relationship. In the second one *Mary* is still understood as the object of *likes*, but *likes* is now the predicate of a complement of the higher verb *says*, and the appropriate annotation for defining *Mary*'s within-clause function would be ($\uparrow$ COMP OBJ) = $\downarrow$. For the third sentence the equation would be ($\uparrow$ COMP COMP OBJ) = $\downarrow$, and in general for every additional level of embedding that might happen to be in the main clause, the path of functions appropriate for *Mary* would be lengthened with an additional COMP. The uncertainty in how to annotate the fronted NP comes from the fact that there is no information available at its surface position to determine exactly which of these possible equations correctly captures its functional relationship to the embedded clause.

Functional uncertainty provides a simple way of defining a family of equations while still leaving open the choice of exactly which member of the family will turn out to be consistent with an embedded f-structure. For this particular construction, the equations in the family all have functional paths that belong to the regular language COMP* OBJ, and the infinite family of appropriate equations can be specified in the single constraint ($\uparrow$ COMP* OBJ) = $\downarrow$. In the general case, suppose that f and g are f-structures and that α is an expression denoting a regular language of functional paths. Then we assert that

(7) (ƒα) = g holds if and only if (ƒ x) = g holds for some string x in the language α.

Kaplan and Zaenen (1989) give a somewhat more precise definition and discuss an initial set of linguistic applications for this device; Kaplan and Maxwell (1988a) show that it has attractive mathematical and computational properties.

Functional uncertainty is a general descriptive mechanism that need not be restricted to the binding of fronted phrases. As we have seen, it is used in rule (1a) to characterize the functional relation between a constituent in a flat c-structure middlefield and a governing verb that can be embedded in the c-structure indefinitely far away in the verb-cluster. A nice result is that the functional uncertainty in (1a) interacts with LFG's formal account of constituent coordination (Kaplan & Maxwell 1988b) to allow for sentences such as (8) (originally due to M. Moortgat, p.c.) where *een liedje* is the OBJ of *schreef* and of *verkopen* in spite of the fact that these verbs are at different levels of embedding.

(8) ...dat Jan   een liedje schreef en   trachtte te verkopen.
     ...that John a   song wrote and tried   to sell.
     ...that John wrote and tried to sell a song.

Rule (1a) uses functional uncertainty to associate the NP's in a flat middlefield with argument positions in the predicate hierarchy. But because there is no c-structure hierarchy to mirror the f-structure dependencies, the linear ordering constraints that are naturally imposed by phrase-structure rules cannot be used to relate the c-structure order of the NP's to their positions in the functional hierarchy. Linear order constraints under these circumstances must be stated in terms of a combination of c-structure and f-structure properties. In rule (1b) we have used the functional precedence relation (f-precedence, notated as $<_f$) as a natural way of picking out the right configurations.

Left-to-right precedence is a native relation among the words and phrases of a c-structure tree, but it is not a native relation among the parts of an f-structure. But as illustrated in (4), LFG establishes a correspondence between nodes in the c-structure and units of the f-structure, and the image of c-structure precedence under the mapping from c-structure to f-structure induces an ordering relation on the f-structure. Its formal definition is given in (9).

(9) For any f-structures ƒ and g, ƒ f-precedes g (written ƒ $<_f$ g) if and only if all the c-structure nodes that map to ƒ precede all the c-structure nodes that map to g.

F-precedence was exploited originally in the analysis of null-anaphora and weak crossover (Bresnan 1995; Kameyama 1989; Dalrymple et al. 2001). In ZK and here we use it to impose the proper ordering constraints on the elements in the middlefield, as this order depends on the level of f-structure embedding of the governing verb.[2] We observed that the constraint $(\uparrow \text{XCOMP}^+ \text{NGF}) \neg <_f$ $(\uparrow \text{NGF})$ is satisfied by the c-structure/f-structure configuration in (4). If we switch the order of the NP's as in (10), the string is still grammatical but the f-structure in (4) is no longer assigned to it. The only possible interpretation has *Marie*, not *Jan*, serving as the subject of the highest (left-most) predicate.

(10) ...dat Marie Jan geneeskunde wil   laten   studeren.
      ...that Marie Jan medicine   wants let-INF study.
    *...that John wants to let Marie study medicine.
      ...that Marie wants to let John study medicine.

The analysis in ZK also uses f-precedence to account for the order of the nominal complements in Swiss German. Their account of Swiss German assigns a flat as opposed to a right-branching structure for the sequence of NP's and verbs. ZK observe that certain topicalization facts argue against such a flat structure for the verb cluster in Dutch.

3.   Variation in the order of verbal elements in Dutch

ZK do not discuss the difference between participles and infinitives nor the different orders that are possible within the verbal complex. In the following sections we give an overview of the facts and propose extensions to our rules to cover them.

3.1   Properties of verbs taking non-tensed verbal complements

It is useful to subdivide the Dutch verbs that take non-tensed verbal complements (henceforth NTV) according to distinctions on three dimensions that only partially coincide: the morphological dimension, the functional dimension, and the c-structure dimension. The morphological dimension specifies the morphological form of the verbal complement, the functional dimension specifies its syntactic function, COMP or XCOMP in the cases under discussion, and the c-structure dimension determines whether the verb is part of a verb cluster or not.

We describe these dimensions first and then discuss the constraints that account for the range of verb-cluster phenomena.

Verbal complements: Morphological distinctions

Morphologically, the verbal complements of an NTV can be participles, bare infinitives or *te*-infinitives. These morphological alternatives will be marked by the value of the VFORM feature in the f-structure that corresponds to the verb. We assume that *te* is a morphological element, just like the *ge*- of the participle, but which accidentally is not written as forming one word with the following infinitive. The four possible values of the VFORM feature are specified by the equations in (11); these are associated by a separate morphological component with the proper verb forms:

(11)   a. $(\uparrow \text{VFORM}) = \text{PART}$ for participles
       b. $(\uparrow \text{VFORM}) = \text{INF}$ for bare infinitives
       c. $(\uparrow \text{VFORM}) = \text{TE-INF}$ for *te* infinitives
       d. $(\uparrow \text{VFORM}) = \text{TENSED}$ for all tensed forms

The lexical entries for different classes of NTV verbs then select for the different morphological forms of their complements by virtue of the constraints in (11a):

(12)   a. $(\uparrow \text{XCOMP VFORM}) \in \{\text{PART, INF}\}$ for auxiliaries
       b. $(\uparrow \text{XCOMP VFORM}) = \text{INF}$ for modals, causatives, perception verbs. . .
       c. $(\uparrow \text{XCOMP VFORM}) = \text{TE-INF}$ for other NTV verbs.

Verbal complements: Functional distinctions

Verbal complements in LFG fall into two broad classes: XCOMPs and COMPs. XCOMP is an open function whose subject is functionally controlled by a function of the higher governing verb. With the COMP function there is no functional control, but we can have either an overt subject or a silent pro subject. In Dutch and German, COMPs with overt subjects are tensed embedded clauses, e.g. that-clauses, whereas the COMPs with silent pro subjects are the extraposed *te*-infinitives as illustrated in (13)

(13)   . . .omdat hij beloofd   heeft een liedje te zingen.
       . . .because he promised-PART has   a   song   to sing.
       . . .because he promised to sing a song.

Infinitival COMPs are always cases of equi-constructions. The relevant part of a lexical entry for a verb like *beloven* is given in (14)

(14)   ($\uparrow$ PRED) = 'beloven<($\uparrow$ SUBJ) ($\uparrow$ COMP)>'
       ($\uparrow$ COMP SUBJ PRED) = 'PRO'

The various non-extraposed verbal complements are XCOMPs.[3] The difference between XCOMPs and COMPs is motivated by the possibility of an impersonal passive,[4] as illustrated by the contrast in (15):

(15)   a.   Er   werd geprobeerd een liedje te zingen.
            There   was   tried-PART a   song   to sing.
       b.   *Er   werd een liedje proberen   te zingen.
            There   was   a   song   try-INF   to sing.

       (Somebody) tried to sing a song.

Proberen is one of the verbs that can have a COMP or an XCOMP as illustrated in (16), but only the extraposed variant allows an impersonal passive.

(16)   a.   ...omdat   hij een liedje heeft proberen te zingen.
            ...because he a   song   has   try-INF   to sing.
       b.   ...omdat   hij geprobeerd heeft een liedje te zingen.
            ...because he tried-PART has   a   song   to sing.

       ...because he has tried to sing a song.

This analysis was first proposed for Dutch by Schuurman (1987) and also adopted by Berman (2000) for German.

   A different argument for the COMP/XCOMP distinction can be derived from the observation made in Evers (1975), that unstressed pronouns in the middle-field cannot be linked to argument positions in extraposed COMPs (extraposed infinitivals or tensed subordinate clauses).

(17)   a.   *...dat zij 't heeft getracht   te doen.
             ...that she it has   tried-PART to do.
       b.   ...dat   zij 't heeft trachten   te doen.
            ...that she it has   try-INF   to do.

       ...that she has tried to do it.

XCOMPs can appear in either equi or raising constructions. (16a) illustrates a subject equi case. The following examples illustrate object equi, subject raising, and object raising.

(18) ...omdat zij hem een liedje heeft helpen   zingen.
      ...because she him a   song has   help-INF sing-INF.
      ...because she has helped him to sing a song.

(19) ...omdat hij een liedje scheen te willen   zingen.
      ...because he a   song seemed to want-INF sing-INF.
      ...because he seemed to want to sing a song.

(20) ...omdat Jan de kinderen een liedje hoorde zingen.
      ...because John the children a   song heard   sing-INF.
      ...because John heard the children sing a song.

The relevant parts of the lexical entries are given in (21).

(21) a. object control: $(\uparrow$ PRED$) =$ 'predicate$<(\uparrow$ SUBJ$) (\uparrow$ OBJ$)(\uparrow$ XCOMP$)>$'
                           $(\uparrow$ OBJ$) = (\uparrow$ XCOMP SUBJ$)$
      b. subject control: $(\uparrow$ PRED$) =$ 'predicate$<(\uparrow$ SUBJ$) (\uparrow$ XCOMP$)>$'
                           $(\uparrow$ SUBJ$) = (\uparrow$ XCOMP SUBJ$)$
      c. subject raising: $(\uparrow$ PRED$) =$ 'predicate$<(\uparrow$ XCOMP$)>(\uparrow$ SUBJ$)$'
                           $(\uparrow$ SUBJ$) = (\uparrow$ XCOMP SUBJ$)$
      d. object raising: $(\uparrow$ PRED$) =$ 'predicate$<(\uparrow$ SUBJ$) (\uparrow$ XCOMP$)>(\uparrow$ OBJ$)$'
                           $(\uparrow$ OBJ$) = (\uparrow$ XCOMP SUBJ$)$

We will assume that the causatives and the perception verbs are object raising verbs. For some of these, however, other analyses have been proposed, especially complex predicate analyses. We follow Rambow's (1996) conclusion for German that, at least under the LFG conception of complex predicates (see Butt 1995; and Alsina 1996), these do not fall into that category.

Verbal complements: C-structure distinctions

A third way verbs can be classified is whether they can combine with the head of their verbal complement to form a verbal cluster or whether they require it to be extraposed. We will call the first class *clustering* and the second *extraposing*. We assume that the clustering verbs have a feature CLUS, specified by an equation $(\uparrow$ CLUS$) = +$ in their lexical entries. Verbs that take participles or bare infinitives as their complements always have this feature but verbs that take *te*-infinitives can be either clustering or extraposing and may or may not have this feature. As we have seen above in (16), a single verb can fall into both categories, but if it does, there will be a difference in its functional complement structure. The occurrence of extraposed or non-extraposed verbs is correlated with their functional complements by virtue of the phrase-structure rule (1a).

As we will see in the next section, we cannot say that the clustering/extraposing distinction coincides with the distinction of taking an XCOMP or COMP. According to the rule in (1b), verb clusters are formed of a verb and its embedded XCOMP, they form a chain of further and further (functionally) embedded complements. We will refer to the most embedded elements as being at the bottom of the verbal cluster.

3.2 Restrictions within the verbal cluster

Morphological restriction: Infinitivus pro participio

The most salient morphological phenomenon is the alternation between the participle and the infinitive for the complements of auxiliary verbs. The following examples illustrate this behavior:

(22) a. ...dat Jan   een liedje heeft gezongen.
        ...that John a   song has   sung-PART.
        ...that John has sung a song.
     b. ...dat Jan een liedje wil   hebben   gezongen.
        ...that John a   song wants have-INF sung-PART.
        ...that John wants to have sung a song.
     c. ...dat Jan   een liedje heeft willen   zingen.
        ...that John a   song has   want-INF sing-PART.
        ...that John has wanted to sing a song.
     d. ...dat Jan   heeft gehoopt   een liedje te zingen.
        ...that John has   hoped-PART a   song   to sing-INF.
        ...that John has hoped to sing a song.
     e. ...dat hij braaf moet zijn geweest.
        ...that he good   must be   been-PART.
        ...that he must have been good.

We see here that the auxiliary *hebben* takes a participle complement when the complement consists of one verb (22a–b), but an infinitive when there is an embedded verb cluster (22c). When instead of a cluster there is an extraposed complement (22d) or a non-verbal complement (22e), the participle is again used. We can insure this behavior by attaching the following constraint to *hebben* and the other auxiliary verbs:

(23)   Auxiliaries: (↑ XCOMP VFORM) = INF ⇔ (↑ XCOMP CLUS)

If the complement verb is an infinitive, then the constraint (↑ XCOMP CLUS) must hold. This will be satisfied if the complement verb is marked with the

CLUS feature and thus does not lie at the bottom of the verbal cluster. Otherwise, by virtue of (12a) the complement verb must be a participle and in that
case it must be the lowest verb. Note that in the case of non-verbal XCOMPs the
bottom verb behaves as non-clustering, as illustrated by the adjectival XCOMP
complement in (22e). This is why the feature CLUS is not redundant with the
XCOMP function.

Ordering constraints in the verb cluster

Auxiliary, modal and modal-like constructions
Apart from the traditional modals there are a certain number of other verbs in
Dutch that take bare infinitives, such as perception verbs (*zien, horen . . .*) and
causatives (*laten*). As far as their ordering constraints and the morphology of
their complement heads, they behave the same as the modals and they also can
only occur in clusters.

All verb clusters allow a right-branching structure. We will call this the
canonical order. We also find left-branching structures with auxiliaries (24)
and modals (25).

(24) a. . . .dat Jan een liedje heeft gezongen.
          . . .that John a   song has   sung-PART.
      b. . . .dat Jan een liedje gezongen heeft.
          . . .that John a   song sung-PART has.

          . . .that John has sung a song.

(25) a. . . .dat Jan een liedje wilde zingen.
          . . .that John a   song wanted sing-INF.
      b. . . .dat Jan een liedje zingen   wilde.
          . . .that John a   song sing-INF wanted.

          . . .that John wanted to sing a song.

When a complement is headed by a cluster verb, however, not all the permutations that (24) and (25) might lead one to expect are grammatical. We find the
following pattern for Standard Northern Dutch:

(26) a.   . . .dat Jan een liedje heeft willen   zingen.
           . . .that John a   song has   want-INF sing-INF.
      b. * . . .dat Jan een liedje willen   zingen   heeft.
           . . .that John a   song want-INF sing-INF has.

    c. *...dat Jan   een liedje zingen   willen   heeft.
       ...that John a   song sing-INF want-INF has.
    d. *...dat Jan   een liedje heeft zingen   willen.
       ...that John a   song has   sing-INF want-INF.
       ...that John has wanted to sing a song.

As shown in (26), a tensed auxiliary must come before a string of infinitives, and the complement infinitives themselves have to be in their canonical right-branching order. The same is true for tensed modals, as shown in (27):

(27) a. ...dat Jan   een liedje wilde   mogen   zingen.
        ...that John a   song wanted be-allowed-INF sing-INF.
    b. *...dat Jan   een liedje wilde   zingen   mogen.
       ...that John a   song wanted sing-INF be-allowed-INF.
    c. *...dat Jan   een liedje mogen   zingen   wilde.
       ...that John a   song be-allowed-INF sing-INF wanted.
    d. *...dat Jan   een liedje zingen   mogen   wilde.
       ...that John a   song sing-INF be-allowed-INF wanted.
       ...that John wanted to be allowed to sing a song.

(28) illustrates that with an infinitival auxiliary taking an infinitival complement, only the canonical order is possible.

(28) a. ...dat Jan   een liedje wou   hebben   mogen
        ...that John a   song wanted have-INF be-allowed-INF
        zingen.
        sing-INF.
    b. *...dat Jan   een liedje wou   mogen   zingen
       ...that John a   song wanted be-allowed-INF sing-INF
       hebben.
       have-INF.
       ...that John wanted to have been allowed to sing a song.

However, when the lowest verb is a participle, it can be freely ordered with respect to the other verbs (28a–c) – this is the participle "creeping" effect. (29d, e) show that the infinitive has to stay in the canonical order relative its governing modal.

(29) a. ...dat Jan   een liedje zal hebben   gezongen.
        ...that John a   song will have-INF sung-PART.

b. ...dat Jan   een liedje zal   gezongen hebben.
...that John a   song will sung-PART have-INF.

c. ...dat Jan   een liedje gezongen zal   hebben.
...that John a   song sung-PART will have-INF.

d. *...dat Jan   een liedje gezongen hebben zal.
...that John a   song sung-PART have-INF will.

e. *...dat Jan   een liedje hebben   gezongen zal.
...that John a   song have-INF sung-PART will.

...that John will have sung a song.

We can summarize the data in (24)–(29) about the relative ordering of the complements of modals and auxiliaries as follows:

(30) a. A tensed modal or auxiliary must precede the head of its complement if this head is a cluster verb (24)–(26).
b. A modal or auxiliary infinitive must precede the infinitival head of its complement (27)–(28).
c. A participle may follow or precede any other verb in the cluster (29).

Our account of these patterns starts from the ZK verb cluster rule in (1b), repeated here for convenience in (31). This rule allows only the canonical ordering, assigning the representation in (32) to (27a).

(31) V' →   V   (V')

$(\uparrow \text{XCOMP}) = \downarrow$

$(\uparrow \text{XCOMP}^+ \text{NGF}) \neg <_f (\uparrow \text{NGF})$

(32)

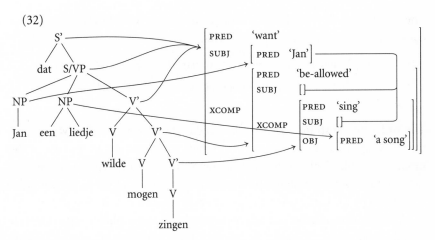

We could allow for the other ordering possibilities by elaborating the c-structure with another category to control order at the top of the cluster. Instead of doing that, we will relax the c-structure order throughout the cluster and then add functional-precedence constraints to the lexical entries of the various types of verbs. We adopt this strategy because it reflects our sense that these are idiosyncratic properties of lexical items that vary from dialect to dialect and language to language. Thus, we allow both orders in (24) and (25) by making the order in the right side of the rule in (30) optional as given in (32). Here we use a standard immediate-dominance notation; Kaplan (1989) shows that this notational extension adds nothing to the formal power of LFG.

(33)   V' →   [V ,   (V')   ]

$(\uparrow \text{XCOMP}) = \downarrow$

$(\uparrow \text{XCOMP}^+ \text{ NGF}) \neg <_f (\uparrow \text{NGF})$

This rule will overgeneralize without further restrictions. It correctly prevents a higher verb (*heeft* in (34)) from appearing between two lower ones, but it incorrectly permits every governing verb to appear on either side of its complement.

(34)   a. *...dat Jan   een liedje willen   heeft zingen.
       ...that John a   song want-INF has   sing-INF.
   b. *...dat Jan   een liedje zingen   heeft willen.
       ...that John a   song sing-INF has   want-INF.

   ...that John has wanted to sing a song.

The restrictions in (30a, b) are encoded by adding the following precedence constraints to the indicated lexical entries:

(35)   Tensed modals or auxiliaries: $(\uparrow \text{XCOMP CLUS}) \Rightarrow \uparrow <_f (\uparrow \text{XCOMP})$

(36)   Infinitival modals or auxiliaries: $(\uparrow \text{XCOMP VFORM}) = \text{INF} \Rightarrow$
       $\uparrow <_f (\uparrow \text{XCOMP})$

The ordering constraint (36) on the modal and auxiliary infinitives insures that they always occur before their infinitival complements. In the case of the modals, an infinitival complement is the only possibility whereas auxiliaries can also take participles. For tensed modals and auxiliaries the canonical order is imposed by (35) only when the complement itself is a clustering XCOMP.

These constraints do not affect participles, but the phrase structure rule (33) does not allow the participle to creep leftward in the verb cluster as illustrated in (29). We remedy this with the following extension:

(37) V' →   (V)   [V ,   (V')   ]

   ($\downarrow$ VFORM) = PART   ($\uparrow$ XCOMP) = $\downarrow$

   ($\uparrow$ XCOMP$^+$) = $\downarrow$ ($\uparrow$ XCOMP$^+$ NGF)¬$<_f$($\uparrow$ NGF)

This rule allows a participle to appear at any position in the verbal complex; by virtue of the uncertainty it functions as an XCOMP at the current level or at some lower level in the functional hierarchy. By the restrictions discussed above, the uncertainty will always resolve to the lowest level in the cluster.

The same creeping phenomenon is found with particles:

(38) a. ...dat Jan een liedje moet willen   meezingen.
          ...that John a   song   must want-INF with-sing-INF.
      b. ...dat Jan een liedje moet mee willen   zingen.
          ...that John a   song   must with want-INF sing-INF.
      c. ...dat Jan een liedje mee moet willen   zingen.
          ...that John a   song   with must want-INF sing-INF.

      ...that John must want to sing along a song.

If participles and particles appear together in the same cluster, they can both creep but they do not have to be adjacent as long as the particle precedes the participle, as shown in (39).

(39) a. ...dat Jan een liedje meegezongen   moet willen
          ...that John a   song   with-sung-PART must want-INF
          hebben.
          have-INF.
      b. ...dat Jan een liedje mee moet gezongen   willen
          ...that John a   song   with must sung-PART want-INF
          hebben.
          have-INF.
      c. ...dat Jan een liedje moet mee willen   gezongen
          ...that John a   song   must with want-INF sung-PART
          hebben.
          have-INF.
      d. ...dat Jan een liedje moet willen   mee hebben gezongen.
          ...that John a   song   must want-INF with have-INF sung-INF.

      ...that John must want to have sung along a song.

In LFG, Dutch particles belong to the post-position morphological category PostP and they contribute the feature PRT to the f-structure of their head. We add this category to the beginning of our phrase structure rule with an uncertainty that allows for the leftward creep:

(40) V' →   (PostP)   (V)   [V ,   (V')   ]

    ($\uparrow$ XCOMP$^+$ PRT) = $\downarrow$ ($\downarrow$ VFORM) = PART   ($\uparrow$ XCOMP) = $\downarrow$

                ($\uparrow$ XCOMP$^+$) = $\downarrow$ ($\uparrow$ XCOMP$^+$ NGF)$\neg<_f$($\uparrow$ NGF)

        $\downarrow\neg<_f$($\uparrow$ PRT)

The precedence constraint now attached to the participle verb asserts that the participle verb cannot come before its particle.[5] In this case the constraint is stated in the negative to cover the vacuous case where there is no particle to associate with the verb.

Equi verbs and raising verbs with te in verb cluster constructions
With clustering equi verbs and raising verbs whose complement head is a *te* infinitive, the situation is rather simple: the equi or raising verb only allows right branching,[6] modulo the behavior of the participle already described in the previous section. This is illustrated in the following examples. The pattern for subject-raising verbs is shown in (41) and (42), and (43) illustrates the behavior of subject equi verbs.

(41) a.   ...dat   Jan   een liedje schijnt te zingen.
        ...that John a   song seems   to sing-INF.
      b. *...dat   Jan   een liedje te zingen   schijnt.
        ...that John a   song to sing-INF seems.
      c.   ...dat   Jan   een liedje schijnt te willen   zingen.
        ...that John a   song seems   to want-INF sing-INF.
      d. *...dat   Jan   een liedje schijnt te zingen   willen.
        ...that John a   song seems   to sing-INF want-INF.

        ...that John seems to want to sing a song.

(42) a.   ...dat   Jan   een liedje schijnt te hebben   gezongen.
        ...that John a   song seems   to have-INF sung-PART.
      b.   ...dat   Jan   een liedje schijnt gezongen   te hebben.
        ...that John a   song seems   sung-PART to have-INF.

    c. ...dat Jan   een liedje gezongen schijnt te hebben.
        ...that John a   song sung-PART seems to have-INF.

        ...that John seems to have sung a song.

(43) a. ...dat Jan   een liedje probeert te zingen.
        ...that John a   song tries   to sing-INF.

    b. *...dat Jan   een liedje te zingen   probeert.
        ...that John a   song to sing-INF tries.

        ...that John tries to sing a song.

    c. ...dat Jan   een liedje probeert te mogen   zingen.
        ...that John a   song tries   to be-allowed-INF sing-INF.

    d. *...dat Jan   een liedje probeert te zingen   mogen.
        ...that John a   song tries   to sing-INF be-allowed-INF.

        ...that John tries to be allowed to sing a song.

The *te*-taking verbs have the lexical constraint $(\uparrow \text{XCOMP VFORM}) = \text{TE-INF}$, and in all their forms they also have the precedence condition $\uparrow <_f (\uparrow \text{XCOMP})$. Their ordering properties follow from these lexical specifications and the phrase structure rules above.

Extraposed verbal complements and the third construction

As indicated above, we analyze extraposed infinitivals as COMPs just like obligatorily extraposed *dat*-clauses. They are handled by the optional VP expansion in the ZK phrase structure rule (1a), but here we propose a slightly restricted version that more accurately reflects the fact that an NP can link to a COMP only at the bottom of the verbal cluster hierarchy.[7]

(44) VP →   NP*   V'   (VP)

                $(\uparrow \text{XCOMP*} (\text{COMP}) \text{NGF}) = \downarrow$ $(\uparrow \text{XCOMP*} \text{COMP}) = \downarrow$

Within the extraposed VP we can of course get all the non-tensed verb cluster orders describe above, as illustrated with the examples in (45), but nothing special needs to be said about this.

(45) a. ...dat Jan hoopt een liedje goed gezongen te hebben.
        ...that John hopes a   song well sung-PART to have-INF.

    b. ...dat Jan hoopt een liedje goed te hebben   gezongen.
        ...that John hopes a   song well to have-INF sung-PART.

        ...that John hopes to have well sung a song.

We assume that the third construction arises from the combination of extra-position and focused elements in the middlefield.[8] That this is a kind of focus construction would also explain the facts illustrated earlier in (17). In this con-struction, just like in topicalization, we cannot link an unstressed pronoun to an NGF of the extraposed COMP. Again this construction has been described in ZK and is covered by the COMP annotation on the NP in rule (44).

Summary: An LFG analysis of Dutch verb clusters

Our account of Dutch verb clusters involves two phrase structure rules and several lexical/morphological specifications. The VP rule (44), repeated in the summary below, is the one given in ZK, modulo the small restriction for the COMP in the NP uncertainty path. The V' rule (40) has been expanded to allow for particles and participles, and it relaxes the ordering of the V' and the V.

(44)   VP →   NP*   V'   (VP)

            $(\uparrow \text{XCOMP}^* (\text{COMP}) \text{NGF}) = \downarrow$ $(\uparrow \text{XCOMP}^* \text{COMP}) = \downarrow$

(40)   V' →   (PostP)   (V)   [V ,   (V')   ]

      $(\uparrow \text{XCOMP}^+ \text{PRT}) = \downarrow$ $(\downarrow \text{VFORM}) = \text{PART}$ $(\uparrow \text{XCOMP}) = \downarrow$

            $(\uparrow \text{XCOMP}^+) = \downarrow$ $(\uparrow \text{XCOMP}^+ \text{NGF}) \neg <_f (\uparrow \text{NGF})$

            $\downarrow \neg <_f (\uparrow \text{PRT})$

Our lexical/morphological specifications make explicit which features and con-straints are needed to account for the ordering in the verb cluster. We make use of a quite standard feature inventory augmented only by the CLUS feature that we introduce to mark verbs that occur in the specific, not universally avail-able, cluster construction. The features assigned to particular morphological forms are described by (11), repeated here; (12) and (23) indicate how those morphological features of complements are selected by governing verbs; and (35) and (36) relate morphological features to the right-branching precedence constraints that restrict the relaxed c-structure order.

(11)   a. $(\uparrow \text{VFORM}) = \text{PART}$ for participles
      b. $(\uparrow \text{VFORM}) = \text{INF}$ for bare infinitives
      c. $(\uparrow \text{VFORM}) = \text{TE-INF}$ for *te* infinitives
      d. $(\uparrow \text{VFORM}) = \text{TENSED}$ for all tensed forms

(12) a. (↑ XCOMP VFORM) ∈ {PART, INF}   for auxiliaries
     b. (↑ XCOMP VFORM) = INF   for modals, causatives, perception verbs...
     c. (↑ XCOMP VFORM) = TE-INF   for other NTV verbs.

(23) Auxiliaries: (↑ XCOMP VFORM) = INF ⇔ (↑ XCOMP CLUS)

(35) Tensed modals or auxiliaries: (↑ XCOMP CLUS) ⇒ ↑ $<_f$ (↑ XCOMP)

(36) Infinitival modals or auxiliaries: (↑ XCOMP VFORM) = INF ⇒ ↑ $<_f$ (↑ XCOMP)

The following lexical entries are examples of how these constraints are realized.

(46) a. hebben: (↑ PRED) = 'perfect<(↑ XCOMP)>(↑ SUBJ)'
               (↑ SUBJ) = (↑ XCOMP SUBJ)
               (↑ CLUS) = +
               (↑ XCOMP VFORM) ∈ {PART, INF}
               (↑ XCOMP VFORM) = INF ⇔ (↑ XCOMP CLUS)
               (↑ XCOMP VFORM) = INF ⇒ ↑$<_f$ (↑ XCOMP)
               (↑ VFORM) = INF

     b. heeft: (↑ PRED) = 'perfect<(↑ XCOMP)>(↑ SUBJ)'
               (↑ SUBJ) = (↑ XCOMP SUBJ)
               (↑ CLUS) = +
               (↑ XCOMP VFORM) ∈ {PART, INF}
               (↑ XCOMP VFORM) = INF ⇔ (↑ XCOMP CLUS)
               (↑ XCOMP CLUS) ⇒ ↑$<_f$ (↑ XCOMP)
               (↑ VFORM) = TENSED

     c. willen: (↑ PRED) = 'want<(↑ SUBJ) (↑ XCOMP)>'
               (↑ SUBJ) = (↑ XCOMP SUBJ)
               (↑ CLUS) = +
               (↑ XCOMP VFORM) = INF
               ↑ $<_f$ (↑ XCOMP)
               (↑ VFORM) = INF

     d. wil: (↑ PRED) = 'want<(↑ SUBJ) (↑ XCOMP)>'
               (↑ SUBJ) = (↑ XCOMP SUBJ)
               (↑ CLUS) = +
               (↑ XCOMP VFORM) = INF
               (↑ XCOMP CLUS) ⇒ ↑$<_f$ (↑ XCOMP)
               (↑ VFORM) = TENSED

e.   proberen (cluster entry):

$(\uparrow \text{PRED}) = \text{'try}<(\uparrow \text{SUBJ}) (\uparrow \text{XCOMP})>\text{'}$

$(\uparrow \text{SUBJ}) = (\uparrow \text{XCOMP SUBJ})$

$(\uparrow \text{CLUS}) = +$

$(\uparrow \text{XCOMP VFORM}) = \text{TE-INF}$

$\uparrow <_f (\uparrow \text{XCOMP})$

$(\uparrow \text{VFORM}) = \text{INF}$

f.   proberen (extraposition entry):

$(\uparrow \text{PRED}) = \text{'try}<(\uparrow \text{SUBJ}) (\uparrow \text{COMP})>\text{'}$

$(\uparrow \text{COMP SUBJ}) = \text{'pro'}$

$(\uparrow \text{COMP VFORM}) = \text{TE-INF}$

$(\uparrow \text{VFORM}) = \text{INF}$

Given that most of the constraints are linked to (classes of) lexical items, accounting for dialect variation consist in many cases simply in removing or adding a constraint. For instance in the dialect of the second author of this paper sentences like the following are grammatical (cf. (26)):

(47) ...dat Jan   een liedje willen   zingen   heeft.
...that John a   song   want-INF sing-INF has.
...that John has wanted to sing a song.

(48) ...dat Jan   een liedje moet willen   zingen   hebben.
...that John a   song   must want-INF sing-INF have-INF.
...that John must have wanted to sing a song.

For this dialect we can simply say that the constraints $(\uparrow \text{XCOMP CLUS}) \Rightarrow \uparrow <_f$ $(\uparrow \text{XCOMP})$ in (35) and $(\uparrow \text{XCOMP VFORM}) = \text{INF} \Rightarrow \uparrow <_f (\uparrow \text{XCOMP})$ in (36) are included for modals but not for auxiliaries.

4.   Prolegomena to a treatment of German verb clusters

In this section we sketch how the Dutch system can be adapted to account for some of the phenomena found in German. We do not attempt to describe a real variant of German here; we just choose some salient aspects of the German verbal cluster ordering and give rules to handle them. A full treatment of any variant of German would need further specifications.

German allows for extraposition and for the third construction, so the Dutch VP rule (44) can be taken over to German without modification. German differs from Dutch in not permitting the creeping of participles or particles. This means that the PostP and participle expansions for Dutch are not needed in the German V' rule, and that we can revert to the basic unordered c-structure arrangement in (33). We also want to account for the following observations about the order of verbs in German clusters:

(49)   a.   ...daß sie ausgehen wollte.
            ...that she outgo-INF wanted.
            ...that she wanted to go out.

       b.   ...daß sie mich ausgehen gesehen hat.
            ...that she me   outgo-INF seen-PART has.
            ...that she has seen me go out.

       c.   ...daß sie hat ausgehen wollen.
            ...that she has outgo-INF want-INF.
            ...that she has wanted to go out.

       d.   ...daß sie wird ausgehen wollen.
            ...that she will outgo-INF want-INF.
            ...that she will want to go out.

       e.   *...daß sie hat ausgehen gewollt.
            ...that she has outgo-INF wanted-PART.
            ...that she has wanted to go out.

       f.   *...daß sie wollte ausgehen.
            ...that she wanted outgo-INF.
            ...that she wanted to go out.

       g.   *...daß sie ist ausgegangen.
            ...that she is   outgone-PART.
            ...that she has gone out.

       h.   *...daß sie das haben tun können muß.
            ...that she that have-INF do-INF be-able-INF must.
            ...that she must have been able to do that.

       i.   ...daß sie das muß haben tun können.
            ...that she that must have-INF do-INF be-able-INF.
            ...that she must have been able to do that.

       j.   *Er versuchte das (zu) mußen haben tun
            He tried   this (to) must-INF have-INF do-INF
            (zu) können.
            (to) be-able-INF.

The patterns in (49) exemplify the following generalizations:

(50)   In German verb clusters the canonical order is left branching, with complements preceding their governors (49a, b).

(51)   Some German verbs optionally govern right-branching complement structures, subject to the following conditions:
   a.   All verbs below a left branching verb also branch to the left (49h, i).
   b.   Right branching can start at a tensed verb (i.e. the highest verb of a cluster) (Oberfeldumstellung) (49c, d, h, j).
   c.   The head of a right-branch complement is always in the infinitive, even when the governing verb is an auxiliary (Ersatzinfinitiv) (49e).

The canonical left-branching order is possible for all German cluster verbs (50), and complements below a left branch are also left-branching (51a). The following two precedence constraints enforce these conditions:

(52)   a. $<_f \uparrow (\uparrow$ XCOMP)
        b.   ($\uparrow$ XCOMP CLUS) $\Rightarrow$ ($\uparrow$ XCOMP) $<_f$ ($\uparrow$ XCOMP XCOMP)

The small number of cluster verbs (including *haben*, *werden* and *wollen*) that optionally allow right-branching complements have as a disjunctive alternative to (52) the simple right-branching constraint (53):

(53) $\uparrow <_f$ ($\uparrow$ XCOMP)

One consequence of constraint (52b) is that right branching can begin only at the top of a clustered XCOMP hierarchy. The top verb of a cluster can either be a tensed form as specified in (51b), or it can be the *zu*-infinitive head of an extraposed COMP. Extraposition verb entries include the variant of (52b) shown in (54) and thus exclude the possibility of right-branching anywhere below the extraposed infinitive.

(54)   ($\uparrow$ COMP VFORM) = *zu*-INF
        ($\uparrow$ COMP CLUS) $\Rightarrow$ ($\uparrow$ COMP) $<_f$ ($\uparrow$ COMP XCOMP)

Finally, the constraint (55) implements the generalization (51c) that right-branching complements of auxiliaries have infnitival heads.

(55)   Auxiliaries: ($\uparrow$ XCOMP VFORM) = INF $\Leftrightarrow$ ($\uparrow$ XCOMP) $<_f \uparrow$

5.   Conclusion

In this paper we have sketched an LFG treatment of verb clusters in West Germanic languages with a particular emphasis on Dutch. Our treatment reflects what we take to be the idiosyncratic nature of the phenomena: we do not see broad, universal generalizations here. However, these phenomena are interesting because they involve several kinds of interactions. There are mutual constraints among local morphological/lexical features and quasi-local ones (for example, the features of the xcomp of an xcomp or comp), and these then correlate with how functional precedence relations and long-distance uncertainties can be resolved. Our account made use only of descriptive devices that are independently motivated and already available in the LFG formalism. Germanic verb-cluster phenomena thus provide further support for the architectural principles of the LFG framework.

Notes

1. We are agnostic about the difference between S and VP nodes in Dutch. Here they are collapsed, in other places we have distinguished them, but this c-structure distinction plays no role in our analysis.

2. The annotations in (1b) do not specify the order of the grammatical functions of a single verb. They can be ordered by adding other f-precedence requirements to the V' rule, for instance (↑ obj) ¬<(↑ obj2) for Dutch. In German such requirements are most likely better associated with the lexical item as there are different orders depending on different lexical classes.

3. It is possible to argue that in auxiliary and perhaps even in some modal constructions, the non-tensed verbs are in fact the head of the construction. See Butt, Niño, and Segond (1996) and Frank and Zaenen (2002) for some discussion. This would complicate but not substantially change the analysis proposed here.

4. Klaus Netter (p.c.) has argued that sentences like (15a) are actually personal passives with an extraposed sentential subject. We could then assign the obj function to the active sentence, extending an analysis proposed for tensed German prepositional complements in Dalrymple and Lødrup (2000). Again, this analysis would not change the account substantially but it would require us to go further into a discussion about the typology of functions in LFG which we don't have space for here.

5. We do not discuss here the separate issue of exactly how a particle and its head mutually select each other.

6. The grammatical pattern illustrated in (i) involves the third construction:

(i)   ...dat Jan een liedje heeft geprobeerd te zingen.
      *...dat Jan een liedje geprobeerd te zingen heeft.
      *...dat Jan een liedje geprobeerd heeft te zingen.

7. The ZK account in (1a) would allow ungrammatical strings such as

(i)   *...omdat   Jan   het liedje   geprobeerd   heeft   te beloven   te zingen.
      ...because John the song   tried   has   to promise   to sing.

8. This does not account for the fact that the third construction is not possible when the extraposed element is introduced by *om*,

(i)   ...dat Jan een liedje heeft geprobeerd om   te zingen.
      ...that John a   song has   tried   COMPL to sing.

We assume that *om* is a complementizer and that it blocks topicalization but we have not formalized this.

CHAPTER 5

Subjects in unexpected places and the notion of "predicate"*

Andreas Kathol
UC Berkeley

1. Introduction

One of the driving forces in Head-Driven Phrase Structure Grammar (HPSG; Pollard & Sag 1994) is the idea that much, if not all, of syntactic combination can be captured in terms of saturation of valence requirements. This is illustrated in (1), where the transitive verb *won* combines with its object dependent *the race*. As a result, the valence requirement, here given in terms of the feature SUBCAT are reduced. At the mother level, only a subject is required.[1] The example in (1) further illustrates how valence requirements can be shared across different components of the sentence. The auxiliary *has* requires precisely the subject that its complement VP is missing (indicated by means of the identity tag "□"). Once that dependent has been identified (here: *an outsider*), the valence requirements are saturated, resulting in an empty SUBCAT list at the top clausal level:

(1)

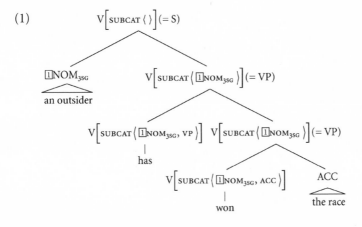

While the combinatorial structure of embedded nonfinite VP complements is pretty much uncontroversial in English, the analysis of the corresponding German constructions has been significantly less uniform. Rather than compare different possibilities, I take as my point of departure a particular approach that has become quite popular within lexicalist approaches to German syntax.

2.   Valence in the verb cluster

Within the literature on German syntax within HPSG, few ideas have proven as influential as Hinrichs and Nakazawa's (1989) idea of "argument composition". Its basic idea is that in verb clusters, that is, clause-final sequences of nonfinite and at most one finite verb, the arguments of a main verb are realized as the dependents projected from any auxiliary that governs that main verb rather than as direct dependents of the main verb as in the English case in (1). For instance in (2a), the tense auxiliary *hat* governs the transitive main verb *gewinnen*. As the head of the cluster *gewonnen hat*, the auxiliary *hat* effectively takes over the arguments from the main verb. In turn, since the unsaturated valence requirements of the head are passed to the mother level, the entire clauster *gewonnen hat* then combines with the phrasal NP dependents (the object *das Rennen* and the subject *ein Außenseiter*). The resulting constituent structure is shown in (2b).

(2)   a.   daß   ein Außenseiter   das Rennen   gewonnen   hat.
          that   an outsider   the race   won   has
          'that an outsider has won the race.'

      b.

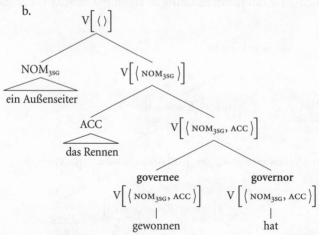

In (2b), I abbreviate valence requirements by means of a simple list representation (" ⟨...⟩"). These include only phrasal dependents, whereas I assume that governees within a verb cluster are selected by means of the selectional feature VCOMPL, not shown in (2b).[2] In more formally precise terms, the valence requirements of the argument raising auxiliary *hat* can be characterized as in (3a):

(3) *hat*

  a.

$$\left[\begin{array}{l} \text{SUBCAT } \boxed{1}\langle \, ... \, \rangle \\[2ex] \text{VCOMPL} \left\langle \begin{array}{c} \text{V} \\ \left[\text{SUBCAT } \boxed{1}\langle \, ... \, \rangle \right] \end{array} \right\rangle \end{array} \right]$$

  b.

$$\left[\begin{array}{l} \text{SUBCAT } \boxed{1}\langle \, \text{NP}[\text{NOM}], \text{NP}[\text{ACC}] \, \rangle \\[2ex] \text{VCOMPL} \left\langle \begin{array}{c} \text{V} \\ \left[\text{SUBCAT } \boxed{1}\langle \, ... \, \rangle \right] \end{array} \right\rangle \end{array} \right]$$

The auxiliary selects a verbal complement by means of VCOMPL. Whatever the phrasal dependents of that complement (represented here by means of the SUBCAT feature), the coreference tag "$\boxed{1}$" guarantees that the auxiliary has precisely the same requirements. For the particular case in (2), this means that the identity in SUBCAT requirements includes a nominative and an accusative NP, as shown in (3b). In what follows I will not include selectional requirements involving VCOMPL, unless such details become important.

Valence information is an important component of HPSG analyses as it constitutes the locus for nominative case marking and and subject agreement for finite verbs. We can characterize a regular third person finite verb as a verbal element that combines with an NP which is marked nominative and which has a 3SG index. This is illustrated for the finite verb *gewinnt* in (4a) and the finite auxiliary *hat* in (4b) for cases such as (3b), in which a subject and an object have been raised:

(4) a. *gewinnt*

    $$\left[\text{SUBCAT}\langle \, \text{NP}[\text{NOM}]_{3\text{SG}}, \text{NP}[\text{ACC}] \, \rangle \right]$$

  b. *hat*

    $$\left[\text{SUBCAT}\langle \, \text{NP}[\text{NOM}]_{3\text{SG}}, \text{NP}[\text{ACC}] \, \rangle \right]$$

In fact, while we have presented the case-marking requirements in (4) as lexical facts, it is rather straightforward to state these as part of a larger generalization. If we assume that subjects are simply marked lexically as bearing structural case ("STR"), which is an abstraction over nominative and accusative case (vs. pre-assigned lexical cases, which are not constructionally determined), then we can express nominative case marking along the lines sketched in (5a). This constraint requires that any verb with finite morphology that takes a structurally case-marked subject NP also imposes a requirement that the subject occur with nominative case. A similar constraint can be stated for structural accusative case as the morphological expression of a nonsubject structural case, cf. (5b):[3]

(5) a.
$$\begin{bmatrix} \text{v[FINITE]} \\ \langle\, \text{NP[STR], ...}\rangle \end{bmatrix} \rightarrow \begin{bmatrix} \langle\, \text{NP[NOM], ...}\rangle \end{bmatrix}$$

   b.
$$\begin{bmatrix} \text{v} \\ \langle\, [\ ], \text{NP[STR] ...}\rangle \end{bmatrix} \rightarrow \begin{bmatrix} \langle\, [\ ], \text{NP[ACC] ...}\rangle \end{bmatrix}$$

The analysis of verb clusters along the lines given in (2b) straightforwardly extends to more complicated governor–governee structures, such as (6a).

(6) a. daß ein Außenseiter das Rennen gewinnen dürfen wird.
       that an outsider   the race   win   may   will
       'that an outsider will be allowed to win the race.'

   b.

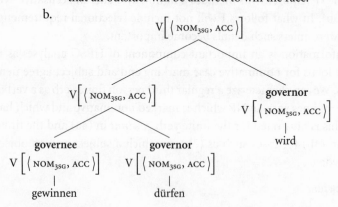

The constituency relations posited for (6a) are supported by the fact that the subcluster *gewinnen dürfen* can be fronted in verb-second constructions, as shown in (7):

(7)   [Gewinnen dürfen] wird ein Außenseiter das Rennen nie.
     win   may   will an outsider   the race   never
    'An outsider will never be allowed to win the race.'

While issues of word order are not at the heart of this study, it may nonetheless be helpful to briefly sketch some of the general assumptions I make here about how constituent relations are mapped onto linear order.

3.   Remarks on linear order

Following Kathol (1998) and Kathol (2000), I assume a "linearization-based approach" to word order in German, specifically the problems of placing finite verbs, positioning of any pre-verbal phrases, and the ordering of elements within the verbal cluster (see also Kempen & Harbusch, this volume for a related approach). As most linearization-based work, I adopt the notion of "order domain" (listed below by means of the feature DOM) as a level of representation, only indirectly linked to constituent structure, on which constraints on linear order operate.

Order domains can be understood as totally ordered lists of information bundles which each contain phonological and syntactic-semantic information. Simplifying somewhat, every time two syntactic elements are combined by some schema of combination, a corresponding order domain is built up involving the domains of the constituents thus far derived. In most combinations of a head with a syntactic argument, that argument is entered into the resulting domain of the mother as a single phonologically encapsulated informational chunk. Consider for instance the combination of a verb and an NP object in (8).

(8)
$$
\begin{bmatrix}
\text{VP} \\
\text{DOM} \left\langle \begin{bmatrix} [\langle gewinnt \rangle] \\ \text{V[FIN]} \end{bmatrix}, \begin{bmatrix} \langle das\ Rennen \rangle \\ \text{NP[ACC]} \end{bmatrix} \right\rangle
\end{bmatrix}
$$

$$
\begin{bmatrix}
\text{V[FIN]} \\
\text{DOM} \left\langle \begin{bmatrix} \langle gewinnt \rangle \\ \text{V[FIN]} \end{bmatrix} \right\rangle
\end{bmatrix}
\qquad
\begin{bmatrix}
\text{NP[ACC]} \\
\text{DOM} \langle [\langle das \rangle], [\langle Rennen \rangle] \rangle
\end{bmatrix}
$$

Here, the domain of the VP consists of two elements, one for the head (*gewinnt*) and one constructed from the complement (*das Rennen*). In the domain resulting from the verb-object combination, the internal linear composition of *das Rennen* can no longer be referenced. In the terminology of Kathol (1995), the object has been *domain-inserted* into that of the head.

What makes the linearization-based approach a powerful tool of syntactic description is the fact that it can easily accommodate discontinuous structures. For instance, if we add a subject to the VP structure in (8), we may do so in a way that breaks up the verb and object within the domain, giving rise to the linear order that one would find, for instance, in a polar interrogative clause:

(9) a. Gewinnt ein Außenseiter das Rennen?
       wins   an outsider   the race
       'Is an outsider winning the race?'

   b.

$$
\begin{bmatrix}
\text{VP} \\
\text{DOM} \left\langle \begin{bmatrix} \langle \textit{gewinnt} \rangle \\ \text{V[FIN]} \end{bmatrix}, \begin{bmatrix} \langle \textit{ein Außenseiter} \rangle \\ \text{NP[NOM]} \end{bmatrix}, \begin{bmatrix} \langle \textit{das Rennen} \rangle \\ \text{NP[ACC]} \end{bmatrix} \right\rangle
\end{bmatrix}
$$

$$
\begin{bmatrix}
\text{V[FIN]} \\
\text{DOM} \left\langle \begin{bmatrix} \langle \textit{gewinnt} \rangle \\ \text{V[FIN]} \end{bmatrix}, \begin{bmatrix} \langle \textit{das Rennen} \rangle \\ \text{NP[ACC]} \end{bmatrix} \right\rangle
\end{bmatrix}
\begin{bmatrix}
\text{NP[NOM]} \\
\text{DOM}[\langle \textit{ein} \rangle], [\langle \textit{Außenseiter} \rangle]\rangle
\end{bmatrix}
$$

So far, we have not addressed the question what constrains order possibilities at the clausal level. Here I assume that clausal order domains quite directly implement the traditional "topological fields" model (cf. for instance Drach 1937; Engel 1970; Höhle 1986).[4] For instance, in terms of the topological organization, the sentence above in (6a) gives rise to an order domain that is organized as follows:

(10)

$$
\begin{bmatrix}
\text{DOM} \left\langle \begin{bmatrix} \textit{cf} \\ \langle \textit{daß} \rangle \\ \text{COMPL} \end{bmatrix}, \begin{bmatrix} \textit{mf} \\ \langle \textit{ein Außenseiter} \rangle \\ \text{NP} \end{bmatrix}, \begin{bmatrix} \textit{mf} \\ \langle \textit{das Rennen} \rangle \\ \text{NP} \end{bmatrix}, \begin{bmatrix} \textit{vc} \\ \langle \textit{gewinnen} \rangle \\ \text{V} \end{bmatrix}, \begin{bmatrix} \textit{vc} \\ \langle \textit{dürfen} \rangle \\ \text{V} \end{bmatrix}, \begin{bmatrix} \textit{vc} \\ \langle \textit{wird} \rangle \\ \text{V[fin]} \end{bmatrix} \right\rangle
\end{bmatrix}
$$

It may be useful to briefly zoom in on the verb cluster part of (10), whose combinatorial structure was already considered above in (6b). In (11) the corresponding order domains are illustrated.[5]

(11)

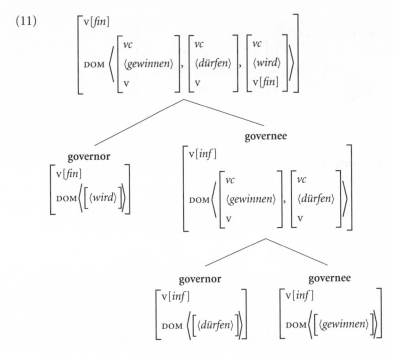

One of the most important consequences of this approach is that there is no equivalent of "verb movement" in terms of actual dislocation of verbal material from its clause-final place of origin. Instead, verb-first structures such as the polar question version of (6a), given in (12a), simply involve the alternative marking of the finite element in the *cf* topological field ("linke Satzklammer"), as illustrated in (12b):

(12) a. Wird ein Außenseiter das Rennen gewinnen dürfen?
          will an outsider   the race   win   may
          'Will an outsider be allowed to win the race?'

      b.

$$\left[\text{DOM} \left\langle \left[\begin{matrix} cf \\ \langle wird \rangle \\ v[fin] \end{matrix} \right], \left[\begin{matrix} mf \\ \langle ein\ Au\beta enseiter \rangle \\ NP \end{matrix} \right], \left[\begin{matrix} mf \\ \langle das\ Rennen \rangle \\ NP \end{matrix} \right], \left[\begin{matrix} vc \\ \langle gewinnen \rangle \\ v \end{matrix} \right], \left[\begin{matrix} vc \\ \langle d\ddot{u}rfen \rangle \\ v \end{matrix} \right] \right\rangle \right]$$

In terms of combinatorial structure, this alternative ordering involves precisely the same steps as in the clause-final case in (11) above. This is illustrated in (13):

(13)

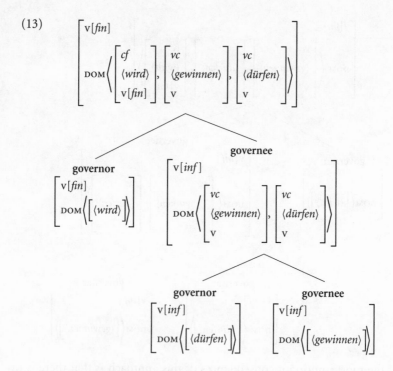

In the present model, linear order can, to some degree, be seen as disconnected from constituent relations. In fact, in Kathol (2000: 58–76), I present extensive arguments why, in the case of verb placement, this is also a desirable result with respect to putative scope differences associated with different tree-structural positions for finite predicates.

As a final aspect of our brief excursion into issues of linear order, let us consider verb-second constructions with a fronted phrasal constituent of the kind seen in (7) above. Following virtually all HPSG work on German, I assume that frontings of this kind are the result of information about a missing constituent ("gap") within a clause being matched against a clause-initial "filler". Like the head-argument structures in (8) and (9b) above, filler-head structures render the information of the non-head (filler) into a single domain element which is inserted into the domain of the head. In addition, the domain element corresponding to the filler receives the topological label *vf*.[6] As a result, examples of the kind seen in (7) above can be given the analysis presented in (14). Here, "/" indicates information about gaps inside a given constituent.

(14)

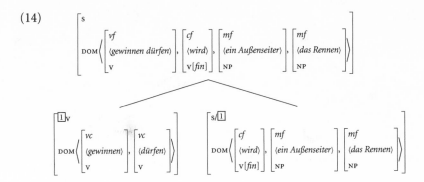

Since the focus of the present paper is on dependency relations across constituent boundaries, I will not further dwell on issues of linearization here. But since constituent relations are not mapped directly onto linear order, it should be kept in mind that in the tree representations below, the tree position of the finite verb (consistently occurring clause-finally), should not be interpreted as indicating that element's actual linear position.

4. Fronted (partial) VPs

The kind of analysis for verb clusters shown in (2b) and (7) at first appears to be at odds with constructions in which a VP or a partial VP is fronted, as for instance in (15).[7]

(15) [Dieses Rennen gewonnen] hat ein Außenseiter noch nie.
      this race   won   has an outsider   yet   never
      'No outsider has ever won this race.'

As the structure in (16) shows, the main verb *gewonnen* combines with its phrasal dependent *dieses Rennen* to form a filler phrase. Valence and other information of this filler phrase are shared with the corresponding gap site inside the clause,[8] indicated in (16) by means of the coreference tag ⬚, while, as in (14) above, "/" indicates gap information. The governing auxiliary *hat* combines with (the gap of) the fronted VP and, via (3a), takes over any unrealized arguments of that VP as its own arguments. In the present case, the one dependent not realized within the fronted phrase is the subject *ein Außenseiter*; as a result, the latter is realized as a dependent of the auxiliary, rather than the fronted main verb *gewonnen*.

(16)

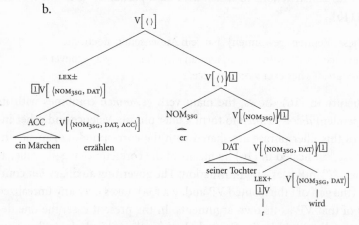

The following example illustrates the case in which the two complements of a main verb are "distributed" across the fronted phrase and the *Mittelfeld*. Again, this is directly accounted for if the auxiliary (here: *wird*) simply takes over any complement that the fronted main verb has not combined with (here, the dative phrase *seiner Tochter*).[9]

(17) a. [Ein Märchen   erzählen] wird er   seiner Tochter.
          a fairy tale.ACC tell   will he   his daughter.DAT
          'He will tell his daughter a fairy tale.'

     b.

One of the issues raised by this construction type is why main verbs should sometimes be allowed to combine with their phrasal dependents (e.g., in (16) and (17b)), while at other times, they first combine with an auxiliary, as in (2b). As has been shown by Müller (1996) and Meurers (1999b), however, such cases can be accommodated if we assume that fillers and gaps may sometimes diverge in their lexical/phrasal status. Thus, while elements inside the verb cluster need to be "lexical" [LEX +],[10] this requirement does not hold of fillers in verb-second constructions. If there is no constraint on the lexical/phrasal status of the initial filler ([LEX ±]), then the initial occurrence of phrases such as *das Rennen gewonnen* is correctly accounted for.

5. Subjects in fronted phrases

As has been pointed out by Grewendorf (1988), Haider (1990), and others,[11] fronted partial VPs in German may sometimes contain a subject, as illustrated in (18) with intransitive *gewinnen*.

(18) [Ein Außenseiter gewonnen] hat hier   noch nie.
      an outsider   won   has here   still never
      'No outsider has yet won here.'

Before addressing the challenges posed by this construction type for the valence-based approach to case-marking and agreement, a few comments on the constraints on phrase-internal subjects may be in order.

5.1 Semantic restrictions on fronted verbal projections

Not all frontings of verbal constituents containing subjects yield acceptable results and the exact nature of the operative constraints is still not properly understood. First, agent-patient verbs with full NP objects appear to generally disallow the construction. This is very clearly the case when the object is part of the fronted constituent, as in (19a), but even when it remains within the *Mittelfeld*, as in (19b), the result appears not to be much better (cf. also Haider 1990:94):

(19) a. *[Ein Außenseiter ein solches Rennen gewonnen] hat noch nie.
          an outsider.NOM a such race.ACC   won   has still never
          Intended: 'No outsider has yet won such a race.'
      b. *[Ein Außenseiter gewonnen] hat ein solches Rennen noch nie.
          an outsider.NOM won   has a such race.ACC   still never
          Intended: 'No outsider has yet won such a race.'

Examples such as the following have prompted some (e.g., Kathol 2000:239 or Grewendorf 1988:295) to assume that the constraints are essentially thematic in nature. I.e. only non-agentive subjects, as those of unaccusative verbs (20a) or stimulus-like subjects (20b) appear to be frontable.

(20) a. [Eine Concorde gelandet] ist hier noch nie.
     a Concorde   landed   is here still never
     'A Concorde has so far never landed here.'
   b. [Ein Fehler unterlaufen] ist ihr noch nie.
     a mistake happen   is her still never
     'She never had a mistake happening to her.'

However, such an account is at odds with the thematic role of the subject of verbs such as *gewinnen*, even in their intransitive variants, as seen above in (18). One piece of evidence arguing against the unaccusative analysis is the fact that such verbs robustly form their perfect with a form of *haben*, rather than *sein*. Moreover, a thematic account would fail to account for the following observation, which Haider (1990:96) attributes to Angelika Kratzer. As is shown in (21), fronted verbal constituents display a "definiteness effect".

(21) a. *[Der Außenseiter gewonnen] hat hier noch nie.
     this outsider   won   has here still   never

A potentially more promising avenue to pursue may be judgment type (cf., e.g., Kuroda 1972).[12] Thus, in the cases in (18) and (20) above, the fronted phrases appear to express thetic judgments, which are generally incompatible with definite subjects. Instead, the use of the demonstratives forces a categorical interpretation on the clause.

Since categorical judgments involve the identification of a predication base (typically the grammatical subject) about which a statement is made, they naturally seem more compatible with root interpretations of modals. Conversely, since no predication base is involved in thetic judgments, it would seem that "wide-scope" (i.e., logical necessity, possibility, etc.) readings of modals are more in line with statements of the thetic judgment types. There is some evidence supporting this proposal. As Meurers (1999a:290) points out, citing an observation originally due to Tilman Höhle, the sentence in (22) which involves a fronted subject together with the otherwise ambiguous modal *können* only allows for the non-root reading of the modal:

(22) [Ein Kollege aus Köln   teilnehmen] kann diesmal leider
     a colleague from Cologne participate can   this time unfortunately
     nicht.
     not
     'Unfortunately, it is not possible that a colleague from Cologne partici-
     pates this time.'
     Not available: 'Unfortunately, a colleague from Cologne is unable to par-
     ticipate this time.'

Meurers attributes the difference to the difference in control vs. raising construal of *können*, but this explanation would again fail to address the definiteness effect. As (23) shows, if the fronted constituent contains a definite subject,
the result is notably worse under either reading. This is fully unexpected in an
analysis that is based on the raising vs. control distinction.

(23) *[Dieser Kollege aus Köln   teilnehmen] kann diesmal
      a colleague   from Cologne participate can   this time
      leider   nicht.
      unfortunately   not

In addition, the constraint against the construal of the fronted verbal constituent as a categorical judgment may also explain why the sole exception
to the above mentioned ban against objects appears to be pronominal elements. Thus, Haider (1990:97) reports that examples such as the one in (24)
are notably more acceptable than those involving full NP objects as in (19b)
above:

(24) [Ein Außenseiter gewonnen] hat das da   noch nie.
     an outsider.NOM won   has that there still never
     'No outsider has yet won that there.'

It has been argued (Vallduví & Engdahl 1996) that pronouns are in a sense "inert" for the purposes of information packaging. That is, unlike full NPs, they
may not be forced into the same information-packaging categories as full NP
dependents. If this can also be maintained for thetic judgments, i.e., if thetic
judgments are possible with pronominal nonsubject dependents, it may explain why examples such as (24) appear to be so much better than their full NP
counterparts. Such an account would offer an alternative to Haider's (1990) explanation in terms of differences in available structural positions for pronouns
vs. full NPs (p. 106).

After these admittedly somewhat speculative remarks I will ignore the issue of how properly to circumscribe the set of frontable subjects for the remainder of this article, even though this is a question that clearly deserves more research.

5.2 The locality of phrase-internal subjects

Recent work by Meurers (1999c, 1999a) and Meurers and De Kuthy (2001) has pointed out that fronted verbal projections containing subjects present a severe challenge to analyses of the verb cluster in terms of argument composition as outlined above in Section 2. The problem is that the subject forms a phrase with the participle *gewonnen*. Given that saturation of valence requirements results in the removal of those elements from the valence list, that subject is consequently not represented on the valence list of the fronted phrase, as illustrated in (25).

(25)

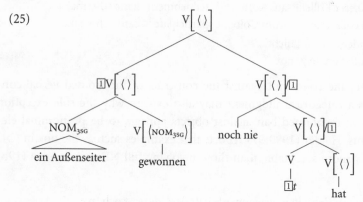

As a result, there is no "communication" between the governing auxiliary *hat* and the phrase-internal subject *ein Außenseiter*. Thus, standard assumptions about nominative case marking and agreement of the kind shown earlier in (5a) cannot apply. It is therefore unclear how the obligatory nominative case marking on the phrase-internal NP and its agreement with the auxiliary can be accounted for. As is illustrated in (26), the construction leaves no choice in this matter; an accusative NP or a mismatch in number leads to ungrammaticality:

(26) a. *Einen Außenseiter gewonnen hat hier noch nie.
          an outsider.ACC   won   has here still never
      b. *Außenseiter gewonnen hat hier noch nie.
          outsider.PL won   has here still never

5.3 Raising spirits

The solution offered for this problem by Meurers (1999c, 1999a) is in terms of "raising spirits". These are representations of dependents which remain on valence-related lists even though the valence requirements have been locally realized. As a result, raising spirits become "accessible" outside the fronted phrase for purposes of case assignment and agreement.

In (27), for instance, the subject requirement of *gewonnen* is satisfied within the fronted phrase, represented as "②". Rather than being removed from the valence list, (as in (25) above), the subject remains part of the valence list of the mother node. To render raising spirits combinatorially inert, that is, to indicate at a higher node that an element has been "found" inside that phrase, Meurers assigns them a special marking. Thus in (27), "②" points toward the same informational content as "②", except that in the former, the NP[NOM] bears a marking as "realized".[13] The resulting structure is given in (27) (Meurers & De Kuthy 2001: 28):

(27)

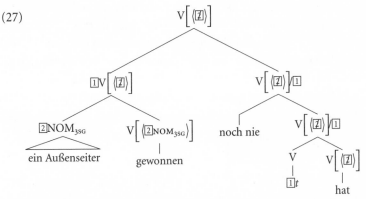

Since ② and ② both contain the same information content as far as case and agreement features are concerned, the puzzle of how to get the finite verb to communicate with the phrase-internal subject appears solved.

However, the solution comes at a steep price. The notion of a "spirit" is antithetical to the overall design of the HPSG theory, in which, as I noted above, syntactic combination is primarily driven by the notion of saturation level. Thus, valence lists with spirits are burdened with information that they were not originally designed to bear. Furthermore, it is not clear whether there is any independent evidence for the notion of spirit apart from the problematic VP fronting construction with subjects in German.

Thus it seems highly desirable to eliminate the notion of spirits from the HPSG theory if the problem of phrase-internal subjects can be solved by means that do not require an extension of the basic theory. As I will show in the next section below, this is indeed the case once the independently motivated notion of argument structure is used to link the various components of a periphrastic predicate.

6.   Argument sharing and periphrastic predicates

6.1   Valence vs. argument structure

The idea of a single representation of all the dependents of some predicator has recently been revived in the form of the ARG-ST feature on lexical elements. By default, the elements of the ARG-ST list are identical with the valence elements given by SUBCAT[14] at the lexical level. The two lists do not always line up in this fashion and the possiblity of mismatches has given rise to a number of analyses of otherwise puzzling phenomena, such as "*pro*-drop".

The standard approach to missing subjects in finite environments has been to posit a null pronoun (*pro*) that instantiates the syntactic subject position. In keeping with HPSG's general avoidance of unpronounced syntactic material, we can instead analyze the unexpressed subject as an ARG-ST element that does not have a corresponding valence expression. The following example from Italian (28a) and the corresponding lexical description of the verb *mangia* in (28b) illustrate this idea:

(28) a.   Mangia un gelato.
           eat.3SG a   ice cream
           'S/he is eating an ice cream.'
      b.
$$\begin{bmatrix} \text{ARG-ST} \; \langle \boxed{1}\text{NP}[\text{3SG}], \boxed{2}\text{NP} \rangle \\ \text{SUBCAT} \; \langle \boxed{2} \rangle \end{bmatrix}$$

Dependencies in which the subject participates, such as binding or agreement, can be accommodated straightforwardly if we assume that their description references the first ARG-ST element, rather than the first member of the SUBCAT list.

While SUBCAT as a valence feature records the level of syntactic saturation for each higher phrase in the tree, ARG-ST is usually taken to be a static representation of the dependents of the lexical head that does not project to higher nodes in the structure (cf. for instance Sag & Wasow 1999: 387 on this point). The rationale behind this assumption is that non-projecting ARG-ST information gives rise to a stronger notion of syntactic locality. That is, if a phrase retains no record of its internal dependents by means of ARG-ST, then selectional dependencies are severely restricted. Thus many nonexisting dependencies are accounted for because the grammatical framework gives us no way to express them. One example of such nonexisting dependencies would be a verb that requires a finite complement clause with a ditransitive head.

The idea that ARG-ST is limited to word-level expressions has recently been challenged by Przepiórkowski (2001:268–271). Among the evidence he presents are examples such as (29) from Polish, in which the main verb *uważać* ('consider') takes two arguments, an accusative marked object (here: *go*, 'him'), and a predicative phrase such as *za szczerego* ('as sincere'). Crucially the predicate (adjective or nominal) inside the PP has to agree in case with the matrix object – in fact they are structurally identical.

(29) Uważałem   go   [{za szczerego/   za studenta}].
      considered.1SG him.ACC   as sincere.ACC as student
      'I considered him to be {sincere/a student}.'

Przepiórkowski shows how a satisfactory solution becomes available once the ARG-ST value of the preposition is projected to the phrasal level, which in turn allows the matrix predicate *uważać* to make reference to it.

Przepiórkowski's arguments involve the visibility of the subject on the embedded ARG-ST list. This could be taken to mean that only subject information is passed to the mother level, while other ARG-ST information is non-projective, as originally proposed. However, there is suggestive evidence from ergative languages that this conclusion does not hold up either.

One such piece of evidence comes from light verb constructions in Urdu, discussed by Andrews and Manning (1999:68):

(30) Anjum ne   d-ii   Saddaf ko   [ciṭʰii   likʰ-ne].
      Anjum ERG give-PERF.F.SG Saddaf DAT letter.F.NOM write-INF
      'Anjum let Saddaf write a letter.'

Andrews and Manning present convincing evidence for the constituent status of *likʰ-ne* ('write') and its object *ciṭʰii* ('letter'). At the same time, since this particular construction displays an ergative case and agreement pattern, the light verb *d-ii* agrees in gender with the object *ciṭʰii* ('letter'). As Andrews and Manning point out, on an analysis based solely on argument composition, the light verb has no access to the embedded object by means of a valence list, hence there is no way to effect the agreement between the light verb and the embedded object. One possible objection may be that, according to Manning's (1996) "inverse linking" hypothesis, the embedded object $citt^hii$ may actually be linked to the grammatical function of subject. If subject information is projected to the phrasal level, then this element should be visible at the phrasal level. However, Manning's idea of inverse linking only applies in cases of syntactic ergativity, of which there is no evidence in a language such as Urdu. Hence, even under Manning's approach to ergativity, the phrase $citt^hii$ would count as a grammatical object. On the analysis proposed here, the entire ARG-ST list of the dependent predicate lik^h-ne ('write'), including both subject and object, is projected to the phrasal level, and thus the agreement marking facts can be readily accommodated.

A similar argument comes from long-distance agreement in Tsez, reported by Polinsky and Comrie (1999). As the following examples show, the matrix predicate ('know') agrees in gender class, not with the matrix dative subject (*enir*), but rather with the absolutive-marked element of the embedded clause. In (31a), this element is the subject, but in (31b), it is the notional object that is marked absolutive.

(31) a. Eni-r   [uži   āy-ru-λi]   iy-xo.
          mother-DAT   boy.ABS   I.arrive-PT.PART-NMLZ   I-know-PRES
          'The mother knows that the boy arrived.'

      b. Eni-r   [už-ā   magalu   b-āc'-ru=λi]
          mother-DAT   boy-ERG   bread.III.ABS   III-eat-PT.PART-NMLZ
          b-iy-xo.
          III-know-PRES
          'The mother knows that the boy ate the bread.'

As before with Urdu, one may think that Manning's (1996) inverse mapping analysis would treat the notional object as a grammatical subject and hence predict visibility, but this proposal has the obvious drawback that it would posit an inverse linking structure for a language that does not elsewhere show any signs of syntactic ergativity (Maria Polinsky, p.c.).

If, instead, argument structure is always projected in full, along the lines suggested here, then agreement relations involving embedded objects can straightforwardly be accounted for and require no further adjustment to the theory. In addition, as I will show in the next section, projecting entire argument structures to the phrasal level also allows us to establish a tighter link among the elements of a verb cluster. In turn, this will allow the agreement and case marking facts involving subjects in fronted verbal constituents to fall out naturally.

6.2 Predicates

Ackerman and Webelhuth (1998) develop a unified theory in which *predicates* are treated as unitary elements of syntactic description regardless of their morpho-syntactic realization. That is, depending on the (sometimes idiosyncratic) details of morphological realization, a given lexeme may be mapped onto a single word or a periphrastic construction involving auxiliaries or other elements. Applied to a concrete example relevant here, this means that, in addition to the synthetic tense forms, the German verb *gewinnen* also possesses a number of complex realizations involving tense and other auxiliaries, sketched here:

(32)   **Extended paradigm for *gewinnen***

	present indicative	past indicative	...	present perfect ...
1sg	gewinne	gewann		gewonnen habe
...				
3SG	gewinnt	gewann		gewonnen hat
...				

Ackerman and Webelhuth (1998) propose that the main verb is the basis for the predicate with accompanying elements selected by means of features such as "AUX". This, however, is at odds with standard HPSG assumptions about the governor–governee relationships holding in such constructions, for instance the fact that the auxiliaries determine the particular form of a main verb, but not the other way round. If the auxiliary is considered the governor, then this situation is fully in line with other head–dependent relationships, such as prepositions governing particular cases on their NP complements.

Despite these implementational differences, however, the thrust of Ackerman and Webelhuth's (1998) idea can be preserved if we assume that a predicate in its periphrastic realization is the domain of a common argument structure list (ARG-ST). That is, in addition to linkages among its parts that are based on valence, the integrity of a predicate is manifested in terms of a common argument structure shared among all of its parts. This is achieved first by assuming that – in valence-preserving cases – the governing element has the same ARG-ST value as its governee (i.e., 1), as shown in (33):

(33)

$$
\begin{bmatrix}
\text{ARG-ST} \boxed{1} \\
\text{SUBCAT} \boxed{2} \\
\text{VCOMPL} \left\langle \begin{array}{c} \text{V} \\ \begin{bmatrix} \text{ARG-ST} \boxed{1} \\ \text{SUBCAT} \boxed{2} \end{bmatrix} \end{array} \right\rangle
\end{bmatrix}
$$

Valence information continues to be shared between governee and governor (here: $\boxed{2}$). If there is no extraction from a verb cluster, ARG-ST and SUBCAT are identical at the lexical level, but, as we will see below, they crucially do not always have to be.

Second, I follow Przepiórkowski (2001) in assuming that the argument structure of the phrasal mother is the same as that of the head, as shown in (34).[15] (For ease of readability, I will from now on abbreviate " $\left[\text{ARG-ST} \langle ... \rangle \right]$ " as " $\langle\langle ... \rangle\rangle$ ".)

(34)

$$
\text{V} \left[\boxed{1} \langle\langle ... \rangle\rangle \right]
$$

governee
$\text{V} \left[\langle\langle ... \rangle\rangle \right]$

governor/head
$\text{V} \left[\boxed{1} \langle\langle ... \rangle\rangle \right]$

As a result, we obtain the following analysis for the structure in (2b) above:

(35)

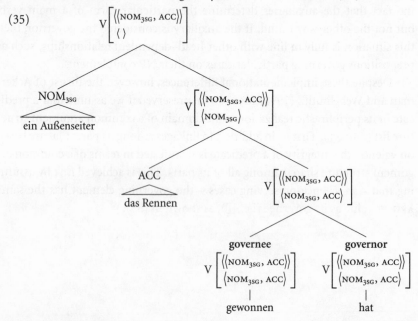

Once the various elements of a predicate are seen as linked via argument sharing, a new perspective on subjects in fronted VPs becomes available. Such constructions can now be understood as involving a single predicate (e.g., *gewonnen hat*). Rather than being contained in a single constituent, as in (35), they
occur discontinuously in structures such as (18), repeated here:

(18) [Ein Außenseiter **gewonnen**] **hat** hier noch nie.
      an outsider   won   has here still never
      'No outsider has yet won here.'

In (35), the finite exponent of this predicate is directly involved in nominative
case marking and subject agreement. In the discontinuous case, by comparison, case marking and agreement is mediated by the nonfinite exponent (i.e.,
the participle *gewonnen*).

Applied to the problem of subjects in fronted VPs, this yields the analysis
outlined in (36), in which the two elements of the periphrastic predicate occur
in boldface:

(36)

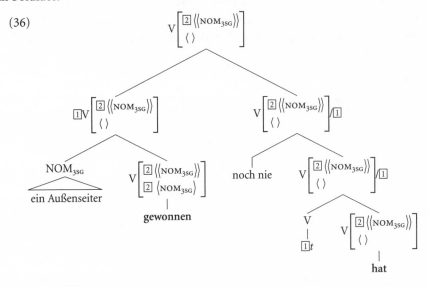

In the lexical representation for the main verb *gewonnen*, the ARG-ST value is
identical with its valence list(s), indicated by means of ②. The main verb combines with its sole dependent inside the fronted verbal projection, saturating its
valence requirement. While there is no phrasal element on the valence list(s) of
the finite auxiliary *hat*, it does have a nonempty ARG-ST list, which is identical
to that of its gapped governee (②). Thus, while in both (35) and (36), the argument structure of the governor is identical to that of the governee, only in (35)

does the governor inherit all of the valence elements of the governee. In (36), only those are inherited by the governor (from the gap of the fronted phrase) that have not already been cancelled within the fronted phrase – in this case, this means an empty list of dependents inherited from the main verb part.

If we assume that case and agreement properties of a finite element are linked to the first element on its ARG-ST list, then the singular marking on *hat* is immediately predicted, as is the nominative case marking on the non-locally realized NP *ein Außenseiter*.[16] This is straightforwardly achieved if case marking is seen not as a constraint on valence representations, but instead of argument structure, as is shown in (37):[17]

(37)
$$
\begin{bmatrix} \text{V[FINITE]} \\ \langle\langle \text{ NP[STR]}, ...\rangle\rangle \end{bmatrix} \rightarrow \begin{bmatrix} \langle\langle \text{ NP[NOM]}, ...\rangle\rangle \end{bmatrix}
$$

As a first prediction of our analysis, we expect that the "communication" of the finite governor with the phrase-internal subject should in principle be able to "pass through" multiple levels of embedding. This is indeed what we find. In (38), we see that the future tense auxiliary *wird* agrees with the subject *ein Außenseiter*, even though it is a dependent of a governee of *können* (cf. also Meurers 1999c: 184).[18]

(38) a. [Ein Außenseiter gewinnen] wird hier nie   können.
         an outsider   win   will here never can
         'No outsider will ever be able to win here.'

     b.

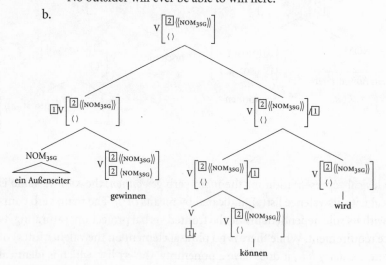

As before, it is the shared argument structure (②) uniting all components of the complex predicate *gewinnen können wird*, which makes this possible. Once case assignment (and agreement) are understood as constraints on ARG-ST, the observed facts fall out without any further stipulation. Thus the analysis proposed here shares with Meurers' solution the idea that information about internal composition needs to remain accessible phrase-externally. However, it approaches the problem from a very different conceptual angle. Instead of seeing the behavior of phrase-internal subjects as a special case that requires modification of the fundamental notion of valence saturation, we can understand it as the result of the convergence of independently justified assumptions about syntactic composition: Przepiórkowski's projectivity of ARG-ST lists and and Ackerman and Webelhuth's conception of "predicate" as a unit in syntactic description.

6.3 Valence increasing environments

The same proposal can be straightforwardly extended to valence increasing environments, such as embeddings under AcI verbs (*accusativus cum infinitivo*, essentially object-raising verbs) such as *sehen*, as seen in the following example from Meurers (1999a: 293):

(39) [Den Kanzler/*der Kanzler   tanzen] sah Oskar.
      the Chancellor.ACC/the Chancellor.NOM dance saw Oskar
      'Oskar saw the Chancellor dance.'

The problem posed by these constructions is quite similar to the ones seen earlier, except that here it is the accusative case on *den Kanzler* which cannot be predicted on the basis of information that is locally available within the fronted phrase.

Since we think of the argument structure of a predicate as being projected from its syntactic head, all that is required to account for such examples is a proper understanding of the ARG-ST properties of valence-increasing heads such as *sehen*. In the valence-preserving case discussed earlier, this entails total identity in ARG-ST values across governor and governee. In valence-increasing cases, the two are linked only by partial identity, outlined in (40), where "⊕" stands for list concatenation:

(40)

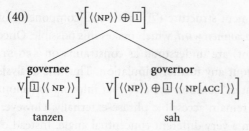

As a result, the subject requirement of *tanzen* is now linked to the second element of *sah*'s ARG-ST list. As the second (structurally case-marked) element on the ARG-ST list of the finite verb *sah*, that NP is marked with accusative case, rather than nominative case, as in the valence-preserving cases seen earlier.

(41)

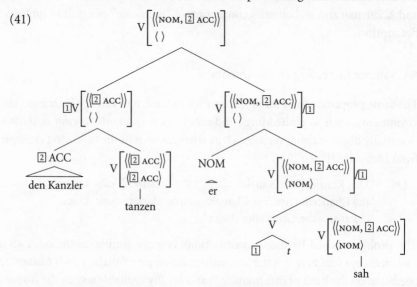

In order to ensure that the fronted NP correctly be marked with accusative case, we only need to change the valence-based constraint from (5b) to one that is based on ARG-ST information, as shown in (42).[19]

(42)
$$\begin{bmatrix} \text{V} \\ \langle\langle \text{NP[STR], NP[STR]} ...\rangle\rangle \end{bmatrix} \rightarrow \begin{bmatrix} \langle\langle \text{NP[STR], NP[ACC]}, ...\rangle\rangle \end{bmatrix}$$

A further illustration of a valence-increasing environment is given in (43), where a transitive predicate (*reparieren*) occurs in the fronted phrase, together with its object and notional subject *den Mechaniker*. That NP also occurs as the second element on the argument composing predicate *lassen*. Due to the constraint in (42), that phrase is marked with accusative case.

(43)   a.   [Den Mechaniker   den Wagen reparieren] ließ der Lehrer
            the mechanic.ACC the car.ACC repair   let   the teacher.NOM

oft.
often
'The teacher often had the mechanic fix the car.'

b.

$$V\left[\begin{matrix}\langle\langle\text{NOM}, \boxed{2}\,\text{ACC}, \text{ACC}\rangle\rangle \\ \langle\,\rangle\end{matrix}\right]$$

$$\boxed{1}V\left[\begin{matrix}\langle\langle\boxed{2}\,\text{ACC}, \text{ACC}\rangle\rangle \\ \langle\,\rangle\end{matrix}\right] \qquad V\left[\begin{matrix}\langle\langle\text{NOM}, \boxed{2}\,\text{ACC}, \text{ACC}\rangle\rangle \\ \langle\,\rangle\end{matrix}\right]/\boxed{1}$$

$$\boxed{2}\,\text{ACC} \qquad \boxed{1}V\left[\begin{matrix}\langle\langle\boxed{2}\,\text{ACC}, \text{ACC}\rangle\rangle \\ \langle\boxed{2}\,\text{ACC}\rangle\end{matrix}\right] \qquad \text{NOM} \qquad V\left[\begin{matrix}\langle\langle\text{NOM}, \boxed{2}\,\text{ACC}, \text{ACC}\rangle\rangle \\ \langle\text{NOM}\rangle\end{matrix}\right]/\boxed{1}$$

den Mechaniker   der Lehrer

$$\text{ACC} \qquad V\left[\begin{matrix}\langle\langle\boxed{2}\,\text{ACC}, \text{ACC}\rangle\rangle \\ \langle\boxed{2}\,\text{ACC}, \text{ACC}\rangle\end{matrix}\right] \qquad\qquad V \qquad V\left[\begin{matrix}\langle\langle\text{NOM}, \boxed{2}\,\text{ACC}, \text{ACC}\rangle\rangle \\ \langle\text{NOM}\rangle\end{matrix}\right]$$

den Wagen $\boxed{1}$ t

reparieren   ließ

A further direct consequence of our approach is that, in order for a phrase to occur in a fronted phrase, it has to be a dependent of the fronted verb. As a result, if an argument-raising predicate introduces phrasal dependents of its own (as for instance *versprechen* 'promise', which takes an optional dative argument), then that dependent cannot be part of the fronted phrase. This is illustrated in (44).

(44)   a.   daß er   ihr   den Wagen zu reparieren versprochen hat.
            that he   her the car   to repair   promised   has
            'that he promised her that he would fix the car.'

       b.   [Den Wagen zu reparieren] hat er   ihr   nie   versprochen.
            the car   to repair   has he   her never promised
            'He never promised her that he would fix the car.'

       c.   *[Ihr den Wagen zu reparieren] hat er   nie   versprochen.
            her   the car   to repair   has he   never promised

To conclude, the current proposal is both conceptually and technically simpler than Meurers' account in terms of raising spirits. In addition, it also immediately accounts for some of the constraints on the phrasal dependents that can occur in fronted verbal constituents. In the final section, I wish to briefly consider another construction in which nominative elements cooccur with nonfinite verbs without the mediation of the finite element.

6.4 An exceptional construction

Verbs such as *anfangen* ('begin') can occur either in so-called "coherent" and "incoherent" constructions. The first, shown in (45a), is generally treated as on a par with verb cluster construction involving auxiliaries, seen above in (2b), see, e.g., Kiss (1995). The second, shown in (45b) involves a dependent VP, which in turn occurs after the verbal complex in *Nachfeld* position.[20]

(45) a. daß der Mond zu scheinen anfing.
          that the moon to shine   began
          'that the moon began to shine.'
      b. daß der Mond anfing [zu scheinen].
          that the moon began   to shine
          'that the moon began to shine.'

Meurers (199a: 291) observes that, in addition to the constructions above, *anfangen* may also cooccur with a postposed verbal projection that contains a nominative subject, as illustrated in (46):

(46) obwohl   damals anfing [der Mond   zu scheinen].
      although then   began   the moon.NOM   to shine
      'although the moon began to shine then.'

This construction type thus constitutes the mirror image of the preposed subject+V phrases discussed earlier.

Meurers does not discuss the range of possibilities further and I find such cases are slightly marginal in comparison to the fronted partial VPs containing subjects.[21] Nonetheless, I would like to offer a very simple way of accommodating such cases within the approach pursued here. First, in (47), I present the lexical description for *anfangen* as a VP-embedding predicate, as it occurs in (45b) above.

(47) *anfing* (VP-embedding)

a.

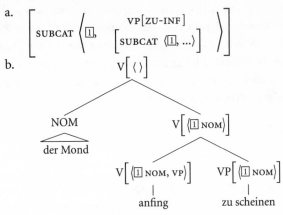

b.

Turning now to the description that is responsible for the unexpected construction in (45) above, it seems that such cases involve the verb taking a fully saturated ("clausal") verbal projection ([SUBCAT ⟨ ⟩]) whose ARG-ST list is shared with that of clausal dependent. Since the subject of the clausal dependent (*der Mond* in (46)) is now also the subject of the finite predicate *anfing*, nominative case marking on *der Mond* and agreement between *anfing* and *der Mond* are correctly accounted for, as illustrated in (48):

(48) *anfing* (clause-embedding)

a.

b.

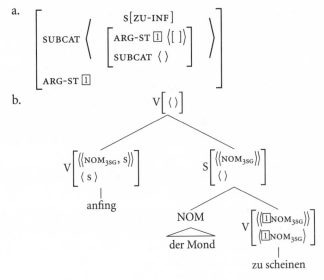

To be sure, the account developed earlier for subjects occurring in fronted verbal phrases does not immediately lead us to expect that sentences such as (46) should be possible as well.[22] Given that the acceptability of (46) is somewhat marginal, this probably is a desired result. Whatever the proper understanding of the constraints exhibited by such constructions, the present proposal provides the proper tools to account for the linkage between phrase-internal subject and the finite matrix predicate.

7.   Summary and final remarks

The proposal advanced in this study may appear at first sight to be just a technical variation of Meurers' original proposal for phrase-internal fronted subjects – specifically the idea that information about the internal dependents of the fronted phrase need to become part of the informational content represented on the fronted phrase itself. However, as I have argued above, this result is achieved here in a way that ties a number of strands in recent research together in a natural way. The first is the idea that information about argument structure needs to be projected to the phrasal level, as argued by Przepiórkowski and further supported here on the basis of evidence from ergative languages. The second is the idea that multiple predicate constructions may be linked by a common argument structure, which allows us to give content to Ackerman and Webelhuth's idea of "predicate" as a unit of syntactic description above the word level.

As a result, we were able to solve the puzzle of how to get the finite auxiliary to agree with and assign nominative to the subject in the fronted constituent. In fact under the present proposal, the required dependencies fall out for free, as the nonfinite fronted verb and the finite auxiliary are really, in a sense, different lexical exponents of the same predicate. Unlike in the case of Meurers' analysis, these results could be achieved without changing the fundamental saturation-driven character of syntactic combination in HPSG.

One of the consequences of this proposal, which does not come out as clearly in Meurers' approach is the fact that any approach to syntax that is entirely driven by saturation appears to be inadequate to deal with the data discussed here. For instance, early HPSG (Pollard & Sag 1987) or standard Categorial Grammar appear to supply no means for recording subject-related information on the fronted constituent.

In fact, some may think that the present proposal is too unconstrained in making phrase-internal information "visible" to phrase-external elements. In particular, our proposal may have the drawback of not ruling out a number of potential selection relations that become available once phrases contain a record of their internal composition in the form of the ARG-ST list. This is indeed a valid concern and I wish to address it in a somewhat new way. While previously the notion of restrictiveness has been thought of entirely in terms of the grammatical relations that are or are not projected to the phrase level, another possibility is to restrict ARG-ST projection to **nonfinite** environments. That is, only nonfinite heads project their ARG-ST information, while ARG-ST is not an appropriate attribute for finite phrases. Under such a proposal, the analysis in (36) would instead be as shown in (49):

(49)

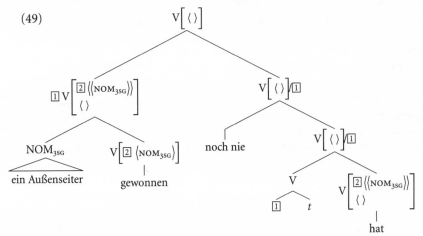

Moreover, the analysis in (41) above would instead be as follows:

(50)

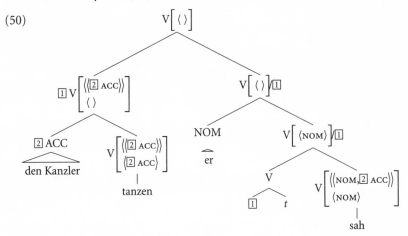

Such a move would severely limit the kinds of selectional possibilities involving dependents within finite clauses. I will leave it for further study to determine whether this proposal makes the right predictions concerning the locality of dependent information in finite contexts.[23]

Notes

* A shortened version of this paper was presented at the Eighth International Conference on HPSG in Seoul, Korea (August, 2002). I would like to thank the audience, in particular Ivan Sag as well as Stefan Müller for helpful discussion and comments.

1. In much recent HPSG work, valence is separated into SUBJ(ECT) and COMP(LEMENT)s requirements. This distinction is largely immaterial for our purposes. Also, as a matter of expository convenience, I often use simple case labels as abbreviations for case-marked NPs (i.e., NOM = NP[nom]).

2. Within the recent HPSG literature, the selection of elements within the verbal cluster is often handled by means of the same selectional feature as that of phrasal arguments, that is, SUBCAT(EGORIZATION) or COMP(LEMENT)s. While this choice is not important for the purposes here, I refer the interested reader to Kathol (1998: 230ff.) for a justification for distinguishing the combinatorial mechanisms operative in verbal clusters from those of regular phrasal combinations.

3. In formally slightly more precise terms, this constraint can be stated as follows:

(i)   a.
$$\left[\begin{array}{l} \text{HEAD} \mid \text{VFORM } \textit{finite} \\ \text{SUBCAT } \langle \text{NP[STR]}, ... \rangle \end{array} \right] \rightarrow \left[\text{SUBCAT } \langle \text{NP[NOM]}, ... \rangle \right]$$

   b.
$$\left[\begin{array}{l} \text{HEAD } \textit{verb} \\ \text{SUBCAT } \langle \, [\ ], \text{NP[STR]} ... \rangle \end{array} \right] \rightarrow \left[\text{SUBCAT } \langle \, [\ ], \text{NP[ACC]}, ... \rangle \right]$$

The reason that the constraints in (ib) and (ab) do not mention finite verbs is that accusative case occurs both in finite and nonfinite environments such as VP complements, as shown in (ii):

(ii)   Hugo versucht [den Wagen zu waschen]
       Hugo tries   the car.ACC to wash
       'Hugo tries to wash the car.'

Nominative case, on the other hand, always requires a finite predicate (at least in clausal contexts). As we will see below, however, finite expressions may sometimes not occur as part of the same phrase as the subject.

4. The topological indices used in this study are hence (in part) inspired by the terms used in the traditional literature: *vf*: *Vorfeld* ('initial field'); *cf*: *Comp/Finite, linke Satzklammer* ('left sentence bracket'); *mf*: *Mittelfeld* ('middle field'); *vc*: *verb cluster, rechte Satzklammer* ('right sentence bracket'); and *nf*: *Nachfeld* ('final field').

5. The basic constraint for ordering within the verb cluster in this example is that governors generally follow governees in German. See Kathol (1998) for extensive discussion of more complicated ordering possibilities in both German and Dutch.

6. The actual implementation of this constraint is somewhat more complex. See Kathol (2000).

7. In Grewendorf (1988:300), this problem is referred to as "inkonsistente Strukturzuweisung" ('inconsistent assignment of structure').

8. The use of a trace ("*t*") in (16) is entirely for expository convenience. Everything is fully compatible with a traceless implementation along the lines suggested by, for instance, Sag and Fodor (1994).

9. Thus, the present approach differs from the one of Hinrichs and Nakazawa (1999:284–292), which assumes that unrealized arguments within the fronted phrase are linked to their realization site by means of a filler-gap dependency. While Hinrichs and Nakazawa's analysis requires the existence of gap information within gaps, the present analysis avoids such recursive gap structures.

Also, to the extent that alternative groupings of the verbal head with its dependents are possible, as for instance in (i), I assume that these are due to different orders on the valence list:

(i)   [Seiner Tochter   erzählen]   wird er ein Märchen.
      his daughter.DAT tell   will he a fairy tale.ACC
      'He will tell his daughter a fairy tale.'

For additional discussion on this point, see Kathol (2000:240–243).

10. Here, I assume that combinations such as *gewinnen dürfen* in (6b) are marked as [LEX +]. Thus, a positive marking for LEX may be more appropriately read as "not having combined with phrasal dependents". See Kathol (1998:225ff.) for more discussion of this point.

11. Grewendorf (1988:295) credits unpublished work by Haider and Tappe from 1982 as being the first to point out such structures.

12. See also Melnik (2002) for a related proposal that approaches inversion constructions in Modern Hebrew from the perspective of judgment type, rather than, e.g., unaccusativity.

13. Technically, this is achieved by means of a relational constraint that maps representations containing a LOCAL value of type *unrealized* into one that is of type *realized* (cf. Meurers 1999a:200).

14. Or SUBJ/COMPS, cf. Note 1 above.

15. In (34), the argument structure of the governee is not explicitly identified with that of the governor, unlike in (33). This is because we will soon need to accommodate valence-increasing governors, whose ARG-ST list is only partially identical to that of their governee, cf. Section 6.3 below.

16. A move along these lines also allows us to accommodate the case of fronted verbal constituents with stimulus nominative dependents, repeated here:

(20) b.   [Ein Fehler unterlaufen] ist ihr noch nie.
           a mistake happen   is her still never
           'She never had a mistake happening to her.'

The nominative element is the first on the ARG-ST list and therefore triggers agreement with the verb. In terms of valence, however, it appears to be a more oblique dependent, which is captured in (i) by means of a misalignment between argument structure and valence:

(i)   *unterlaufen*

$$
\begin{bmatrix}
\text{V}[\text{FINITE}] \\
\langle\langle\, \text{NP}[\text{STR}]_i,\, \text{NP}[\text{DAT}]_j\,\rangle\rangle \\
\langle\, \text{NP}[\text{DAT}]_j\; \text{NP}[\text{STR}]_i\,\rangle
\end{bmatrix}
$$

The stimulus nominative subject, by virtue of occurring non-initially on the SUBCAT list, combines with the verb before the stimulus dative dependent (here: *ihm*) does. As a result, the dative has to occur in the *Mittelfeld*. In fact, we would expect that the opposite order of occurrence is not possible, which appears to be borne out by the unacceptability of examples such as (ii).

(ii) *[Einem Profi unterlaufen] ist dieser Fehler   noch nie.
       a pro.DAT   happen   is this mistake.NOM still never
       Intended: 'A pro has never had such a mistake happening to him.'

However, native speaker judgments do not appear to be uniform on this issue.

17. The reader is reminded that [⟨⟨ ... ⟩⟩] abbreviates [ARG-ST ⟨ ... ⟩]. A more formally precise rendition of the constraint in (37) is as follows:

(i)
$$
\begin{bmatrix}
\text{HEAD} \mid \text{VFORM}\; \textit{finite} \\
\text{ARG-ST}\; \langle\, \text{NP}[\text{STR}],\, ...\rangle
\end{bmatrix}
\rightarrow
\begin{bmatrix}
\text{ARG-ST}\; \langle\, \text{NP}[\text{NOM}],\, ...\rangle
\end{bmatrix}
$$

See also Przepiórkowski (1999a) for a very similar idea.

18. Of course, there is nothing in our analysis that would prevent the fronted verbal constituent from containing a more complex verbal cluster. As the grammaticality of (i) shows, this prediction is correct.

(i)   [Ein Außenseiter gewinnen können] wird hier nie.
       an outsider   win   can   will here never
       'No outsider will ever be able to win here.'

19. Again, the more formally precise version of this constraint is as follows:

(i)
$$
\begin{bmatrix}
\text{HEAD}\; \textit{verb} \\
\text{ARG-ST}\; \langle\, \text{NP}[\text{STR}],\, \text{NP}[\text{STR}]\, ...\rangle
\end{bmatrix}
\rightarrow
\begin{bmatrix}
\text{ARG-ST}\; \langle\, \text{NP}[\text{STR}],\, \text{NP}[\text{ACC}],\, ...\rangle
\end{bmatrix}
$$

20. There are well-known complications arising in the form of the "Third Construction", which I will ignore here. See Kathol (2000: 243–250) and Hinrichs and Nakazawa (1998), among others, for some discussion.

21. In particular, it seems that there is quite a strong requirement that predicates occurring in such constructions take non-agentive subjects, cf. the ungrammaticality of the examples in (i):

(i)　a.　*weil　　anfing,　[ein Außenseiter　zu gewinnen].
　　　　because　began　　an outsider　　　　to win
　　　b.　*weil　　anfing,　[ein Kind　zu lachen].
　　　　because　began　　a child　　to laugh

22. This is a property shared by Meurers' raising spirits account.

23. There is some evidence suggesting that, at least in English, subject information must be projected to the clausal level in finite contexts. However, in proposals such as Bender and Flickinger (1999), this has been achieved by accessing the verb's agreement information by means of Kathol's (1999) AGR head feature. This still leaves as an open question whether selectional dependencies ever require access to nonsubject dependents of finite clauses.

CHAPTER 6

Dutch and German verb constructions in Performance Grammar

Gerard Kempen and Karin Harbusch

Psychology, Leiden University & Max Planck Institute for
Psycholinguistics, Nijmegen / Computational Linguistics, University of
Koblenz-Landau

o. Introduction

Within the psycholinguistically motivated syntactic framework of *Performance Grammar*, we develop a linearization model that we claim captures a broad range of linear order phenomena in Dutch and German clauses, including the verb constructions focused in this volume. In Section 1, we lay out the essentials of Performance Grammar (PG hereafter). Sections 2 and 3 are devoted to the PG treatment of verb constructions in Dutch and German respectively. In Section 4, we draw some conclusions.

1. Essentials of Performance Grammar

Performance Grammar (Kempen & Harbusch 2002; Harbusch & Kempen 2002)[1] consists of separate components generating, respectively, the hierarchical and the linear structure of sentences.[2] Hierarchical structures in PG are unordered trees ('mobiles') composed out of elementary building blocks called *lexical frames*. Every lexical entry (*lemma*) in the *Mental Lexicon* has associated with it a lexical frame encoding its information concerning word class (part of speech), subcategorization features, and morphological diacritics (person, gender, case, etc.). Lexical frames are retrieved from the Lexicon by a *lexicalizer* in response to a conceptual 'message' (during language production) or to a word string (during language perception). Associated with every lexical frame is a one-dimensional array called *topology*, which specifies a fixed number of positions (or *slots*, *landing sites*) where segments (branches, constituents) of lexical frames can be stored in left-to-right order. The segments stored in a topology may include constituents originating from a lexical frame lower in the hierarchy. As we will see below, this happens without affecting the frame hierarchy.

In this section, we discuss the hierarchical and linear grammar components in turn. For the empirical psycholinguistic arguments in support of the separation between hierarchical and linear structure we refer to Kempen and Harbusch (2002).

1.1   Hierarchical structures in Performance Grammar

PG's hierarchical component generates unordered trees by combining 3-tiered 'mobiles' called lexical frames. Figure 1 shows the eight lexical frames expressing how each of the words in Dutch example (1) is used.[3]

(1)   *Denk   je,   dat   hij   de   auto   gerepareerd   heeft?*
        Think you   that   he   the car   repaired   has
        'Do you think that he has repaired the car?'

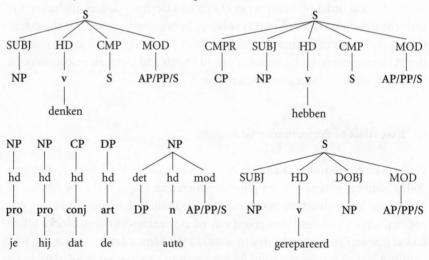

Figure 1. Simplified lexical frames underlying the eight words of sentence (1). Left-to-right order of branches is arbitrary. The basic shape of lexical frames is retrievable from the Mental Lexicon in response to contents of the to-be-expressed conceptual message; however, certain branches (e.g. CMPR) are added as a consequence of local syntactic constraints (CMPR = CoMPlementizeR; CP = Complementizer Phrase).

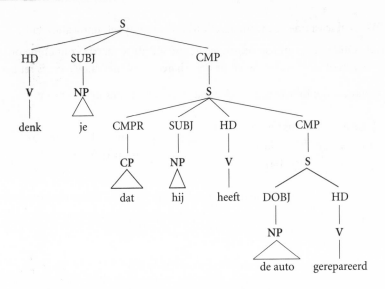

Figure 2. Verb frame hierarchy underlying example (1). The root S-node of the verb frame associated with *heeft* and the CoMPlement S-node of *denk* have merged as a result of substitution, and so have the S-CMP of *heeft* and the root S-node dominating *gerepareerd*. Left-to-right order of branches is arbitrary.

The top layer of a frame consists of a single *phrasal node* (the 'root'; e.g. S, NP, DP, CP), which is connected to one or more *functional nodes* in the second layer (e.g., SUBJect, HeaD, Direct OBJect, CoMPlement, PREDicate, MODifier). At most one exemplar of a functional node is allowed in the same frame, except for MOD nodes, which may occur zero or more times. Every functional node dominates exactly one phrasal node ('foot') in the third layer, except for H(ea)D which immediately dominates a lexical (part of speech) node. Each lexical frame is 'anchored' to exactly one lexical item, which is printed below the categorial node serving as the frame's HeaD.

Lexical frames are combined to form larger mobiles by a *substitution* operation which replaces phrasal foot nodes by lexical frames. More precisely, substitution involves a simple, non-recursive form of unification called *feature unification,* and merges the root of one frame with one phrasal foot of another frame (Figure 2). Unification of two feature matrices proceeds as follows:

(A) For each attribute shared by the two matrices, take the value sets, compute their intersection, and delete the members that do not belong to the intersection. (Attributes occurring in one matrix only will not be affected.)

(B)   If at least one of the intersections is the empty set, unification fails.

(C)   Otherwise, unification succeeds, and a feature matrix containing one token of each of the shared or non-shared attribute-value pairs is returned.

For instance, the following matrices have two attributes in common:

$$\begin{bmatrix} \text{case} = \{\text{nominative, accusative}\} \\ \text{number} = \{\text{singular}\} \\ \text{person} = \{\text{3rd, 1st}\} \end{bmatrix} \quad \begin{bmatrix} \text{person} = \{\text{1st, 2nd, 3rd}\} \\ \text{case} = \{\text{nominative}\} \end{bmatrix}$$

The intersections of these disjunctive value sets are {1st, 3rd} and {nominative} respectively. Since none of these sets is empty, unification succeeds and the following matrix is returned:

$$\begin{bmatrix} \text{case} = \{\text{nominative}\} \\ \text{number} = \{\text{singular}\} \\ \text{person} = \{\text{3rd, 1st}\} \end{bmatrix}$$

It follows that if a feature matrix contains at least one feature whose value set is empty, it cannot successfully unify with any other feature matrix. In Sections 2 and 3 below we introduce order-related features and apply unification as a mechanism for assigning constituents to positions in a linear structure.

Unification uses the lexical frame as its domain of locality and serves, among other things, to select the value of agreement features (e.g. entailing second person singular *denk* of the verb *denken*; agreement features are not shown in the figure). Unification operates on features stored in the *feature matrix* that is associated with every categorial node (i.e., lexical or phrasal node). Such a matrix is a set of pairs, each consisting of an attribute and a finite set of values. Features are instantiated with a non-empty value set. An attribute is a character string (e.g., "gender", "person", "number"). A value set contains a non-zero finite number of character strings (e.g., {sing}, {1st, 2nd, 3rd}), each representing a possible value of the attribute (disjunctive value sets).

1.2   Linear structure in PG

In order to assign a left-to-right position to the branches of lexical frames, we introduce an additional type of data structure. Associated with every lexical frame is a *topology*, a one-dimensional array specifying a fixed number of positions (or *slots*, *landing sites*) for its constituents. The topology of a verb frame (i.e., of a finite or non-finite clause) allocates storage space for each of vari-

Fore-field			Midfield				Endfield	
F1	M1	M2	M3	M4	M5	M6	E1	E2

Figure 3. Slot labels used in topologies for Dutch and German clauses.

F1	M1	M2	M3	M4	M5	M6	E1	E2
	denk	je						•

⇑

	M1	M2	M3			M6		
	dat	hij	de auto			repareert		

Figure 4. Linearization of example (2). The dashed slots of the embedded topology denotes 'topology sharing', to be discussed below.

ous grammatical functions that can be fulfilled by its constituents, e.g., to the HeaD verb, to the SUBJect NP, the Direct OBJect NP, etc. The topology that we use for Dutch and German clauses specifies nine different slots, labeled as indicated in Figure 3.

Table 1 illustrates which clause constituents select which slots as their landing sites. Constituents may select different positions depending on their shape. For instance, if the Direct OBJect role is fulfilled by a Wh-phrase, it will end up in the Forefield of the clause rather than in the Midfield. A CoMPlement clause will land in slot E2 if it is finite; non-finite CoMPlements have several additional placement options.

We show linearization at work on sentence (2), an abbreviated version of (1). As we assume that every lexical item launches its own lexical frame and topology, a sentence containing more than one verb instantiates several clausal topologies. This applies to verbs of any type, whether main, auxiliary or copula. It follows that sentence (2) needs two topologies (Figure 4).

(2) *Denk je   dat hij de   auto repareert?*
     think you that he the car repairs
     'Do you think that he repairs the car?'

Slot F1 of the interrogative main clause remains empty in the absence of a Wh-constituent. The pronominal Subject NPs of the main and the subordinate clause go to slot M2 of their respective topologies. The HeaD verb selects slot M1 in the main clause, and M6 in the CoMPlement. The CoMPlementizeR *dat* goes to M1 of the CoMPlement's topology. Finally, the root S-node domi-

Table 1. Examples of topology slot selection rules (Dutch and German clauses). Precedence between constituents landing in the same slot is marked by "≪". The details of the placement of HeaD verbs, CoMPlement clauses, and PaRTicles are explained in Sections 2 and 3.

Slot	Filler
F1	*Declarative main clause*: SUBJect, Topic or Focus (one constituent only) *Interrogative clause*: Wh-constituent, including Du. *of* and Ger. *ob* 'whether' *Complement clause*: Wh-constituent
M1	*Main clause:* HeaD verb *Complement clause*: CoMPLementizeR *dat/om* (Du.) and *dass* (Ger.) 'that'
M2	Subject NP (iff non-Wh), Direct Object (iff personal pronoun)
M3	Indirect OBJect (iff non-Wh) ≪ Direct OBJect (iff non-Wh and non-pers.pro.)
M4	PaRTicle (Du. only)
M5	Non-finite CoMPlement of Verb Raiser
M6	*Subordinate clause*; Du.: Pre-INFinitive *te* 'to' ≪ HeaD verb Ger.: PaRTicle ≪ Pre-INFinitive *zu* 'to' ≪ HeaD
E1	Non-finite Complement of Verb Raiser (Du. only)
E2	Non-finite CoMP of VP Extraposition verb Finite Complement

nating the finite CoMPlement clause lands in E2, as indicated by the bullet and upward double arrow.

In case of more than one verb, the topologies associated with them are allowed to *share* certain identically labeled slots, conditionally upon several restrictions. *After two slots have been shared, they are no longer distinguishable; in fact, they are the same object.* In example (2), the embedded topology shares its F1 and E2 slots with their namesakes in the matrix topology. This is indicated by the dashed border of the two bottom slots.

Now consider example (3), where the Direct OBJect of *repareert* is a Wh-phrase (*welke auto* 'which car'). This constituent lands in the shared F1 slot: see Figure 5. As a consequence, the Wh-phrase gets 'fronted' and seems to have been 'extracted' from the complement. This behavior, caused by *lateral topology sharing* manifests itself as upward movement of constituents in shared slots. We will call this effect *promotion*. In the topology diagrams, promotion is indicated by an upward single arrow, and a bullet located at the landing site of the promoted constituent.

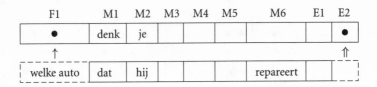

Figure 5. Linearization of example (3).

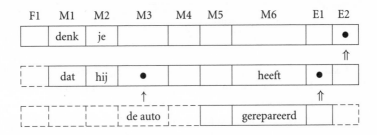

Figure 6. Linearization of example (1).

(3)   *Welke auto denk je dat hij repareert?*
      'Which car do you think that he repairs?'

Example (1) embodies a more radical case of cross-clause topology sharing. The topologies associated with *heeft* and *gerepareerd* share the entire region extending from F1 through M4. The result is promotion of Direct OBJect *de auto*, as shown in Figure 6.

The overt constituent order of a sentence is determined by a *Read-out module* that traverses the hierarchy of topologies in depth-first, left-to-right manner, scanning shared slots only once. Any lexical item it 'sees' in a slot, is appended to the output string. E.g., *welke auto* in example (3) is seen while the Reader scans the matrix topology rather than during its traversal of the embedded topology. Consider the artificial example of lateral topology sharing in Figure 7. The uppermost clause shares lateral (peripheral) slots at, respectively, positions P1 and P5 of its topology with its downstairs neighbor. The lower topology has landed in slot P2 to the right of item *A*. The Read-out module first processes item *a* at P1 and *A* at P2, then proceeds to the non-shared region P2 through P4 of the lower topology, and outputs the sequence *bcd*. Having reached shared slot P5 it returns to slot P2 of the upper topology and processes there the remaining slots P3 through P5, which yields the sequence *Be*. The resulting string is *aAbcdBe* (cf. lower panel of Figure 7).

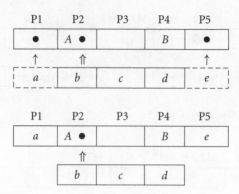

Figure 7. Read-out of topologies in case of lateral topology sharing. *Upper panel*: P1 through P5 are labels of the slots in both the upper and lower topology. Shared slots are indicated by dashed rectangles. Bullets above single arrows represent the position of items that have been 'promoted' into the upper topology. The double arrow points to the landing site of the non-shared region of the topology at its tail. *Lower panel*: The shared slots P1 and P5 of the embedded topology have not been drawn because they are the same objects as slots P1 and P5, respectively, of the governor's topology. Therefore, items *a* and *e* are 'seen' during read-out of the matrix topology. The output sequence reads *aAbcdBe*.

We postulate that cross-clause lateral topology sharing in Dutch and German is subject to the restrictions in (4) below. The combination of constraints (4b) and (4c) implies that topology sharing may divide a clausal topology into three parts, as follows:

–   a left-peripheral shared region up to but not including the position of the HeaD verb,
–   a non-shared region including at least the position assigned to the HeaD verb, and
–   a right-peripheral shared region.

The two shared peripheral regions will be called "lateral", the non-shared region "central". (Notice that the central region need not coincide with the Midfield; actually, in most cases they are different.)

(4)   *General Constraints on cross-clause lateral topology sharing in Dutch and German*

   a.   A verb frame can left-peripherally share part of its clausal topology with that of another verb frame only if they are located at adjacent levels of the verb frame hierarchy.

b.   Only lateral (i.e., left- and right-peripheral) regions of a topology are sharable.

c.   The HeaD of a lexical frame, i.e. the verb, does not participate in topology sharing: it cannot be promoted outside of its own topology, nor can the slot serving as its landing site be the promotion target of any constituent from a lower topology.

Whether or not two clausal topologies share some lateral region(s), and which slots will be affected, depends on a *language-specific cross-clause lateral topology sharing rule*. The topology sharing rules for Dutch and German are shown in Table 2. The variables *LS* and *RS* stand for, respectively, the number of left- and right-peripheral slots that the complement clause shares with the topology of its governor. For instance, the first row of the Table indicates that if a Dutch or German complement clause is interrogative, it shares no slots with its upstairs neighbor. The last row deals with declarative non-finite complements of Verb Raisers (auxiliaries in particular; see beginning of Section 2): In both Dutch and German, the right-peripherally shared area includes one slot only, i.e. E2. The left-peripherally shared areas in the two languages differ: In German it covers five slots (F1 through M4); in Dutch it varies optionally between four (F1 through M3) and six (F1 through M5). Figure 4 and Figure 5 above illustrate sharing of the F1 slot of a finite declarative complement clause.[4] Figure 6 shows sharing of the entire left-peripheral region F1 through M4, due to the fact that *de auto gerepareerd* is the declarative non-finite complement of the auxiliary *heeft* 'has'.

Table 2. Size of the left- and right-peripheral shared topology areas (*LS* and *RS*) in diverse complement constructions. Numbers separated by a colons denote the minimum and the maximum size of a shared region.

Type of CoMPlement clause	Dutch	German
Interrogative	$LS = 0$ $RS = 0$	$LS = 0$ $RS = 0$
Declarative & Finite	$LS = 1$ $RS = 0$	$LS = 1$ $RS = 0$
Declarative & Non-Finite, VP Extraposition	$LS = 1$ $RS = 0{:}1$	$LS = 1$ $RS = 0{:}1$
Declarative & Non-Finite, Third Construction	$LS = 1{:}6$ $RS = 0{:}1$	$LS = 1{:}6$ $RS = 0{:}1$
Declarative & Non-Finite, Verb Raising	$LS = 4{:}6$ $RS = 1$	$LS = 5$ $RS = 1$

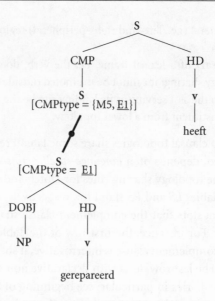

Figure 8. Positional features for two verbs of sentence (1). The underlined slot label in the CMPtype features refers to the value of CMPtype *after* unification of the two S-nodes.

The final ingredient of PG's linearization system utilizes the non-recursive feature unification mechanism introduced in Section 1.2. We allow lexical frames to carry not only agreement features but also positional features. Their values are determined as part of the unification process. A simplified example is provided in Figure 8 by the placement of the past participle *gerepareerd* of example (1). The "CMPtype" feature on the CoMPlement S-node in the lexical frame of the Dutch auxiliary *heeft* 'has' specifies the disjunctive value "{M5, E1}". This means that the complement of *heeft* is free to land either in slot M5 or in slot E1. Because the root S-node of *gerepareerd* happens to have a CMP-type feature with one of these values, its unification with *heeft*'s complement S-node succeeds. This licenses the CoMPlement clause headed by *gerepareerd* to land in slot E1 of *heeft*'s topology (see Figure 6). As will become clear shortly, unification of positional features offers a simple but effective method to control verb order in Dutch and German clause-final verb clusters.

Now that the essentials of PG's linear ordering component are in place, we can proceed to the verb constructions in the target languages.

2.   Dutch verb constructions

The rule for cross-clause topology sharing in Dutch is shown in Table 2. It contains provisions for three different types of non-finite CoMPlement clause constructions traditionally called 'Verb Raising', 'VP Extraposition', and 'Third Construction'[5] (Den Besten & Rutten 1989). We now discuss some examples that illustrate the joint effect of slot selection (Table 1) and topology sharing.

In sentence (5), the finite middle clause lands in slot E2 of the matrix. The lower clause is governed by the verb *moeten* 'must, have to', a Verb Raiser. Therefore, it shares the entire left-peripheral region from F1 through M3 ($LS = 4$; cf. Table 2), and possibly even M4 + M5 ($LS = 4{:}6$), with its upstairs neighbor. This causes promotion of the Direct OBJect and the PaRTicle of the lower clause. If slot M4 of the lower topology were not shared, PaRTicle *op* would end up after *moet*.

(5) a. *Zei je   dat ik haar op moet   bellen?*
         said you   that I   her   up have-to call
         'Did you say that I have to call her up?'

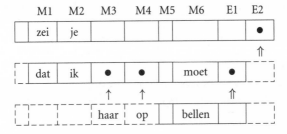

The examples in (6) exemplify the Third Construction, with *vergeten* 'forget' as governing verb. The topology-sharing rule now licenses varying amounts of topology sharing in the left periphery, and thereby several alternative output strings. Sentences (6a) and (6b) represent the extremes: no promotion of any constituent in (6a) vs. all constituents dependent on the infinitival verb promoted in (6b). Intermediate amounts of topology sharing yield acceptable sentences *provided that sharing is indeed left-peripheral*: see the grammaticality contrast between items (6b/c) on the one hand and (6d/e) on the other. The grammaticality contrast between examples (6f/g) illustrates VP Extraposition: *vragen* 'ask' governs a VP Extraposition construction. This rules out promotion of Direct OBJect *de fiets* into the same slot as *vragen*'s Indirect OBJect *Jan*.

(6) a.   ... *dat   Jan   vergat   Marie   het   boek   terug   te geven*
       that John   forgot   Mary   the   book   back   to give
     '... that John forgot to give Mary the book back'

M1	M2	M3	M4	M6	E2
dat	Jan			vergat	●

		Marie het boek	terug	te geven	

b.   ... *dat Jan Marie het boek terug vergat te geven*

M1	M2	M3	M4	M6	E2
dat	Jan	●	●	vergat	●

		Marie het boek	terug	te geven	

c.   ... *dat Jan Marie vergat het boek terug te geven*

M1	M2	M3	M4	M6	E2
dat	Jan	●		vergat	●

		Marie	het boek	terug	te geven	

d.   *... *dat Jan het boek vergat Marie terug te geven*

M1	M2	M3	M4	M6	E2
dat	Jan	●		vergat	●

		Marie	het boek	terug	te geven	

e.   *... *dat Jan het boek terug vergat Marie te geven*

M1	M2	M3	M4	M6	E2
dat	Jan	●	●	vergat	●

		Marie	het boek	terug	te geven	

f.   ... *dat   Marie   Jan   vraagt   (om)   de   fiets   te repareren*
    that Marie Jan asks   (CMPR) the bike to repair
    'that Marie asks Jan to repair the bike

M1	M2	M3			M6		E2
dat	Marie	Jan			vraagt		•

⇑

(om)		de fiets			te repareren		

g.   *... *dat Marie Jan de fiets vraagt (om) te repareren*

M1	M2	M3			M6		E2
dat	Marie	Jan	•		vraagt		•

↯   ⇑

(om)		de fiets			te repareren		

The rules discussed so far may cause a congestion of verbs at the end of a
finite clause. Such a *verb cluster* contains one finite verb, one or more non-
finite dependent verbs (infinitive or past participle), possibly with one PaR-
Ticle and/or one or more PreINFinitives *te* 'to'. Some representative examples
are given in (7). They include three Verb Raisers (the auxiliaries *hebben* 'have',
zullen 'will/shall' and *kunnen* 'can/to be able to'), one main verb that cannot
take a non-finite complement clause (*zingen* 'to sing'), and a Third Construction verb (*hopen* 'to hope'). The sentences also exemplify the 'infinitivus pro
participio' (IPP) phenomenon. If the perfective auxiliary *hebben* takes another
Verb Raiser (VR) as its complement, this verb surfaces as an infinitive rather
than as a past participle. In (7m), for instance, the infinitival form *kunnen* sub-
stitutes for the past participle *gekund* as complement of *hebben*. The subscripts
in the examples denote levels in the verb frame hierarchy.

(7)   a.   ... *dat   ze   deze   liedjes   zullen$_1$ zingen$_2$*
            that they these songs will   sing
            '... that they will sing these songs'

      b.   ... *dat ze deze liedjes zingen$_2$ zullen$_1$*

      c.   ... *hebben$_1$ gezongen$_2$* ('... have sung')

      d.   ... *gezongen$_2$ hebben$_1$*

      e.   ... *zullen$_1$ hebben$_2$ gezongen$_3$* ('... will have sung')

      f.   ... *zullen$_1$ gezongen$_3$ hebben$_2$*

      g.   ... *gezongen$_3$ zullen$_1$ hebben$_2$*

      h.   *... *hebben$_2$ zullen$_1$ gezongen$_3$*

      i.   *... *hebben$_2$ gezongen$_3$ zullen$_1$*

j.   *... *gezongen$_3$ hebben$_2$ zullen$_1$*

k.   ... *zullen$_1$ kunnen$_2$ zingen$_3$* ('... will be able to sing')

l.   *... *zullen$_1$ zingen$_3$ kunnen$_2$* (all other permutations unacceptable)

m.   ... *hebben$_1$ kunnen$_2$ zingen$_3$* ('have been able to sing')

n.   *... *hebben$_1$ zingen$_3$ kunnen$_2$* (all other permutations unacceptable)

o.   ... *hadden$_1$ zullen$_2$ zingen$_3$* (all other permutations unacceptable)
     would-have will   sing
     '... would have intended/promised/planned to sing'

p.   ... *zullen$_1$ hebben$_2$ kunnen$_3$ zingen$_4$* ('will have been able to sing')

q.   *... *zingen$_4$ zullen$_1$ hebben$_2$ kunnen$_3$* (all other permutations bad)

r.   ... *dat   ze   deze   liedjes hopen$_1$ te zingen$_2$*
          that they these songs   hope   to sing
     '... that they hope to sing these songs'

s.   *... *dat ze deze liedjes te zingen$_2$ hopen$_1$*

t.   ... *dat ze deze liedjes hopen$_1$ te kunnen$_2$ zingen$_3$* (all other permutations unacceptable)
     '... that they hope to be able to sing these songs'

u.   ... *zouden$_1$ kunnen$_2$ hebben$_3$ gezongen$_4$*
     'it might be possible that they have sung (these songs)'

v.   ... *zouden$_1$ kunnen$_2$ gezongen$_4$ hebben$_3$*

w.   ... *zouden$_1$ gezongen$_4$ kunnen$_2$ hebben$_3$*

x.   ... *gezongen$_4$ zouden$_1$ kunnen$_2$ hebben$_3$*

y.   *... *hebben$_3$ gezongen$_4$ zouden$_1$ kunnen$_2$* (all other permutations unacceptable)

Our approach to controlling word order in verb constructions deploys the unification mechanism for positional features introduced at the end of Section 1.1 (cf. Figure 8). We postulate that whenever a verb frame is instantiated as a finite or non-finite complement, its root S-node contains the *CoMPlement type* feature. The values of the "CMPtype" feature simultaneously represents three aspects of the complement:

(A) verb status:[6] the HeaD verb is a bare infinitive (coded as "Infin"), an infinitive preceded by a Pre-INFinitive[7] ("PInfin"), a past participle ("PastP") or a finite verb ("Fin")

(B) landing site (slots M5, E1 or E2), and

(C) pattern of left-peripheral topology sharing allowed by the HeaD verb (cf. Table 2): VP Extraposition (VE), Verb Raising (VR) Third Construction (VT), or finite complementation (VF). Verbs that take no complement at all will be designated as 'simple verbs' (VS). In order to abbreviate notation we propose to let the symbol "V" in a CMPtype feature cover any of the verb types distinguished here: V = {VE, VF, VR, VS, VT}.

For instance, the feature "CMPtype = {M5-VR-Infin}" represents the option "non-finite complement clause that is headed by an infinitival Verb Raiser without Pre-INFinitive and lands in slot M5". The feature "CMPtype = E2-V(E, T)-PInfin" indicates that the clause carrying it will be realized as a non-finite clause in slot E2 of its governer, that the HeaD verb of this clause takes a VP Extraposition or a Third Construction complement, and that the HeaD verb will be preceded by Pre-INFinitive *te*. Notice that characters between parentheses denote optional elements. E.g. "V(E, S)" is matched by an Extraposition verb or by a simple verb without a complement; the code "(P)Infin" stands for an infinitive with or without a PINF. "(M5, E1)" indicates that M5 or E1 can be chosen as landing sites. Importantly, the symbol "V" is an abbreviation of "V(E,F,R,S,T)" and matches any verb type from the set {VE, VF, VR, VS, VT}.

We assume that every root S-node of a complement clause is instantiated with a CMPtype feature whose value set includes one or more such tripartite options. Furthermore, the CMP-S foot node in the lexical frame of verbs that take finite or non-finite complements, also includes a CMPtype feature. Unification of such a foot S-node with the root S-node of another verb frame succeeds only if this operation yields a non-empty CMPtype value set (cf. the definition of feature unification in Section 1.1).

Figure 9 shows the CMPtype features for the verbs in (7). The modal auxiliaries have two entries each.[8] Sentence (7a) involves unification of the CMP-S node in the lexical frame for *zullen2* with the root node of the *zingen* frame. The one remaining option "E1-V-Infin" directs the infinitive *zingen* to slot E1 in the topology of *zullen2*. The inverse order in (7b) ensues in the case of selection of verb frame *zullen1*, with the main verb in slot M5 (*zingen zullen*). The past participle *gezongen* that complements the perfect auxiliary *hebben* in (7c/d), has two landing site options: M5 and E1.

The six examples in (7e–j) include all permutations of *zullen, gezongen,* and *hebben*. They are acceptable only if *zullen* precedes *hebben*; the position of *gezongen* seems irrelevant. *Zullen2*'s CoMPlement unifies successfully with *hebben*, forcing the latter to land in E1 and to trail behind its governor. Past participle *gezongen* is offered two possible landing sites: M5 and E1. Figure 10 portrays the latter option. If *gezongen* selects M5, the verb cluster surfaces as *zullen gezongen hebben*. This presupposes, in agreement with the middle option in the topology sharing rule in Table 2, that *zullen2* does NOT share its M5 slot

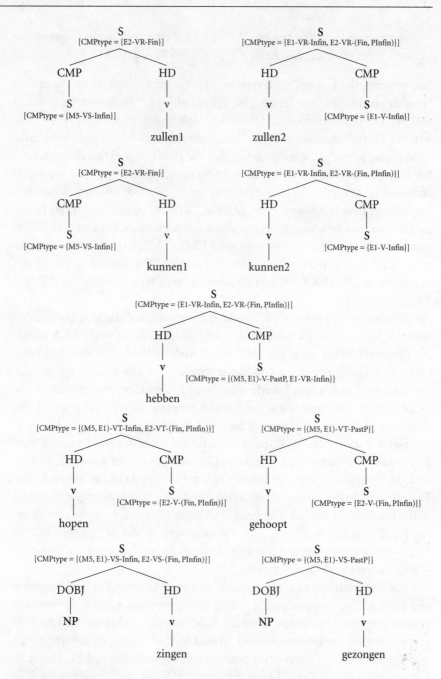

Figure 9. Partial lexical frames for the verbs in (7). The CMPtype features, which control the placement of finite and non-finite clauses, have been printed between square brackets below the S-nodes.

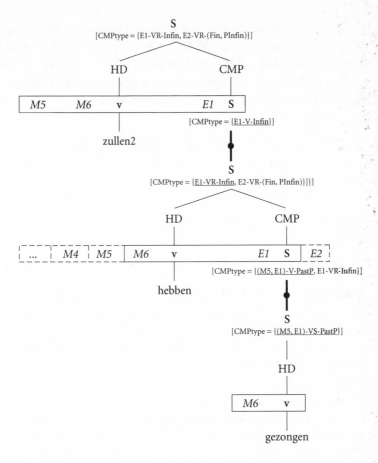

Figure 10. Analysis of sentences (7e–j). The complement headed by *gezongen* selects position E1 from the two alternatives licensed by the unification of its root S with the CMP-S of *hebben*. (The legal M5 option, yielding *gezongen hebben*, is not depicted here.) Sharing of slots M4 and M5 in the middle topology is optional. If *zullen2* selects the sharing option for M5, and *gezongen* indeed goes to M5 of *hebben*, the sequence *gezongen zullen hebben* results, i.e. example (7g). The black dots denote unification with substitution of S-nodes; the CMPtype values selected by unification have been underlined. Remember that "V" abbreviates for "V(E,F,R,S,T)".

with that of its complement *hebben*. If *zullen2* chooses the other option and does share its M5 slot with that of its complement, *gezongen* will end up as the first member of the verb cluster.

The IPP effect exemplified in (7m–q) is due to the interaction between *hebben* and *kunnen/zullen* at unification. (*Hadden* is the past tense plural of *hebben.*) *Hebben* and *kunnen2/zullen2* are successful unification partners, given that *hebben* is the governor and a Verb Raiser its complement. We assume that the IPP effect is restricted to VR complements of *hebben*. However, the effect also occurs – optionally – when *hebben* takes a complement clause headed by a Third Construction verb with all non-verbal constituents promoted. Sentence (8) is an example.

(8) a. ... *dat zij   dit   lied   hebben proberen/geprobeerd te zingen*
          that they this song have   try/tried   to sing
          '... that they have tried to sing this song'
     b. ... *dat zij hebben *proberen/geprobeerd dit lied te zingen*

We can handle this by granting verbs like *proberen* the double status of Third Construction verb *and* Verb Raiser:

(9) [CMPtype = {(M5, E1)-VT-Infin, E2-VT-(Fin, PInfin), E1-VR-Infin}]

If the latter option is chosen, the infinitive *proberen* (heading the complement clause landed in E1 of *hebben*'s topology) is obligatory, and the topology sharing rule forces promotion of all non-verbal constituents: see (8b). The grammatical alternative in (8b) with *geprobeerd* is analyzable as a Third Construction without promotion of its dependents.

The verb *hopen* in (7r–t) takes a Third Construction complement at slot E2. All other placements are illegal. E2 is also the only possible landing site for complements of VP Extraposition verbs (VE; not illustrated here).

Examples (7u–y) feature the past tense *zouden* of *zullen* because this form is better suited to bring out the *irrealis* meaning; this has no consequences with respect to word order. The various positions of *gezongen* depend on the level(s) at which a topology shares slot M5 with its upstairs neighbor – through the same promotion mechanism that is illustrated in example (7g) and Figure 10. The linear structure of the verb cluster of (7x) looks as follows:

M1	M2	M3	M4	M5	M6	E1	E2
dat	ze	●		●	zouden	●	
		↑		↑		⇑	
					kunnen	●	
		↑		↑		⇑	
					hebben		
		↑		⇑			
		deze liedjes			gezongen		

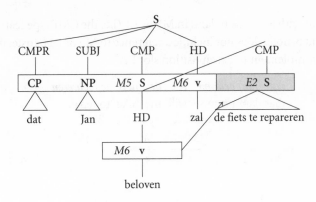

Figure 11. Right-peripheral topology sharing (shaded area E2) in sentence (11a).

We propose a similar approach to the placement of particles of so-called separable verbs. A case in point is sentence (10), which is identical to (7u) except for the particle *mee* 'together' preceding the past participle *gezongen* (*meezingen* = to sing together).

(10)   ... *dat ze deze liedjes zouden₁ kunnen₂ hebben₃ meegezongen₄*

The particle can be placed at any position in the verb cluster as long as it precedes the verb it belongs to (*zingen*). Since *zouden, kunnen* and *hebben* are only allowed to occur in this order while *gezongen* may occupy four different positions, there are ten different permutations. This is exactly the set licensed by the promotion mechanism:

- the CMPtype features in the three auxilaries guarantee they occur in the correct order,
- *gezongen* may follow or precede its governor *hebben*, and may even precede the other auxiliaries because the sharing configurations permit a promotion path to slot M5 in any of the three higher topologies, and
- since the PaRTicle can only land in an M4 slot while it may be promoted into any of the higher topologies, it will always precede *gezongen*.

In the sentences discussed so far, topology sharing was restricted to the left-periphery of the clausal topology. Cases such as (11a), however, with 'extraposed' constituents, require *right-peripheral topology sharing* as well. The rule for right-peripheral topology sharing is stated in (12), which partly repeats Table 2. The verb *beloven* 'promise' precedes its governor *zal* while its complement *de fiets te repareren* is clause-final (Figure 11). This discontinuity is due to the fact that *beloven* is a Third Construction verb and does not fit out its complement with a license to land in M5 or E1 (i.e. the CMPtype feature of the complement S-node does not include a reference to M5 or E1). Instead, *beloven* directs its complement to extraposition slot E2.

(11) a. ... *dat Jan beloven zal de fiets te repareren*
     that Jan promise will the bike to repair
     '... that Jan will promise to repair the bike'

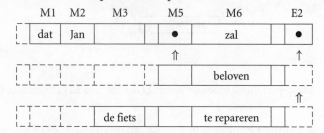

b. *... *dat Jan de fiets te repareren beloven zal*
c. ... *dat Jan zal beloven de fiets te repareren*
d. ... *dat Jan beloven zal aan Marie de fiets te repareren*
   '... that Jan will promise (to) Marie to repair the bike'

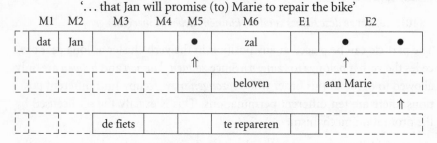

(12) *Right-peripheral topology sharing in complement clauses of Dutch and German*

a. Right-peripheral topology sharing is restricted to E2 slots ($RS = 1$ in Table 2).
b. Lexical frames headed by a Verb Raiser *obligatorily* share slot E2 of their topology with that of their complement ($RS = 1$).
c. Lexical frames headed by a VP Extraposition or a Third Construction verb *optionally* share slot E2 of their topology with that of their complement ($RS = 0$:1).
d. A finite complement clause does not right-peripherally share its E2 slot with that of its governor ($RS = 0$).
e. If CoMPlement clauses from several clausal topologies land in the same E2 slot, they line up in increasing clause depth order.

The CMPtype features in the lexical frames of the modal auxiliaries in Figure 9 also account for the ordering phenomenon illustrated in (13) below. The order of modal auxiliary and main verb in clause-final verb clusters is arbitrary as long as the main verb does not take a sentential complement. If the auxiliary governs a complement-taking verb, Aux-MainV is the only acceptable sequence: see the grammaticality contrast between (13a/b) on the one hand and (13c/d) on the other.

(13) a. ... *dat Jan de fiets zal proberen te repareren*
          '... that Jan will try to repair the bike'
      b. *... *dat Jan de fiets proberen zal te repareren*
      c. ... *dat Jan de fiets zal (uit)proberen*
          '... that Jan will try (out) the bike'
      d. ... *dat Jan de fiets (uit)proberen zal*
      e. *Ik weet niet welke fiets Jan zal proberen te repareren*
          'I don't know which bike Jan will try to repair'
      f. **Ik weet niet welke fiets Jan proberen zal te repareren*
      g. *Ik weet niet welke fiets Jan zal (uit)proberen*
          'I don't know which bike Jan will try (out)'
      h. *Ik weet niet welke fiets Jan (uit)proberen zal*

The lexical frames for *zullen1* and *kunnen1* have a much narrower range of applicability than their counterparts *zullen2* and *kunnen2*. They can head finite clauses only, licensing MainV-Aux order exclusively to 'simple' verbs, which do not take sentential complements. The phenomenon holds irrespective of whether the dependent NP is promoted within the Midfield (*de fiets* in M3) or within the Forefield (*welke fiets* in F1) – cf. (13e–f).

A construction of Dutch which has no counterpart in German or English, is governed by verbs such as *zitten* 'sit', *staan* 'stand' and *liggen* 'lie'. They take an infinitival complement expressing an ongoing action performed by the referent of the SUBJect NP (cf. Progressive aspect in English) and simultaneously mention the bodily position assumed by the SUBJect referent during the action. The examples in (14) demonstrate, interestingly, that the status of the complement's HeaD verb varies in function of the status the governor: If the governing verb is finite, the complement has PInfin status (with *te*); in all other cases, the complement's HeaD verb is a bare infinitive without *te* (status = Infin).

(14) a. ... dat Jan een boek zit/staat/ligt   te lezen
          that Jan a   book   sits/stands/lies to read
          '... that Jan is reading a book (while sitting/standing/lying)'

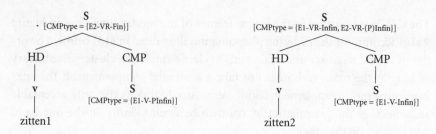

Figure 12. Lexical frames for the complement-taking verb *zitten* in example (14).

> b. ... dat Jan een boek zou zitten/staan/liggen lezen
> '... that Jan would be reading a book'
> c. ... dat Jan een boek heeft zitten/staan/liggen lezen
> '... that Jan has been reading a book'

We propose to treat these complement-takers in a way similar to the modal verbs in Figure 9 (e.g. *kunnen* and *zullen*), that is, to associate with them separate lexical frames for use in finite and infinitival constructions. (The verbs cannot take participial status.) Figure 12 shows the CMPtype features.

We finally turn to verb clustering in passive constructions, as exemplified by the examples (15) and (16), which are more or less synonymous. (15a–f) list all six permutations of two past-participles *(aangeboden* and *geworden)* and the finite passive auxiliary *was*. Three of these are ungrammatical. Version (15g) is the sole (marginally) acceptable ordering where the particle *aan* and the main verb *geboden* are not contiguous. The past-participle *geworden* is nearly always omitted in modern standard Dutch. So, in everyday usage, the verb cluster has three possible orderings: *was aangeboden, aangeboden was* and *aan was geboden*. The grammaticality ratings of the seven versions of (16) run parallel to their counterparts in (15). We take this as evidence for a parallel treatment of *aangeboden gekregen had* and *aangeboden geworden was*. That is, we analyze not only *geworden* but also *gekregen* as a complement-taking verb, and they both can take *aangeboden* as non-finite complement. The lexical frames of the verbs involved are depicted in Figure 13. (The entry for *had* 'had', the past tense of *hebben* 'have', has been copied from Figure 9; *zijn* 'be' is the infinitival form of *was*.) The reader may verify for her/himself that, in conjunction with the cross-clausal topology sharing rule (Table 2), these lexical frames generate exactly the set of (marginally) acceptable verb orderings.

> (15) a. ... *dat deze baan haar niet aangeboden₃ (geworden₂) was₁*
> that this job her not PRT-offered been was
> '... that this job had not been offered to her'

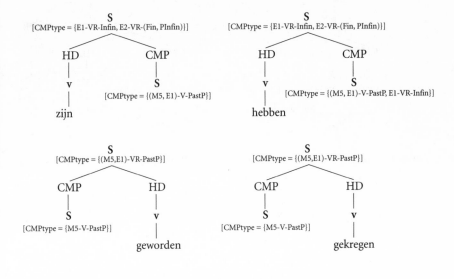

Figure 13. Lexical frames and CMPtype features for the verbs in (15) and (16).

b.   ... *aangeboden was (geworden)*

c.   *... *(geworden) was aangeboden*

d.   *... *(geworden) aangeboden was*

e.   *... *was (geworden) aangeboden*

f.   ... *was aangeboden (geworden)*

g.   ?... *aan was geboden (geworden)*

(16) a.   ... dat ze   deze baan niet aangeboden₃ gekregen₂ had₁
               that she this job   not   PRT-offered   gotten   had
               '... that she had not been offered this job'

b.   ... *aangeboden had gekregen*

c.   *... *gekregen had aangeboden*

d.   *... *gekregen aangeboden had*

e.   *... *had gekregen aangeboden*

f.   ... *had aangeboden gekregen*

g.   ?... *aan had geboden gekregen*

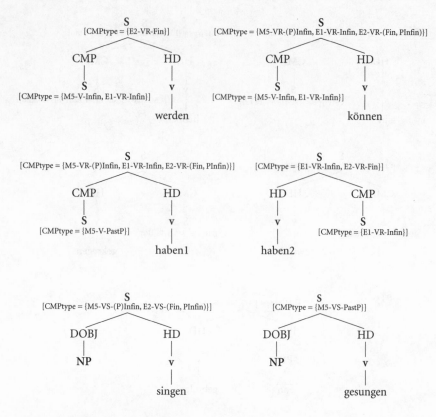

Figure 14. The CMPtype features which control the placement of complement clauses in the lexical frames for the verbs in (17).

3.   German verb constructions

Our treatment of word order in German clauses is based on the topology slot selection rules in Table 1, the topology sharing rule in Table 2, and CMPtype features such as those listed in the lexical items of Figure 14 and Figure 16. The German slot selection rules closely resemble the Dutch ones, the main difference being that the PaRTicle of separable verbs goes to M6 rather than M4. The left-peripheral topology sharing rule is essentially the same as the one for Dutch, except that Verb Raisers like *wollen* do not want their complements to share slot M5. As to right-peripheral sharing, we assume that the Dutch rule in (12) above also applies to German.

In designing the German linearization system we were guided by the numerous facts discussed by Kathol (2000) and Meurers (2000). They present de-

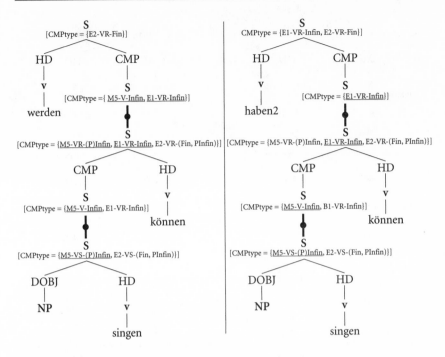

Figure 15. Left-hand side: unification in the verb cluster of examples (17c–h). Right-hand side: idem for (17i). *Werden* licenses both M5 and E1 as legal landing sites for its VR complement, yielding *werden singen können* and *singen können werden*. The order *singen werden können* ensues if the upper and middle topologies share their M5 slots. Of the two lexical entries for *haben*, only *haben2* can unify with infinitival *können*.

tailed surveys of both traditional and contemporaneous linguistic proposals for dealing with word order in German, and develop their own HPSG-style solutions. Other publications we consulted include Uszkoreit (1987); Engelkamp, Erbach and Uszkoreit (1992); Reape (1993); Haider (1993); Nerbonne, Netter and Pollard (1994); Hinrichs and Nakazawa (1994, 1998); Seuren (1996); Bouma and Van Noord (1998); Richter (2000), and Seuren (this volume). The confines of the present paper do not allow us to describe in detail the numerous phenomena and concomitant theoretical explanations in these sources.

Figure 15 illustrates how the value of CMPtype features constrains linear order within the verb clusters in (17). Figure 16 shows the CMPtype feature values of the lexical frames referenced in (18) – examples mostly due to Seuren (this volume). Figures 17 and 18 illustrate the analyses of four of them. The notational conventions are identical to those for Dutch (see previous section). Notice that the figures do not contain lexical frames for past participles

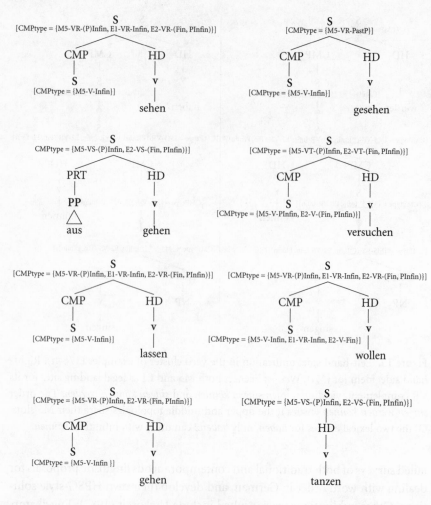

Figure 16. Partial lexical entries for the verbs in examples (18).

of modal auxiliaries. We have assumed that, in standard German, forms like *gekonnt* 'been able' and *gewollt* 'wanted' do not subcategorize for non-finite clausal complements. Thus we can account for the unacceptability of examples like (17j) and (18c).

(17) a. ... *dass sie das Lied singen₂ können₁/werden₁*
          that they the song sing   be-able/will
          '... that they can/will sing the song'

      b. *... *dass sie das Lied können₁/werden₁ singen₂*

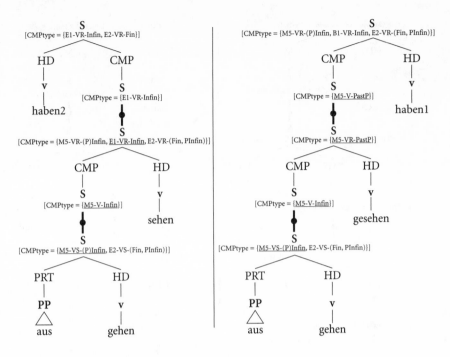

Figure 17. Analysis of examples (18e–f).

c. ... *dass sie   das Lied   singen₃ können₂ werden₁*
that they the song sing   be-able will
'... that they will be able to sing the song'

d. ... *werden₁ singen₃ können₂*

e. *... *singen₃ werden₁ können₂*

f. *... *werden₁ können₂ singen₃*

g. *... *können₂ werden₁ singen₃*

h. *... *können₂ singen₃ werden₁*

i. ... *haben₁ singen₃ können₂*
have sing be-able
'... (that they) have been able to sing'

j. *... *singen₃ gekonnt₂ haben₁*

(18) a. ... *dass sie   ausgehen₂ will₁*
that she out-go   wants
'... that she wants to go out'

b. ... *dass sie   hat₁ ausgehen₃ wollen₂*
that she has out-go   want
'... that she has wanted to go out'

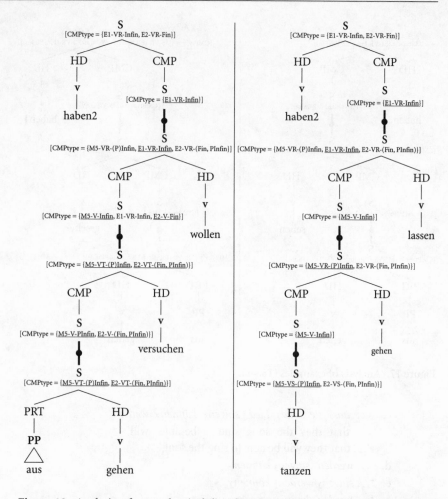

Figure 18. Analysis of examples (18k/l). Alternative (18k′) ensues if option E2-V-PInfin is selected for *versuchen*'s complement (due to obligatory sharing of E2 slots).

c. *... *dass sie ausgehen₃ gewollt₂ hat₁*
   that she out-go   wanted has
   '... that she has wanted to go out'

d. ... *dass sie mich ausgehen₂ sah₁*
   that she me   out-go   saw
   '... that she saw me go out'

e. ... *dass sie mich hat₁ ausgehen₃ sehen₂*
   that she me   has out-go   see
   '... that she has seen me go out'

f. ... *dass sie mich ausgehen$_3$ gesehen$_2$ hat$_1$*
    that she me out-go seen has
    '... that she has seen me go out'

g. *... *dass sie wird$_1$ ausgehen$_2$*
    that she will out-go
    '... that she will go out'

h. ... *dass sie ausgehen$_2$ wird$_1$*
    that she out-go will
    '... that she will go out'

i. ... *dass sie wird$_1$ ausgehen$_3$ wollen$_2$*
    that she will out-go want
    '... that she will want to go out'

j. ... *dass sie ausgehen$_3$ wollen$_2$ wird$_1$*
    that she out-go want will
    '... that she will want to go out'

k. ... *dass sie wird$_1$ haben$_2$ auszugehen$_5$ versuchen$_4$ wollen$_3$*
    that she will have out-go try want
    '... that she will have wanted to try to go out'

k'. ... *dass sie wird$_1$ haben$_2$ versuchen$_4$ wollen$_3$ auszugehen$_5$*

l. ... *dass ich sie habe$_1$ tanzen$_4$ gehen$_3$ lassen$_2$*
    that I her have dance go let
    '... that I have let her go dance'

The lexical entry of the future auxiliary *werden* in Figure 14 assumes – in line with a suggestion by Meurers (2000:223) – that this verb can only occur in finite form. This property accounts, among other things, for the grammaticality contrast between (19a) and (19b). *Können* but not *werden* is allowed to head the complement of *haben2*, as shown in the CMPtype features of these auxiliaries (Figure 14).[9] Furthermore, *haben2* is not allowed to head a complement clause with PInfin status. The verb *behaupten* – similarly to *versuchen* (Figure 16) – licenses slot E2 but not E1 as a landing site for its complement. This rules out (19d) while (19c), with *haben1*, is unproblematic.

(19) a. ... *dass er es hätte$_1$ singen$_3$ können$_2$*
    b. *... *dass er es hätte$_1$ singen$_3$ werden$_2$*
    c. *Er behauptete, es gesungen$_2$ zu haben$_1$*
       he claimed it sung to have
       'He claimed to have sung it'
    d. *Er behauptete, es zu haben$_1$ singen$_3$ können$_2$*
       he claimed it to have sing be-able-to
       (intended) 'He claimed to have been able to sing it'

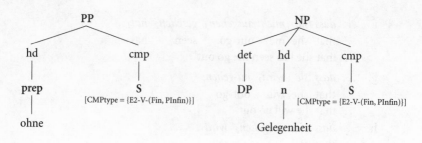

Figure 19. Analysis of example (20d).

The latter observation relates to the fact that *haben2* cannot head the non-finite complement of a preposition or a noun (Haider 1993). While (20a) below, with a finite complement of *ohne* 'without', is perfectly grammatical, the IPP version (20b) is ruled out. *Ohne* can take a non-finite complement headed by *haben2*, as illustrated by (20c). Example (20d), with the complement-taking noun *Gelegenheit* 'opportunity', is ill-formed for the same reason as (20b). We can account for these phenomena on the assumption that CMP-S nodes of nouns and prepositions contain a CMPtype feature that specifies slot E2 as the only possible landing site for non-finite complements, thus preventing unification of these CMP-S nodes with the *haben2* frame (see Figure 19).[10]

(20) a. ... *ohne   dass sie es hat₁ singen₃ können₂*
            without that she it has sing be-able-to
            '... without her being able to sing it'
      b. *... *ohne es zu haben₁ singen₃ können₂*
            (intended) '... without having been able to sing it'
      c. ... *ohne es gesungen₂ zu haben₁*
            '... without having sung it'
      d. *... *eine Gelegenheit es zu haben₁ singen₃ können₂*
                an   opportunity it to have sing be-able-to
            (intended) '... an opportunity to have been able to sing it'

Various scrambling phenomena in German involve *fronting* of constituents – in our terminology: placement of focused or topicalized constituents in slot F1 of a main clause. Examples (21a) through (21f), from Engelkamp, Erbach, and Uszkoreit (1992), represent *Simple Fronting*: slot F1 hosts exactly one constituent – a single NP, AdvP, Head verb, or clause. In cases of *Complex Fronting*, slot F1 seems to accommodate several phrases, as exemplified by (21g) and (21h), also from Engelkamp et al. (1992). Such cases seem to challenge the widely held view that in main clauses of German no more than one constituent is allowed to precede the finite verb. The mechanism of left-peripheral topology sharing can solve this problem on the assumption that the focus/topic relations within the complement clause overrule the topology sharing defaults stated in Table 2. Auxiliaries like *wollen* and *sollen* standardly cause sharing of slots F1 through M4 of the complement topology. This default presumably does not apply to focused or topicalized constituents of the complement. These do not undergo promotion and are fronted while the promoted parts of the complement are slotted into the standard Midfield positions of the matrix topology.[11]

(21)   a.   *Der Kurier   sollte   nachher einem Spion den Brief zustecken*
             the   courier should later   a   spy   the letter slip
             'The courier was later supposed to slip a spy the letter'
       b.   *Zustecken sollte der Kurier nachher einem Spion den Brief*
       c.   *Den Brief sollte der Kurier nachher einem Spion zustecken*

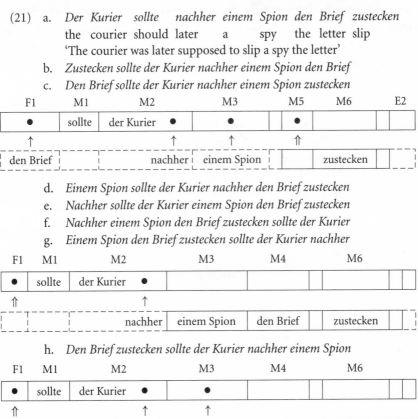

       d.   *Einem Spion sollte der Kurier nachher den Brief zustecken*
       e.   *Nachher sollte der Kurier einem Spion den Brief zustecken*
       f.   *Nachher einem Spion den Brief zustecken sollte der Kurier*
       g.   *Einem Spion den Brief zustecken sollte der Kurier nachher*

       h.   *Den Brief zustecken sollte der Kurier nachher einem Spion*

Complex Fronting may involve a stack of non-finite complement clauses. The sentence in (22a), from Kathol (2000), contains two complements headed by the verbs *können* and *finden*. The six logically possible variants embodying simple or complex fronting are shown in (22b) through (22g). These are all grammatical, except for (22d) and (22f). When drawing the linear structures, we have assumed that the complements either go to slot M5 of their governor or, if focused or topicalized, to F1.[12] All five grammatical cases can be generated by our linearization system. With respect to (22e) we assume, like we did in the context of some of the examples in (21) above, that focus/topicalization can prevent promotion of phrasal arguments (here the Direct OBJect *das Buch*). The ill-formedness of variants (22d) and (22f) follows from the fact that *können* cannot be fronted without taking *finden* along: if *finden* is not going to F1, it can only land in M5 – a slot that Verb Raisers like *können* never share with their complement. Interestingly, the system does not rule out a (marginally) acceptable case such as (23), from Kathol (2000:234). The basic reason is that the complement of *versprochen*, unlike the complement of *können*, is free to land in E2 as well as in M5.

(22) a. *Peter wird das Buch finden können*
          Peter will the book find   be-able-to
          'Peter will be able to find the book'
      b. *Das Buch wird Peter finden können*
      c. *Finden wird Peter das Buch können*

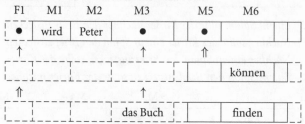

      d. **Können wird Peter das Buch finden*

e. *Das Buch finden wird Peter können*

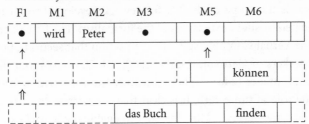

f. **Das Buch können wird Peter finden*

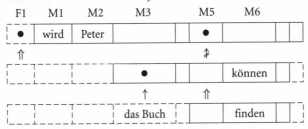

g. *Finden können wird Peter das Buch*

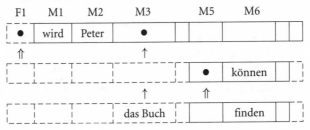

(23) ?*Versprochen wird er ihr nicht haben den Wagen zu waschen*
      promised   will he her not   have the car   to wash
      'He will not have promised her to wash the car'

We now turn to some special German word order phenomena whose explanation exceeds the scope of the PG framework developed so far but may be accommodated by slight extensions of the formalism. The first example is provided by the Verbal Complex Split, a construction that seems to be acceptable to many speakers of German. Kathol (2000:204–205) gives four illustrations, one of them sentence (24a).[13] They all feature the auxiliaries *werden* or *haben* (IPP) in the role of finite verb. It is clear that the current linearization model only generates the variant (24b). In order to enable the Verbal Complex Split, we need to add a special subcategorization property to the lexical items *werden* and *haben2*, namely, that they license the embedded clause to share slot M5 – over and above the slots F1 through M4 that are already shared by virtue of the default rule in Table 2. The clause headed by *bestehen* will then get promoted into the matrix, there preceding *hat/wird* in slot M5. However, because an extension of the model along this line may have undesirable side-effects, and in view of the insecure status of the Verbal Complex Split as a construction of standard German, we have not explored this approach any further. (Interestingly, the modified version of the German cross-clause topology sharing rule resembles the Dutch one more closely than the original one; see Table 2.)

(24) a. ... *dass er das Examen bestehen wird/hat können*
          that he the exam   pass   will/has be-able-to
          '... that he will be/has been able to pass the exam'

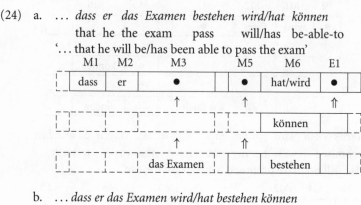

     b. ... *dass er das Examen wird/hat bestehen können*

The rule for left-peripheral topology sharing in Table 2 states that Verb Raisers like *wollen* and other auxiliaries cause their complements to share the slots F1 through M4. Because, in subordinate clauses, the finite Verb Raiser and the governed non-finite verb land in adjacent slots (the Verb Raiser itself in M6, the HeaD verb of the governed clause in M5 or E1), it follows that the region M5 through E1 of the subordinate clause can only be populated by verbs. This implication is falsified by examples like (25), from Kathol (2000:233), where *geben*'s Direct OBJect interrupts the verb cluster. Such cases, although relatively rare, call for a somewhat more lenient version of the topology sharing rule for Verb Raisers – one that offers a wider range of Midfield locations where to put the boundary between shared and non-shared constituents than just at the end of slot M4. It is not clear, however, which conditions control the exact position of the boundary.

(25)   ... *dass Karl dem Mann wird das Buch haben geben wollen*
      that Karl the   man   will   the book   have   give   want-to
      '... that Karl will have wanted to give the man the book'

M1	M2	M3	M4	M5	M6	E1
dass	Karl	●			wird	●
		↑				⇑
			●		haben	●
		↑	↑			⇑
				●	wollen	
		↑	↑	⇑		
		dem Mann	das Buch		geben	

4. Conclusion

We have presented a linearization formalism capable of capturing a broad range of verb constructions in Dutch and German. It is part of the psycholinguistically motivated formalism of Performance Grammar, which has separate but interrelated components for assembling the hierarchical and the linear structure of sentences. Particularly importantly in the present context, PG's linearization component deals not only with 'horizontal' position assignment (left-to-right arrangement of constituents within clauses) but also with a broad class of (vertical) 'movement' (constituents being left-right arranged at a clause level higher than their level in clause hierarchy). Unlike what happens in other grammar formalisms, these movement types take place without affecting the hierarchical structure. (Another class of movement phenomena, we assume, does affect the clause hierarchy, in particular the PG equivalents of Subject-to-Subject and Subject-to-Object Raising. The distinction between movement classes at issue here corresponds to the distinction between Ā and A-movement in Chomskyan Generative Grammar.) Responsible for this behavior are a data structure called *topology* and the mechanism of *lateral topology sharing*. A topology is a one-dimensional array of positions ('slots') serving as landing sites for syntactic constituents. For every pair of a grammatical category (NP, PP, V, etc.) and a grammatical function (Subject, Object, Head, etc.), there is a set of one or more landing sites. The topology sharing mechanism causes unification of left- or right-peripheral slots of clausal topologies at adjacent levels of the clause hierarchy, and thereby virtual vertical movement of constituents landed in a shared slot.

The treatments we proposed for the two target languages are uniform both from a cross-linguistic and from an intralinguistic perspective (see Harbusch & Kempen 2002, for a treatment along the same lines of *movement* phenomena). The topologies, the topology sharing rules, the constraints on topology sharing, and the CoMPlement-type features are very similar across languages. Word order contrasts between the target languages largely reduce to a few narrowly confined and relatively minor differences concerning topology slot fillers and topology sharing rules. The most salient contrasts between Dutch and German verb constructions are caused by lexical factors – the detailed composition of the CMPtype value in the S-nodes of verb frames.

Acknowledgement

We are indebted to Camiel van Breugel (Leiden Institute for Advanced Computer Science, Leiden University) for implementing, in his Performance Grammar Workbench, a PG for Dutch that includes the rule system described in Section 2. The PGW is accessible through the internet and can be run as an applet in JAVA-enabled browsers (www.liacs.nl/home/cvbreuge/pgw).

Notes

1. For predecessors of PG, see Kempen and Hoenkamp (1987) and De Smedt and Kempen (1990a, b).

2. Other grammar formalisms that assign hierarchical and linear computations to separate rule systems, are GPSG (Gazdar, Klein, Pullum, & Sag 1985) and HPSG (Pollard & Sag 1994).

3. For readers who are more familiar with German than with Dutch: the syntactic structure of the German translation of this example (*Denkst du, dass er das Auto repariert hat*) is identical in all currently relevant aspects.

4. The complement clause in Figure 5 is declarative notwithstanding the fact that it includes a Wh-phrase. Compare sentence (3) with the following English paraphrase, which brings out the scope of the Wh-phrase: 'For which car x is it the case that he repairs x?'.

5. Verbs that allow their non-finite complements to be introduced by CoMPlementizeR *om* 'in order to' will be treated as Extraposition Verbs.

6. We borrow this term from Bech (1955).

7. The PINF is realized as *to* in English, as *te* in Dutch, and as *zu* in German.

8. In order to distinguish different verb frames that belong to the same verb, we use numerical *suffixes*, e.g. *zullen1* and *zullen2*. They should not be confused with numerical *subscripts* that in sample sentences refer to verb hierarchy level (e.g. $zullen_1$ and $zullen_2$). The numerical suffixes serve to differentiate between lexical frames; they do not imply that the meanings associated with these frames are also different.

9. Interestingly, the Dutch translation equivalent of (19b), with clause-final verb cluster had_1 $zullen_2$ $zingen_3$, is perfectly acceptable. It requires the lexical frame *zullen2* rather than *zullen1*. See example (7o) above.

10. Meurers (2000:70–71) argues that this construction occurs frequently enough to consider it well-formed, *contra* Haider (1993) who does not accept it. Interestingly, if we make the same CMPtype assumption for CMP-S nodes of Dutch nouns and prepositions, the Dutch counterparts of (20a) and (20d) are predicted to be grammatical: The CMPtype feature in the root S-node of *hebben* does include E2 as an optional landig site (see Figure 9). This prediction is indeed verified by the full grammaticality of literal translations (i) and (ii):

(i)   zonder het te hebben kunnen zingen

(ii) een gelegenheid het te hebben kunnen zingen

11. Table 1 does not specify landing sites for Adverbial Phrases. Here, we assume that the adverbial modifier *nachher* is assigned a late position in slot M2, unless focused or topicalized.

12. The lexical item *werden*, shown in Figure 14, also allows its complement to land in slot E1. This additional possibility does not affect our account of the examples in (22).

13. Kathol (o.c.) refers to an unpublished workshop paper by Meurers (1994) as the original source of these examples. See Meurers (2000) for additional examples.

CHAPTER 7

Coherent constructions in German
Lexicon or syntax?

Owen Rambow
Columbia University

1. Introduction

This paper addresses the issue of embedded *zu*-infinitival clauses in German from the perspective of a formal grammatical framework, Tree Adjoining grammar (TAG) and related tree rewriting systems.[1] Two radically different analyses have been proposed for this construction. According to the 'syntactic' analysis, embedded infinitivals in German are analyzed essentially as in English, namely as clausal complementation. The 'incorporation' analysis suggests that there is a process by which two verbs are combined into a single lexical unit (in some sense), which is head of a single syntactic projection. The incorporation analysis has become widely (in fact, nearly universally) accepted in one form or another in both the transformational and non-transformational literature, and has an undeniable intuitive appeal to the native-speaker linguist. However, this paper argues that there is empirical evidence against the incorporation analysis. Furthermore, methodological parsimony requires that the introduction of machinery to handle the merging of argument lists of two verbs (as required under the incorporation analysis) be motivated by the data, and that no alternate account (which does not rely on the additional mechanism) be available. Unfortunately, the status of much of the crucial data is quite murky. As a consequence, theoretically significant choices in the machinery of syntactic theories need to be made on the basis of difficult grammaticality judgments.

This paper does not argue for a syntactic solution as such. Instead, it suggests that the stark contrast between the two analyses is in fact an artifact of the grammatical frameworks in which the construction has been analyzed. The paper proposes an analysis in a grammatical formalism in which all phrase structure is built incrementally in a formal derivation, and in which node labels are represented largely as features. In such a system, it is argued, the difference between the syntactic and the incorporation analyses can be interpreted as a difference in the ordering of steps in the derivation.

This paper is structured as follows. In Section 2 I introduce TAG and lexicalized tree-rewriting systems. In Section 3 I summarize the relevant data and describe the incorporation analysis. I then discuss why this analysis is problematical for TAG. In Section 4 I present arguments against the incorporation analysis, and propose a solution using a tree-rewriting system in Section 5.

2.   Tree Adjoining Grammar

Work in non-transformational frameworks including LFG (Kaplan & Bresnan 1982), HPSG (Pollard & Sag 1994), categorial systems such as CCG (Steedman 1996, 1997), and Tree Adjoining Grammar (TAG) (Joshi et al. 1975; Joshi 1985), has stressed the importance of the lexicon in the development of a theory of syntax, and these approaches share a desire to locate syntactic variation within and between languages in the lexical component of grammar. In TAG-based linguistic theories[2] (Kroch 1987; Frank 1992, 2001), the lexicalist orientation of the linguistic theory is expressed in a *lexicalized* mathematical formalism (a tree-rewriting system): a Tree Adjoining Grammar is a set of elementary trees, each of which represents a single lexical item and its syntactic projection. The lexicon is thus a grammar in the formal sense defined by TAG.[3]

The elementary trees are combined using the operations of substitution and adjunction. In substitution, a frontier node is replaced by a tree; in adjunction, an interior node is replaced by a tree.

Substitution is illustrated schematically in Figure 1. We can substitute tree β into tree α if there is a nonterminal symbol on the frontier of α which has the same label as the root node of β ('A' in Figure 1). We can then simply append β to α at that node. Nodes at which substitution is possible are called 'substitution nodes' and are usually indicated with a downarrow (↓).

Adjunction is shown in Figure 2. Tree α contains a nonterminal node labeled *A* (not on its frontier); the root node of tree β (an 'auxiliary tree') is also labeled *A*, as is exactly one non-terminal node on its frontier (the 'foot node'). All other frontier nodes are terminal nodes or substitution nodes. We take tree α and remove the subtree at its node *A*, insert in its stead tree β, and then add at the footnode of β the subtree of α that we removed earlier. The result is tree γ.

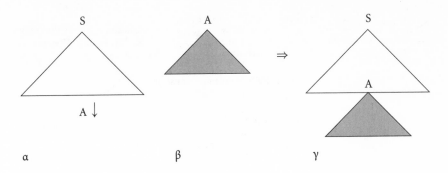

Figure 1. The Substitution Operation

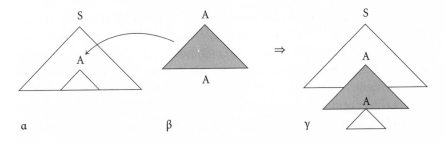

Figure 2. The Adjunction Operation

The interest of the TAG-based approach derives from the fact that the combination of syntactic structures is a formal operation. This has both formal and linguistic advantages. From a formal point of view, the restricted nature of the operations that derive larger structure means that the generative capacity of the formalism is restricted and that efficient (polynomial) parsers can be built. From a linguistic point of view, it means that syntactic theory is restricted in its scope to local domains. More precisely, syntactic theory must specify how to project structure from single lexical items, and how to derive variants (such as trees with *wh*-movement), be it by lexical rules (Abeillé 1990), metarules (Becker 2000; Evans et al. 2000), or by a principles-and-parameters type transformational theory based on move-α (Frank 2001). I will refer to this phase as the *lexical derivation* (since it affects the syntax of a single lexical projection). Note that in TAG-based linguistic theories, the lexical derivation is not a derivation in the TAG formalism; rather, this phase produces a grammar in the TAG formalism. Structures from this grammar are then combined using the formal operations of TAG. There is no other way of combining two lexical items. For example, there can be no additional restrictions on movement; ef-

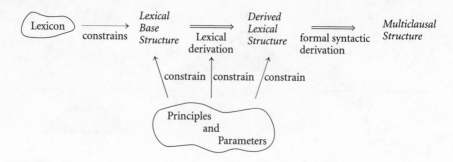

Figure 3. The 'basic TAG approach': Using TAG as a metalanguage for linguistics

fects such as long-distance *wh*-movement and island constraints must fall out of the way in which elementary structures are defined in the lexical derivation, and the way in which the formalism combines them in the syntactic derivation.[4] I will refer to this phase as the *syntactic derivation* (since it combines the syntax of more than one lexeme). The syntactic derivation is restricted only by the definition of the elementary trees and the formal definitions of substitution and adjunction – the linguist using TAG as a metalanguage cannot formulate new or language-specific operations for the syntactic derivation (unlike HPSG or CCG (Steedman 1991), in which the syntactic derivations are subject to cross-linguistic variation). As a result, if a linguist wants to develop a principles-and-parameters theory, its scope is limited to the lexical derivation.[5] The methodology is illustrated in Figure 3.

3.   Coherence and clause union: The incorporation approach

3.1 Coherent constructions

Properties of German embedded infinitivals led Bech (1955) to descriptively identify two classes of constructions, the *coherent* constructions in which two or more verbs are adjacent and in which the verbs' arguments appear to behave as if they were arguments of a single verb, and the *incoherent* constructions, in which the verbs are not (necessarily) adjacent and which displays expected biclausal behavior. Purely descriptively, the following properties have been noted (this list is based on Von Stechow & Sternefeld 1988, and is not exhaustive):[6]

– Sentences with extraposed clauses and sentences in which only one verb has been fronted are always incoherent constructions:

(1) a. daß Hans versucht, das Auto zu reparieren
         that Hans tries   the car   to repair
         'that Hans tries to repair the car'
     b. Zu reparieren hat Hans das Auto versucht.
         to repair   has Hans the car   tried
         'Hans has tried to repair the car.'

– Fronting of multi-verb sequences without their arguments is possible only in coherent constructions:

(2) Zu reparieren versucht hat Hans das Auto.
     to repair   tried   has Hans the car
     'Hans has tried to repair the car.'

– Long scrambling[7] is possible only in coherent constructions:[8]

(3) a. daß es Hans zu reparieren versucht
         that it Hans to repair   tries
         'that Hans tries to repair it'
     b. *daß es Hans repariert zu haben bereut
         that it Hans repair   to have regrets
         intended meaning: 'that Hans regrets having repaired it'

(3–b) shows that long scrambling is restricted to certain verbs. I will call verbs that allow for coherent constructions with their complements *coherent* verbs, and those that do not, *incoherent* verbs. (3–b) also shows that the juxtaposition of center-embedded infinitivals is not a sufficient condition for coherence. In fact, most authors assume that in the center-embedded construction with *zu* infinitives, coherence is optional even if the matrix verb is a coherent verb.

– Coherent verbs allow for a transposition of the matrix and embedded verbs (the 'Third Construction'):

(4) daß Hans das Auto versucht zu reparieren

– In incoherent constructions, negation in the embedded clause cannot have matrix interpretation, while in coherent constructions, it must.

(5) a. weil   Hans versucht, das Auto nicht zu reparieren
         because Hans tries   the car   not to repair
         only reading: 'because Hans is trying not to repair the car'

b. weil Hans das Auto nicht zu reparieren versucht
reading 1: 'because Hans is trying not to repair the car'
reading 2: 'because Hans is not trying to repair the car'

Note that (5–b) has two readings since the string is ambiguous between a coherent and an incoherent construction.

– In coherent constructions, embedded reflexives can take their antecedent among the matrix arguments:

(6) Hans$_i$ hat sich$_i$ zu rasieren versucht
Hans has himself to shave   tried
'Hans has tried to shave.'

– As pointed out by Höhle (1978), it is possible in coherent constructions to promote the embedded object to matrix subject through passivization. It is not possible to passivize only the matrix clause:

(7) Zu reparieren versucht wurde der   Wagen/*den Wagen schon
to repair   tried   was   the$_{NOM}$ car   the$_{ACC}$ already
dreimal
thrice
'It has already been tried three times to repair that car.'

Note that many speakers find the version with the nominative quite marginal as well.

Bech (1955) claims that only subject-control verbs without nominal objects can participate in a coherent construction. Haider (1993) shows that this is not true. For example, in (8) (Haider's 56b), an object-control verb is involved in a coherent construction (as evidenced by the long scrambling of the embedded object).[9]

(8) ?daß ihn   mir   jemand zu konsultieren geraten   hat
that him$_{ACC}$ me$_{DAT}$ someone to consult   recommended has
'that someone has recommended to me to consult him'

3.2 Clause union: An incorporation analysis

The descriptive distinction between coherent and incoherent constructions is interpreted by Evers (1975) in the formal context of transformational grammar.[10] He proposes that sentences with recursively embedded clauses in Continental West Germanic languages differ significantly in their syntactic analysis from their non-center-embedded counterparts in the same languages and in other languages such as English and French. In constructions in which verbs are adjacent to each other, he proposes a two-pronged process for coherent matrix verbs, which he calls 'clause union':

1. ￼ The embedded verb moves up to its governing verb and forms a single morphological unit through incorporation ('verb cluster formation'). The argument lists of the two verbs are merged.
2. The process of verb raising dissolves the clause boundary of the embedded clause ('clause pruning').

This approach has been followed by many other researchers in other frameworks as well, though of course analyses differ greatly as they are expressed in the different frameworks. For example, Haider (1993), working in the Chomskyan transformational framework of the day, rejects the notion that a morphologically complex verb can be formed in the syntax, and instead proposes that the verbs provide a complex basis for single projection. I will refer to all analyses in which the two verbs are explicitly given properties of a single verb as the *incorporation analysis*. I will use the terms 'incorporation analysis' and 'clause union' interchangeably.

3.3 Tree Adjoining Grammar and lexicalism

It should by now be clear that the operation of verb cluster formation is potentially troubling for TAG-based approaches: the strict separation between a grammar (= lexicon) on the one hand and formal rules for deriving larger multi-lexemic structures from the lexicon on the other hand would be blurred by a pure incorporation analysis of the coherent construction. More precisely, an incorporation analysis leads to two problems, one linguistic and one formal:

- Linguistically, the scope of syntactic theory is extended beyond the definition of projections from lexical items and of lexical rules to be performed on these projections, since now we need a new mechanism to combine structures for two initially independent lexical items. The principal linguistic advantage of TAG, that the scope of syntactic theory is restricted and that derivations involving multiple projections are handled by the formal machinery of TAG, is lost.
- Formally, a mechanism to include in the lexicon complex verbal forms of potentially unbounded size means that the lexicon (as a formal entity) is no longer finite. This means that we no longer have a TAG (since a TAG

requires a finite grammar), and we lose the formal advantages (restricted generative capacity and efficient parsing).

Neither problem is necessarily fatal for TAG. Linguistically, it is probably uncontroversial that we want a productive lexical mechanism, for example to combine a preposition and a verb to create particle verbs (*weggucken, wegfahren, wegwischen* 'to look/drive/wipe away'), even if certain combinations are restricted and certain combinations give rise to idiosyncratic meanings. This mechanism could be extended in order to handle the manipulation of argument lists needed for the cases at hand. On the formal front, the grammar used for parsing could be 'tailored' to the input, since the grammar is lexicalized. This means that only those recursive lexical rules need be applied which are justified by the input string, resulting in a finite *ad hoc*-grammar. Nonetheless, the clause union analysis is, basically, at odds with the spirit of TAG. It is therefore not surprising that Kroch and Santorini (1991), in providing a TAG analysis for German and Dutch embedded clauses, suggest that these constructions should not, in fact, be analyzed as forming a clause union.

4. Arguments against clause union

While TAG-based linguistic frameworks may have a particularly acute interest in avoiding an incorporation analysis of the coherent construction, the incorporation analysis needs to be justified in any framework: given the existence of the incoherent constructions, it is clear that we need to have a syntactic mechanism for subordination of infinitival clauses in German in any case. Therefore, methodological parsimony requires that the introduction of additional machinery to handle the coherent constructions by lexical means be justified, and in particular, it needs to be firmly established that the syntactic machinery is not empirically adequate. It may be objected that there is ample independent evidence in German for a lexical process of incorporation, e.g. the aforementioned particle verbs. However, unlike embedded infinitivals, these processes are not recursive, and furthermore, they do not require the merging of argument lists from two originally independent lexical items. It may also be objected that the causative, which in many languages is a morphological affix, provides independent cross-linguistic evidence for the need for lexical manipulation of argument lists. However, the morphological causative, like the passive, is a manipulation of the argument structure linked to the morphology of a single lexeme, not to a lexical derivation involving two (open-class) lexemes.

Thus, the apparatus of argument list merger is not independently motivated in syntax, and is unique to the proposed clause union analysis for Continental West Germanic.

In this section, I question the validity of some of the arguments for an independent lexical process of clause union formation by sketching an alternative account in a transformational framework, and discuss additional empirical evidence against it.

4.1 Is clause union necessary?

I will now sketch accounts of the data presented in Section 3.1 in an informal transformational framework. These accounts do not rely on the notion of clause union and instead are purely syntactic in that lexical items retain their individual projections. Some of these accounts have been proposed and discussed previously in the literature (as noted) and can be characterized as an 'evacuation' account: the syntactic phenomena are derived by long scrambling out of a constituent and an independent operation performed on the remnant constituent.

Suppose that the only difference between coherent and incoherent verbs were the fact that coherent verbs allowed scrambling out of their complement clause, but incoherent verbs did not. Such a proposal is motivated by the difference between bridge and non-bridge verbs in many languages including English and German, which differ with respect to allowing *wh*-extraction from their finite complement clause. This proposal is supported by the observation that the bridge verbs in German appear to be exactly the coherent verbs. In the case of scrambling, the difference between coherent and incoherent verbs could be represented as a difference in the category or feature content of the maximal projection of the selected clause.

Suppose furthermore a general process of clausal extraposition (independently needed), and suppose that scrambling can also occur from extraposed clauses. Following the proposal of Den Besten and Rutten (1989), we can derive the coincidence of the Third Construction with coherent verbs by suggesting that it is the result of extraposition and subsequent long scrambling of the arguments out of the extraposed clause. Incoherent verbs do not allow long scrambling from the extraposed clause, and hence do not allow the third construction, as required. A similar approach (following Webelhuth & Den Besten 1987) can predict that fronted multi-verb sequences are restricted to coherent verbs: we front the matrix VP after scrambling all arguments of both verbs out of it. Since for the embedded arguments, this represents long scrambling, the construction cannot be derived if the matrix verb is incoherent. Finally, if we assume simply that the negation marker *nicht* modifies the verb into whose projection it is adjoined, we can derive the ambiguity in coherent constructions by assuming that for the matrix negation reading, the embedded arguments have been scrambled to the left of the *nicht* adjoined into the matrix clause. Again, an incoherent verb would not allow this long scrambling. (For an alternative account of the negation facts that resorts neither to clause union nor to long scrambling in the overt syntax, see Kroch & Santorini 1991.) Finally, the binding facts can be straightforwardly explained if we assume that the embedded subject, whether or not represented in the phrase structure as PRO, is coreferential with the matrix argument and can serve as local antecedent. This analysis is in fact confirmed by the fact that incoherent verbs also allow this kind of binding: *Hans bereut, sich rasiert zu haben.* (We return to long passives in Section 5.4.)

4.2 Is clause union sufficient?

The syntactic analyses proposed above make additional predictions: if the word orders which are taken to be indicative of the coherent construction are derived by long scrambling, what happens if we only scramble some elements and leave others *in situ*? First, consider the Third Construction. Since it is derived by scrambling arguments from an extraposed clause, we expect that we can leave arguments or adjuncts in the extraposed clause, while scrambling others out. This is indeed the case:

(9) a. daß er die Schweine vergessen hat dreimal zu füttern
         that he the pigs   forgotten has thrice   to feed
         'that he forgot to feed the pigs three times'   (Bayer 1992)

     b. daß uns   Hans versuchte, seinen Wagen zu zeigen
         that us$_{DAT}$ Hans tried   his   car   to show
         'that Hans tried to show us his car'   (Kroch & Santorini 1991)

     c. daß ich diesen Beruf   nach   Fähigkeit und
         that I   this   profession according-to ability   and
         Neigung   glaube am besten ausfüllen zu können
         inclination think   at best   exercise   to can$_{INF}$
         'that I think that it is this profession that my abilities and inclinations make me most suited for'
         (Uwe Johnson (German novelist), in a letter reproduced in his memoires, *Die Katze Erinnerung*)

d. daß sie   sie   glaubten mit Augen zu sehen und
    that they_{NOM} them_{ACC} believed with eyes to see and
    mit den Händen zu erfassen
    with the hands   to grasp
    'that they believed to see them with their eyes and to grasp them with
    their hands'   (Ludwig Tieck, *Franz Sternbalds Wanderungen*)

These sentences contradict the characterization of coherent constructions. In
these examples, embedded arguments or adjuncts appear between matrix arguments or adjuncts and the matrix verb, stranded from the embedded verb. If
they have scrambled from the extraposed embedded clause, we must conclude
we have a coherent construction. At the same time, the presence of embedded
arguments or adjuncts between the two verbs means the examples cannot form
a coherent construction.[11]

In the case of verb fronting, the syntactic analysis, but not the incorporation analysis, predicts that we should be able to front only the embedded verb,
even if long scrambling takes place:[12]

(10) Zu repaRIEren hat das Auto der HANS versprochen.
      to repair   has the car the Hans promised
      'It is Hans who has promised to rePAIR the car.'

Again, this sentence is problematic for the incorporation analysis, since the
long scrambling forces a coherent analysis, while the fronting of a single verb
precludes it.

Similarly, under the syntactic analysis, we expect to be able to front two
verbs while leaving behind arguments of both, and while extraposing the embedded verb in the fronted position along with a remaining argument. Again,
this is the case:

(11) Versucht, einen Freund vorzustellen, hat er ihr   noch nie.
      tried   a_{ACC} friend to-introduce has he her_{DAT} yet   never
      'He has never yet tried to introduce a friend to her.'   (Netter 1991)

The presence of arguments and adjuncts of both verbs in the Mittelfeld forces
an analysis as a coherent construction, while the extraposed embedded verb
(with argument) precludes it.

In the case of negation, we expect, under the syntactic analysis, to be able
to have *nicht* with scope only over the embedded clause (by being adjoined to
it) even when long scrambling takes place out of that clause. This prediction is
borne out:

(12)   A: Wieso redet Jutta so behutsam mit Karsten?
       Why is Jutta speaking so carefully with Karsten?
       B: ?Weil   ihn   Jutta nicht zu beleidigen versucht
            because him$_{ACC}$ Jutta not   to insult   tries
            'Because Jutta is trying not to insult him.'

In the incorporation analysis, the long scrambling forces the coherent construction, which in turn predicts that only the matrix reading of the negation should be available.

Finally, consider a sentence that allows us to test for binding facts without interference from the control reference:[13]

(13)   Zu rasieren erlaubt hat der Meister$_i$ dem   Lehrling$_j$ nur
       to shave   allowed has the master   the$_{DAT}$ apprentice only
       ihn$_{i,*j}$/sich$_{j,*i}$ selber
       him/himself self.
       'The master has allowed the apprentice to shave only him/himself.'

The possible readings are exactly as expected if the construction were incoherent, and are incompatible with a coherent construction under the assumption that the verbs form a single domain for anaphor binding, as would be natural in the clause union analysis. But under the incorporation analysis, the verb sequence can only be fronted without arguments if the construction is coherent.

In conclusion, we see that there is empirical evidence against the incorporation analysis. At the same time, much of the relevant evidence is somewhat degraded, and in corpora it is rare.

5.   Coherence and tree rewriting: The syntactic approach

5.1   A formalism for (relatively) free word order

In (14), the embedded verb, *geben* 'to give', has two overt nominal arguments, one of which has topicalized into sentence-initial position, and the other of which has scrambled beyond the matrix subject.

(14)   [Dieses Buch]$_i$ hat [den Kindern]$_j$ niemand [PRO t$_j$ t$_i$ zu geben]
       [this book]$_{ACC}$ has [the children]$_{DAT}$ [no-one]$_{NOM}$ to give
       versucht.
       tried
       'No-one has tried to give this book to the children.'

If we associate the nominal arguments of each verb with their verb, and the matrix auxiliary with the matrix verb, we get the following pattern:

(15) Dieses Buch hat den Kindern niemand zu geben versucht
      n^{emb} v^{matrix} n^{emb} n^{matrix} v^{emb} v^{matrix}

This sentence cannot be derived by any TAG, if we assume that nominal arguments and auxiliaries are substituted/adjoined into the tree of their main verb. This is because upon adjunction, the frontier of one tree is divided into three segments (as can be seen in Figure 2), and the frontier of the other into two, giving us five segments, but in the string above we have six segments! Simple TAG is therefore not sufficiently powerful to handle the word order variation found in German.

If TAG is not adequate for the description of syntax, what options do we have? The relatively free word order found in German suggests that what is needed is not a formalism whose elementary structures are trees, but one in which the elementary structures are underspecified trees, i.e., *descriptions* of trees. Such a formalism is D-Tree Substitution Grammar (DSG) (Rambow et al. 2001). In lexicalized TAG, elementary objects of a grammar are completely specified trees which fix the syntactic context for the lexical anchor. In DSG, the elementary objects are descriptions of trees ('d-trees'), which represent possible syntactic contexts for the anchor. D-trees are formalized in a logic for describing nodes and the relationships that hold between them, namely dominance, immediate dominance, and linear precedence.[14] A relation of underspecified dominance between two nodes is called a *d-edge*. An example is shown in Figure 4.[15] Immediate dominance is represented as always with a solid line, while d-edges are represented with a dashed line. D-edges may be annotated with

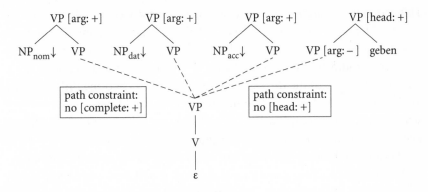

Figure 4. D-tree for German verb *geben* 'to give'

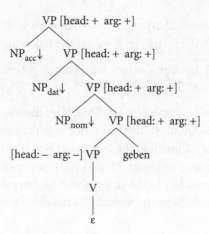

Figure 5. Tree for German verb *geben* which is a minimal reading of the d-tree in Figure 4

path constraints, which restrict the sets of node labels (or features of node labels) that may occur on the path in the derived tree which corresponds to the d-edge. A set of nodes which are connected (directly or indirectly, through other nodes) by immediate dominance relations are referred to as a *component*. In Figure 4, there are five components.

If a d-tree has a single component, it is a tree. If a d-tree has more than one component, we can associate with it the set of trees which represent minimal readings of the d-tree, i.e. which have been obtained from the d-tree by identifying pairs of nodes of the d-tree in order to eliminate d-edges, but without introducing new nodes. Furthermore, in identifying nodes, we can only identify nodes that are at the top end of a d-edge with root nodes of components. This requirement means that the components of a d-tree will not 'disappear' through identification of multiple pairs of nodes – structure, once defined in a d-tree, must be preserved when reading off trees. Figure 5 shows a tree which is a minimal reading of the d-tree in Figure 4. It is clear that we can obtain all six possible orderings of the three arguments of *geben* by choosing different ways of eliminating the d-edges. Note that in TAG we would need six elementary structures in order to capture the relevant syntactic behavior of *geben*, while in DSG we need only one, the d-tree in Figure 4.

Because of the underspecification, we do not need the operation of adjunction to intermingle the projections of different lexical items, and there is only the operation of substitution. Its definition is basically the same as in TAG: we identify frontier nodes which are labeled with nonterminals as *substitution nodes* (again marked with a downarrow ↓), and then append another d-tree at such nodes. But since we are appending d-trees, we can choose the root node of any of the d-tree's components as the node which we append to the substitution node. Formally, the operation of substitution consists in forming the union of two tree descriptions and of identifying two nodes, a substitution node and a root node of a component. A derivation consists of a sequence of substitutions. At the end of a derivation, we can obtain trees associated with the derived d-tree in exactly the same manner as explained above for elementary d-trees.

We illustrate a derivation in DSG using an example of long scrambling.

(16) a.   daß die Kinder   dem Lehrer   das Buch   zu geben
           that [the children]$_{NOM}$ [the teacher]$_{DAT}$ [the book]$_{ACC}$ to give
           versuchen
           try
           'that the children try to give the teacher the book'
      b.   daß dem Lehrer die Kinder das Buch zu geben versuchen
      c.   daß dem Lehrer das Buch die Kinder zu geben versuchen

We can represent the matrix verb as shown in Figure 6, and the result of substituting the d-tree for *geben* (at the root of the component containing the verb) into the substitution node for the clausal complement in the d-tree for *versuchen* is shown in Figure 7. From this we can still obtain all six possible word orders, which would be impossible using simply LP rules that order sister nodes. (It would also be impossible in LTAG, but see Joshi et al. 2000 for an alternate discussion of long scrambling in LTAG). In fact, we also get another two orders, which correspond to cases in which the entire clause has scrambled:

(17) a.   daß dem Lehrer das Buch zu geben die Kinder versuchen
      b.   daß das Buch dem Lehrer zu geben die Kinder versuchen

Note that because of the d-edges, we cannot derive word orders in which embedded arguments follow the embedded verb, which are not grammatical:

(18) a.   *daß dem Lehrer zu geben das Buch die Kinder versuchen
      b.   *daß das Buch zu geben die Kinder dem Lehrer versuchen

Formally and computationally, DSG is an appealing formalism for the description of natural languages: if lexicalized, the formalism generates only context-sensitive languages (Rambow 1994a), and it is polynomially parsable (Rambow et al. 2001).[16]

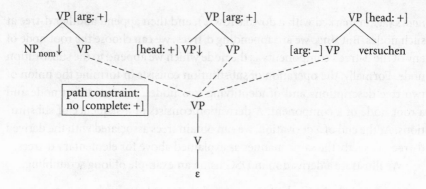

Figure 6. D-tree for German verb *versuchen* 'to try'

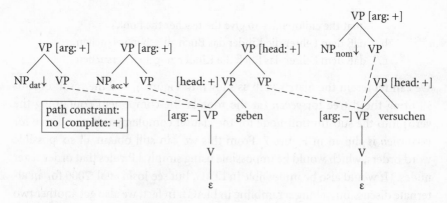

Figure 7. DSG derivation for complex sentence

5.2 DSG as a metalanguage for syntax

DSG, like TAG, is a mathematical formalism and not a linguistic theory. There are many ways in which it can be used to develop a linguistic theory. In particular, it would be possible to use the same approach used for simple TAG, illustrated above in Figure 3: we define basic projections from lexical items along with procedures outside the formalism for deriving related projections (with scrambled arguments, *wh*-movement, and the like). However, the fact that the elementary structures are now tree descriptions suggests a different approach, not previously available. Under the new 'unified' approach, all projections from a lexical item are derived *within* the formalism. More precisely, a full derivation proceeds in two steps:

- In the *lexical* derivation, further specifications are added to a d-tree. The lexical derivation may, but need not form a (fully specified) tree. The resulting d-tree corresponds to the (extended) projection from that lexical item.
- In the *syntactic* derivation, the d-trees derived during the lexical derivation are combined using substitution in the usual way to form larger, multi-lexemic structures. At the end of the syntactic derivation, a tree is read off from the derived d-tree.

Thus, there no longer are two *formally* different types of derivations, lexical and syntactic. Instead, both types of derivation are formal operations within DSG, the difference being that the lexical derivation removes underspecification from a single d-tree, while the syntactic derivation combines d-trees and then removes underspecification from the resulting derived tree. This is illustrated schematically in Figure 8.

An important aspect of the linguistic theory for DSG is the use of fewer node labels. This is imposed on us because the lexical entry is underspecified with respect to how the head projects. For example, in German we use the same lexical entry for verb-final clauses and verb-second (V2) clauses. Normally, the head in verb-final position would be dominated by a VP node, and the head in V2 position by, say, a $\overline{C}$ node. In our approach, both nodes must be labeled VP, since the label is given in the lexical entry common to both constructions. Instead, the difference between the different levels of projection from a lexical item is expressed using a system of binary features, called *categorial features*. The categorial features are independently motivated by semantic or morphological facts. They constrain the lexical derivation. For example, they make sure that, upon choosing a verbal tree set, we can derive tree sets that correspond to a finite clause with a complementizer, a finite V2 clause, a finite V1 clause

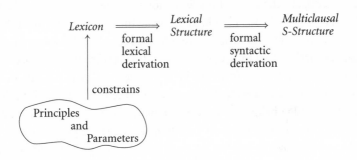

Figure 8. Using V-TAG as a metalanguage for linguistics

(question), or a finite or non-finite verb-final clause. These different lexical derivations are determined by an assignment of features to the lexical head of the tree set and to morphologically independent heads (auxiliaries, complementizers, determiners). There is not necessarily a one-to-one correspondence between features and heads. For a cross-linguistic discussion of how categorial features can derive a range of verb-second behavior, see Rambow and Santorini (1995). V2 will not be discussed further in this paper.

Since we are only interested in verb-final clauses in this paper, we omit all features related to V2. We assume that there is a tense feature which is related to case assignment in the usual manner, so that only tensed verbs can assign nominative case, and so that non-finite verbs must have an empty PRO subject. Furthermore, we assume that the component containing the origin of the projection (but not the lexical head) is lacking a feature which all other components have.

In addition, we will use the following three features related to the lexical head and its arguments:[17]

- The binary feature [head] has the value + at all levels of projection that dominate the lexical head.
- The binary feature [arg] has the value + at all levels of projection that dominate at least one syntactic argument of the head. A VP with feature [arg: −] corresponds, in some sense, to the node label V in traditional systems.
- The binary feature [complete] has the value + at all levels of projection that dominate *all* of the syntactic arguments of the lexical head. It designates the completion of the lexical predicate-argument structure in syntax.

This means that at the origin of the projection, all features have the value −. Once a head or an argument introduces a value +, the feature will have that value all the way up the projection.

Consider again the d-tree for *geben* shown in Figure 4. The head component has the feature [head: +] at its root, while the components that introduce arguments have [arg: +]. Furthermore, the d-edge below the nominal components have a path constraint [complete: +] (this feature may not occur along the path corresponding to the d-edge in the derived tree), since clearly the predicate is not complete at a node if a nominal argument dominates it in the projection. The d-edge below the head has a path constraint of [head: +]. Note that the path constraints follow naturally from the same principle that introduces features: below the level in the projection at which the feature is set to +, it must be −.

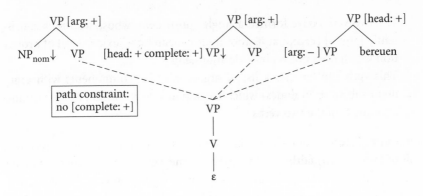

Figure 9. D-tree for incoherent verb *bereuen* 'to regret'

5.3 Deriving coherent and incoherent constructions

In this approach, the difference between coherent verbs such as *versprechen* 'to promise' and incoherent verbs such as *bereuen* 'to regret' is expressed by the feature content on the clausal substitution node in the matrix verb. We will assume that all clausal substitution nodes have feature [head: +], meaning that they must dominate the head of the embedded clause. Incoherent verbs furthermore select for a VP with [complete: +], i.e., for a syntactically complete predicate (Figure 9). As a result, the entire structure projected from the embedded verb must be dominated by the substitution node, since the path constraints on the dominance links preclude any component from being inserted above the substitution node. Put differently, in the lexical derivation we can fully specify both the matrix and the embedded d-trees, since no interleaving of components will occur during the syntactic derivation.

For the coherent verbs, we assume that the VP substitution node is marked only for [head: +], and that both features [arg] and [complete] are undefined. Now we can substitute any component of the *geben* d-tree into the substitution node (other than the origin of the projection). If we choose an argument component, we derive a sentence with at least one embedded argument in the embedded clause. If we choose the head component, we obtain the derived d-tree shown in Figure 7. Because of the d-edges, we can then read off trees that correspond to the word orders in (16) and (17).[18] If we first eliminate the d-edge which connects the components containing the clausal substitution node, the matrix head *versuchen*, and the matrix and embedded origins of the projections, we obtain the structure in Figure 10. It can be seen immediately that this stage of the derivation represents quite faithfully the incorporation analysis:

- The two verbs have formed a single constituent, whose feature is consistently [arg: –] (except at its root node), meaning a 'lexical' level of projection which does not yet include arguments.
- This verb 'cluster' has a list of arguments (i.e. components with argument substitution nodes) which corresponds to the union of the nominal arguments of the two verbs.

Of course, Figure 10 and the associated derivation do not implement the analysis of Evers (1975) faithfully. In particular, the 'verb complex' does not in any way appear to have undergone a special morphological process.[19] And, as mentioned, the clauses were never 'pruned', since this is a non-transformational system. However, I would like to claim that this derivation captures the underlying intuition of the lexical analysis, which has proved compelling to most native speaker linguists (even if the arguments put forward in favor of it have not necessarily proved compelling). However, unlike the incorporation analysis, the representation in Figure 10 is just an artifact of our choice of how to read off a tree from the derived tree description: we chose to first eliminate underspecification around the two verbs. We could also have proceeded first to eliminate underspecification of the (matrix) arguments, in which case we would not have obtained an intermediate representation corresponding to a 'verb complex'. Put differently, we obtain a verb complex in a derivation if the

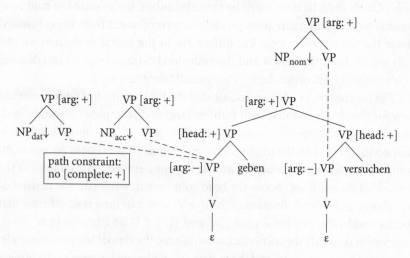

Figure 10. Possible intermediate point in DSG derivation for complex sentence, corresponding to 'verb complex'

lexical derivation is kept very short and very little fully specified structure is associated with the lexemes prior to the syntactic derivation.

There is another option: we can mark the clausal substitution node with [arg: –] (with [complete] undefined). Now, there is only one derivation possible: the only component that can substitute at a node labeled VP [head: + arg: –] is the component containing the head. As a result, the lexical derivation of the embedded component can at most eliminate the dominance link between the origin of the projection and the head component. All arguments will have to be inserted in the matrix clause. As a result, we cannot derive any of the word orders in Section 3.1, and in fact, in terms of empirical predictions, this analysis corresponds to the original incorporation analysis.

As we saw in Section 4.2, there are empirical reasons for choosing the syntactic analysis over the incorporation analysis. However, using DSG, these two analyses are not as starkly different as they are in a transformational framework (where the incorporation analysis requires machinery not needed for similar constructions in other languages) or a pure TAG approach (where the incorporation analysis cannot naturally be represented at all). In fact, the difference is in the value of a single feature, [arg], which is either undefined (syntactic analysis) or – (incorporation analysis). This rather slight difference corresponds to the sometimes slight difference in acceptability: usually, the relevant judgments are not clear-cut. By deriving different syntactic behavior from lexically determined features, it becomes more plausible to expect not only lexically idiosyncratic behavior, but also extensive dialectal and even individual variation. And in either analysis, we can obtain the 'verb cluster' representation of Figure 10 as an intermediate step in the reading-off process.

5.4 Accounting for the data

It can easily be seen that the analyses of the coherent constructions discussed in Section 4.1 can be implemented straightforwardly in this framework if we assume that coherent verbs only specify [head: +] on their clausal complements. Furthermore, the cases discussed in Section 4.2 that are problematic for a clause union analysis can also be derived. Under this view, as desired, the difference between coherent and incoherent verbs reduces to the fact that coherent verbs allow scrambling out of their complement.

The long passive facts remain to be explained.[20] I will only sketch a solution here. Long passives pose a problem for a purely syntactic account of coherent constructions in German, since passive is typically assumed to be a lexical transformation, and therefore cannot intervene after the syntactic derivation has started. However, in the framework proposed here, the lexical and the syntactic derivations are formally identical, and differ only in whether trees from one or from more than one set are combined. In Rambow (1994b) I suggest that lexical processes such as passive and object-shift can be captured by assigning different features to heads (just as in the case of V2). For example, the double-object construction and the NP-PP construction would both result from assembling the components of phrase structure in the lexical d-tree of a ditransitive verb in different manners, depending on the assignment of features to heads. In the case of the passive, the absorption of the ability to assign (say) accusative case by the verb (represented by the shifting of a feature representing case-assignment or case-agreement) is accompanied by an additional operation: the subject (or agent) is either marked as optional or removed entirely from the lexical tree set. There is no inherent reason why all feature assignments must be made to elementary d-trees. Suppose instead we perform some initial feature assignment to the d-tree, and then start the syntactic derivation to the point shown in Figure 10. We can then finish the feature assignment to the verbal heads in such a way that the embedded verb loses its ability to assign case. At the same time, we mark the matrix subject as being optional. We then obtain the long passive, in a manner quite analogous to the regular passive. (The embedded object would, as required, be assigned nominative case from the matrix verb. The embedded subject could not be marked optional since then there would not be enough case assigners to finish the derivation.) In the case of the incoherent construction, the same procedure could be followed, except that the embedded object could not get case in the matrix clause because the matrix verb has marked its complement with [complete: +], so the embedded argument cannot leave the embedded clause.

It may be objected that the idea of passivizing what is in effect a complex clause is unappealing. However, there is cross-linguistic evidence from Italian causatives that such an operation is needed. In Italian causatives, the causative auxiliary and the main verb do not form a morphological word, but the construction allows long passives (Burzio 1986; Heycock & Santorini 1988).

6. Conclusion

The analysis presented in this paper is based on a formalism whose elementary structures are descriptions of trees. It suggests that the difference between the incorporation analysis and a purely syntactic analysis is really an artifact of the systems that are used to express them. If the mechanisms for projecting from a lexical item (lexical derivation) and for combining one or more such projections (syntactic derivation) are quite different and if this difference is furthermore expressed by differences in node labels (V and VP), then the German data will require a choice. The incorporation solution means that the standard syntactic mechanism for combining two lexical items with separate argument lists cannot be used, and a new lexical mechanism must be invented for German coherent constructions. The incorporation analysis does not appear to be empirically adequate, but the syntactic solution appears not to capture certain intuitions about coherent constructions. However, if we choose to assemble phrase structure incrementally from underspecified descriptions during both the lexical and the syntactic derivations, we see that the incorporation analysis and the syntactic analysis differ only in the value of one (or two) features in the projection level selected by the matrix verb. And the 'verb cluster' is an effect of the derivation (in both the 'syntactic' and the 'incorporation' analyses), not expressible explicitly in the competence grammar on its own.

Notes

1. I would like to thank Tony Kroch and Beatrice Santorini for helpful discussions.

2. Tree Adjoining Grammar, unlike HPSG or LFG, is simply a mathematical formalism. Hence the need to refer to 'TAG-based linguistic theories' rather than simply 'TAG'.

3. For general introductions to TAG, see (Joshi 1987, 1994; Abeillé & Rambow 2000).

4. See (Kroch 1987, 1989; Frank 2001) for discussions of *wh*-movement in TAG.

5. The term 'principles-and-parameters theory' refers to a type of linguistic theory, not a particular one.

6. The terms 'matrix' and 'embedded' are used purely descriptively to refer to the two verbs involved and to their arguments. The use of this terminology does not imply a bias against the incorporation analysis.

7. The term 'long scrambling' is used to refer descriptively to cases in which an argument or adjunct of a verb appears to the left of an argument of the matrix verb, or to the left of the matrix verb if it precedes the embedded verb. One often finds the claim that German has no long scrambling. This claim is not an empirical claim, but a theoretical claim, since it is based on the clause union analysis: if coherent constructions (the only context in which long scrambling is licensed) are in fact monoclausal constructions, then of course there is no theoretical distinction between local and long scrambling. That scrambling is syntactically different from *wh*-movement in that *wh*-movement can escape from finite clauses while scrambling never can (a statement occasionally made to show that long scrambling does not exist), is both uncontroversial and irrelevant to the issue.

8. I ignore differences between clitic climbing and scrambling for the sake of the argument in this paper.

9. The somewhat reduced acceptability can be attributed to the multiple scrambling, and the sentence is clearly better than would be expected if *raten* were coherent.

10. I leave aside the issue to what extent the transformational theory of the '70s was 'formal' – the term is used here to contrast Evers' work with the purely descriptive work of Bech.

11. It could be argued that elements such as *dreimal* in (9c) are incorporated into the verbal complex. However, there is no independent motivation for such a proposal, and it clearly cannot account for the other examples, in which full phrases intervene between the two verbs, in the case of (9d) even including two conjoined verbs with adjuncts!

12. These cases are not very good if the fronted verb and the matrix subject are not stressed (which we indicate through capitalization).

13. This sentence should be compared to that in Haider (1993, Note 20). The contrast in judgments suggests that other factors are at work in Haider's example, given the relative clarity of the judgments here.

14. In DSG, precedence is always fully specified. It is fairly straightforward to extend the formalism to allow for underspecified linear precedence, but we will use the underspecified dominance relation to describe word order phenomena.

15. We will discuss this example from a linguistic point of view shortly; right now, it serves to illustrate the formalism.

16. Recall that a grammar is *lexicalized* if each tree set is associated with at least one lexical item, as will be the case for linguistically motivated formal grammars.

17. We could use names for these features which relate them more clearly to traditional node labels, but these feature names make their use clearer, and it is quite plausible to assume that we have access to a system of features that describe the lexical predicate-argument relations.

18. Note that some word orders can be obtained by assuming that an embedded constituent is either in the embedded clause, or in the matrix clause.

19. The fact that the dominance links of the embedded verb's argument impinge lower in the verb cluster than those of the matrix verb is irrelevant, since the embedded arguments cannot be added except above the matrix verb.

20. The partial VP fronting data also needs to be derived. To do so in DSG, we must assume that arguments can either dominate the origin of the projection, or the lexical head component itself. The details are left to further work.

CHAPTER 8

Verb clusters and branching directionality in German and Dutch

Pieter A. M. Seuren

Max Planck Institute for Psycholinguistics, Nijmegen

0. Introduction

The analysis and description of Dutch and German Verb clusters proposed here is cast in terms of the theory of *Semantic Syntax* (SeSyn; Seuren 1996). In SeSyn, a grammar is an algorithm that takes as input a Semantic Analysis (SA), formulated in a regimented variety of the *language of predicate calculus*, and produces a Surface Structure (SS) as output. The relevant details, as well as the wider cognitive environment of the SeSyn model, are given in the Sections 1, 2 and 3. One important parameter, allowing for crosslinguistic variation, is *branching directionality* (Section 1.2). Tree structures in specific parts of the grammar of a language are marked for left branching (LB) or right branching (RB); the rules that operate on them conform automatically. Dutch and German V-clusters ('coherent constructions'; Bech 1955) are discussed in the Sections 4 and 5, respectively. They result from similar syntactic systems, but with overall RB for Dutch, and overall LB for German V-clusters. Yet when in a derivation a German (LB) V-cluster headed by an *R-verb* (e.g. *können, wollen, dürfen*) stands directly under the perfective auxiliary *haben* or under the futuricity auxiliary *werden*, the remaining derivation of the cluster becomes RB, obligatorily for *haben* and optionally for *werden*. Given the specific SA-regimentation posited for the Germanic (and many other) languages, the relevant German facts follow automatically. The same regimentation explains the defective paradigm of the English modals, as well as many other similar phenomena. This analysis crucially fits the *uncontroversial* facts of Standard German. There are, however, also many *controversial* facts, especially in German, due to the complexity of the constructions, the rich array of admissible topicalizations, and the considerable dialectal variation. Section 6 discusses the data problem. It is concluded that the norms for Standard German are too flexible to allow for a description that yields *all* the possibly correct constructions. Instead, we must be content with a description that yields *only* correct constructions, leaving room for some parametric variation for less clear cases. Even so, it is felt that the description approximates the norms of Standard German in a nontrivial way. The last section gives a *mise au point* of what is actually claimed, in terms of linguistic reality, by the analysis presented. The central claim is that the *derivational* character of the system proposed is indispensable to its explanatory value: any physical implementation of the system must be derivational and cannot be just representational.

1.   The Semantic Syntax model

1.1   General architecture

Semantic Syntax (SeSyn; Seuren 1996) is a *transformational mediational* model of grammar. It considers a natural language grammar to be a mediating device mapping Semantic Analyses (SAs) of sentences onto corresponding Surface Structures (SSs) and vice versa. SAs are formulated in a *regimented version of the language of modern predicate calculus* or LPC, consisting of a lexical nucleus or matrix commanded by a number of operators.[1] The regimentation differs crosslinguistically but stays within the broad syntactic format of LPC. The differences concern mostly the build-up of the Auxiliary System of the language in question, containing tenses, aspects, modalities, negation, quantification and other (adverbial) operators. It is assumed that Auxiliary Systems of languages are built up according to language-specific semantic *auxiliary checklists* (see Note 5 below).

In this study we concentrate exclusively on the top-down or generative part, the transforming of SAs into SSs, leaving out the bottom-up part where SSs are parsed into SAs. The reason for this restriction is mainly practical: the description of the top-down transformational process has been strikingly successful in that significant generalizations could be captured, both within the languages described and crosslinguistically. No such successes have been achieved so far in specifying the bottom-up parsing process. It is felt that a parser, one which transforms input surface structures of sentences into corresponding semantic analyses, will have to rely heavily on the top-down generative mechanism, besides being dependent also on cognitive factors that filter out pragmatically improbable meanings.

SeSyn is embedded in an overall architecture linking it up with, on the one hand, cognition and, on the other, the physical media of sound and script. It is premissed on the assumption that cognition produces discourse-linked *thoughts*, i.e. mental propositions combined with a commitment operator. The latter defines the modality of the speaker's personal responsibility or commitment with respect to the former. Linguistic interaction is not primarily a matter of transfer of information, as superficial theorizing usually has it, but is primarily a matter of social position-taking with respect to a proposition: the speaker guarantees the truth of the proposition concerned, or enquires about its truth, or expresses a hope or wish or order to see the propositional representation realized, and so on.

We are, however, not concerned with the speech-act quality of uttered sentences; only with the propositional component. A proposition is, in principle, the mental act of assigning a property to some (concrete or abstract, existing or imagined) entity or entities. Little is known about the precise mechanisms and structures involved in the coming about of propositions. Here we assume that thoughts are generally structured as shown in Figure 1.

Any particular thought is a unique discourse-linked token occurrence, which has to be processed by a type-level linguistic machinery to be converted into a token utterance. The type-level machinery is what has been called the speaker's *linguistic competence*, a complex processor whose functioning is for the most part automatic and inaccessible to introspection. It is assumed that a lexical search order is issued by the machinery for the main lexical predicate expressing the property assigned, and for the predicates to be used in forming the nominal and other terms of the sentence to be. When the proper lexical choices have been made, a syntactic structure is built up largely according to (a) the restrictions imposed by the predicates found, (b) the instructions issuing from the regimented LPC in question (the auxiliary checklist), and (c) the discourse structure at hand (topic-comment modulation). The result is a Semantic Analysis (SA), a linguistic tree structure cast in a typologically restricted variety of LPC. The overall 'skeletal' format of a right-branching SA as found in all European and many non-European languages is given in Figure 2 below. The SA is then fed into a GRAMMAR, which transforms SAs into SSs. A morphological and a phonological component subsequently specify the phonetic (or orthographic) form of the ensuing token utterance. The transformational grammar is our central concern here.

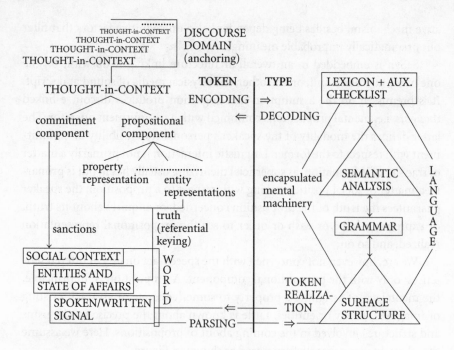

Figure 1. More detailed environment of a mediational grammar

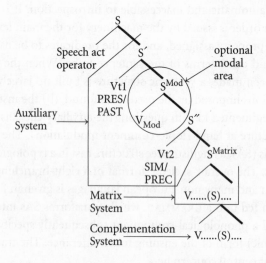

Figure 2. Skeletal structure of SA in VSO-format (right-branching)

Apart from the speech act operator, an SA consists of an Auxiliary System, a Matrix System, and optionally a Complementation System. The Auxiliary System specifies at least the tenses and optionally also modality, quantifiers and all kinds of possible adverbial adjuncts, in particular negation, that can be added to the Matrix sentence. In most European and many other languages there are two tenses, whose values have to be be specified for a sentence to come about. The first tense (Vt1) is deictic and is specified as either PRESENT or PAST, the second (Vt2) is relational with regard to the time denoted by Vt1 and is specified as SIMULTANEOUS or PRECEDING.

The Auxiliary System consists of predicates called *operators* since they modify or restrict the semantic applicability of the Matrix sentence. The Matrix System contains the main clause of the sentence, with the main lexical predicate and its terms. If any of the terms is again of a sentential nature, it is called a Complement-S, to be processed by the Complementation System of the Grammar, recursively.

It is assumed, furthermore, in keeping with an old tradition in Transformational Grammar, that the rule system that converts SAs into SSs falls into two main components. First the *cyclic rules* apply, at each successive S-cycle starting from the bottom of the tree. When the Cycle is over, i.e. when the highest S has been processed, the result is called *Shallow Structure* (ShS). The ShS is then input to a set of linearly ordered *postcyclic rules*. The cyclic rules are, for the most part, induced by the V-constituent at each cycle. They are also assumed to be highly constrained by universal principles, and thus very uniform across languages. The postcyclic rules are much more language-specific and much less tied up with lexical predicates.

1.2 Branching directionality

It appears that one of the main parameters in grammars is branching directionality. Main sections or subsections of the grammar are defined for right branching (RB) or left branching (LB). If the syntax of a language L is defined as RB for overall sentence structure (i.e. S-projections are programmed for RB), the verb comes first, followed by its terms, typically in the order Subject–Indirect Object–Direct Object (V-S-IO-DO), normally known as VSO-order. If the S-syntax is defined as LB, the verb comes last and is preceded by its terms, in the same order (S-IO-DO-V), normally known as SOV-order. Figure 3 below shows the two general formats for SA-structures. When L has a surface SVO-order, canonical SSs will consist of an NP followed by a VP, so that, in practice, SVO-order equals NP-VP order.[2] It is shown below how a surface SVO(=NP-

$$S \rightarrow (V-) \ NP/S \ (-V)$$
$$ subj.$$

$$S \rightarrow (V-) \ NP/S - NP/S \ (-V)$$
$$ subj. \quad dir.obj.$$

$$S \rightarrow (V-) \ NP/S - NP \ - \ NP/S \ (-V)$$
$$ subj. \quad ind.obj. \quad dir.obj.$$

Figure 3. General format of SA-structures in (V)-S-IO-DO-(V)

VP)-order results naturally from a particular transformational processing of underlying VSO-order structures.

If L has overall VSO-order, the main parts of the syntax will also be RB, and analogousy for SOV-order and LB. There are, however, exceptions, as languages do occasionally shift from one main word order to the other (mostly as a result of language contact), in which case mixed forms are found.[3] Thus, in German, V-clusters are predominantly LB, even if the syntax as a whole is probably best taken to be RB. In Dutch, on the other hand, V-clusters are predominantly RB, just as S-syntax: V-projections are programmed for LB in German, for RB in Dutch. Morphological *flection* and *declension* processes tend to be LB in the languages of the world: an overwhelming majority has verbal and nominal suffixes, rather than prefixes, to indicate tense, modality, case, agreement and the like.[4] Morphological *lexical derivation*, on the other hand, varies a great deal between LB and RB. In the present study, the directionality parameter is a major factor in the explanation of the facts and thus of prime importance.

In the diagrams the branching directionality has been marked by heavy lines wherever appropriate. In *S-syntax* the branching directionality is taken to be rooted in (programmed for) the S-nodes of SAs. In *category syntax* the directionality is taken to be rooted in (programmed for) the category symbols in the SA-structure at hand, in particular those whose lexical fillers induce cyclic or postcyclic rules. How precisely branching directionality is best implemented in the grammar machinery is a technical question.

The general format specified in Figure 3 is taken to apply across the board, to all main and embedded structures, both in the lexicon and in the grammar. This means that many elements that are labeled 'V' (predicate) in SA-trees must be *relabeled into the appropriate surface category*, which is specified in the lexicon. The grammar carries out this relabeling during the transformational process when the element in question is up for treatment, mostly during, but sometimes after the cycle.

1.3   The Auxiliary System

Since, in the theory at hand, verb clusters contain both matrix lexical material and material from the Auxiliary System, something must be said about that. In doing so we will restrict ourselves to the tenses and the modals, other aspects of the Auxiliary System being less relevant for the present purpose.

1.3.1   *The tenses*
The tense system follows Beauzée (1767) and Reichenbach (1947), who made a distinction between *utterance time* (S), *event time* (E), i.e. the time in which the event or situation described in the proposition is or was actually situated, and *reference time* (R), i.e. the discourse-related time focused on by the speaker at S, the time of speaking. These authors found that E is pointed down linguistically by a two-tiered system: first R is located with regard to S, then E is located with regard to R. It has been found that this framework provides an adequate syntactic as well as semantic basis for the description of the tenses in the European and many other languages.[5]

We therefore posit two tense operators (predicates), Vt1 expressing R and Vt2 expressing E (S is given anyway). Vt1 is either a deictic 'present' (PRES) or an anaphoric 'past' (PAST); Vt2 is defined relative to Vt1 and is either 'simultaneous' (SIM) or 'preceding' (PREC) with respect to Vt1. In most European languages, PRES and PAST are manifest as verbal suffixes. SIM is usually not lexicalized (except in English, where the dummy verb *do* acts for SIM and is deleted under certain conditions). PREC is realized as a perfect tense auxiliary (*have* or *be*). There are, however, also languages such as Ijo or Berbice Dutch (Kouwenberg 1994) where Vt1 is manifest as an auxiliary verb and Vt2 as a suffix, or, as in Latin and Ancient Greek, where both Vt1 and Vt2 are manifest as verbal suffixes, or, as in Creole languages, where both Vt1 and Vt2 tend to be lexicalized as preverbal particles or preverbs.

Futurity does not fit into the tense system, but is part of the modal system and mixed in with the tense system, as shown in §1.3.2 below. The fact that many languages express futurity by morphological means is no sufficient ground for treating it as a tense. (Turkish, for example, expresses possibility by means of an affix, yet possibility is clearly not a tense.)

The SA of every main sentence has to have the two tense operators, but embedded clauses may either have two tenses, in which case the embedded clause is S´, i.e. it contains a finite verb, or have only Vt2 (embedded clause is S″), or even be without any tense operator at all (S^{Matr}; see §1.4). In the latter two cases the embedded clause, S″ or S^{Matr}, is infinitival or participial. The SA

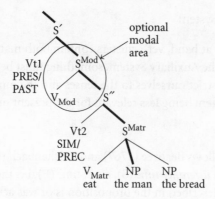

Figure 4. The position of the tenses

position of Vt1 and Vt2 is shown in Figure 4, which also gives the optional modal area between the two tenses, discussed in §1.3.2 below.

The four main tenses of English and, analogously, German, Dutch, French etc., are composed as follows:

PRES + SIM   → simple present   (I walk)

PAST + SIM   → simple past   (I walked)

PRES + PREC → present perfect   (I have walked)

PAST + PREC → pluperfect   (I had walked)

Figure 5. The composition of the tenses

The grammatical processing leading from SA to SS is discussed below.

1.3.2   *Auxiliation*

There is a peculiar phenomenon regarding predicates with lexically weak meanings and whose main function is to modify the meaning or the application range of stronger lexical predicates. The phenomenon affects mainly predicates expressing a modality, especially futuricity, but also other predicates expressing temporal aspect, aktionsart or appearance. All these predicates require an embedded complement-S in subject position.

The phenomenon consists in the fact that such predicates normally originate, in the history of any given language, as lexical matrix predicates, occurring in the position of V_{Matr} in Figure 4, but then show a tendency to 'climb' into the Auxiliary System via a number of distinct steps. This process we call *auxiliation*. Sometimes we also find that such verbs, besides undergoing auxiliation, still retain a parallel existence as old-fashioned matrix verbs.

The details of auxiliation are not well understood. It seems, however, that an early step may well be a tendency of the verb in question to develop a preference for the position of Vt2. Once this has grown into a fixture in the grammar, the verb can no longer occur in a perfective tense, since the Vt2 position has been taken, nor can it be followed by a perfective infinitive, for the same reason. As a result, their past participle form, which only occurs in the perfective tenses, is lost from the paradigm, and the status of their infinitival form is considerably weakened, as these verbs can no longer occur in an infinitival complement clause. This appears to have happened, for example, with Italian *bisogna* (it is necessary) and French *il faut* (it is necessary; with dative personal pronoun). It also seems to be beginning to break through with Italian *importa* (it matters).

If this is correct, it may provide an explanation for the fact that French allows, for example, for (1a, b) but not for (1c–f).

(1) a. Il lui faut/fallait partir.   (he has/had to leave)
     b. Il lui faudra/faudrait partir.   (he will/would have to leave)
     c. *Il lui faut être parti.   (he has to have left)
     d. *Il lui a fallu partir.   (he has had to leave)
     e. *Il va/peut/doit lui falloir partir.   (he will/may/must have to leave)
     f. *Il vient de lui falloir partir.   (he has just had to leave)

Similarly for Italian *bisogna*:

(2) a. Bisogna/bisognava partire.   (one has/had to leave)
     b. Bisognerà/bisognerebbe partire.   (one will/would have to leave)
     c. *Bisogna essere partiti.   (one has to have left)
     d. *Ha bisognato partire.   (one has had to leave)
     e. *Va/può/deve bisognare partire.   (one will/may/must have to leave)

In general, the relation between so-called 'defective' verbal paradigms and auxiliation processes requires a great deal of further research, which cannot be carried out here (cp. Erb 2001). One thing, however, stands out with relative clarity: many such lexically weak verbs end up in a position between Vt1 and Vt2, that is, the area in the Auxiliary System marked as 'optional modal area' in Figures 2 and 4. This clearly applies to the English modal auxiliaries *can*, *may*, *will*, *must*, *shall* and *ought to*, which are, of course, known for their defective paradigm lacking infinitives and participles. Their SA position between Vt1 and Vt2 guarantees that they can occur only in the simple present or past tense. Since, moreover, complement-Ss are either fully or partially tensed or untensed, but never modal, they cannot occur as infinitives.[6]

Clear cases of full auxiliation in German are the auxiliary verb of futuricity *werden* as well as epistemic (not deontic) *müssen* (Erb 2001) and the 'half-modals' (Halbmodalen) *drohen, scheinen, versprechen* and *pflegen* in their impersonal meanings (Richter 2000: 136–149):

(3) a. Er wird es schaffen.   (he will manage)
     b. *Er hofft, es schaffen zu werden. (he hopes that he will manage)
     c. Das muß wahr sein.   (that must be true)
     d. *Das hätte wahr sein müssen.   (that should have been true)
     e. Er scheint gegessen zu haben.   (he seems to have eaten)
     f. *Er wird zu essen scheinen.   (he will seem to eat)
     g. Es drohte zu sinken.   (it threatened to sink)
     h. *Es hat gedroht zu sinken.   (it has threatened to sink)
     i. Es pflegte zu regnen.   (it used to rain)
     j. *Es kann zu regnen pflegen.   (it may habitually rain)
     k. Es verspricht zu regnen.   (it promises to rain)
     l. *Es wird zu regnen versprechen. (it will promise to rain)

Interestingly, the corresponding verbs in Dutch have so far not or hardly been affected by auxiliation: the direct translations of (3a–l) sound reasonably correct, in any case not clearly incorrect, in Dutch. Only the verb *schijnen* (seem, Ger. *scheinen*) is beginning to show auxiliation tendencies, as it no longer seems to allow for the perfective tenses.

It will become clear below that the auxiliation of German futuricity *werden* and the non-auxiliation of its Dutch equivalent *zullen* are directly relevant for the proper description of German and Dutch V-clusters. Here we merely note that the Dutch direct translation of (3b):

(4) Hij hoopt het te zullen klaren.   (he hopes that he will manage)

is fully grammatical in Dutch, contrary to the German original (3b). This fact is explained by the auxiliation hypothesis.

1.4 Complementation types

SeSyn assumes there to be six types of complementation at SA level. Embedded argument clauses can be a fully tensed S′ (with Vt1 and Vt2), or a partially tensed S″ (with only Vt2), or an untensed S^Matr. Moreover, each of these three types can occur with or without a directly dominating NP. In English, both bare

S′ → *that*-clause	$_{NP}[S']$ → *that*-clause
S″ → infinitival	$_{NP}[S'']$ → participial
S^{Matr} → infinitival	$_{NP}[S^{Matr}]$ → participial

Figure 6. Six possible Complement-S-types in European languages

S′ and $_{NP}[S']$ become a finite subordinate clause (the default complementizer is *that*),[7] and both bare S″ and bare S^{Matr} become infinitive constructions. $_{NP}[S'']$ and $_{NP}[S^{Matr}]$ become participial constructions. Figure 6 gives a survey of these six possibilities in English grammar.

The important thing to note here is that there is no complementation type 'Modal', which would allow for the embedding of an S^{Mod} without a higher S′ containing Vt1. That is, clauses that contain a modal predicate can only be embedded together with the highest tense which secures the finiteness of the verb form immediately below it, as will be shown below.

2. The rule system and some examples

The rule system of SeSyn takes as input a given SA structure. It consists, first, of a set of *cyclic rules*, whose application starts with the most deeply embedded S and subsequently through each higher S-node, till the highest S has been processed. The resulting structure is called *Shallow Structure* (ShS). This is then input to a set of linearly ordered *postcyclic rules*, which add final trimmings to the sentence structure and prepare it for the morphological component, which is left unspecified here. The cyclic rules have a high degree of universality and are, for the most part, induced by the predicate on each S-cycle, in which case they are given between angled brackets in each tree structure until they have been applied. The postcyclic rules are much more language-specific and are, for the most part, structure-induced.

Let us now, by way of illustration, follow the generation process of some simple example sentences. Consider first the English sentence (5):

(5)   John slept on the roof.

The derivation is given in (6a–h). 'OI' stands for (cyclic) 'Object Incorporation', 'Lp' for (cyclic) 'Peripheral Lowering', 'L' for (cyclic) 'Lowering onto V', 'SR' for (cyclic) 'Subject Raising', and 'AH' for the postcyclic rule of 'Affix Handling'. The filler 'Ø' for Vt2 stands for 'SIM'.

(6)

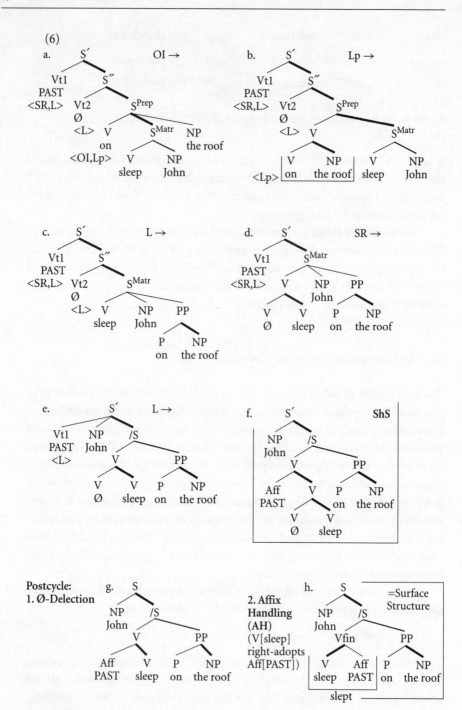

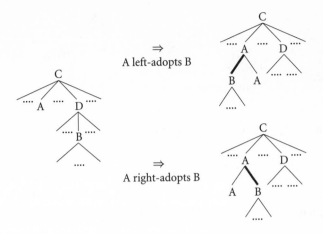

Figure 7. Adoption of the constituent B by the constituent A

Structure (6a) is the SA-structure. The first rule to apply, on the S^{Matr}-cycle, is OI , which takes the object NP and unites it with V by means of *adoption*, a standard unification procedure illustrated in Figure 7.

That is, the highest node A of the constituent A forms a copy of itself above itself; then constituent B is attached to the new copy node A. The right or left attachment ensures the correct directionality for the A-cluster. Since English V-clusters are RB, the attachment is to the right, as shown in (6b).

The entire complex predicate $_V$[on the roof] is now subject to *Peripheral Lowering* (Lp), which lowers the element in question to the far right of the argument-S. The result is shown in (6c), which marks the end of the S^{Matr}-cycle. Note that while Lp applied, the labeling of the constituent changed: the highest V has become Preposition Phrase (PP) and the V-node immediately dominating *on* has been relabeled as 'Preposition' (P). This follows from the general principle that surface categories are assigned during the cyclic processing.

Now we move up to the S″-cycle, where $_V$[Ø] must undergo Lowering (L), i.e. adoption by V_{Matr}. Since the structure involved is RB, and since $_V$[Ø] comes from higher up in the tree, there is left adoption, resulting in a RB V-cluster, as shown in (6d).[8]

On the next cycle, the S′-cycle, the first rule to apply is Subject Raising (SR). The general format of SR is shown in Figure 8.

That is, the subject-NP of the argument-S_{n+1} is removed from its position and given the position of its own immediately dominating S-node, which is moved one position to the right. This S-node is demoted to the status of /S, i.e. an S that has lost its subject-NP. What is called '/S' in SeSyn corresponds

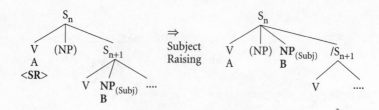

Figure 8. Rule schema of Subject Raising (SR)

to 'VP' in traditional terminology. We prefer '/S' because it shows the fact that VPs are nothing but Ss that have lost their subject-NP one way or another. An /S still has some characteristics of S-structures, but not all of them: /Ss are weakened Ss.

SR applies to NP constituents in subject position. The S from which the subject-NP is removed may be a subject or an object S. In the former case the raised subject-NP becomes a new subject to the higher V; in the latter case it becomes a new direct object to the higher V, normally marked for accusative case in languages that mark cases. The latter form of SR corresponds to the *Accusative-cum-Infinitive* (AcI) construction known from Latin and Ancient Greek. The result of SR on the S′-cycle is shown in (6e).

The next and last rule to apply on the S′-cycle is, again, L, resulting in (6f). Note that $_V$[PAST] has been relabeled as $_{Aff}$[PAST]: 'V' has become 'Affix', with consequences for the Postcycle and for the morphology.

We have now completed the Cycle, and the postcyclic rules apply from here on. The two rules that apply in this case are *Ø-Deletion*, resulting in the deletion of $_V$[Ø], as in (6-g), and *Affix Handling* (AH), by which $_V$[sleep] right-adopts $_{Aff}$[PAST], surprisingly resulting in a LB V-cluster. The branching directionality has been inverted on account of the fact that affixes are flectional morphological elements and flectional morphology is LB. The final result is (6-h), which, when processed by the morphology, is the surface structure corresponding to (5).

The V-cluster $[_V$[sleep]$_{Aff}$[PAST]] has been relabeled 'Vfin' (finite verb). Special stipulations within the rule AH may cause relabeling. Thus, after AH a structure $_V[_V$[X]$_{Aff}$[PRES/PAST]] is relabeled $_{Vfin}[_V$[X]$_{Aff}$[PRES/PAST]]; $_V[_V$[X]$_{Aff}$[EN]] is relabeled $_{PaP}[_V$[X]$_{Aff}$[EN]]; $_V[_V$[X]$_{Aff}$[ING]] is relabeled $_{PrP}[_V$[X]$_{Aff}$[ING]]. Vt1 is responsible for the finiteness of a verb form.

The inverted branching directionality as part of AH is neatly shown by the processing of French future verb forms. The French futurity modal predicate changes its category from V to Affix during the cyclic processing, losing verbal status. This means that a French finite verb form may have two affixal elements, as opposed to only one in English. Example (7) shows how the finite verb *mangera* ('he will eat') is generated from the SA (7a) representing *Jean mangera* (Jean will eat). The Cycle combines PRES and FUT into the V-cluster (7b) ($_{Vt2}[\varnothing]$ is unrealized). (7b) then undergoes AH twice: first $_{Aff}[FUT]$ is right-adopted by $_V[manger]$; then $_{Aff}[PRES]$ is right-adopted by the complex constituent $_V[_V[manger]_{Aff}[FUT]]$. The result is the LB V-cluster (7c), corresponding to the finite verb form *mang-er-a*.

(7)

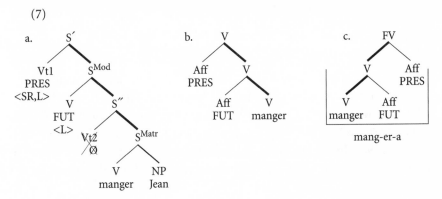

Finally, consider (8), whose abbreviated derivation is shown in (9a–e):

(8) Mary may have eaten the cake.

(9)

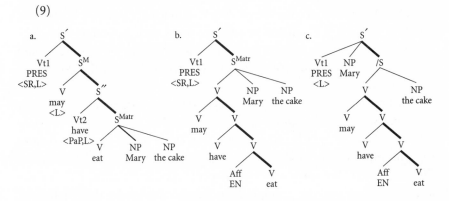

(9)   d.   POSTCYCLE: AH (2x)

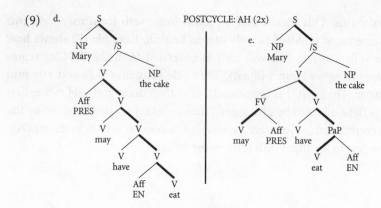

The first cyclic rule to apply is PaP: $_V$[eat] left-adopts the new element $_{Aff}$[EN], later to be processed as the past participle morpheme. Then $_V$[have] is lowered onto the lower V by L. On the S^M-cycle, $_V$[may] likewise undergoes L. The result is (9b). SR on the S'-cycle gives (9c) and L gives the NP-/S (=NP-VP) structure (9d). In the Postcycle, AH makes $_V$[may] attract $_{Aff}$[PRES] into a LB FV-constituent, and makes $_V$[eat] attract $_{Aff}$[EN] into a LB PaP-constituent.

3.   Matrix Greed

S^{Matr} being the main frame of the sentence, elements from the Auxiliary System as well as elements from complement-Ss are, as much as possible, incorporated into S^{Matr} (the limits of what is possible are set by each individual language). Languages go a long way to secure the fattening of S^{Matr} at the expense of both the Auxiliary and the Complementation Systems. We call this the *Principle of Matrix Greed.*

We have seen that auxiliary elements tend to be incorporated into S^{Matr} by Lowering, which is either *Lowering onto V* (L), leading to V-clusters, or *Peripheral Lowering* (Lp), which makes the lowered element land at the far right of the embedded S. In general, complex auxiliary elements, such as Preposition Phrases, take Lp, but single auxiliary elements may do the same. The German and Dutch negations, for example, take peripheral lowering (Lp), unlike the negation in English, which takes lowering on V (L).

The only case running counter to Matrix Greed is Subject Raising (SR) induced by Vt1 and leading to surface NP-/S (=NP-VP) structures with SVO basic constituent order. Why so many languages do this, is not clear, but there may be something to the contention, which is sometimes heard, that a middle position of the main verb enhances ease of comprehension. Creole languages, which maximize semantic transparency (Seuren & Wekker 1986), are all SVO. If this view is correct, there is a good functional reason for SR induced by Vt1. It is, anyway, interesting to observe that without Vt1-induced SR the result is a straightforward RB VSO language, and that SVO languages are likewise predominantly RB in their syntax.[9]

In the Complementation System we also find a pressure to incorporate elements into S^{Matr}, yet less strongly than in the Auxiliary System, perhaps because of the less abstract and more lexically prominent status of complement-Ss. Finite, i.e. fully tensed, subordinate clauses are largely left alone. But embedded S″ or S^{Matr} is always affected. A variety of strategies is found. In some languages, for example, there is a tendency to nominalize untensed or partially tensed complement-Ss. In other languages the subject-NP is removed and, consequently, the dominating S is reduced to /S, or the dominating S-node is removed, and its constituents are amalgamated with S^{Matr}. We shall have a closer look at the latter two strategies, removal of the lower subject-NP and removal of the lower S-node.

Removal of the lower subject-NP occurs in two different ways. When the lower subject-NP is referentially bound by a controlling NP term in the Matrix-S (i.e. the lower NP takes its reference value from the controlling NP), the regular process is Subject Deletion (SD), which deletes the lower subject-NP and reduces its dominating S to /S. In most cases the controlling Matrix-NP is the subject, but object NPs also frequently act as controllers of SD. This form of SD is called *vertical SD*, as the deletion occurs in an embedded complement-S. There is, however, also *horizontal SD*, deleting the referentially controlled subject-NP in untensed or partially tensed SA object-Ss with a preposition like *by* or *in* or *on* as SA predicate. Horizontal SD is found in sentences like:

(10)   a.   Sophie escaped by breaking the lock.

derived as shown in (10b, c) (details omitted):

(10)

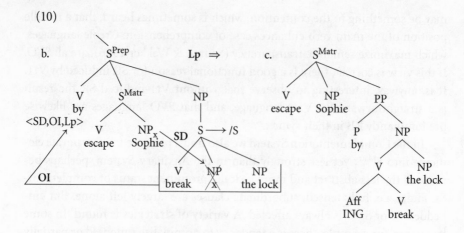

The general formats of the various forms of SD are given in Figure 9.

The second form of subject-NP removal is Subject Raising (SR), illustrated above in Figure 8. SR occurs when the lower subject-NP is not referentially controlled by a higher NP in the Matrix-S. Often, in languages that have SR,

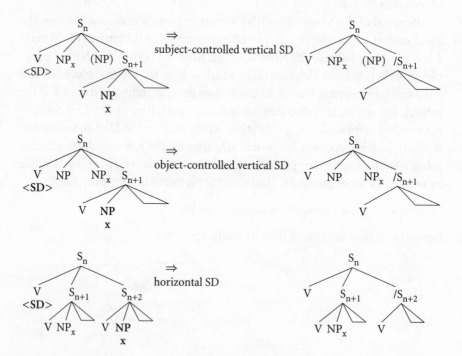

Figure 9. Rule schemata for Subject Deletion (SD)

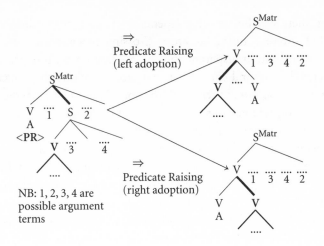

Figure 10. Rule schemata for Predicate Raising

SD and SR alternate in that SD applies when there is coreferentiality between the designated higher term and the lower subject-NP, while SR applies when there is not, as in English *I want to go* versus *I want you to go*.

The other strategy, besides subject-NP removal, is Predicate Raising (PR). PR implies the removal of the whole dominating S- or /S-node, whose constituents are amalgamated with the higher S. This is the regular procedure in languages that have PR, as opposed to SR. PR takes the V-constituent of the embedded S, which must be a bare S″ or S^{Matr} (unmodified by negation or adverbial operators), and unites it by means of RB or LB adoption with the higher V, as shown in Figure 10. A general universal principle is assumed implying that an S-structure that loses its V thereby loses its S-status, so that the S-node in question disappears and all remaining material is simply re-attached higher up in the order of occurrence. PR is the farthest a grammar can go in incorporating material from a complement-S into S^{Matr}.

There appears to be a typological distinction between languages that have SR and those that have PR in their Complementation System (both in combination with SD). For example, English, Portuguese, Latin, Ancient Greek, Ijo are SR-languages. But German, Dutch, Aztec, Luiseño, Japanese, Sre, and many more, are PR-languages. French is mixed: it takes SR for subject clauses, but predominantly PR for object clauses.

One striking result of PR is that the matrix-S with the complex V-cluster will often end up with more argument terms than the original matrix-S with the non-complex lexically defined predicate. Moreover, when PR is right-branching, there will be crossing dependencies – a fact that has attracted a great deal of attention in the literature. Crossing dependencies make a structure less semantically transparent and put a strain on on-line processing. In fact, it seems that natural comprehension capacity allows for a maximum of four accumulated argument terms. With more than four terms, the structure is no longer interpretable other than by explicit (pen and paper) analysis.

A further consequence is that a lower subject-NP often surfaces as the middle term between the higher subject and the original lower direct object, and thus occupies the position of indirect object (see Figure 3 above). In fact, one sees that in many languages the original lower subject term turns up in SS as a DATIVE (indirect object) when flanked by a direct object in the embedded S (see Seuren 1972[2001] for extensive discussion). Thus, in the French sentence (11a) the dative *à Pierre* (to Pierre) is the original semantic subject of the verb *voir* (see), and likewise in the Dutch sentence (11b), where the dative *aan Pieter* (to Pieter) is the original semantic subject of the verb *zien* (see):

(11) a. Je ferai   voir la   lettre à Pierre.
          I   will-make see the letter to Pierre
          'I will make Pierre see the letter'
      b. Ik zal de brief aan Pieter laten zien.
          I   will the letter to Pieter let   see
          'I will make Pieter see the letter'
      c. Ich werde den   Mann den   Brief sehen lassen.
          I   will the$_{ACC}$ man the$_{ACC}$ letter see   let
          'I will make the man see the letter'

Such 'derived' datives are typically, but not always, found with PR constructions in the languages of the world. German is among the exceptions: as can be seen from (11c), German assigns accusative case to the raised subject term (although there are signs in colloquial spoken German that the dative is beginning to gain ground).[10]

4. Dutch V-clusters

4.1 Optional and obligatory PR

It is now time to have a closer look at the Dutch V-clusters, which result from the application of Matrix-Verb-induced PR.

Consider the Dutch subordinate clauses (12a–d), all meaning 'that Jan wanted to try to teach the dog to fetch the newspaper'.

(12) a. ... dat Jan wilde proberen de hond te leren de krant te halen
       b. ... dat Jan wilde proberen de hond de krant te leren halen
       c. ... dat Jan de hond wilde proberen te leren de krant te halen
       d. ... dat Jan de hond de krant wilde proberen te leren halen

We can now show that they all derive from the SeSyn rule system as set out so far, provided the predicates involved are given the right rule specifications. *Willen* (want) induces the rules SD and PR; both *proberen* (try) and *leren* ('teach') induce SD and optional PR. Moreover, *proberen* adds the particle *te* (to) to the following infinitive, whether PR has applied or not; *leren* adds *te* only if PR has not applied. Note, finally, that in Dutch as well as in German the postcyclic rule V-Final applies. In main clauses, this rule moves the non-finite part of the V-cluster, in non-main clauses and infinitival or participial constructions the entire V-cluster to the far right, but never across an embedded S or /S (German does allow V-Final to cross an embedded /S). Since in subordinate clauses the entire V-cluster is left intact, whereas it is cut up into two parts in main clauses, it is customary, in grammatical studies of the two languages concerned, to present examples in the form of subordinate clauses, as these give a clearer picture of the syntactic structure of the sentence. Dutch V-clusters are predominantly RB.

The common SA of (12a–d) – without the Auxiliary System – is (13a). Application of SD on the S_6-cycle gives (13b); subsequent optional application of PR on the same cycle gives (13c).

(13)

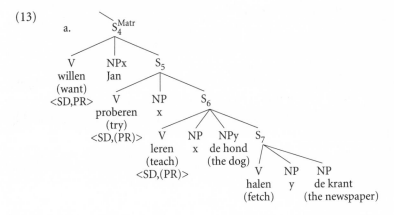

(13)

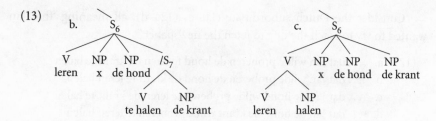

On the S_5-cycle SD is obligatory but PR is optional. If only SD is applied, then (13b) leads to (13d), while (13c) leads to (13e). However, when PR is applied additionally, then (13b) gives (13f), while (13c) gives (13g).

(13)

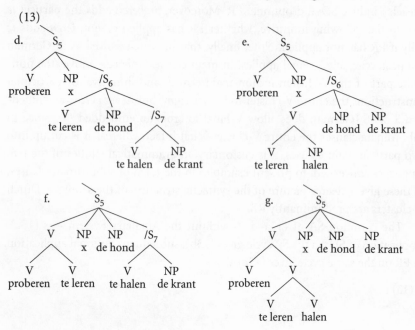

We now have four versions. On the S_4-cycle both SD and PR apply obligatorily, so that there will be no further increase in the number of possible variants. (13d) becomes (13h); (13e) becomes (13i); (13f) goes to (13j), and (13g) to (13k).

(13)

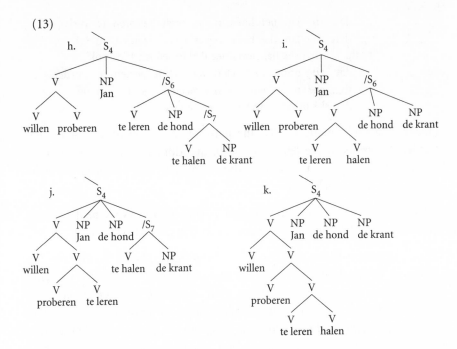

The ordinary tense routine and postcyclic V-Final within each S-structure then give (12a–d), respectively.

In Dutch, PR has as a secondary consequence that the cyclic PaP-rule induced by the perfective auxiliary is cancelled whenever the lower V is clustered with one or more other Vs. The expected past participle then surfaces as an infinitive, the so-called *Infinitivus pro Participio* (IPP), as in (14), where the form *willen* (want) is infinitival despite its direct dependence on the perfective auxiliary *hebben* (have):

(14) ... dat zij het boek heeft *willen* verkopen
      ... that she the book has   want   sell
      '... that she has wanted to sell the book'

4.2 The Third Construction

In spite of the preceding, clauses like (15a–c) are common, especially in spoken Dutch:

(15) a. ... dat zij Jan nooit heeft besloten   het boek te verkopen
          ... that she Jan never has   decided_PaP the book to sell

    b. ... dat zij Jan het boek nooit heeft besloten te verkopen
        ... that she Jan the book never has decided to sell
        both: '... that she has never decided to sell Jan the book'
    c. ... dat zij nooit met Han verwachtte gezien te worden
        ... that she never with Han expected   seen   to be
        '... that she never expected to be seen with Han'

(15a–c) are problematic in that the leftmost main constituent of the embedded /S occurs to the left of the /S in question, somewhere between the
higher subject-NP and the commanding V-cluster. The regular forms would
be (16a, b), respectively:

(16) a. ... dat zij nooit heeft besloten $_{/S}$[Jan het boek te verkopen]
      b. ... dat zij nooit verwachtte $_{/S}$[met Han gezien te worden]

The construction shown in (15a, b) has been called *Third Construction* (Den
Besten & Rutten 1989). In order to avoid confusion, we speak of the Third
Construction when *there is evidence of an embedded /S whose leftmost non-
verbal constituent or constituents are found to the left of the /S in question, i.e.
as a direct dependent of the commanding higher verb.* This means that the term
and the concept 'Third Construction' are theory-dependent. Since the term is
now used rather widely in different theoretical frameworks, one should realize
that it may have different meanings in different theories.

    The Third Construction is thus a phenomenon that is conditional upon
the occurrence of an embedded infinitival object clause (/S), whose underlying
subject has been deleted through SD.[11] It cannot be a variant of PR, since it
never occurs with verbs that take obligatory PR. It does occur, however, with
verbs that take optional PR, such as *proberen* (try) or *hopen* (hope). The conclusion seems obvious that when it occurs with the latter class of verbs, PR has not
applied, so that an embedded /S automatically results (after SD). This explains
why a clause like the following is ruled out, at least in standard Northern Dutch:

(17) *... dat hij Jan heeft proberen het boek te verkopen
      ... that he Jan has try$_{INF}$ the book to sell
      '... that he has tried to sell Jan the book'

The infinitive *proberen* shows that PR has been applied, which must result
in a V-cluster and not in an embedded /S. (In many varieties of Southern
Dutch (17) is fully acceptable, as they allow for PR clustering with one or more
arguments united with the raised V, so-called VP-Raising.)

    The Third Construction has so far resisted attempts at providing a convinc-
ing treatment in terms of transformational grammar. Den Besten and Rutten

(1989:50) posit a Scrambling rule, 'which is held responsible for (part of) the relatively free word order in the middlefield of Dutch and German sentences.'[12] A possible explanation may be found in the assumption of a process of *weak topicalization*: for reasons of focus or emphasis, the constituent in question is moved to the left out of its /S and into the superordinate /S. The movement is restricted to the superordinate /S, so that the subject NP forms a left-hand-side barrier. Within the superordinate /S the focused constituent moves as far to the left as possible (there may be obstacles due to scope, as shown in (19) below). We shall leave the details of such a *Left Extraposition* (LE) rule undiscussed here, (a) because it seems that the Third Construction facts can be treated as an isolated set of phenomena with a somewhat marked sociolinguistic and discourse status, left over after an otherwise convincing analysis in terms of optional or obligatory PR, and (b) because a full discussion would go way beyond the restrictions of size imposed on the present study.

To see the complexity of the matter, one is invited to note that certain forms of LE appear to be banned. To give just one example, it does not seem possible to let LE generate (18a) or (18b) from the regular (18c). Apparently, there is something about the external dative *aan Jan* (to Jan) that blocks LE:

(18)   a.   *... dat zij aan Jan nooit heeft besloten het boek te verkopen
       b.   *... dat zij het boek aan Jan nooit heeft besloten te verkopen
       c.   ... dat zij nooit heeft besloten /S[het boek aan Jan te verkopen]

Yet there is no general blocking of LE-induced movement of PPs, witness (15c). There, however, as one will have noticed already, LE stops short of the adverb *nooit* (never), whereas in (15a, b) the extraposed NP happily crosses *nooit*. The variant (19) is not entirely ruled out, but definitely less natural:

(19)   ?... dat zij met Han nooit verwachtte gezien te worden

The linguistic expert's intuition says that this is probably connected with the fact that both *nooit* and *met Han* represent scope-bearing operators, with *nooit* taking scope over *met Han*. Given the general tendency in language to position larger scope operators to the left of smaller scope operators, it is to be expected that (19) is less acceptable than (15c). To make this general statement, however, is a great deal simpler than to implement this tendency in a grammatical mechanism.

Not surprisingly with such a complicated system, speakers often make mistakes. Note, for example, the sentence (20a) (uttered by the great soccer coach Rinus Michels):

(20) a. *Ik heb die jongen altijd   geprobeerd z'n gevoelens te sparen.
        I   have that boy   always tried   his feelings   to spare
        'I have always tried to spare that boy's feelings.'
      b.   Ik heb altijd geprobeerd /S[die jongen z'n gevoelens te sparen]

The sentence is, though actually uttered, grossly ungrammatical, no doubt be-
cause NP[die jongen] is not an argument-NP. The grammatical version is (20b).
In (20a) NP[die jongen] has been moved into the superordinate /S, out of the
complex NP NP[die jongen z'n gevoelens] (that boy's feelings) in the embedded
/S. Native intuition suggests that what was meant was probably something like
'I have, as far as that boy is concerned, always tried to spare his feelings'.

4.3 Directionality

As has been said, Dutch V-clusters are, on the whole right-branching (RB).
Occasionally, however, LB V-clusters are observed, as in (21b), which is as
acceptable as the normal RB (21a) (both: 'that she wanted to leave'):

(21) a. ... dat ze wilde[1] vertrekken[2]
      b. ... dat ze vertrekken[2] wilde[1]

The LB variety is possible only in the simple present or simple past, not in
the perfective tenses, and only, normally speaking, with a small class of modal
verbs, including *willen* 'want'. V^2, moreover, must not be clustered. All Dutch
modal verbs are full nuclear lexical verbs, and all induce PR without the particle
te. The class of verbs allowing for LB – let us say the *L-class* – contains at least
the following verbs:

> **L-class:**
>
> *zullen* (shall, will)   *willen* (want)   *mogen* (may, be allowed)
> *kunnen* (be able, can)   *moeten* (must, have to)

Other PR-inducing verbs, such as *zien* (see), *horen* (hear), *voelen* (feel), *laten*
(let, allow), (all without the particle *te*) can marginally be treated as L-verbs,
but LB then provokes a literary or poetic effect:

(22) ... dat ze mij dansen[2] zag[1]
      ... that she me dance   saw
      '... that she saw me dance'

*We posit that V-nodes are programmed for the directionality of their projections:
RB in principle but with an optional switch to LB when an unclustered V^2 stands*

under a non-perfective V¹ of the L-class. For a literary style register the L-class is extended with verbs of perception and *laten.* All L-verbs, both unmarked and marked, induce PR without *te.*

We shall see below that directionality switch also occurs, though under different conditions, in German, where it is much more conspicuous.

4.4 CREEPING

One final phenomenon in Dutch V-clusters, which we have decided to call CREEPING (following Evers and also Kaplan & Zaenen, both in this volume; Seuren 1996 speaks of 'End Cluster Arrangement'), must be dealt with. This concerns the fact that verbal particles as well as past participles have the freedom to move upward, or 'creep', within V-clusters, as can be seen from the following examples:

(23) a. ... dat ze mij [zou¹ kunnen² hebben³ gegroet⁴]
... that she me would can have greeted
'... that she would have been able to greet me'

b. ... dat ze mij [zou¹ kunnen² gegroet⁴ hebben³]

c. ... dat ze mij [zou¹ gegroet⁴ kunnen² hebben³]

d. ... dat ze mij [gegroet⁴ zou¹ kunnen² hebben³]

e. *... dat ze gegroet⁴ mij zou¹ kunnen² hebben³

(24) a. ... dat ze het boek [zou¹ willen² mogen³ opbergen⁴]
... that she the book would like be allowed put away
'... that she would like to be allowed to put away the book'

b. ... dat ze het boek [zou¹ willen² op mogen³ bergen⁴]

c. ... dat ze het boek [zou¹ op willen² mogen³ bergen⁴]

d. ... dat ze het boek [op zou¹ willen² mogen³ bergen⁴]

e. *... dat ze op het boek zou¹ willen² mogen³ bergen⁴

(25) a. ... dat ze het boek [zou¹ kunnen² hebben³ opgeborgen⁴]
... that she the book would can have put away
'... that she might have put away the book'

b. ... dat ze het boek [zou¹ kunnen² op hebben³ geborgen⁴]

c. ... dat ze het boek [zou¹ kunnen² opgeborgen⁴ hebben³]

d. ... dat ze het boek [zou¹ op kunnen² hebben³ geborgen⁴]

e. ... dat ze het boek [zou¹ op kunnen² geborgen⁴ hebben³]

f. ... dat ze het boek [zou¹ opgeborgen⁴ kunnen² hebben³]

g. ... dat ze het boek [op zou¹ kunnen² hebben³ geborgen⁴]

h. ... dat ze het boek [op zou¹ kunnen² geborgen⁴ hebben³]

i. ... dat ze het boek [op zou¹ geborgen⁴ kunnen² hebben³]

j.   ... dat ze het boek [**opgeborgen⁴** zou¹ kunnen² hebben³]
k.   *... dat ze **op** het boek zou¹ kunnen² hebben³ **geborgen⁴**
l.   *... dat ze **opgeborgen⁴** het boek zou¹ kunnen² hebben³
m. *... dat ze het boek **geborgen⁴** zou¹ **op** kunnen² hebben³

Note that, at least in standard Northern Netherlandic, PPs that have become lexically incorporated into a verb creep obligatorily to the very top of the V-cluster. Consider the compound verb *in de steek laten* (leave in the lurch; German: *im Stich lassen*):

(26) a.   ... dat   ze   haar broer   niet **in de steek** zou   hebben
           ... that she her   brother not   **in the lurch** would have
           gelaten
           left
           '... that she would not have left her brother in the lurch'
     b.   ... dat ze haar broer niet **in de steek** zou **gelaten** hebben
     c.   ... dat ze haar broer niet **in de steek gelaten** zou hebben
     d.   *... dat ze haar broer niet **gelaten in de steek** zou hebben
     e.   *... dat ze haar broer niet zou hebben **in de steek gelaten**
     f.   *... dat ze haar broer niet zou **in de steek** hebben **gelaten**

The variants (26e) and (26f) are ungrammatical in standard Northern Netherlandic but grammatical in standard Belgian Dutch.

These phenomena require a postcyclic rule like the following:

CREEPING (**Northern Netherlandic**):
Past participles, verbal particles and other adverbial or adjectival elements in a V-cluster (see the next section) may climb through the V-cluster without limit. PPs that have become a lexical part of a verb must climb to the top of the V-cluster. A past participle may never climb across a verbal particle or PP belonging to the same verb.

It is important to note that the CREEPING phenomena, and in particular the ungrammatical cases in (23)–(25), are strong independent confirmation of the reality of V-clusters in Dutch: the 'creeping' of elements up the V-cluster is restricted to the V-cluster itself; further movement outside the V-cluster leads to ungrammaticality. Since it is only rarely that one sees transformations at work so clearly (in terms of a canonical form and its transformational variants), and so clearly within the bounds of one particular type of constituent structure, CREEPING deserves a prominent place in the theory of grammar.

4.5 Non-verbal (pseudo)complements

In Dutch, as well as in German and many other languages, it is not always lower surface *verbs* that are attracted by PR. In some cases, the higher V attracts lower predicates that have different, in particular adverbial or adjectival, surface labelings. The usual term for such non-verbal raising products is *small clauses*, but this term seems misleading since, I argue, they are not clauses at all in surface structure, but raised elements in a V-cluster, originating from embedded complement-Ss whose predicate is marked for a non-V surface category, such as adjective, adverb, past participle, or particle. Instead, we speak of *non-verbal complements* (many or most of which are *pseudo*complements, as will be explained presently).

The elements thus raised partake in CREEPING, as explained in the previous section. In Dutch, these raisings differ from the V-raisings that have been discussed so far in that they are subject to left-branching, not to the customary right-branching, directionality. (In German they are likewise LB, just like the V-raisings.)

The following clauses are cases in point (the elements that have been raised by PR are printed in italics):

(27) a. ... dat Jan de deur had willen   *blauw* verven
         ... that Jan the door had wanted blue   paint
         '... that Jan had wanted to paint the door blue'
     b. ... dat Dan de ladder *rechtop* heeft gezet
         ... that Dan the ladder upright has   put
         '... that Dan has put the ladder up'
     c. ... dat Han mij *arm* heeft gegeten
         ... that Han me poor has   eaten
         '... that Han has made me poor by his eating'

CREEPING allows the alternative orderings *had blauw willen verven* and *blauw had willen verven* for (27a); *heeft rechtop gezet* for (27b), and *heeft arm gegeten* for (27c).

Let us consider the relevant part of the derivation of, for example, (27a).

(28)

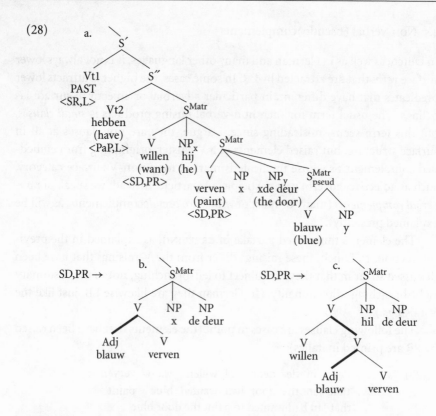

We note first that in the SA (28a) the verb *verven* (paint) has an irregular argument assignment. Besides the normal subject-NP and object-NP, there is an extra S_{pseud}^{Matr} that does not figure in its lexical subcategorization frame. Such additional complements, which we call *pseudocomplements*, occur, one way or another, in all languages (see Seuren 2002 for extensive discussion). Their subject term is normally controlled by an argument of the higher verb (in this case by the object-NP *de deur* of the verb *verven*).

Pseudomplements express either a purpose, or a result (as in (27a)), or a concomitant circumstance with regard to the embedding S. They are the source of the well-known *serial verb constructions* found in many Asian, African and Creole languages (see Seuren 1991, 2002). They are also the source of most verb-particle constructions, usually fully lexicalized with specialized meanings, such as English *put up, hand out, stow away, pay off*, etc., or German separable verbs like *weglaufen* (run away), *wiedersehen* (see again), etc., as well as many similar verbs in Dutch.

Moreover, as has often been observed in the literature, Dutch has constructions with verbs of movement or position, like *zitten* (sit), *lopen* (walk), *staan* (stand), *gaan* (go), that are used semantically as durative or progressive auxiliaries while their original lexical meaning is bleached considerably, as in *Hij ligt te slapen* (he is asleep <while lying down>). Grammatically, however, these verbs function as full lexical verbs, allowing for the full range of tenses and moods, and it seems to make sense to treat the embedded complement-S as a conventionalized (lexicalized) subject-controlled pseudocomplement in the sense discussed here (with the meaning of concomitant circumstance). It is clear that the V of the complement-S is raised to the higher verb by PR, forming a V-cluster. In this case the cluster is right-branching, as the raised element is a surface verb.

Generally, in Dutch and German, verbs that take a pseudocomplement acquire the rule feature <PR>, but in both languages the PR is left-branching whenever the element raised is non-verbal.[13] The lower predicate is relabeled appropriately ('Adjective' in the case of (27a)). If there is control, the rule feature <SD> is likewise added automatically.[14]

Let us now consider the question of the derivation of (29a) (also discussed in Kempen & Harbusch, this volume), which is not a case of pseudocomplementation but merely of non-verbal raising. (29a) is somewhat problematic since this construction appears to have quite a few idiosyncrasies. It has also hardly been studied in the literature in a way that serves our purpose. This is the best we can do.

(29) a. ... dat zij die baan had *aangeboden* gekregen
         ... that she that job had offered   got$_{PaP}$
         '... that she had been offered that job'

Given the general premises of the theory, it seems reasonable to assume an SA of the form (29b). The complement $_S[[worden]_S[aanbieden,die baan]]$ is not a pseudocomplement but a regular passive object-S that Dutch *krijgen* (get, receive) is subcategorized for. Following normal procedure, this object-S is converted into $_S[_V[_V[worden]_{PaP}[aangeboden]],die baan]$ (=(29c)). Now we must get rid of $_V[worden]$, so as to be left with the bare $_{PaP}[aangeboden]$. The simplest assumption is that the deletion of $_V[worden]$ is induced by the conditions that must be assumed to come with the passive object-S, but it must be admitted that no detailed analysis of this kind of construction is available. On this assumption we get (29d). Then, on the *krijgen*-cycle, $_{PaP}[aangeboden]$ is adjoined to $_V[krijgen]$ by PR. The resulting cluster is left-branching since the raised element is not labeled 'V'. This gives (29e). The next step is the cyclic processing of the perfective auxiliary $_V$[hebben], which induces the rules PaP and Lowering, in that order. PaP assigns past-participle morphology to the first lexical V down the V-cluster (the PaP rule is not canceled because the V-cluster contains just one lexical V). Lowering then results in (29f). Further processing gives the shallow structure (29g), converted into the surface structure (29h) in the postcycle.

(29)

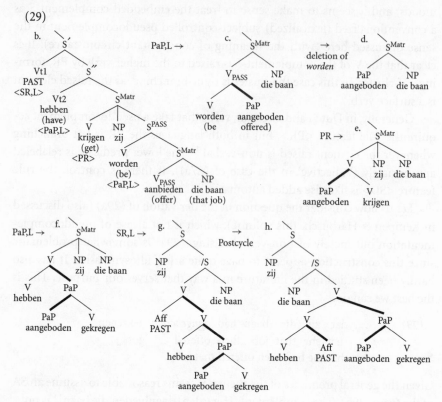

(29a) thus represents the form without any postcyclic CREEPING. With CREEPING the forms *aangeboden had gekregen* (leftmost PaP moved) and *aangeboden gekregen had* (entire PaP-cluster moved) are possible. No other variant is generated.

5. German V-clusters

We turn now to German V-clusters. As in the case of Dutch, we limit ourselves in principle to *standard modern German* (SMG), realizing that the dialects of Dutch and German deviate significantly from the respective standard languages, in particular with respect to V-cluster phenomena. A full study of all dialects is not feasible given the inherent limits of this study. Moreover, the status of dialectal data is, on the whole, doubtful, partly because native dialect speakers are hard to question on syntactic matters, but also because every dialect is profoundly affected by the standard language. But we do claim that the data in (30) unambiguously represent standard modern German.

The subdomain of German V-clusters is, in principle, LB, as can be read from the descending order of superscripts on the verb forms in (30). There are, however, infractions of this principle. (30b, e, g, j, l, n, q) show a RB arrangement at the top end of the V-cluster, a phenomenon known as *Oberfeldumstellung*. The question is: how do we catch these phenomena into a rule, thereby excluding the ungrammatical cases (30c, h, m, o, r, s)?

(30) a. ..., daß sie ausgehen^2 will^1
      ... that she out-go   wants
      '... that she wants to go out'

     b. ..., daß sie hat^1 ausgehen^3 wollen^2
      ... that she has out-go   want
      '... that she has wanted to go out'

     c. *..., daß sie ausgehen^3 gewollt^2 hat^1
      ... that she out-go   wanted   has
      '... that she has wanted to go out'

     d. ..., daß sie mich ausgehen^2 sah^1
      ... that she me   out-go   saw
      '... that she saw me go out'

     e. ..., daß sie mich hat^1 ausgehen^3 sehen^2
      ... that she me   has   out-go   see
      '... that she has seen me go out'

     f. ..., daß sie mich ausgehen^3 gesehen^2 hat^1
      ... that she me   out-go   seen   has
      '... that she has seen me go out'

     g. ..., daß ich sie habe^1 tanzen^4 gehen^3 lassen^2
      ... that I   her have   dance   go   let$_{INF}$
      '... that I have let her go dance'

h. *..., daß sie wird[1] ausgehen[2]
  ... that she will   out-go
  '... that she will go out'

i. ..., daß sie ausgehen[2] wird[1]
  ... that she out-go   will
  '... that she will go out'

j. ..., daß sie wird[1] ausgehen[3] wollen[2]
  ... that she will   out-go   want
  '... that she will want to go out'

k. ..., daß sie ausgehen[3] wollen[2] wird[1]
  ... that she out-go   want   will
  '... that she will want to go out'

l. ..., daß sie das wird[1] haben[2] tun[4] können[3]
  ... that she that will   have   do can_{INF}
  '... that she will have been able to do that'

m. *..., daß sie das haben[2] tun[4] können[3] wird[1]
  ... that she that have   do can_{INF} will
  '... that she will have been able to do that'

n. ..., daß sie das muß[1] haben[2] tun[4] können[3]
  ... that she that must   have   do can_{INF}
  '... that she must have been able to do that'

o. *..., daß sie das haben[2] tun[4] können[3] muß[1]
  ... that she that have   do can_{INF} must
  '... that she must have been able to do that'

p. ..., daß sie das tun[3] können[2] muß[1]
  ... that she that do can_{INF} must
  '... that she must have been able to do that'

q. ..., daß sie das wird[1] müssen[2] haben[3] tun[5] können[4]
  ... that she that will $must_{INF}$ have   do can_{INF}
  '... that it will be so that she must have been able to do that'

r. *..., daß sie das müßen[2] haben[3] tun[5] können[4] wird[1]
  ... that she that $must_{INF}$ have   do can_{INF} will
  '... that it will be so that she must have been able to do that'

s. *..., daß sie das muß[1] werden[2] haben[3] tun[5] können[4]
  ... that she that must $will_{INF}$ have   do can_{INF}
  '... that it must be so that she will have been able to do that'

Note, incidentally, that the Dutch equivalent of (30s) is fully grammatical:

(31) √..., dat zij dat moet[1] zullen[2] hebben[3] kunnen[4] doen[5]
     ... that she that must will$_{INF}$ have can$_{INF}$ do
     '... that it must be so that she will have been able to do that'

To avoid misunderstanding, let us see first how a simple sentence like (30a) is generated in SeSyn. The derivation is as in (32a–f). (32a) is the input SA, (32e) the Shallow Structure, and (32f) the Surface Structure:

(32)

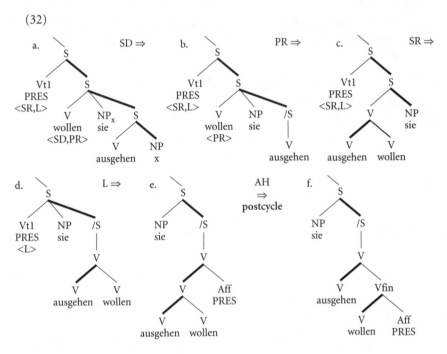

To account for the switch from LB to RB in V-clusters we posit a class of **R-verbs**, consisting at least of the following members (*sehen*, *hören*, *fühlen* are full members in SMG but optional members in some almost standard dialects):

    R-class:

sehen 'see'	*können* 'be able'	*mögen* 'like','may'
hören 'hear'	*müssen* 'must'	*dürfen* 'be allowed'
fühlen 'feel'	*sollen* 'must'	
lassen 'let, allow, make'	*wollen* 'want'	

We posit that these verbs are subject to the **R-Condition**, which applies at the appropriate moment in the Cycle and turns the directionality of all further additions to the V-cluster from the default LB to marked RB under the following conditions:

When an R-verb V_R is the highest matrix-V of a (LB) V-cluster below an Auxiliary System, then all subsequent Lowerings onto V in the Auxiliary System are right-branching (i.e. with left-attachment):

(a) obligatorily when V_R stands directly under a perfective auxiliary (*haben* in all cases) and the clause contains Vt1;[15]

(b) optionally when V_R stands directly under the modal verb of futuricity *werden* ('will').

When the R-Condition applies, the rule *Past Participle* is inoperative (resulting in a so-called 'Ersatzinfinitiv', the German counterpart of Dutch IPP).[16]

This gets all the data of (30) right, provided the modal predicate of futuricity *werden* is placed, in the SA, between Vt1 and Vt2, and may never occur without Vt1, as specified above in Figures 2 and 4 (cp. the examples (3a–l) in Section 1.3.2 above). (33b) shows the shallow structure of (30l) cyclically derived from the SA (33a):

(33)

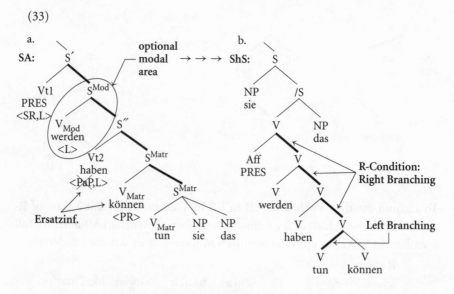

Here the order must be [werden¹–haben²–tun⁴–können³], since the V-cluster is RB as from the addition of *haben*, owing to the R-Condition which says that all subsequent Lowerings must be RB as well. Therefore, the later addition of *werden* must proceed in the RB fashion. This explains why (30j, k) are both grammatical: the R-Condition leaves the switch to RB optional for R-verbs under *werden*. However, the corresponding form with the perfective *haben* only allows for the RB version, as in (30l); (30m) is judged to be ungrammatical (Duden 1995:787; Heidolph et al. 1981:724).[17] ((30h) is ungrammatical because *ausgehen* is not an R-verb.)

It is thus clear that the intertense position of the modal auxiliaries, together with the classification of German *werden* as a modal auxiliary, is a crucial element of the analysis. The analysis is, moreover, cast in general theoretical terms applicable to groups of languages, while the specific values on the various parameters have been restricted largely to the lexicon or anyway defined in close relation with classes of lexical items. This gives the analysis a firm footing in the general theory of grammar.

If CREEPING occurs in German, it is much more restricted than in Dutch. It may pay off to assume optional CREEPING to the top of the V-cluster for PPs that have become a lexical part of a verb, as in *im Stich lassen* (leave in the lurch). This assumption is warranted if (34b), which is identical in meaning to (34a), is considered grammatical.

(34) a. ... weil   ich den Jungen nie   hätte   **im Stich**   lassen
          ... because I   the boy   never had$_{SUBJ}$ in the lurch leave
          können
          can
          '... because I could never have left the boy in the lurch'
      b. ... weil ich den Jungen nie **im Stich** hätte lassen können

If (34b) is grammatical in standard German (which it does seem to be), then PP[im Stich] has 'crept' up to the very top of the V-cluster.

Moreover, it seems that past participles, with or without the passive auxiliary *werden*, are allowed to creep (cp. Haider, this volume, ex. (23a–d)):

(35) a. ... daß es getan⁴ hätte¹ werden³ sollen²
          ... that it done had$_{SUBJ}$ be   shall$_{INF}$
          (hätte getan werden sollen)
      b. ... daß es getan⁴ werden³ hätte¹ sollen²
          both: '... that it should have been done'

Then, optional *Left /S-Extraposition*, probably induced by some form of *weak topicalization* (cp. the Dutch Third Construction), must be posited for German, but not for Dutch (see Zifonun et al. 1997, Vol. 3:2186–2214 for many examples). This allows for one single /S-constituent, but without any possible embedded /Ss, to be moved leftward into the superordinate /S. This gives, e.g., (36a, b) but not (36c) (cp. 5, 11 of Table 1 below):

(36) a.   ... weil   er   sich   /s[den Wagen abzuholen] schon
           ... because he himself   the car to fetch   already
           vorgenommen hatte
           proposed   had
           '... because he had already planned to fetch the car'
      b.   ... weil   er /s[zu versuchen] verspricht /s[das Fahrrad zu
           ... because he   to try   promises   the bicycle to
           reparieren]
           repair
           '... because he promises to try to repair the bicycle'
      c. *... weil   er /s[zu versuchen /s[das Fahrrad zu reparieren]]
           ... because he   to try   the bicycle to repair
           verspricht
           promises
           '... because he promises to try to repair the bicycle'

But note that (36b), though with a different structure, is also generated through
PR induced by *versuchen* (try).

It appears, moreover, that /S-topicalization in subordinate clauses is also
permitted to the top of the clause, as in 9 of Table 1 below, where the complex
/s[zu versuchen /s[das Fahrrad zu reparieren]], has been thus topicalized, or in
17 and 20, where this has happened to only /s[das Fahrrad zu reparieren]. We
must, however, refrain from giving explicit rules for such phenomena, whose
treatment is contingent upon the system proposed.

6.   The data problem (with special reference to German)

After all the work of the previous sections, we still face the question of the
empirical adequacy of the machinery. The question has a certain urgency with
respect to German, because there is an especially acute problem as regards the
German data. German speakers' acceptability judgements, as well as forms used
by competent speakers in well-monitored speech, appear to vary beyond what
can be captured in terms of one single system. On the other hand, there is
a core of clearly well-formed, unmarked construction types that are accepted
by all speakers as being representative of SMG. The large range of variation
is perhaps due to dialectal variation, which is considerable among speakers of
German. What we have aimed for in this study is a generative rule system that
captures the core of those SMG data that are beyond suspicion in terms of one

single system, leaving out of account the variant forms that are acceptable to some but not to all speakers. To what extent we have been successful in doing so is a question that should be settled by further systematic data collection.

Meanwhile, a spot check has been carried out on 11 competent speakers of SMG, who were asked to rank 30 variants of a single German subordinate clause (taken from Rambow 1994a) on a scale of 'fully grammatical' or '√', 'doubtful' or '?', and 'fully ungrammatical' or '*'. Their judgments are given in Table 1 below, where the judgments presented in Rambow (1994a) have been counted as those of one individual (although in fact they represent the judgments of a group of native speakers). On the whole, the results support SeSyn, whose output is given in the right hand side column, though not unambiguously. It must be taken into account, however, that the test conditions were far from optimal: when confronted with 30 variants of one clause, subjects are likely to get confused. Moreover, the number of 11 respondents is too low to be statistically relevant. An improved test, with a greater variety of forms to be judged, a larger number of test subjects and better controls is obviously called for. In defense of the SeSyn generative system it may be mentioned that a distinct correlation was found between those variants that are marked '(√)' under SeSyn (that is, left open by SeSyn; to do with weak topicalization) on the one hand, and specific groups of respondents on the other: one group (5 persons) was clearly in favor of these variants, a second group (2 persons) was systematically against, and a third group (4 persons) systematically hesitated.

(37)

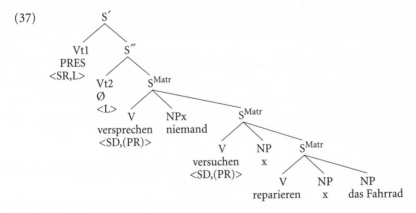

The Rambow clause has the SA (37). All the variants are assumed to be derivations from this one SA, some illicit and others legitimate. (The fact that

Table 1. Grammaticality judgments by 11 speakers of German
NB: ($\sqrt{}$): left open by SeSyn; to do with weak topicalization

		$\sqrt{}$	?	*	SeSyn
1	weil niemand das Fahrrad zu reparieren verspricht zu versuchen		6	5	*
2	weil das Fahrrad niemand zu versuchen zu reparieren verspricht	1	4	6	*
3	weil das Fahrrad niemand zu reparieren zu versuchen verspricht	2	6	3	*
4	weil das Fahrrad niemand zu versuchen verspricht zu reparieren		4	7	*
5	weil niemand zu versuchen verspricht, das Fahrrad zu reparieren	7	2	2	$\sqrt{}$
6	weil zu versuchen niemand das Fahrrad zu reparieren verspricht		2	9	*
7	weil das Fahrrad niemand verspricht zu versuchen zu reparieren		5	6	*
8	weil niemand das Fahrrad verspricht zu reparieren zu versuchen	1	6	4	*
9	weil zu versuchen, das Fahrrad zu reparieren, niemand verspricht	9	2		($\sqrt{}$)
10	weil niemand das Fahrrad zu reparieren zu versuchen verspricht	6	3	2	$\sqrt{}$
11	weil niemand zu versuchen, das Fahrrad zu reparieren, verspricht	4	5	2	*
12	weil niemand das Fahrrad verspricht zu versuchen zu reparieren	2	1	8	*
13	weil niemand das Fahrrad zu versuchen zu reparieren verspricht	2	6	3	*
14	weil das Fahrrad niemand zu reparieren verspricht zu versuchen	2	3	6	*
15	weil das Fahrrad zu versuchen zu reparieren niemand verspricht	4	5	2	*
16	weil das Fahrrad niemand verspricht zu reparieren zu versuchen		4	7	*
17	weil das Fahrrad zu reparieren niemand zu versuchen verspricht	8	2	1	($\sqrt{}$)
18	weil das Fahrrad zu versuchen niemand zu reparieren verspricht	1	2	8	*
19	weil zu versuchen niemand verspricht, das Fahrrad zu reparieren	1	3	7	*
20	weil das Fahrrad zu reparieren niemand verspricht zu versuchen	5	4	2	($\sqrt{}$)
21	weil niemand verspricht, das Fahrrad zu versuchen zu reparieren	5	4	2	*
22	weil niemand zu versuchen das Fahrrad verspricht zu reparieren			11	*
23	weil niemand verspricht, das Fahrrad zu reparieren zu versuchen	8	2	1	$\sqrt{}$
24	weil das Fahrrad zu versuchen niemand verspricht zu reparieren		4	7	*
25	weil zu versuchen niemand das Fahrrad verspricht zu reparieren		1	10	*
26	weil niemand verspricht zu versuchen, das Fahrrad zu reparieren	11			$\sqrt{}$
27	weil niemand das Fahrrad zu versuchen verspricht zu reparieren		3	8	*
28	weil zu versuchen das Fahrrad niemand zu reparieren verspricht			11	*
29	weil zu versuchen das Fahrrad niemand verspricht zu reparieren		1	10	*
30	weil das Fahrrad zu reparieren zu versuchen niemand verspricht	6	5		($\sqrt{}$)

NP[niemand] represents a negative existentially quantified NP has not been taken into account in the SeSyn rule system.)

The SeSyn system is supported by the responses to the clauses 1, 2, 4, 6, 7, 8, 9, 12, 14, 16, 18, 19, 22, 24, 25, 26, 27, 28 and 29. Supportive evidence is also provided by 5, 10, 17, 23, and 30, in sofar as these clauses are favored by speakers who, apparently, have stored the verbs *versprechen* and *versuchen* as inducing PREDICATE RAISING. Doubtful are 3, 11, 13, 15, 20 and 21. 11 may be seen as an instance of *Left /S-Extraposition* of two embedded /Ss, disallowed in

SeSyn, but apparently considered acceptable by some spreakers. The doubtful cases 13, 15 and 21, all ruled out by SeSyn, show right branching (RB), just like 1 and 2, where German normally has left branching (LB). This does seem to occur, at least in spoken German (I have not been able to check whether this RB feature correlates with certain dialects). Recently I heard a competent German speaker utter the sentence:

(38)   Ich glaube, ich habe Ihnen etwas vergessen^1 zu sagen^2.

which may be taken to have the RB V-cluster $_V$[vergessen^1 zu sagen^2], where SMG would have the left-branching $_V$[zu sagen^2 vergessen^1], provided SMG allowed for *vergessen* to induce PREDICATE RAISING (which, for many speakers, apparently, it does not do).

A striking contrast in the position of SeSyn with regard to the responses is seen between 20 and 21: the responses are identical (though the respondents differ greatly among themselves), but SeSyn comes out with opposite results. 20 is not ruled out by SeSyn, but not ruled in either, as it appears to involve a form of subordinate clause topicalization of $_{/S}$[das Fahrrad zu reparieren] from the embedded $_{/S}$[zu versuchen $_{/S}$[das Fahrrad zu reparieren]]. 21 is ruled out, as has been said, because it involves RB.

Note, moreover, that 16 is ruled out because $_{NP}$[das Fahrrad] has been moved from a /S containing a V-cluster, a form of extraposition (or scrambling) that we have not considered so far for German. 3 is structurally ambiguous. It may have arisen from a structure with the LB V-cluster $_V$[zu reparieren zu versuchen verspricht]. It may also have arisen from Left Extraposition of $_{/S}$[das Fahrrad $_V$[$_V$[zu reparieren] $_V$[zu versuchen]]]. In both cases, however, $_{NP}$[das Fahrrad] must follow, and not precede, $_{NP}$[niemand], as in 10, which scores much better. The fact that 3 does not score too badly may be due to special rules (not gone into here) applying to the positioning of German indefinite pronouns, such as *niemand* (nobody). In fact, it would seem that 3 with, for example, *er* (he) instead of *niemand* would score dramatically worse.

Many more aberrations from the standard system have been observed, as one would expect given the complex character of the German system. A well-known case (Berry 1989)[18] is the North-Swabian dialect form (39a), which not only has a right-branching V-cluster but also the past participle on the wrong verb. According to Berry (1989) sentences like (39a) are common and considered acceptable among North-Swabian dialect speakers, though apparently lexically restricted to the verb *helfen* 'help'. The subordinate clause form (39b) is also commonly accepted, much more than the fully right-branching (39c):

(39) a. Ich habe¹ das Gras helfen² gemäht³.
          I   have the grass help   mowed
          'I have helped mow the grass'
      b. ... daß ich das Gras helfen² gemäht³ habe¹
      c. *?... daß ich das Gras habe¹ helfen² gemäht³

These and similar complications are left out of account in the present study, which is restricted to SMG and concentrates on less controversial cases.

7. Discussion

What are the real empirical claims inherent in the analysis presented in this study? This question is important if we want to do justice to the facts while avoiding empty notational claims. That is, we need to specify what we take to be necessary elements, regardless of nonessential notational aspects, in whatever will turn out to be the physical implementation of the grammars of German and Dutch (and other languages showing similar phenomena) in the brains of competent speakers. In the following we will survey the relevant real claims of our analysis, including those that are inherent both in the notation used and in the overall architecture and environment of the theory as explained in Section 1 above.

One central element is the *assumption of V-clusters*, more precisely the amalgamation of embedded and superordinate propositional structures by means of V-clustering and argument unification. It certainly is one claim of the present analysis that some such procedure is needed to establish a systematic link between the surface structures in question and their semantic interpretation. Strong empirical evidence for V-clustering has been adduced, in addition to the arguments already presented in the existing literature such as Bech (1955), Evers (1975) or Haider (1993, 1994, this volume). Among the arguments developed here we mention, in particular, the CREEPING facts of Dutch (Section 4.4), the emergence of 'derived' datives (Section 3), and the branching phenomena, including the German 'Oberfeldumstellung' (Sections 1.2; 5).

Further evidence consists in reflexivization phenomena. For example, Dutch has clauses like (40a) (German has analogous counterparts), with the SA matrix-S (40b)

(40) a. ... dat Karelᵢ zichᵢ   het pakje liet bezorgen
          ... that Karelᵢ himselfᵢ the parcel let deliver
          '...that Karel had the parcel delivered to him'
      b. ... ₛ[ᵥ[laten] ₙₚ[hijᵢ] ₛ[ᵥ[bezorgen_PASS] ₙₚ[hemᵢ] ₙₚ[het pakje]]]

In our treatment, the lower $_V$[bezorgen] is obligatorily clustered with the superordinate $_V$[laten] (which is categorized for obligatory PR) and their arguments are serialized under one S-node, making the higher subject $_{NP}$[Karel$_i$] and the lower indirect object $_{NP}$[hem$_i$] clause-mates under one S. The latter is thus subject to reflexivization (assuming that reflexive pronouns are transformationally sensitive morphological variants of their non-reflexive counterparts). This contrasts with cases that have the same embedding structure as (40b) but disallow V-clustering, such as (41):

(41) ... dat Karel$_i$ opdroeg hem$_i$ / *zich$_i$ het pakje te bezorgen
     ... that Karel$_i$ ordered him$_i$ / *himself$_i$ the parcel to deliver
     '... dat Karel gave the order to deliver the parcel to him'

Here no V-clustering has taken place, since the verb *opdragen* (order) does not induce PR. This means that the surface structure has an embedded $_{/S}$[$_{NP}$[hem$_i$] $_{NP}$[het pakje] $_V$[te bezorgen]]. Now $_{NP}$[Karel$_i$] and $_{NP}$[hem$_i$] have not become clause mates and no reflexivization can take place.

In the face of all this evidence, and in the absence of convincing evidence to the contrary, we feel justified in claiming that V-clustering is a real element in the physical implementation of the grammars of Dutch and German (and many other languages as well), no matter what biological form this implementation will eventually turn out to take.

If, however, the assumption of V-clusters and clause unification were all there is to the present analysis, then, within certain limits, most of the formalism used would be arbitrary. For it is perfectly possible to express this idea in a variety of different ways. One may, for example, subcategorize PR verbs for the incorporation of any other verb and develop a mechanism for the proper unification of the arguments of both verbs, placing the whole operation within the lexicon, so to speak. Conversely, one may undo PR constructions by a well-defined system of categorial function analysis that reveals the proper semantic relationships. Such techniques make it appear as if no SA, i.e. no level of semantically analytic representation, is needed, though in fact, of course, any structural composition or functional unraveling requires a specification of the semantic relationships, and thus some form of SA.

The real question is whether the relation between surface structures and their SAs is to be specified in terms of a purely semantic calculus or in terms of formal mappings from linguistic structures onto linguistic structures involving (a) a semantically and formally well-defined SA-structure that lays out the semantic relationships explicitly and unambiguously, (b) a formally well-defined surface structure, and (c) any number of intermediate structures. The semantic interpretation of the surface structures is then defined jointly by their form and the mapping machinery that relates them to an appropriate SA. This latter class is often called *derivational*, whereas the systems working with a purely semantic calculus are known as *representational*. Transformational grammars, and thus also the analysis presented in the present paper, are by definition derivational.

Mainly for reasons of computational convenience, a body of opinion has formed lately holding that grammars should be representational, not derivational. Not only do representational techniques appear to facilitate automatic parsing procedures (still problematic in derivational systems), it is also felt that the semantic computations envisaged are not, or much less, subject to the methodological requirement of maximal crosslinguistic universality. Unfortunately, this feeling of liberty is totally unjustified, due as it is to a general lack of methodological reflection. One may, with good reason, raise many objections against currently fashionable forms of generative or transformational grammar, but its insistence on universal constraints is a powerful positive factor. Given the variety of languages in the world, the criterion of a universal charter constraining linguistic structures and processes is undeniably an indispensable element in any study of linguistic machinery. Obviously, the drawing up of such a charter is typically a long-term bootstrapping process. No such universal charter has so far been formulated, but partial hypotheses have been and are being put forward, and in circles of generative or transformational grammar the criterion of crosslinguistic unity is an important element in the evaluation of linguistic analyses. (As far as my own analysis of verbal clusters is concerned, the reader will easily check that the universality criterion has been prominent in all my work in this respect since 1972.)

The main point here, however, is that the derivational approach is to be preferred not only because it stands in a tradition where universal constraints play an active role in evaluating proposals, but also, decisively, on empirical grounds. This means that no matter how convenient the representational approach may be for a limited range of practical purposes, it is claimed to be insufficient for an adequate understanding of the machinery at work in linguistic processing. Such an understanding requires an apparatus of successively ordered constituent tree structures and well-defined mapping operations on them of at least roughly the kind specified above, together with the surrounding environment as specified in Figure 1 above.

What makes us say so? Again we may refer to the importance of branching directionality and, in particular, to the analysis presented of the German phenomenon of Oberfeldumstellung, i.e. the conditions under which German left-branching embedding operations shift to right-branching ones. For this analysis to work a detailed analysis of the Auxiliary System is necessary, in particular the assumption of a class of modal auxiliaries, with futuricity as a prime case, occurring between the two tenses, as specified in Figures 2 and 4 above. The members of this class have undergone *auxiliation* (Section 1.3.2 above): their status as lexical verbs has been weakened, a process resulting in their 'moving up' the auxiliary tree to land in the intertense position. Their occurrence in this position automatically accounts for their well-known defective paradigm: they only occur as finite forms and lack infinitives and participles (see Seuren 1996: 84–87, 113–114). This, it is claimed, explains the defective paradigm of English modals like *will, can, may, must*, and a few others, as it explains similar phenomena in many other languages.

In the Germanic languages futuricity appears in surface structure as a verb, but in the Romance languages as a morphological element, while in most Creole languages it surfaces as a particle word (with clearly verbal origin). In SeSyn these differences are reduced to different relabelings during the transformational process. The nature of the new label determines further grammatical treatment, either in the open syntax or in the morphology of the language in question.

It has been argued that the German futuricity verb *werden* has undergone auxiliation, in contrast with its Dutch counterpart *zullen* which has so far remained a full lexical verb. This explains the fact that German (42a) is ungrammatical whereas its word-by-word Dutch counterpart (42b) is fully grammatical (cp. (3b) above):

(42) a. *Ich hoffe, das Kapitel morgen   abschließen zu werden.
          I   hope the chapter tomorrow off-close   to will$_{INF}$
      b. Ik hoop het hoofdstuk morgen   te zullen afsluiten.
          I hope the chapter   tomorrow to will$_{INF}$ off-close
          both: 'I hope to round off the chapter tomorrow.'

German futuricity *werden* is thus taken to occupy the position between the two tenses, as specified in Figures 2 and 4 and in (33a) above.

This, in turn, is a necessary element in the explanation of the fact that Oberfeldumstellung of *werden* is obligatory when *werden* is followed by the perfective auxiliary *haben*, but optional when it directly commands a non-perfective R-verb, as shown in (30j–m) above, repeated here for rhetorical emphasis:

(30) j. ..., daß sie wird^1 ausgehen^3 wollen^2
          ... that she will   out-go   want

k. ..., daß sie ausgehen³ wollen² wird¹
    ... that she out-go   want   will
    both: '... that she will want to go out'
l. ..., daß sie das wird¹ haben² tun⁴ können³
    ... that she that will have do   can$_{INF}$
m. *..., daß sie das haben² tun⁴ können³ wird¹
    ... that she that have do can$_{INF}$ will
    both: '... that she will have been able to do that'

This follows from the R-Condition (Section 5), which says that V-clustering becomes, and stays, right-branching:

(a) obligatorily when an already clustered verb V_R of the R-class stands directly under a perfective auxiliary (*haben* in all cases) and the clause contains Vt1;

(b) optionally when V_R stands directly under the modal futuricity verb *werden* ('will').

Since *wollen* (want) and *können* (be able) are both members of the R-class, it follows that both (30j) and (30k) are grammatical, while of the second pair only (30l) can be.

Moreover, given that epistemic *müssen* has likewise undergone full auxiliation (Section 1.3.2), it follows that (43a) and (43c) should be grammatical, while (43b) and (43d) should not be. This prediction is indeed borne out by native speakers' judgments:

(43) a. ... daß er das sagen können muß
          ... that he that say can$_{INF}$ must
      b. *... daß er das muß sagen können
          ... that he that must say   can$_{INF}$
          both: '... that he must be able to say that'
      c. ... daß er das muß haben sagen können
          ... that he that must have say can$_{INF}$
      d. *... daß er das haben sagen können muß
          ... that he that have say can$_{INF}$ must
          both: '... that he must have been able to say that'

This follows from the fact that (43a, b) do not contain the perfective auxiliary *haben*, so that the R-Condition does not apply even though the R-verb *können* occurs, whereas in the SA of (43c, d) the R-verb *können* is directly commanded by the perfective *haben*, so that here the R-Condition applies obligatorily for the whole remainder of the derivation. Clearly, this system will only work on the assumptions we have made about SA-structure and about the transformational rule system.

These may seem relatively insignificant details of the entire V-cluster story, yet they constitute crucial evidence in favor of a derivational and against a representational treatment of the relevant facts. Other theories, in particular those of the representational kind, will no doubt be able to *accommodate* these facts one way or another, but only, one fears, as isolated idiosyncrasies. In the derivational system of SeSyn, however, these facts are seen to follow from a treatment that is cast in terms of *general principles of linguistic theory.*

To summarize, we claim that the analysis presented here, complete with the SA-structures, the rule systems and the constituent-tree-structure notation proposed, is a necessary, but obviously far from sufficient, condition for a proper understanding of the linguistic machinery as it is implemented in the brain as a result of both innate predispositions and acquired programming. Any actual implementation of the linguistic system in the brain of language users must be taken to express, in some regular way, the significant generalizations caught in terms of tree structures and operations on them. This claim will be upheld until a more powerful theory is presented, with greater explanatory power, in which these elements have been subsumed under more general principles. Meanwhile, it makes sense to take a closer look at the formal and empirical properties of the derivational theory at hand, including its potential for a proper parsing procedure.

Notes

1. One should note that the *semantics* of LPC is not necessarily that of modern predicate calculus: the semantic definitions of the logical terms of LPC are likely to be different in natural language from what they are in modern standard logic. They also differ considerably from language to language.

2. I do not follow the new habit to speak of 'DP' (Determiner Phrase) instead of the more traditional 'NP' (Noun Phrase). The modern usage of 'DP' is motivated by the desire to have a uniform terminology for phrases, whereby phrases are called after their functional head: a PP (Prepositional Phrase), for example, is so called because the semantic value of a PP is the value of the function 'Preposition', which takes an NP as argument. Analogously, a DP would be so called because its semantic value is taken to be the value of the function 'Determiner' with a noun as argument. This analysis appears correct for NPs with definite articles and perhaps also (depending on the theory adopted) for NPs with quantifiers. However, there are many NPs where no Determiner is in sight. For example, in the PP *by breaking the lock* the prepositional argument *breaking the lock* is best taken to be an NP, just as in other, more canonical, PPs. Yet to treat either *breaking* or *the lock* as a Determiner seems very far-fetched

indeed. Given the present, still highly underdeveloped, state of NP-theory, it looks as if we have to conclude that DPs are best taken to be a subclass of NPs. We shall let the matter rest here.

3. For example, the Germanic languages, which were originally SOV, changed to surface SVO, some with a strong V2-Constraint, probably as a result of intensive contact with Celtic speakers. The Celtic languages are predominantly VSO, but some are also prone to the preposing of argument terms, most often subjects, that function as topic in a given discourse (e.g. Borsley & Kathol 2000), a process that may give rise to a surface SVO-order, with a V2-Constraint.

4. Matthew Dryer, personal communication, based on his survey of ±900 languages.

5. The precise *semantics* of the tenses in question in those languages that conform to this scheme is a great deal more detailed and more varied from language to language, and from dialect to dialect, than has been indicated here. But these complications are not germane to the topic at hand. Neither are others, such as those caused by the passé défini (aorist) in Greek and the Romance languages. We make the general assumption that auxiliary systems are built up according to what we may call *auxiliary checklists*, which specify the kind of information required for a well-formed sentence or clause. These differ considerably from language to language. Thus English has no parameter for 'reported information', but Turkish does. It is assumed that in tenseless languages, such as Chinese or Malay, the auxiliary checklist contains no time-related questions.

6. This account of the defective paradigm of certain modals in English, French and German was first presented in Seuren (1996).

7. The difference between bare S′ and $_{NP}$[S′] is manifest in the ungrammaticality of a preposed *that*-clause, which requires NP-status (e.g. *That John left seems*, versus *That John left is likely*), or in semantic differences (see Seuren 1989, 1996: 145–149).

8. In most European languages $_V$[∅] is unlexicalized. In English, however, $_V$[∅] is replaced postcyclically with a dummy verb $_V$[do] when not immediately followed by V_{Matr}. Otherwise $_V$[∅] is postcyclically deleted.

9. John Hawkins (pers. com.) informs me that statistically VSO languages have rich verb agreement, whereas SOV languages tend to have rich NP marking, and SVO languages typically have neither. Since this means that languages with little flectional morphology are predominantly SVO, one might expect a tendency for languages that are losing morphological endings to become SVO. However, little is known about such phenomena.

10. In Seuren (1972[2001]) it is argued, in line with the Generative Semantics tradition (e.g. McCawley 1968b), that causative verbs often incorporate a hidden syntactic structure resulting from PR. Evidence for this view is found in the fact that many causative verbs that may occur not only as ditransitives but also as simple transitives assign dative case to the semantic subject of the semantically embedded lower verb when used ditransitively, but accusative case when used transitively. For example, English *serve* assigns dative and accusative case when used with two objects, as in *serve soup to the client*, but accusative case when accompanied by only one object, whether direct or indirect: *serve soup* or *serve the client*. (Hence the story of the two ladies in a restaurant who are told by the waiter 'We only serve men', upon which one of them answers 'We'll have one each, then.') Other such verbs are, e.g., *teach*,

advise, pay, refuse, delegate, prompt. Similar sets of verbs are found in many other languages. Such facts are typically neglected in non-transformational theories of grammar.

11. But note that the Third Construction is impossible (a) when the higher verb is reflexive, such as *zich voornemen te* (to plan to), (b) when the higher verb takes a pronominal uptake of the embedded clause, as in *erop rekenen te* (to count on it to), or (c) when the higher verb itself takes an NP-complement, as in *het besluit nemen te* (to take the decision to), or any combination of these. It does not matter whether or not the higher verb is itself clustered by PR, as in (i). In such cases, the irregularly placed constituent, here *de hond* (the dog), simply jumps the whole V-cluster:

(i) ... dat Jan de hond heeft moeten willen besluiten uit te laten
     ... that Jan the dog has must want decide out to let
     ... that Jan must have had to want to decide to take the dog out

It would be wrong to conclude that *besluiten* (decide) takes optional PR, given the ungrammaticality of:

(ii) ... *dat Jan de hond heeft besluiten uit te laten

with the IPP *besluiten* for what must be the past participle *besloten*. Note that this is further confirmation for the reality of PR-induced V-clusters.

12. *Middlefield* is a term commonly used in the grammars of German and Dutch for the section of the sentence between the *forefield*, i.e. the subject plus finite verb form in main clauses or just the subject in subordinate clauses, and the verbal final part or *endfield*. The middlefield contains mainly NPs and adverbial expressions (cp. Kathol 2000). So far, our theory has made no use of the 'field' terms, unlike some other, more structuralist, theories of Dutch and German grammar, where they play a central role in the various mechanisms proposed.

13. In English, the higher V's rule feature for adverbial pseudocompements is either SUBJECT RAISING, leading to constructions like *He put the ladder up*, or PREDICATE RAISING, giving *He put up the ladder*. There is thus no need for a rule of PARTICLE MOVEMENT, generally assumed in the early transformational literature.

14. Except in some cases where reflexivization takes place, as in *Hij lachte zich dood* (he laughed himself dead; more idiomatically: he laughed himself silly). Here, the lower controlled subject $_{NP}[x]$ is not deleted but kept as a full argument and then reflexivized as a result of its coreference relation with the new subject term. Clearly, a more detailed study of the precise conditions, including the lexical licensing conditions, would transgress the necessary confines of the present paper.

15. Most competent German speakers dislike Oberfeldumstellung when the V-cluster lacks a finite verb form at the top and even more so when the cluster contains *zu*, as in:

(i) ^{??}... ohne ihn $_V$[haben warten zu lassen]
    ... without him have wait to let
    ($\sqrt{}$/ohne ihn $_V$[warten gelassen zu haben])
    '... without having made him wait'   (Haider, this volume, ex. (29a, b))

Note that it is not the infinitival form *haben*, but rather the absence of a finite verb in the cluster and/or the presence of the particle *zu* that make (i) suspect: (30l) above is fine. Cp. also Zifonun et al. (1997, Vol. 2:1286) where the following are all accepted:

(ii) a. ... weil Hans ihn kommen^4 sehen^3 haben^2 will^1 (with Ersatzinfinitiv *sehen!*)
  b. ... weil Hans ihn will^1 kommen^4 sehen^3 haben^2 (idem)
  c. ... weil Hans ihn will^1 haben^2 kommen^4 sehen^3 (but: *will kommen sehen)
  '... because Hans wants to have seen him come (says that he has seen him come)'

Clearly, the phenomena connected with V-clustered object-complement-Ss (here under *wollen*) will have to be investigated further.

16. The Ersatzinfinitiv also occurs in discourse-conditioned cases of ellipsis:

(i) A: Wir haben es vorgezogen, nicht sofort   die ganze Summe zu zahlen.
    We have it preferred   not   at-once the whole amount to pay
    'We have preferred not to pay the entire amount at once.'

(ii) B: Aber Sie hätten   können.
    But you would-have can-INF
    'But you would have been able to.'

Sentence (ii) is fully grammatical, provided the material deleted by ellipsis is supplied by the discourse, i.c. the preceding sentence (i), uttered by speaker A. This, incidentally, is strong evidence in favor of the reality of ellipsis as a grammatical process.

17. Strangely, the voluminous German grammar Zifonun et al. (1997) (2569 pages!) makes no mention at all of the position of futurity *werden* together with perfective *haben* in V-clusters.

18. I am indebted to Manfred Kripka for bringing this to my attention, and to Tilman Höhle for providing me with the material.

References

Abeillé, Anne (1990). Lexical and syntactic rules in a Tree Adjoining Grammar. *28th Meeting of the Association for Computational Linguistics (ACL'90)*, Pittsburgh.

Abeillé, Anne & Danièle Godard (1994). The complementation of tense auxiliaries in French. *Proceedings of the West Coast Conference on Formal Linguistics, 13*, 157–172. Stanford: CSLI Publications.

Abeillé, Anne & Owen Rambow (2000). Tree Adjoining Grammar: An overview. In Abeillé & Rambow (Eds.), 1–68.

Abeillé, Anne & Owen Rambow (Eds.). (2000). *Tree Adjoining Grammars: Formalisms, Linguistic Analyses and Processing.* Stanford: CSLI Publications.

Ackema, Peter & Ad Neeleman (2002). Effect of short-term storage in processing rightward movement. In S. Nooteboom, F. Weerman, & F. Wijnen (Eds.), *Storage and Computation in the Language Faculty.* Dordrecht: Kluwer.

Ackerman, Farrell & Gert Webelhuth (1998). *A Theory of Predicates.* Stanford: CSLI Publications.

Alshawi, Hiyan & Richard Crouch (1992). Monotonic semantic interpretation. *30th Annual Meeting of the Association for Computational Linguistics*, 32–39. Newark, DE.

Alsina, Alex (1996). *The Role of Argument Structure in Grammar.* Stanford: CSLI Publications.

Andrews, Avery & Christopher Manning (1999). *Complex Predicates and Information Spreading in LFG.* Stanford: CSLI Publications.

Ans (1997). *Algemene Nederlandse Spraakkunst.* 2 Vols. (2nd edition). By W. Haeserijn, K. Romijn, G. Geerts, J. de Rooij, & M. C. van den Toorn. Groningen: Martinus Nijhoff / Deurne: Wolters Plantijn.

Baker, M. (1988). *Incorporation. A Theory of Grammatical Function Changing.* Chicago: University of Chicago Press.

Bayer, J. (1992). *Zum* in Bavarian and scrambling. Ms., Universität Aachen.

Beauzée, Nicolas (1767). *Grammaire générale, ou exposition raisonnée des éléments nécessaires du langage, pour servir de fondement à l'étude de toutes les langues.* (2 Vols.) Paris: J. Barbou. [Modern edition: B. E. Bartlett (Ed.), Stuttgart-Bad Cannstatt: Frommann-Holzboog, 1974, 2 Vols.]

Bech, G. (1955). *Studien über das Deutsche Verbum Infinitum, Band I.* Det Kongelige Danske videnskabernes selskab. Historisk-Filosofiske Meddelelser, 35(2) (1955) and 36(6) (1957). Copenhagen: Munksgaard. [2nd unrevised edition 1983 Niemeyer, Tübingen (Linguistische Arbeiten 139).]

Becker, T. (2000). Patterns in metarules for TAG. In Abeillé & Rambow (Eds.), 331–342.

Beedham, C. (1982). *The Passive Aspect in English, German and Russian.* Tübingen: Narr.

Bender, Emily & Dan Flickinger (1999). Peripheral constructions and core phenomena: agreement in tag questions. In Webelhuth et al. (Eds.), 199–214.

Bennis, Hans (1992). Long Head Movement: The position of particles in the verbal cluster in Dutch. In R. Bok-Bennema & R. van Hout (Eds.), *Linguistics in the Netherlands* (pp. 37–47). Amsterdam & Philadelphia: John Benjamins.

Benvéniste, Émile (1962). Le parfait périphrastique. *Hittite et Indo-Européen: études comparatives,* 40–65. (Series: Bibliothèque archéologique et historique de l'Institut français d'archéologie d'Istanbul 5). Paris: Maisonneuve.

Berman, Judith (1995). Linear Order, Syntactic Rank, and Empty Categories: on Weak Crossover. In Dalrymple et al. (Eds.).

Berman, Judith (2000). Topics in the Clausal Syntax of German. PhD thesis, University of Stuttgart.

Berry, Darcy Bruce (1989). *Mir hen s Gras helfa gmät. Bewegung und Flexionsmorphologie im Nordschwäbischen.* Internal paper University of Tübingen, German Studies.

Borsley, Robert D. & Andreas Kathol (2000). Breton as a V2 language. *Linguistics,* 38 (4), 665–710.

Bos, J. (1995). Predicate logic unplugged. *Proceedings of the Tenth Amsterdam Colloquium.* Amsterdam: ILLC/Department of Philosophy, University of Amsterdam.

Bouma, Gosse & Ivan Sag (2001). Satisfying constraints on adjunction and extraction. *Natural Language and Linguistic Theory,* 19, 1–65.

Bouma, Gosse, Rob Malouf, & Gertjan Van Noord (1998). Word order constraints on verb clusters in German and Dutch. In Hinrichs et al. (Eds.), 43–72.

Bresnan, Joan (1995). Linear Order, Syntactic Rank, and Empty Categories: On Weak Crossover. In M. Dalrymple et al. (Eds.).

Burzio, L. (1986). *Italian Syntax: A Government-Binding Approach.* Dordrecht: Reidel.

Butt, Miriam (1995). *The Structure of Complex Predicates in Urdu.* Stanford: CSLI Publications.

Butt, Miriam, Maria Eugenia Niño, & Frédérique Segond (1996). Multilingual processing of auxiliaries in LFG. In D. Gibbon (Ed.), *Natural Language Processing and Speech Technology: Results of the 3rd KONVENS Conference.* Bielefeld.

Chomsky, N. (1995). *The Minimalist Program.* Cambridge, MA: MIT Press.

Cinque, G. (1993). A null theory of phrase and compound stress. *Linguistic Inquiry,* 24 (2), 239–297.

Conradie, C. (1979). Die Diachronie van die Afrikaanse Voltooide Deelwoord. PhD thesis, University of Johannesburg.

Copestake, Anne, Dan Flickinger, Ivan Sag, & Carl Pollard (1999). Minimal recursion semantics: An introduction. Ms., Stanford University.

Corley, Steffan, Martin Corley, Frank Keller, Matthew W. Crocker, & Shari Trewin (2001). Finding syntactic structure in unparsed corpora: The Gsearch corpus query system. *Computers and Humanities,* 35 (2), 81–94.

Dalrymple, Mary (1993). *The Syntax of Anaphoric Binding.* Stanford: CSLI Publications.

Dalrymple, Mary & Helge Lødrup (2000). The Grammatical Functions of Complement Clauses. In M. Butt & T. King (Eds.), *Proceedings of the LFG00 Conference.* Stanford: CSLI Publications.

Dalrymple, Mary, Ronald Kaplan, & Tracy Holloway King (2001). Weak crossover and the absence of traces. In M. Butt & T. King (Eds.), *Proceedings of the LFG01 Conference*. Stanford: CSLI Publications.

Dalrymple, Mary, Ronald Kaplan, John Maxwell, & Annie Zaenen (Eds.). (1995). *Formal Issues in Lexical Functional Grammar*. Stanford: CSLI Publications.

De Hoop, Helen (1992). Case Configuration and Noun Phrase Interpretation. PhD thesis, Groningen University.

De Hoop, Helen & Jaap van der Does (1998). Type-shifting and scrambled definites. *Journal of Semantics, 15*, 393–416.

De Kuthy, Kordula & Detmar Meurers (1999). Argument raising meets adjunct-as-dependents and traceless extraction. *Proceedings of the Sixth International Conference on HPSG*, 45–50. Edinburgh University.

De Kuthy, Kordula & Detmar Meurers (2001). On partial constituent fronting in German. *The Journal of Comparative German Linguistics, 3*, 143–205.

De Smedt, Koenraad & Gerard Kempen (1990a). Segment Grammar: A formalism for incremental sentence generation. In C. L. Paris, W. R. Swartout, & W. C. Mann (Eds.), *Natural Language Generation and Computational Linguistics* (pp. 329–349). Dordrecht: Kluwer Academic.

De Smedt, Koenraad & Gerard Kempen (1990b). Discontinuous constituency in Segment Grammar. *Proceedings of the Symposium on Discontinuous Constituency*. Tilburg: University of Brabant. [Reprinted in: H. Bunt & A. Van Horck (Eds.), *Discontinuous Constituency* (pp. 141–163), 1996. Berlin/New York: Mouton de Gruyter]

Den Besten, H. & J. Rutten (1989). On Verb Raising, Extraposition and free word order in Dutch. In Jaspers et al. (Eds.), 41–56.

Di Sciullo, A. M. & E. Williams (1988). *On the Definition of Word*. Cambridge, MA: MIT Press.

Drach, Erich (1937). *Grundgedanken der deutschen Satzlehre*. Frankfurt: Diesterweg.

DUDEN (1995). *Duden Grammatik der deutschen Gegenwartsprache* (5th edition). By Peter Eisenberg, Herman Gelhaus, Helmut Henne, Horst Sitta, & Hans Wellmann. (=Duden Band 4.) Mannheim: Dudenverlag.

Emonds, J. (1976). *A Transformational Approach to English Syntax: Root, Structure-preserving, and Local Transformations*. New York: Academic Press.

Engel, Ulrich (1970). Regeln zur Wortstellung. In Ulrich Engel (Ed.), *Forschungsberichte des Instituts für deutsche Sprache Mannheim, 5* (pp. 1–148). Tübingen: Narr.

Engelkamp, J., G. Erbach, & H. Uszkoreit (1992). Handling linear precedence constraints by unification. *Proceedings of the 30th Annual Meeting of the Association for Computational Linguistics*, 201–208.

Erb, Marie Christine (2001). Finite Auxiliaries in German. PhD thesis, Tilburg University.

Evans, R., G. Gazdar, & D. Weir (2000). 'Lexical rules' are just lexical rules. In Abeillé & Rambow (Eds.), 71–100.

Evers, Arnold (1975). The Transformational Cycle in Dutch and German. PhD thesis, Utrecht University. [Also: Bloomington: Indiana University Linguistics Club.]

Evers, Arnold (1976). Predicate Raising and the syntax of German. *Proceedings of the 8th Conference on Linguistics*. Leuven, 19–22 September 1973.

Evers, Arnold (1981). Two functional principles for 'Move V'. In W. Abraham (Ed.), *Groninger Arbeiten zur germanistischen Linguistik* (GAGL), *19* (pp. 96–110). University of Groningen.

Evers, Arnold (1986). Clause Union in German and French. In W. Abraham (Ed.), *Groninger Arbeiten zur germanistischen Linguistik* (GAGL), *28* (pp. 170–201). University of Groningen.

Evers, Arnold (1993). West-Germanic V-to-V raising and the incorporation trigger. *Proceedings of the Parasession 'The Cycle in Linguistic Theory' 1992*, 77–94. Chicago: Chicago Linguistic Society.

Evers, Arnold (1994). A note on particle stress. Ms., Utrecht University.

Evers, Arnold & R. Huybregts (1972/1977). *Transformationele Kern-grammatika's van het Nederlands en het Duits.* (=Utrecht Working Papers in Linguistics 1.) Utrecht University.

Evers, Arnold & J. van Kampen (2000). E-language, I-language and the order of parameter setting. Ms., Utrecht University.

Fanselow, G. (1989). Coherent Infinitives in German: restructuring vs. IP-complementation. Ms., University of Passau.

Frank, Anette & Uwe Reyle (1995). Principle-based semantics. *Seventh Conference of the European Chapter of the Association for Computational Linguistics*, 9–16, Dublin. New Brunswick, NJ: Assocation for Computational Linguistics.

Frank, Anette & Annie Zaenen (2002). Tense in LFG: Syntax and morphology. In H. Kamp & U. Reyle (Eds.), *How do we say WHEN it happens?* Tübingen: Niemeyer.

Frank, R. (1992). Syntactic Locality and Tree Adjoining Grammar: Grammatical, Acquisition and Processing Perspectives. PhD thesis, Department of Computer and Information Science, University of Pennsylvania.

Frank, R. (2001). *Phrase Structure Composition and Syntactic Dependencies.* Cambridge, MA: MIT Press.

Gazdar, G., E. Klein, G. Pullum, & I. Sag (1985). *Generalized Phrase Structure Grammar.* Oxford: Blackwell / Cambridge, MA: Harvard University Press.

Giegerich, H. J. (1985). *Metrical Phonology and Phonological Structure. German and English.* Cambridge: Cambridge University Press.

Grewendorf, Günter (1988). *Aspekte der deutschen Syntax.* Tübingen: Narr.

Grimm, J. (1837). *Deutsche Grammatik IV.* Göttingen: Dieterich.

Haegeman, L. (1992). *Theory and Description in Generative Syntax, a Case Study in West Flemish.* Cambridge: Cambridge University Press.

Haegeman, L. & H. van Riemsdijk (1986). Verb Projection Raising, scope and the typology of rules affecting verbs. *Linguistic Inquiry, 17*, 417–466.

Haider, Hubert (1986). Fehlende Argumente: Vom Passiv zu kohärenten Infinitiven. *Linguistische Berichte, 101*, 3–33.

Haider, Hubert (1990). Topicalization and other puzzles of German syntax. In Günter Grewendorf & Wolfgang Sternefeld (Eds.), *Scrambling and Barriers* (pp. 93–112). Amsterdam & Philadelphia: John Benjamins.

Haider, Hubert (1992). Branching and Discharge. *Arbeitspapiere des SFB, 340* (23). Univ. Stuttgart, Univ.Tübingen & IBM Heidelberg. [Reprinted 2000. In P. Coopmans, M. Everaert, & J. Grimshaw (Eds.), *Lexical Specification and Insertion. Proceedings of the 1991 Utrecht Conference* (=Current Issues in Linguistic Theory 197) (pp. 135–164). Amsterdam & Philadelphia: Benjamins.]

Haider, Hubert (1993). *Deutsche Syntax, generativ. Vorstudien zu einer projektiven Grammatik.* (=Tübinger Beiträge zur Linguistik 325.) Tübingen: Narr.

Haider, Hubert (1994). Fakultativ kohärente Infinitkonstruktionen im Deutschen. In A. Steube & G. Zybatow (Eds.), *Zur Satzwertigkeit von Infinitiven und Small Clauses* (pp. 75–106). Tübingen: Niemeyer. [Earlier 1991. *Arbeitspapiere des SFB* 340.17. Univ. Stuttgart, Univ.Tübingen & IBM Heidelberg.]

Haider, Hubert (1997). Precedence among predicates. *The Journal of Comparative Germanic Linguistics, 1*, 3–41.

Haider, Hubert (1999). The License to License. In E. Reuland (Ed.), *Argument & Case: Explaining Burzio's Generalization* (pp. 31–54). Amsterdam & Philadelphia: Benjamins.

Haider, Hubert (2001). Heads and Selection. In N. Corver & H. van Riemsdijk (Eds.), *Semilexical Categories* (pp. 67–96). Berlin: Mouton de Gruyter.

Harbusch, Karin & Gerard Kempen (2002). A quantitative model of word order and movement in English, Dutch and German complement constructions. *Proceedings of the 19th International Conference on Computational Linguistics (COLING-2002), Taipei, Taiwan,* 328–334. San Francisco: Morgan Kaufmann.

Heidolph, K. E., W. Flämig, & W. Motsch (1981). *Grundzüge einer deutschen Grammatik.* Berlin: Akademie-Verlag.

Heycock, C. & B. Santorini (1988). Remarks on Causative and Passive. Ms., University of Pennsylvania.

Hinrichs, Erhard & Tsuneko Nakazawa (1989). Flipped out: Aux in German. *Papers from the 25th Meeting, Chicago Linguistic Society,* 193–202. Chicago: Chicago Linguistic Society.

Hinrichs, Erhard & Tsuneko Nakazawa (1994). Linearizing AUXs in German verbal complexes. In Nerbonne et al. (Eds.), 11–38.

Hinrichs, Erhard & Tsuneko Nakazawa (1998). Third construction and VP extraposition in German: An HPSG analysis. In Hinrichs et al. (Eds.), 115–157.

Hinrichs, Erhard & Tsuneko Nakazawa (1999). Partial VP and split NP topicalization in German: an HPSG analysis. In Levine & Green (Eds.), 275–331.

Hinrichs, Erhard, Andreas Kathol, & Tsuneko Nakazawa (Eds.). (1998). *Complex Predicates in Nonderivational Syntax.* (= Syntax and Semantics 30.) San Diego: Academic Press.

Hoeksema, J. (1988). A constraint on governors in the West-Germanic verb cluster. In M. Everaert, A. Evers, R. Huybregts, & M. Trommelen (Eds.), *Morphology and Modularity: in Honor of Henk Schultink* (pp. 147–161). Dordrecht: Foris.

Höhle, Tilman (1978). *Lexikalische Syntax: Die Aktiv-Passiv-Relation und andere Infinitiv-konstruktionen im Deutschen.* Tübingen: Niemeyer.

Höhle, Tilman (1986). Der Begriff 'Mittelfeld', Anmerkungen über die Theorie der topologischen Felder. In Albrecht Schöne (Ed.), *Kontroversen, alte und neue: Akten des 7. Internationalen Germanisten-Kongresses, Göttingen 1985, Band 3* (pp. 329–340). Tübingen: Niemeyer.

Jaspers, D., W. G. Klooster, Y. Putseys, & P. A. M. Seuren (Eds.). (1989). *Sentential Complementation and the Lexicon. Studies in Honour of Wim de Geest.* Dordrecht: Foris.

Joshi, A., T. Becker, & O. Rambow (2000). A new twist on the competence/performance distinction. In Abeillé & Rambow (Eds.), 167–182.

Joshi, A. K. (1985). Tree Adjoining Grammars. In D. R. Dowty, L. Karttunen, & A. M. Zwicky (Eds.), *Natural Language Parsing. Psychological, Computational, and Theoretical Perspectives* (pp. 206–250). Cambridge/New York: Cambridge University Press.

Joshi, A. K. (1987). An introduction to Tree Adjoining Grammars. In Manaster-Ramer (Ed.), 87–115.

Joshi, A. K. (1994). Preface to special issue on Tree-Adjoining Grammars. *Computational Intelligence, 10* (4), vii–xv.

Joshi, A. K., L. Levy, & M. Takahashi (1975). Tree adjunct grammars. *Journal of Computing Systems Science, 10*, 136–163.

Kameyama, Megumi (1989). Functional Precedence Conditions on Overt and Zero Pronominals. Ms., MCC, Austin, Texas.

Kaplan, Ronald M. (1989). The formal architecture of Lexical-Functional Grammar. *Journal of Information Science and Engineering, 5.* [Reprinted in Dalrymple et al. 1995.]

Kaplan, Ronald M. & Joan W. Bresnan (1982). Lexical-functional grammar: A formal system for grammatical representation. In J. W. Bresnan (Ed.), *The Mental Representation of Grammatical Relations.* Cambridge, MA: MIT Press.

Kaplan, Ronald M. & John Maxwell (1988a). An algorithm for functional uncertainty. *Proceedings of COLING-88*, Budapest. [Reprinted in Dalrymple et al. 1995.]

Kaplan, Ronald M. & John Maxwell (1988b). Constituent coordination in Lexical-Functional Grammar. *Proceedings of COLING-88*, Budapest. [Reprinted in Dalrymple et al. 1995.]

Kaplan, Ronald M. & Annie Zaenen (1989). Long-distance dependencies, constituent structure, and functional uncertainty. In M. Baltin & A. Kroch (Eds.), *Alternative Conceptions of Phrase Structure.* Chicago: University of Chicago Press. [Reprinted in Dalrymple et al. 1995.]

Kathol, Andreas (1995). Linearization-Based German Syntax. PhD thesis, Ohio State University.

Kathol, Andreas (1998). Constituency and linearization of verbal complexes. In Hinrichs et al. (Eds.), 221–270.

Kathol, Andreas (1999). Agreement and the syntax-morphology interface in HPSG. In Levine & Green (Eds.), 209–260.

Kathol, Andreas (2000). *Linear Syntax.* Oxford/New York: Oxford University Press.

Kempen, Gerard & Karin Harbusch (2002). Performance Grammar: a declarative definition. In A. Nijholt, M. Theune, & H. Hondorp (Eds.), *Computational Linguistics in the Netherlands 2001* (pp. 148–162). Amsterdam: Rodopi.

Kempen, Gerard & Ed Hoenkamp (1987). An incremental procedural grammar for sentence formulation. *Cognitive Science, 11*, 201–258.

Kiss, Tibor (1994). Obligatory coherence. An investigation into the syntax of modal and semi-modal verbs in German. In Nerbonne et al. (Eds.), 71–107.

Kiss, Tibor (1995). *Infinite Komplementation: neue Studien zum deutschen Verbum.* (= Linguistische Arbeiten 333.) Tübingen: Niemeyer.

Kiss, Tibor (2001). Configurational and relational scope determination in German. In Meurers & Kiss (Eds.), 141–175.

Koopman, H. & A. Szabolcsi (2000). *Verbal Complexes*. Cambridge, MA: MIT Press.

Koster, Jan (1978). *Locality Principles in Syntax*. Dordrecht: Foris.

Koster, Jan (1987). *Domains and Dynasties: The Radical Autonomy of Syntax*. Dordrecht: Foris.

Kouwenberg, Silvia (1994). *A Grammar of Berbice Dutch Creole*. Berlin/New York: Mouton de Gruyter.

Kroch, A. (1987). Subjacency in a Tree Adjoining Grammar. In Manaster-Ramer (Ed.), 143–172.

Kroch, A. (1989). Asymmetries in long distance extraction in a Tree Adjoining Grammar. In M. Baltin & A. Kroch (Eds.), *Alternative Conceptions of Phrase Structure* (pp. 66–98). Chicago: University of Chicago Press.

Kroch, A. & B. Santorini (1991). The derived constituent structure of the West-Germanic Verb Raising construction. In R. Freidin (Ed.), *Principles and Parameters in Comparative Grammar* (pp. 269–338). Cambridge, MA: MIT Press.

Kuroda, S.-Y. (1965). Causative forms in Japanese. *Foundations of Language, 1*, 30–50.

Kuroda, S.-Y. (1972). The categorical and the thetic judgment: evidence from Japanese. *Foundations of Language, 9*, 158–185.

Levine, Robert D. & Georgia M. Green (Eds.). (1999). *Studies in Contemporary Phrase Structure Grammar*. Cambridge/New York: Cambridge University Press.

Lieber, R. (1983). Argument linking and compounds in English. *Linguistic Inquiry, 14*, 251–285.

McCawley, James D. (1968a). The role of semantics in a grammar. In E. Bach & R. Harms (Eds.), *Universals in Linguistic Theory* (pp. 124–169). New York: Holt, Rinehart & Winston. [Reprinted in McCawley 1973, 59–98.]

McCawley, James D. (1968b). Lexical insertion in a transformational grammar without deep structure. *Papers from the Fourth Regional Meeting, Chicago Linguistic Society*, 71–80. Chicago: Chicago Linguistic Society. [Reprinted in McCawley 1973, 155–166.]

McCawley, James D. (1973). *Grammar and Meaning. Papers on Syntactic and Semantic Topics*. Tokyo: Taishukan.

Manaster-Ramer, Alexis (Ed.). (1987). *Mathematics of Language*. Amsterdam & Philadelphia: John Benjamins.

Manning, Christopher (1996). *Ergativity: Argument Structure and Grammatical Relations*. Stanford: CSLI Publications.

Manning, Christopher, Ivan Sag, & Masayo Iida (1999). The lexical integrity of Japanese causatives. In Levine & Green (Eds.), 39–79.

Melnik, Nurit (2002). Free Inversion in Modern Hebrew. PhD thesis, UC Berkeley.

Meurers, Walt Detmar (1994). *A modified view of the German verbal complex*. Paper read at the 1994 HPSG Workshop, Heidelberg.

Meurers, Walt Detmar (1999a). German partial-VP topicalization revisited. In Webelhuth et al. (Eds.), 129–141.

Meurers, Walt Detmar (1999b). Raising spirits (and assigning them case). *Groninger Arbeiten zur Germanistischen Linguistik* (GAGL), *43*, 173–226.

Meurers, Walt Detmar (1999/2000). Lexical Generalizations in the Syntax of German Non-Finite Constructions. PhD thesis, Univerity of Tübingen. *Arbeitspapiere des SFB, 340.*

Meurers, Walt Detmar & Kordula de Kuthy (2001). Case assignment in partially fronted constituents. In Christian Rohrer, Antje Rossdeutscher, & Hans Kamp (Eds.), *Linguistic Form and its Computation.* Stanford: CSLI Publications.

Meurers, Walt Detmar & Tibor Kiss (Eds.) (2001). *Constraint-Based Approaches to Germanic Syntax.* Stanford: CSLI Publications.

Miller, Philip (1992). *Clitics and Constituents in Phrase Structure Grammar.* New York: Garland.

Moortgat, Michael (1988). Mixed Composition and Discontinuous Dependencies. In Richard T. Oehrle, Emmon Bach, & Deirdre Wheeler (Eds.), *Categorial Grammars and Natural Language Structures* (pp. 319–348). Dordrecht: Reidel.

Müller, Stefan (1996). Yet another paper about partial verb-phrase fronting in German. *Proceedings of COLING-96*, 800–805. Copenhagen.

Müller, Stefan (1999). *Deutsche Syntax, deklarativ. Head-Driven Phrase Structure Grammar für das Deutsche.* Tübingen: Niemeyer.

Neeleman, A. (1994a). Complex Predicates. PhD thesis, Utrecht University.

Neeleman, A. (1994b). Scrambling as a D-structure phenomenon. In Norbert Corver & Henk van Riemsdijk (Eds.), *Studies on Scrambling. Movement and Non-Movement Approaches to Free Word Order Phenomena* (pp. 387–429). Berlin: Mouton de Gruyter.

Nerbonne, John (1994). Partial verb phrases and spurious ambiguities. Nerbonne et al. (Eds.), 109–149.

Nerbonne, John, Klaus Netter, & Carl Pollard (Eds.). (1994). *German in Head-Driven Phrase Structure Grammar.* Stanford: CSLI Publications.

Netter, Klaus (1991). *Clause Union Phenomena and Complex Predicates in German.* Technical Report R1.1.B (Part 1), DYANA.

Nordlinger, Rachel (1998). *Constructive Case: Evidence from Australian Languages.* Stanford: CSLI Publications.

Overdiep, Gerrit S. (1936). *Stilistische grammatica van het moderne Nederlandsch.* Zwolle: Tjeenk Willink.

Paardekooper, P. C. (1955). *Syntaxis, Spraakkunst en Taalkunde.* Den Bosch: Malmberg.

Polinsky, Maria & Bernard Comrie (1999). Agreement in Tsez. *Folia Linguistica, 33*, 4–25.

Pollard, Carl J. & Ivan A. Sag (1987). *Information-Based Syntax and Semantics. Vol. I.* CSLI Lecture Note Series 13. Stanford: CSLI Publications.

Pollard, Carl J. & Ivan A. Sag (1994). *Head-Driven Phrase Structure Grammar.* Stanford: CSLI Publications.

Pollock, J.-Y. (1989). Verb Movement, universal grammar and the structure of IP. *Linguistic Inquiry, 20* (3), 362–424.

Przepiórkowski, Adam (1999a). Adjuncts as complements: evidence from case assignment. In Andreas Kathol, Jean-Pierre Koenig, & Gert Webelhuth (Eds.), *Lexical and Constructional Aspects of Linguistic Explanation* (pp. 231–246). Stanford: CSLI Publications.

Przepiórkowski, Adam (1999b). On complements and adjuncts in Polish. In Robert D. Borsley & Adam Przepiórkowski (Eds.), *Slavic in HPSG* (pp. 183–210). Stanford: CSLI Publications.

Przepiórkowski, Adam (2001). ARG-ST on phrases: Evidence from Polish. In Dan Flickinger & Andreas Kathol (Eds.), *Proceedings of the Seventh International HPSG Conference, UC Berkeley* (pp. 267–284). Stanford: CSLI Publications.

Quirk, R., S. Greenbaum, G. Leech, & J. Svartvik (1986). *A Comprehensive Grammar of the English Language.* London: Longman.

Rambow, Owen (1994a). Formal and Computational Aspects of Natural Language Syntax. PhD thesis, Department of Computer and Information Science, University of Pennsylvania, Philadelphia. Available as Technical Report 9408 from the Institute for Research in Cognitive Science (IRCS). [Also at: ftp://ftp.cis.upenn.edu/pub/rambow/thesis.ps.Z.]

Rambow, Owen (1994b). Mobile Heads and Strict Lexicalization. MA thesis, Department of Linguistics, University of Pennsylvania, Philadelphia.

Rambow, Owen (1996). Word Order, Clause Union and the Formal Machinery of Syntax. In M. Butt & T. King (Eds.), *Proceedings of the First LFG Conference.* Stanford: CSLI Publications.

Rambow, Owen & B. Santorini (1995). Incremental phrase structure generation and a universal theory of V2. In J. Beckman (Ed.), *Proceedings of NELS 25* (pp. 373–387). Amherst, MA: GSLA.

Rambow, Owen, K. Vijay-Shanker, & D. Weir (2001). D-Tree Substitution Grammars. *Computational Linguistics, 27* (1), 87–121.

Reape, M. (1993). A Formal Theory of Word Order: A Case Study in West Germanic. PhD thesis, University of Edinburgh.

Reichenbach, Hans (1947). *Elements of Symbolic Logic.* New York: Macmillan.

Richter, Frank & Manfred Sailer (2001a). On the left periphery of German finite sentences. In Meurers & Kiss (Eds.), 257–300.

Richter, Frank & Manfred Sailer (2001b). Polish negation and lexical resource semantics. *Proceedings of the Conference on Formal Grammar and Mathematics of Language.* (=Electronic Notes in Theoretical Computer Science 53.) Berlin: Springer.

Richter, Michael (2000). Verbkonstruktionen im Deutschen. Eine transformationelle Analyse syntaktischer Erscheinungen innerhalb des deutschen Verbsystems im Rahmen der semantischen Syntax. PhD thesis, University of Nijmegen.

Robbers, K. (1997). Non-finite Verbal Complements in Afrikaans. PhD thesis, University of Amsterdam.

Roberts, I. (1991). Excorporation and minimality. *Linguistic Inquiry, 22,* 209–218.

Rutten, J. (1991). Infinitival Complements and Auxiliaries. PhD thesis, University of Amsterdam.

Ruys, Eddy (2001). Dutch scrambling and the strong-weak distinction. *The Journal of Comparative Germanic Linguistics, 4* (1), 39–67.

Sag, Ivan A. & Janet D. Fodor (1994). Extraction without traces. In Raul Aranovich, William Byrne, Susanne Preuss, & Martha Senturia (Eds.), *Proceedings of the Thirteenth West-Coast Conference on Formal Linguistics* (pp. 365–384). Stanford: CSLI Publications.

Sag, Ivan A. & Thomas Wasow (1999). *Syntactic Theory: A Formal Introduction.* Stanford: CSLI Publications.

Schuurman, Ineke (1987). *A Lexical-Functional treatment of cross-serial dependencies.* Paper presented at the XIVth International Congress of Linguistics.

Seuren, Pieter A. M. (1972). *Predicate Raising and Dative in French and Sundry Languages.* Magdalen College, Oxford/Linguistic Agency University Trier (LAUT). [Reprinted in Seuren 2001, 139–184.]

Seuren, Pieter A. M. (1989). A problem in English subject complementation. In Jaspers et al. (Eds.), 355–375.

Seuren, Pieter A. M. (1991). The definition of serial verbs. In Francis Byrne & Thom Huebner (Eds.), *Development and Structures of Creole Languages. Essays in Honor of Derek Bickerton* (pp. 193–205). Amsterdam & Philadelphia: John Benjamins.

Seuren, Pieter A. M. (1996). *Semantic Syntax.* Oxford: Blackwell.

Seuren, Pieter A. M. (2001). *A View of Language.* Oxford: Oxford University Press.

Seuren, Pieter A. M. (2002). Pseudoarguments and pseudocomplements. In Bruce E. Nevin (Ed.), *The Legacy of Zellig Harris* (pp. 179–207). Amsterdam & Philadelphia: John Benjamins.

Seuren, Pieter A. M. & Herman Chr. Wekker (1986). Semantic transparency as a factor in Creole genesis. In Pieter C. Muysken & Norval Smith (Eds.), *Substrata versus Universals in Creole Genesis. Papers from the Amsterdam Creole Workshop, April 1985* (pp. 57–70). Amsterdam & Philadelphia: John Benjamins.

Steedman, M. (1983). On the generality of the nested dependency constraint and the reason for an exception in Dutch. *Linguistics, 21,* 35–66.

Steedman, M. (1984). A categorial theory of nesting dependencies in Dutch infinitival complements. In Wim de Geest & Ivan Putseys (Eds.), *Sentential Complementation. Proceedings of the International Conference held at UFSAL, Brussels, June 1983* (pp. 215–226). Dordrecht: Foris.

Steedman, M. (1991). Structure and Intonation. *Language, 68* (2), 260–296.

Steedman, M. (1996). *Surface Structure and Interpretation.* Cambridge, MA: MIT Press.

Steedman, M. (Ed.). (1997). *The Syntactic Interface.* Cambridge, MA: MIT Press.

Steedman, M. (2002). Scope alternation and the syntax-semantics interface. Ms., Edinburgh University.

Sturtevant, E. (1933). *A Comparative Grammar of the Hittite Language.* Philadelpia: Linguistic Society of America (Whitney Linguistic Series).

Uszkoreit, Hans (1987). *Word Order and Constituent Structure in German.* Stanford: CSLI Publications.

Vallduví, Enric & Elisabeth Engdahl (1996). The linguistic realization of information packaging. *Linguistics, 34,* 459–519.

Van Kampen, J. (2000). An Alternative Scenario for the Acquisition of Syntactic Categories. Ms., Utrecht University.

Van Noord, Gertjan & Gosse Bouma (1994). Adjuncts and the processing of lexical rules. *Proceedings of the 15th International Conference on Computational Linguistics (COLING 1994),* 250–256. Kyoto.

Van Noord, Gertjan & Gosse Bouma (1997). Dutch verbal clustering without verb clusters. In Patrick Blackburn & Maarten de Rijke (Eds.), *Specifying Syntactic Structures* (pp. 123–153). Stanford: CSLI Publications.

Van Riemsdijk, H. (1978). *A Case Study in Syntactic Markedness: The Binding of Prepositional Phrases.* Lisse: Peter de Ridder.

Von Stechow, A. & W. Sternefeld (1988). *Bausteine syntaktischen Wissens*. Opladen: Westdeutscher Verlag.

Webelbuth, Gert (1992). *Principles and Parameters of Syntactic Saturation*. Oxford: Oxford University Press.

Webelbuth, Gert & Hans den Besten (1987). Remnant topicalization and the constituent structure of VP in the Germanic SOV languages. *GLOW Newsletter, 18*, 15–16.

Webelbuth, Gert, Jean-Pierre Koenig, & Andreas Kathol (Eds.) (1999). *Lexical and Constructional Aspects of Linguistic Explanation*. Stanford: CSLI Publications.

Williams, E. (1994). *Thematic Structure in Syntax*. Cambridge, MA: MIT Press.

Wöllstein-Leisten, A. (2001). *Die Syntax der dritten Konstruktion*. Tübingen: Stauffenburg.

Wurmbrand, S. (2001). *Infinitives. Restructuring and Clause Structure*. Berlin: Mouton de Gruyter.

Zaenen, Annie & Ron Kaplan (1995). Formal devices for linguistic generalizations: West-Germanic word order in LFG. In J. Cole, G. Green, & J. Morgan (Eds.), *Linguistics and computation*. Stanford: CLSI Publications. [Reprinted in Dalrymple et al. (1995).]

Zifonun, Gisela, Ludger Hoffmann, Bruno Strecker et al. (1997). *Grammatik der deutschen Sprache*. 3 Vols. (=Schriften des Instituts für deutsche Sprache 7.) Berlin: Walter de Gruyter.

Zwart, C. Jan-Wouter (1993). Dutch Syntax. A Minimalist Approach. PhD thesis, Groningen University.

Zwart, C. Jan-Wouter (1996). *Morphosyntax of Verb Movement: A Minimalist Approach to the Syntax of Dutch*. Dordrecht: Kluwer Academic.

Index

CURRENT ISSUES IN LINGUISTIC THEORY

Dr. E.F.K. Koerner
Zentrum für Allgemeine Sprachwissenschaft, Typologie
und Universalienforschung, Berlin

The *Current Issues in Linguistic Theory* (CILT) series is a theory-oriented series which welcomes contributions from scholars who have significant proposals to make towards the advancement of our understanding of language, its structure, functioning and development. CILT has been established in order to provide a forum for the presentation and discussion of linguistic opinions of scholars who do not necessarily accept the prevailing mode of thought in linguistic science. It offers an alternative outlet for meaningful contributions to the current linguistic debate, and furnishes the diversity of opinion which a healthy discipline must have. A complete list of titles in this series can be found on the publishers website, **www.benjamins.com/jbp**

203. NORRICK, Neal R.: *Conversational Narrative. Storytelling in everyday talk.* 2000.
204. DIRVEN, René, Bruce HAWKINS and Esra SANDIKCIOGLU (eds.): *Language and Ideology. Volume 1: cognitive theoretical approaches.* 2001.
205. DIRVEN, René, Roslyn M. FRANK and Cornelia ILIE (eds.): *Language and Ideology. Volume 2: descriptive cognitive approaches.* 2001.
206. FAWCETT, Robin P.: *A Theory of Syntax for Systemic Functional Linguistics.* 2000.
207. SANZ, Montserrat: *Events and Predication. A new approach to syntactic processing in English and Spanish.* 2000.
208. ROBINSON, Orrin W.: *Whose German? The* ach/ich *alternation and related phenomena in 'standard' and 'colloquial'.* 2001.
209. KING, Ruth: *The Lexical Basis of Grammatical Borrowing. A Prince Edward Island French case study.* 2000.
210. DWORKIN, Steven N. and Dieter WANNER (eds.): *New Approaches to Old Problems. Issues in Romance historical linguistics.* 2000.
211. ELŠÍK, Viktor and Yaron MATRAS (eds.): *Grammatical Relations in Romani. The Noun Phrase.* 2000.
212. REPETTI, Lori (ed.): *Phonological Theory and the Dialects of Italy.* 2000.
213. SORNICOLA, Rosanna, Erich POPPE and Ariel SHISHA-HALEVY (eds.): *Stability, Variation and Change of Word-Order Patterns over Time.* 2000.
214. WEIGAND, Edda and Marcelo DASCAL (eds.): *Negotiation and Power in Dialogic Interaction.* 2001.
215. BRINTON, Laurel J.: *Historical Linguistics 1999. Selected papers from the 14th International Conference on Historical Linguistics, Vancouver, 9-13 August 1999.* 2001..
216. CAMPS, Joaquim and Caroline R. WILTSHIRE (eds.): *Romance Syntax, Semantics and L2 Acquisition. Selected papers from the 30th Linguistic Symposium on Romance Languages, Gainesville, Florida, February 2000.* 2001.
217. WILTSHIRE, Caroline R. and Joaquim CAMPS (eds.): *Romance Phonology and Variation. Selected papers from the 30th Linguistic Symposium on Romance Languages, Gainesville, Florida, February 2000.* 2002.
218. BENDJABALLAH, S., W.U. DRESSLER, O. PFEIFFER and M. VOEIKOVA (eds.): *Morphology 2000. Selected papers from the 9th Morphology Meeting, Vienna, 24–28 February 2000.* 2002.
219. ANDERSEN, Henning (ed.): *Actualization. Linguistic Change in Progress.* 2001.
220. SATTERFIELD, Teresa, Christina TORTORA and Diana CRESTI (eds.): *Current Issues in Romance Languages. Selected papers from the 29th Linguistic Symposium on Romance Languages (LSRL), Ann Arbor, 8-11 April 1999.* 2002.
221. D'HULST, Yves, Johan ROORYCK and Jan SCHROTEN (eds.): *Romance Languages and Linguistic Theory 1999. Selected papers from 'Going Romance' 1999, Leiden, 9-11 December.* 2001.
222. HERSCHENSOHN, Julia, Enrique MALLÉN and Karen ZAGONA (eds.): *Features and*

Interfaces in Romance. Essays in honor of Heles Contreras. 2001.
223. FANEGO, Teresa, María José LÓPEZ-COUSO and Javier PÉREZ-GUERRA (eds.): *Eng-lish Historical Syntax and Morphology. Selected papers from 11 ICEHL, Santiago de Compostela, 7-11 September 2000.* 2002.
224. FANEGO, Teresa, Belén MÉNDEZ-NAYA and Elena SEOANE (eds.): *Sounds, Words, Texts and Change. Selected papers from 11 ICEHL, Santiago de Compostela, 7-11 September 2000.* 2002.
225. SHAHIN, Kimary N.: *Postvelar Harmony.* 2002.
226. LEVIN, Saul: *Semitic and Indo-European. Volume II: comparative morphology, syntax and phonetics; with observations on Afro-Asiatic.* 2002.
227. FAVA, Elisabetta (ed.): *Clinical Linguistics. Theory and applications in speech pathology and therapy.* 2002.
228. NEVIN, Bruce E. (ed.): *The Legacy of Zellig Harris. Language and information into the 21st century. Volume 1: philosophy of science, syntax and semantics.* n.y.p.
229. NEVIN, Bruce E. and Stephen JOHNSON (eds.): *The Legacy of Zellig Harris. Language and information into the 21st century. Volume 2: computability of language and computer applications.* 2002.
230. PARKINSON, Dilworth B. and Elabbas BENMAMOUN (eds.): *Perspectives on Arabic Linguistics XIII-XIV. Papers from the Thirteenth and Fourteenth Annual Symposia on Arabice Linguistics.* 2002.
231. CRAVENS, Thomas D.: *Comparative Historical Dialectology. Italo-Romance clues to Ibero-Romance sound change.* 2002.
232. BEYSSADE, Claire, Reineke BOK-BENNEMA, Frank DRIJKONINGEN and Paola MONACHESI (eds.): *Romance Languages and Linguistic Theory 2000. Selected papers from 'Going Romance' 2000, Utrecht, 30 November - 2 December.* 2002.
233. WEIJER, Jeroen van de, Vincent J. van HEUVEN and Harry van der HULST (eds.): *The Phonological Spectrum. Part I: Segmental structure.* 2003.
234. WEIJER, Jeroen van de, Vincent J. van HEUVEN and Harry van der HULST (eds.): *The Phonological Spectrum. Part II: Suprasegmental structure.* 2003.
235. LINN, Andrew R. and Nicola MCLELLAND (eds): *Standardization. Studies from the Germanic languages.* 2002.
236. SIMON-VANDENBERGEN, Anne-Marie, Miriam TAVERNIERS and Louise RAVELLI: *Grammatical Metaphor. Views from systemic functional linguistics.* n.y.p.
237. BLAKE, Barry J. and Kate BURRIDGE (eds.): *Historical Linguistics 2001.Selected papers from the 15th International Conference on Historical Linguistics, Melbourne, 13–17 August 2001.* 2003.
238. NÚÑEZ-CEDENO, Rafael, Luis LÓPEZ and Richard CAMERON (eds.): *A Romance Perspective in Language Knowledge and Use. Selected papers from the 31st Linguistic Symposium on Romance Languages (LRSL), Chicago, 19–22 April 2001.* n.y.p.
239. ANDERSEN, Henning (ed.): *Language Contacts in Prehistory. Studies in Stratigraphy. Papers from the Workshop on Linguistic Stratigraphy and Prehistory at the Fifteenth International Conference on Historical Linguistics, Melbourne, 17 August 2001.* 2003.
240. JANSE, Mark and Sijmen TOL (eds.): *Language Death and Language Maintenance. Theoretical, practical and descriptive approaches.* 2003.
241. LECARME, Jacqueline (ed.): *Research in Afroasiatic Grammar II. Selected papers from the Fifth Conference on Afroasiatic Languages, Paris, 2000.* n.y.p.
242. SEUREN, Pieter A.M. and G. KEMPEN (eds.): *Verb Constructions in German and Dutch.* 2003.
243. CUYCKENS, Hubert, Thomas BERG, René DIRVEN and Klaus-Uwe PANTHER (eds.): *Motivation in Language. Studies in honor of Günter Radden.* 2003.
244. PÉREZ-LEROUX, Ana Teresa and Yves ROBERGE (eds.): *Romance Linguistics. Theory and acquisition.* 2003.
245. QUER, Josep, Jan SCHROTEN, M. SCORRETTI, Petra SLEEMAN and Els VERHEUGD (eds.): *Romance Languages and Linguistic Theory 2001. Selected papers from 'Going Romance' 2001, Amsterdam, 6–8 December.* n.y.p.

UNIVERSITY LIBRARY
NOTTINGHAM